Cinema and Secularism

Cinema and Secularism

Edited by
Mark Cauchi

BLOOMSBURY ACADEMIC
NEW YORK • LONDON • OXFORD • NEW DELHI • SYDNEY

BLOOMSBURY ACADEMIC
Bloomsbury Publishing Inc, 1385 Broadway, New York, NY 10018, USA
Bloomsbury Publishing Plc, 50 Bedford Square, London, WC1B 3DP, UK
Bloomsbury Publishing Ireland, 29 Earlsfort Terrace, Dublin 2, D02 AY28, Ireland

BLOOMSBURY, BLOOMSBURY ACADEMIC and the Diana logo are trademarks
of Bloomsbury Publishing Plc

First published in the United States of America 2024
Paperback edition published 2025

Copyright © Mark Cauchi and contributors, 2024

For legal purposes the Acknowledgments on p. x constitute an extension
of this copyright page.

Cover design: Eleanor Rose
Cover image © Photofest

All rights reserved. No part of this publication may be: i) reproduced or transmitted in any form, electronic or mechanical, including photocopying, recording or by means of any information storage or retrieval system without prior permission in writing from the publishers; or ii) used or reproduced in any way for the training, development or operation of artificial intelligence (AI) technologies, including generative AI technologies. The rights holders expressly reserve this publication from the text and data mining exception as per Article 4(3) of the Digital Single Market Directive (EU) 2019/790.

Bloomsbury Publishing Inc does not have any control over, or responsibility for, any third-party websites referred to or in this book. All internet addresses given in this book were correct at the time of going to press. The author and publisher regret any inconvenience caused if addresses have changed or sites have ceased to exist, but can accept no responsibility for any such changes.

Library of Congress Cataloging-in-Publication Data
Names: Cauchi, Mark, editor.
Title: Cinema and secularism / edited by Mark Cauchi.
Description: New York : Bloomsbury Academic, 2024. | Includes bibliographical references and index.
Identifiers: LCCN 2023025566 (print) | LCCN 2023025567 (ebook) | ISBN 9781501388873 (hardback) | ISBN 9781501388842 (paperback) | ISBN 9781501388866 (epub) | ISBN 9781501388859 (pdf) | ISBN 9781501388835 (ebook other)
Subjects: LCSH: Film criticism. | Motion pictures. | Secularism.
Classification: LCC PN1995 .C48637 2024 (print) | LCC PN1995 (ebook) |
DDC 791.4301–dc23/eng/20230802
LC record available at https://lccn.loc.gov/2023025566
LC ebook record available at https://lccn.loc.gov/2023025567

ISBN: HB: 978-1-5013-8887-3
PB: 978-1-5013-8884-2
ePDF: 978-1-5013-8885-9
eBook: 978-1-5013-8886-6

Typeset by Deanta Global Publishing Services, Chennai, India

For product safety related questions contact productsafety@bloomsbury.com.

To find out more about our authors and books visit www.bloomsbury.com and sign up for our newsletters.

For WMC,
with infinity-times-infinity amounts of love

CONTENTS

List of Figures ix
Acknowledgments x

Introduction: Screening the Secular Mark Cauchi 1

PART I Is Cinema Secular? Genealogy, Theory, Philosophy 27

1 Secularist Film Studies and the Occlusion of the Secular Mark Cauchi 29

2 Deleuze's "Conversion of Belief": The Time-Image and the Disruption of Cinema's Secularist Origins John Caruana 64

3 The Secular as Sacred: Cinema and Buddhist Ritual Francisca Cho 86

PART II Situating Secularism: Culture, Politics, and Cinema 107

4 Ousmane Sembène's *Moolaadé*: Sacred Space as Refuge and Political Agency Nikolas Kompridis 109

5 Cinema as a Secularizing Medium in the Middle East Walid El Khachab 144

6 The Impossible Possible: Secularism and Hindi Popular Cinema Sheila J. Nayar 163

7 Observational Secular: Religion and Documentary Film in the United States Kathryn Lofton 182

PART III The Dis/Enchantment of the World in Moving Images 207

8   The Wonder of Film: Science, Magic, and the Endurance of Enchantment *Catherine Wheatley* 209

9   Vegetal Life, Plant-Soul: Early British Film Flowers *Sarah Cooper* 225

10 "There's a sort of evil out there": Uncanny Secularity in Lynch's *Twin Peaks: The Return* *Robert Sinnerbrink* 242

List of Contributors 265
Index 268

FIGURES

0.1   Opening title, still from *PlayTime* 2
0.2   Office building, still from *PlayTime* 2
0.3   Two nuns, still from *PlayTime* 3
2.1   Irene and Andrea, still from *Europa '51* 80
4.1   Rope, still from *Moolaadé* 116
4.2   Anthill, still from *Moolaadé* 126
4.3   Mosque, anthill, radios, still from *Moolaadé* 129
4.4   Ostrich egg, still from *Moolaadé* 139
4.5   Antenna, still from *Moolaadé* 139
9.1   Narcissus, still from *The Birth of a Flower* 226
9.2   Garden anemone, still from *The Birth of a Flower* 226
9.3   Roses, still from *The Birth of a Flower* 227
9.4   Still from *Gathering Moss* 234
9.5   Still from *Nature's Double Lifers* 237

ACKNOWLEDGMENTS

This project on the relationship between cinema and secularism evolved out of work I had begun doing with John Caruana, when we worked on our collection, *Immanent Frames: Postsecular Cinema Between Malick and von Trier* (2018). It was during our many conversations on postsecular cinema and the various conference presentations given around that time that the awareness started to dawn on me that what the secular means in relation to cinema, theory, and criticism was not by any means self-evident. I would never have arrived at this question were it not for the intellectual exchange, comradery, and challenge of those discussions with John, and for that and for his friendship I am deeply grateful. This intellectual background was enriched by collaborations with others as well, including the contributors to that collection, especially Robert Sinnerbrink and Catherine Wheatley, with whom John and I both collaborated on other, related projects as well. Indeed, my first formulation of the problem at the center of this project was in a talk I gave on a panel organized by John, Catherine, Russell Killbourn, and myself for the SCMS meeting in Chicago in 2017; I am grateful to them, and to the participants in that session, for the opportunity and feedback. A complementary project, long delayed, with John Caruana, Chris Irwin, and Isabel Rocamora also helped nourish the discovery of, and thinking about the present topic.

A special word of gratitude must be given to the organizers of and participants in the annual Film-Philosophy conference. I have presented there on topics adjacent to the present project many times over several years. While this conference is focused on the intersections, parallels, mutual enrichments, and overlappings of film and philosophy, it has repeatedly proven itself to be receptive to my effort to triangulate those practices and discourses with religion and secularism. I could not have advanced my thinking on the present topic, nor felt confident about its relevance to the study of film, without the hospitality of the organizers, friends made there, my various co-panelists at my sessions and their attendees—to them all I am very grateful.

This book obviously would not be what it is without the chapters it includes by John Caruana, Francisca Cho, Sarah Cooper, Walid El Khachab, Nikolas Kompridis, Kathryn Lofton, Sheila J. Nayar, Robert Sinnerbrink, and Catherine Wheatley. I am enormously grateful to each of them for the thoughtfulness and creativity of their chapters, and for the patience and perseverance they demonstrated while we all worked through a disheartening and entropic pandemic and faced numerous delays. I am also grateful to the scholars I won't name to whom I had reached out and who either agreed to be part of the project and then dropped out, or who could not join but who offered feedback and encouragement. They all contributed in some way to my feeling that this virtually unheard-of topic was worth pursuing, if not to the actual shape of its completed form.

This book would also obviously not be what it is without its publisher, Bloomsbury, and I thank everyone I've worked with there. This project was begun before the Covid-19 pandemic, but naturally it was delayed by that event. I'm especially grateful to my editor, Katie Gallof, for being unfailingly understanding about the delays and persistently cheerful, supportive, and efficient in our exchanges, and to Alyssa Jordan for her keen eye, precision, and warmth in communications. I am also grateful to the two anonymous reviewers who offered valuable feedback on the first draft of my Introduction and the general plan for the book. I am very happy with the design of the cover, which was gracefully overseen by Stephanie Grace-Petinos. Derek and Todd at Photofest were very helpful in the production of some of the images in and on the cover of the book.

This project was partially funded by a bursary from the York University YUFA Sabbatical Fund and by a York University Small Research Grant. Those allowed me to hire my research assistant, Sarwar Ahmed Abdullah, for whose work and care in formatting and finalizing the manuscript I am grateful. I also thank the *Journal of Cinema and Media Studies* for granting permission to include Kathryn Lofton's "Observational Secular."

All thinking is always already inter-subjective, inter-affective, interdependent, and worlded, which is to say conditioned and unconditioned by our world and the others in it. Still, thinking and writing can be (or become) a solitary, insular, and even narcissistic activity. I am grateful to be a teacher for many reasons, but two of them are its capacity to keep my words connected to the act of helping others and to broadening my sense of what is worthy of thought by forcing me to confront the interests, projects, and challenges of students. Besides the many students in my undergraduate and graduate courses who especially help with the first reason mentioned earlier (especially those in my Postsecular Thought and Postsecular Cinema courses), the students with whom I work most closely and who challenge my thinking and my insularity most powerfully are my past and present graduate students, and I want to acknowledge them: Sarwar Ahmed Abdullah, Kiran Chahal, Suraiya Farzana, Anthony Ferrara, Tapji Garba, Amelie Jerome, Forrest Johnson, Nuzhat Khurshid, Ryan Lee, Colin Lennard-White, Anthony Nairn, Avesta Naseer, Chris Satoor, Michael Sherbert, Jeff Sidivy, and Nick Valkanis.

Besides the people already mentioned, this project and its ideas, not to mention the psychological well-being required to carry it out, were fostered and nurtured at different times by long-standing relationships, as well as brief but important conversations, with many people: Anders Bergstrom, Shai Biderman, Sarah Blake, William Brown, John Caruana, Theresa Caruana, David Cecchetto, Sarah Cooper, Juliana Ramírez Herrera, Chris Irwin, Anna Isacsson, Ryan Johnson, Selmin Kara, Joe Kickasola, Russell Killbourn, Nikolas Kompridis, Ron Kuipers, Avron Kulak, Terri Kulak, Nancy Levene, Charlotte Lombardo, Philip Maciak, Azed Majeed, Rui Pimenta, Brayton Polka, Brian Price, Isabel Rocamora, Daniele Rugo, Sarah Sharkey Pearce, Robert Sinnerbrink, Shawn Thomson, Caleb Yong, Alia Fortune Weston, Cate Wheatley, and Jonathan Wright. I am fortunate to have been nourished and supported in the final, weary stages of preparation especially by Julia Walter. There is no doubt that I could not have arrived where I am without my family, both for their various forms of support and for the various forms of impediment they bequeath; indeed, my thinking about secularism was no doubt spawned by growing up Catholic and by the process of trying to contend critically with that inheritance.

The project of making the secular in cinema visible involves, among other things, coming to re-see what is no longer seen, rethinking what one assumes one knows, receiving anew as a source of possibility and inspiration what one usually takes for granted. Over the time of working on this project, the person who more than any other persistently expanded and deepened my capacities to do that in ways big and small, overt and subtle, intentionally and unpredictably, was my son, WMC. This book is lovingly dedicated to you.

As I argue in the Introduction, secularism affects and shapes more than most of us realize. Many debates and discussions in the academy would be better conceived and executed if secularism were made explicit in the discussion. When one can see the effects of secularism, then many of our most pressing issues today—anti-Black racism, Indigenous resurgence, decolonization, and so forth—can also be seen in new light. As I will briefly explain in the Introduction and Chapter 1, secularism was an essential part of the racializing discourses that enabled putatively secularizing white peoples to regard themselves as superior to putatively religious non-white peoples and thus to the enacting of colonialism, Black enslavement, and Indigenous genocide. Many secular institutions today proclaim land acknowledgments, yet do not acknowledge the role of secularity itself in the dispossession of Indigenous lands, including the land on which I carried out the work for this book, Tkaronto (now Toronto). Prior to the establishment of the modern discourses of religion and secularity, Tkaronto had been the traditional territory of many Indigenous Nations, including the Anishinabek Nation, the Haudenosaunee Confederacy, and the Huron-Wendat, and is now home to many First Nation, Inuit, and Métis communities. This land, subject to several treaties held by the Mississaugas of the Credit First Nation, was cared for under the auspices of the Dish with One Spoon

Wampum Belt Covenant, an agreement among several neighboring First Nations to peaceably share and care for the land. Acknowledging the role of secularism in the dispossession of this land from these communities, and in the transformation of the status and meaning of the land (not to mention its health) for all its subsequent and current inhabitants, may contribute to opening more just ways of understanding and living together on and with the land.

Introduction

Screening the Secular

Mark Cauchi

The Visibility of Religion

In the beginning of Jacques Tati's 1967 masterpiece, *PlayTime*—his plotless and laconic comedy that loosely tracks the random misadventures of its protagonist for twenty-four hours through a modernist Parisian suburb—we are led by a sequence of shots from beyond the world into it. We move from its opening image of a luminous summer sky, full of fluffy, nebulous clouds (Figure 0.1), to an upward wide-angle shot of an imposing, dark gray, modernist office building standing starkly against the sky (Figure 0.2), and then to the inside of such a building, whose interior space is carved up by multiple geometrical angles and lines (Figure 0.3). In the latter shot, the first human figures to appear in the film—two nuns in full habit—walk toward us in a 45-degree angle on the other side of a glass wall. As they walk in lockstep, with their cornetts comically and mechanically flapping in sync like earthbound wings that cannot fly, they are framed by a grid-like series of windows. It is through these that we see them abruptly make an unnaturally sharp 90-degree left-turn and walk toward the out-of-frame, as if the geometry of their setting has infiltrated their being and shaped their very comportment. The presence of these nuns attests to the fact that, even though we move in this opening from beyond the world into it, from the indefinite or infinite (sky, clouds, heavens) to the delimited and finite (geometry, buildings, world), and thus from something like the transcendent to the immanent, this movement is not one that wholly erases religion. Religion remains visible through the immanent window frame, although, cloistered behind glass, it is highly circumscribed. Thus, even though religion is visible here, what confines or regulates religion—let us call it the secular—

FIGURE 0.1 *Opening title, still from* PlayTime *(dir. Jacques Tati, 1967).*

FIGURE 0.2 *Office building, still from* PlayTime *(dir. Jacques Tati, 1967).*

is nearly unseen in its transparency.[1] While commentators on *PlayTime* recognize that the film renders the invisible boundaries (the "windows") of modernism visible, they never to my knowledge entertain the thought that the film's disclosure of modernity is also a disclosure of secularity.[2] It is as if, to such scholars, religion is visible (although ignorable), while the secular is not.

The visibility of religion in *PlayTime* is not a unique occurrence in the histories of cinema and the study of film and, in fact, carries on traditions that go right back to the very origins of the medium at the turn of the previous century. Very early in this history, both filmmakers and critics

FIGURE 0.3 *Two nuns, still from* PlayTime *(dir. Jacques Tati, 1967).*

were alive to the religious possibilities and actualities of moving pictures. Already in 1897, Albert Kirchner made *La Passion du Christ* and Mark Klaw and Abraham Erlanger made *The Horitz Passion Play*, both now lost, initiating a tradition of global religious filmmaking.[3] As Jolyon Mitchell and S. Brent Plate show, immediately following these first forays, writers in the early century began to reflect on the relationship between the new moving images and religion, some worried about the deleterious effects of this novel phenomenon, others seeing in it opportunities for attracting congregants, spreading and inculcating piety and morality, and developing new theological aesthetics.[4]

While the level and nature of the attention to religion by both filmmakers and film writers have undergone many changes since then, the fact of the attention has not abated. In recent decades among professional film scholars, there has been a steady flow of work on the relationship between religion and film, albeit primarily from within religious studies.[5] Since 2000 alone, there have been no less than five major and hefty, reader-type collections on the topic.[6] This group does not include all the collections on more specialized sub-areas of religion and film, focused on different regions, various religions, specific periods, or particular aspects of religion, like theology, ritual, divinities, and so forth, or particular aspects of cinema, like the medium, genres, reception, auteurs, and so forth.[7] At the same time, there have also been many dozens of monographs on religion and film.[8] And, on top of all of these books, there are two dedicated journals (*Religion and Film*; *Journal for Religion, Film, and Media*), several special issues in various other journals, and a great many one-off articles. "Religion and Film" is evidently a well-established and thriving topic of scholarly enquiry, if not its own field.

Here the central topic of the present book begins to emerge. For by taking note of this abundance of scholarship on film and religion, we are able to confront the seemingly banal yet elemental fact that, for scholars of film, *religion is conspicuous in cinema*, it stands out as a distinct phenomenon, and so requires special consideration. Indeed, the conspicuousness of religion in cinema is presumably the central reason that scholars in *film studies* are able largely to avoid discussing religion directly or to discuss it only as subsumed under another category (like ideology), while scholars in *religious studies* can focus on it. For religion to be circumvented or circumscribed by film studies, for it to be relegated to and quarantined in religious studies, it must first be visible to scholars of both disciplines. The fact that religion in film stands out to such scholars, however, invites the critical question, *from what does religion stand out? From what is it distinct?* The obvious, although usually unstated, answer to this question is that religion can only be distinct from, and stand out against, a background that is, or that is taken to be, nonreligious, which is to say, secular. Now, if religion in film stands out to scholars, then the secular background from which it stands out—like the secular windows of *PlayTime*—obviously does not itself stand out. Indeed, as we shall see in the next section, in contrast to the abundance of work on religion and film noted above, if one were to search for work devoted to what one might assume is the related and perhaps even more expected topic—film and secularism—one would find almost nothing. In neglecting the secular, film scholars are not different from most in the humanities and the social sciences, who have, until very recently, also largely neglected thinking critically about secularism. But while questions about secularity have in the last couple of decades been reinterrogated and pursued in new ways in what some call "secular studies" or "postsecularism" (more on these further in the Introduction), the study of film in both film studies and religious studies has largely remained untouched by these concerns.

Before sketching in more depth in the following sections what this neglect of the secular looks like in the academic study of film, how it can be conceived, and what it might mean to study the secular in cinema, I want to pause here and clarify the language being used. Up to now, I have been using in this introduction and in the collection's title the term "secular" and its cognates—the secular, secularity, secularism, secularization—in a very general, loose, and mostly interchangeable sense. To be precise, it is important to distinguish between three different, related concepts: secularism, secularity (or "the secular"), and secularization. Leaving aside for now how these concepts can be theorized, which I will take up gradually throughout the introduction, these terms can be minimally defined in the following ways: (1) *secularism* can refer either to the political doctrine wherein there is an institutional separation of religion and political power (e.g., the American "wall of separation," French *laïcité*) or to the whole philosophico-ideological framework or outlook that encompasses all of these terms; (2)

secularity or *"the secular"* refer to an epistemological category or ontological condition of being (e.g., when we distinguish between religious music and secular music, or a religious society and a secular one, where "secular" and "religious" function as categories to differentiate the respective ontological features of two phenomena); and (3) *secularization* refers to the historical process by which something (a society, an institution, a concept, a practice, a person) changes from being putatively religious to being putatively secular. Despite their important differences, these meanings are overlapping and interdependent, and they form a kind of conceptual constellation. Thus, when I say in this introduction that film scholars ignore the relationship between cinema and secularism, I am not referring exclusively to political secularism, or any of the other individual terms, but to the relationship between cinema and this whole constellation of interrelated concepts and problematics (close to the second meaning of number 1). Similarly, by entitling this collection *Cinema and Secularism*, I am likewise referring to the whole constellation of secular-concepts, although different chapters will focus on different facets of it, as I shall spell out later.

The Neglect of the Secular in the Contemporary Study of Film

The neglect of the secular indicated earlier is evident throughout contemporary film scholarship in the Anglo and European academies. The one consistent exception is scholarship on Indian cinema, where the question of secularism has long been a vital one, as Sheila Nayar will discuss in Chapter 6. Even though the parameters of the work on secularism in Indian cinema are fairly narrow, focused primarily on questions of representation and religious pluralism (for understandable reasons) while downplaying other potential issues like humanism, atheism, immanence, naturalism, and science, it is still regrettable that this body of work has not prompted film scholars in other areas to consider that secularism can be a worthwhile topic for the study of film.[9] Consequently, outside the context of Indian cinema, one will find barely any specialized monographs,[10] no edited collections, no dedicated journals or special issues, and only handfuls of journal articles and book chapters[11]—certainly nothing constituting an established topic or field. As Sophie Sunderland succinctly observes in one of the earliest of these rare essays (specifically on the work of Jane Campion), "Secularism is rarely visible as an organizing trope in film."[12]

Beyond the paucity of studies devoted specifically to secularism and cinema, when the secular does show up in film scholarship, whether in film studies or religious studies, it is usually briefly, offhandedly, and/or uncritically, with most occurrences simply assuming that film is secular. When

Leo Braudy, for instance, sees in cinema an attribute commonly associated with secularism, he simply asserts, without much explanation, that "Film is potentially the most atheistic of the arts."[13] What could that possibly mean? And why does that seem so obvious that there is no felt need to explain it? Leaving aside the few exceptions for the moment as I try to make evident the norm, let us consider a few revealing moments in academic film scholarship, beginning with film studies (some of these examples are taken up in more depth by me in Chapter 1). Here I disagree with Phillip Maciak's recent contention in his excellent and important book on silent film and secularism (discussed below) that, even though "film studies scholars have been slow to turn to secularism as an analytic category," "it has been a while since film studies ... has been gripped by anything so monolithic as the secularization thesis" (the latter is the idea that, as societies and cultures modernize, they also secularize).[14] Consider Charles Musser's magisterial history of early American cinema, in which he situates the emergence of moving pictures in a long history of projected images going back to early modern magic lanterns and phantasmagorias. He frames this history through a textbook account of European secularization, the kind we will see Charles Taylor criticize in the next section as a "subtraction story" (the secular results when religion is subtracted). This history involves an intellectual shift from "proof by authority" (i.e., Bible, Aristotle, the Church, tradition) to "rationalism," and a corresponding shift in which "belief in ghosts declined" and "witch burnings ceased,"[15] ultimately resulting, he says, in the "demystification of the projected image."[16] Such a narrative, while not wholly wrong obviously, does not account for the persistent ways that putatively non-rational elements remain in society, for ongoing ways that mystery and myth inhabit culture (e.g., spirit photographs), for the metamorphoses rather than the waning of religion in modernity, not to mention for the *contributions* these make to the evolution and reception of moving images, as is discussed in my chapter and those in Part III.

Shifting attention from cinema's origins to a hegemonic cinematic tradition (Hollywood) and a landmark essay in professional film studies, a taken-for-granted secularism is also visible in a different way in Laura Mulvey's "Visual Pleasure and Narrative Cinema" (1975).[17] In the essay, she argues that classic Hollywood cinema configures women as objects for a scopophilic male gaze. While her analyses of various films, particularly those of Hitchcock, arguably presuppose a rather Christian moral framework about virtuous and fallen women, it is notable that this presence is merely presupposed: illustrating a point I will make in Chapter 1 through Bruno Latour about how modern secularist discourses are always defied by persisting subtle, latent, or transmogrified forms of religiosity, Mulvey seems unaware of, and uninterested in, what roles secularism or religion might play in her own gaze and in the aesthetic regime she identifies.[18] She does not consider, for instance, that the related ascendancy of the female nude in early modern European art historically coincides with what is often considered a secularization of European art, and that the latter involved, in part, a shift from aesthetic artifacts functioning within cultic parameters to being made for (defined by) being displayed.[19] On the other hand, in her later work, *Death 24x a Second* (2006), where she examines Iranian filmmaker Abbas Kiarostami's *Through the Olive Trees* (1994), she does not fail to observe that the particular representation of female sexuality in that film is due, in part, to Kiarostami having to work around the supposed "outstanding blind spot of Islamic culture, the status and representation of women," referring to women's alleged concealment in Islam, an idea common in Western media after 9/11.[20] "Islamic *culture*" is probably her (liberal secular) effort not to blame the *religion* of Islam for the alleged blind spot, but she evidently regards Islam (a religion, after all) as the determining factor, otherwise she would say Persian or Middle Eastern culture. Given these facts, it would seem that Islam's alleged blindness toward women's visibility, and Kiarostami's filmic circumvention of it, are conspicuous ("outstanding") to Mulvey's evidently secularist gaze. This is a surprising and telling inversion of her earlier position: while the possible secularity of Hollywood's scopophilic gaze was unnoticed by Mulvey's secular gaze, Islam's allegedly scopo-phobic gaze—its veiling of women, sometimes connected to its supposedly aniconic stance toward images of the Prophet (discussed by Walid El Khachab in a later chapter)—stood out to her. That is, Mulvey's secular gaze cannot see the secularity of a filmic gaze, but it can see the religiosity of one.

The problem of the missing secular in film studies affects not only how scholars understand films but also how they understand, in a meta-reflective mode, the study of film itself. As I shall expand upon in Chapter 1, in a post-Althusserian intellectual climate driven by the distinction between science and ideology, Christian Metz in his epoch-making work, *The Imaginary Signifier* (1977), regards earlier phenomenological film theory (Bazin, Ayfre, Mitry, etc.) as being "duped" or "lured"[21] by a "fetishistic"[22] film image instead of, like him, scientifically disclosing those mechanisms. In framing the distinction between his own work and that of the phenomenologists in these terms, Metz has straightforwardly appropriated the classic, proto-secular, post-Enlightenment discourse about religion, configuring the object of critique (phenomenological theory) in the terms classically imputed to religion and configuring his own position (science) as having been purged of it. Later still, and engaging in a critique of the very form of film theory pioneered by Metz, Mulvey, and others, David Bordwell essentially turns the tables on Metz, but still manages to repeat his secularist moves. In *Making Meaning: Inference and Rhetoric in the Interpretation of Cinema* (1989), he undertakes to show that film criticism "ignores the extent to which its premises derive from the fundamental analogies laid down in postwar literary criticism," and that, in turn, "Literary interpretation seldom acknowledges the degree to which it models itself . . . upon mythological and scriptural exegesis," and, as such, is "a secular version of biblical criticism" (reductively assuming that biblical criticism is religious).[23] As a secular version of biblical criticism, film criticism is, for Bordwell, clearly not secular enough. This shortcoming is due to its alleged latent "Christian" "contempt for appearances" which "wrap[s] the text's sensory qualities in a cocoon of abstractions."[24] Thus, when Bordwell develops his "historical poetics,"[25] averse as it is to the cultural specificity of meaning and aiming instead at "transcultural" and "panhuman" meanings,[26] it is a decidedly secularist criticism, although he never interrogates carefully or critically the meanings of "biblical," "Christian," or "secular," or how the genealogy of his own position, like the one he provides for film theory, would actually link him back to Enlightenment treatments (constructions) of religion.

Turning to the religious studies scholarship on film, the effort there to establish a relationship between religion and film, when it does not outright ignore questions about secularism, is often self-consciously conceived as challenging the opposition between religion and secularism. This challenge sometimes leads to critical reflection upon the secular, as in Joel Martin's Introduction to the volume *Screening the Sacred: Religion, Myth, and Ideology in Popular American Film* (1995) (the title of which I play on in my own title here). In it, he rightly criticizes film studies scholars for "ignor[ing] religion and the academic study of religion" and for simply "assum[ing] secular values . . . matter more than religious ones," both of which "take secularization for granted."[27] Perhaps limited by the fact that he is expressing this thought in an introduction, he does not develop what it would mean not to take secularization for granted and what this would tell us about cinema itself. John Lyden's book, *Film as Religion* (2003), advances these concerns a little further by being attentive to the constructedness of the categories of "religion" and "the secular," often putting them in quotation marks and judiciously attempting to move beyond the Christian bias in the concept of "religion." But the text regularly aligns the relationship between film and religion with the relationship between the secular and the religious, as if it is given that film is secular. This assumption is further evident when he devotes a chapter to thoughtfully articulating the difficulties with defining religion[28] and when he criticizes both Darrol Bryant for his perjorative definition of "secular culture" and Conrad Ostwalt for an inadequate explanation of how cinema is a "secular religion,"[29] but then never offers his own substantive discussion of the secular. He does suggestively propose at one brief moment that secularity should be thought as religious pluralism, which allows him to posit that secularism is a form of religion, but the suggestion is not developed substantially or applied consistently (sometimes "secular culture" just seems to mean nonreligion).[30] Following Lyden's criticism of him, Conrad Ostwalt later further develops his ideas about secularism in his book *Secular Steeples: Popular Culture and Religious Imagination*, which is one of the most substantive discussions of secularism in relation to cinema.

The book proposes many innovative ideas in this regard: religion is part of the secular world,[31] and, as such, is a "secular cultural form" like film itself, which is what allows film to "function religiously."[32] But unlike his effort to define religion, and despite his critique of the secularization thesis, he never once to my knowledge defines the secular or explains why cinema is, as he says repeatedly, a "secular medium."[33] The fundamental questions—what does secularity consist in? and what makes cinema secular?—are not only left unanswered but unasked.

One promising area where the secular is addressed critically is among the small interdisciplinary group of scholars exploring the notion of "postsecular cinema," which is, in fact, the background out of which the current project emerged.[34] The concept of the postsecular itself has evolved in the last two decades or so in response to the so-called return of the religious in politics, social theory, and philosophy. The occurrence has prompted a flurry of new theoretical work on secularism in the humanities and the social sciences and has even spawned the new area of "secular studies,"[35] as mentioned earlier. Theorists of the postsecular have argued that the long-regnant secularization thesis and the complimentary notion that secularity and religiosity have an oppositional relation are inadequate for thinking through the ongoing presence of religion in allegedly secular societies and cultures. Instead, they have undertaken to conceive a form of secularism that is not the same as the classical model, without simply abandoning secularism altogether. As Jurgen Habermas succinctly puts it, "a *post*-secular society must at some point have been in a secular condition," suggesting that it retains some secular features, even if it has also undergone a "change in consciousness" about its relation to religion, rendering it what Hent de Vries calls a "reflective secularism."[36] A handful of works have emerged that explicitly adopt this critical stance toward secularism in relation to cinema: the edited book by Costica Bradatan and Camil Ungureanu, *Religion in Contemporary European Cinema: The Postsecular Constellation* (2014), and the book coedited by John Caruana and myself, *Immanent Frames: Postsecular Cinema between Malick and von Trier* (2018), as well as a series of articles by Catherine Wheatley and Robert Sinnerbrink, and one-offs by others.[37] In a slightly different way, the book by M. Gail Hamner, *Imaging Religion in Film: The Politics of Nostalgia* (2011), while not using the locution "postsecular cinema," interprets film and the treatment of it by scholars in a manner explicitly informed by a postsecular stance. The most substantive examination of cinema and secularism to emerge out of this debate is Philip Maciak's *The Disappearance of Christ: Secularism in the Silent Era*. Maciak shows how silent era cinema operated with an aesthetic he calls "spectacular realism," which he describes as "the aesthetic of the contact zone between realism and fantasy, the uncanny superimposition of disbelief and its suspension, the seamless balancing of the naïve pleasure of credulity with the smug pleasure of incredulity."[38] This aesthetic, concretely demonstrating how transcendence might appear in immanence, allowed silent cinema to function as "a training ground for belief in a secular age."[39] But, as I said, besides this one, specialized, and very recent area of research, for the most part, one consistently and overwhelming finds throughout film scholarship, across both film studies and religious studies, the *assumption* that cinema is secular and, consequently, little effort to define the secular, to spell out its relationship to cinema, or to specify what is secular about cinema (if it is).

While the present project has admittedly grown out of this latter area of research, it is not limited to problematizing the relationship between secularism and religion or to focusing on the silent era, although these issues will inevitably need to be addressed. Its main intention, rather, is to investigate explicitly and critically in various ways the relationships between cinema and secularism broadly construed in all eras, in popular and art cinema, in fiction and documentary, and in global film cultures. Before suggesting in broad terms what might be involved in this relationship and then going on to sketch out the particular ways the contributors to this volume pursue these questions, I want to pause for a moment to reflect theoretically on the absence of attention to secularism in general and in film scholarship.

Discerning the Secular

In largely overlooking the relationship between cinema and secularism, contemporary scholars of film in film studies and religious studies have not deviated from academics in other humanities and social science disciplines, who have, until very recently, also largely failed to develop critical analyses of the secular. What is the cause of this neglect? Talal Asad, the eminent anthropologist at CUNY and one of the major contemporary theorists of secularity, asks the startling question in his 2003 book, *Formations of the Secular*, "what would an anthropology of secularism look like?"[40] The question is startling because, historically, anthropology was typically interested in what we have come to call the "religious" practices of non-Western and allegedly non-modern peoples. But, tellingly, classical anthropology never undertook to do an anthropology of the very point of view—a secular point of view—from which it carried out its own self-given mandate, a point made in a different but related way by Bruno Latour, to whose work I shall turn in my chapter.[41] Why is that? Employing something of a fish-in-water argument, Asad answers, "because the secular is so much part of our modern life, it is not easy to grasp it directly."[42] The sheer pervasiveness of the secular, in which the secularity of things becomes unremarkable, renders the secular invisible to a secular gaze. A secular gaze can generally see ostentatious religion (like the nuns in *PlayTime* or the

Islamic blindspot in Mulvey), or sometimes discern the presence of latent or transmogrified religion (like Bordwell's secular biblical criticism, but not like Mulvey on Hitchcock), but will generally seek to circumscribe and quarantine it.[43] What this secular gaze generally does not see, or see with equal attentiveness, clarity, or rigor, is secularity itself. But if the gaze itself is secular, and this gaze cannot see the secular, then it follows that this gaze also cannot see (at least a dimension of) itself. This is a gaze that is not adequately self-reflexive or self-critical and which thus looks at the world through its secular frame or lens in something of a self-blind and, therefore, ideological manner. Such a gaze may be described not only as secular but as secularist.

In thus functioning ideologically, the invisibility of the secular to the secular gaze is not unlike other such invisible categories that have played constitutive roles in social and cultural formations but which, for a long time, escaped thematic notice. The invisibility of the secular is thus analogous to the long-standing invisibility of, say, whiteness in discourses of race, or masculinity in discourses of gender. In his now-classic text, *White*, Richard Dyer observes that "[t]here has been an enormous amount of analysis of racial imagery in the past decades," and yet "until recently a notable absence from such work has been the study of images of white people."[44] This absence, and the turning of attention to it, is not undetermined. For "[a]s long as race is something only applied to non-white peoples, as long as white people are not racially seen, they/we function as a human norm. Other people are raced, we are just people."[45] Although this introduction is not the place to pursue this point at length, we should note that it is not only that these relations of secularism, whiteness, and masculinity are analogous, but they also in many ways overlap or intersect. Here it is important to see how the proto-secular critique of religion that develops in and follows the Enlightenment becomes intertwined with evolving discourses of racialization, in various ways: white European and American Christians increasingly impute religion, or disparaged forms of religion, to non-white peoples; on the flipside of that move, as John Lardas Modern shows, nineteenth-century white American Evangelicals aligned their practices with the growing discourse, sensibility, and techniques of secularism, leading him to speak of "evangelical secularism"; dominant religio-racial communities, like WASPs in Britain or America, begin to racialize other seemingly "white" religions, as occurs with nineteenth-century debates about whether Irish Catholics or Jewish people are white.[46] In all of these different moves, we can see how "The unmarked racial category and the unmarked religious category jointly mark their others," as Vincent Lloyd argues in the Introduction to *Race and Secularism in America*, leading him to conclude, perhaps too sweepingly, that "whiteness is secular, and the secular is white."[47] The ideological dimension of secularism does not always have to be this glaringly and politically nefarious, although sometimes it no doubt is. Other times, it endemically and silently guides scholars (film or otherwise) away from considering the religious or secular dimensions of various phenomena. Secularism can thus function ideologically to obscure or screen out numerous issues, including the issue of itself.

To claim, as I did earlier, that a secularist gaze cannot see its own secularity is not to claim that it does not have any account of secularity whatsoever, just that it has an ideological or assumed one. Asad's metatheoretical disclosure of anthropology's blindness to secularity is, in fact, indicative of a broader manner of thinking about, or not thinking about, the secular in modernity. We get a helpful articulation of this (non)thinking in Charles Taylor's 2007 book, *A Secular Age*, where he argues, among other things, that the dominant way of conceiving secularity in modernity is through what he calls "subtraction stories." What he means by these are

> stories of modernity in general, and secularity in particular, which explain them [modernity and secularity] by human beings having lost, or sloughed off, or liberated themselves from certain earlier, confining horizons, or illusions, or limitations of knowledge. What emerges from this process—modernity or secularity—is to be understood in terms of underlying features of human nature which were there all along, but had been impeded by what is now set aside.[48]

In the dominant (secularist) conception of secularity, then, secularism is often "defined negatively," as Craig Calhoun notes;[49] it is the *non*-religious, produced through the negation and purgation of whatever we (the self-defined nonreligious academy) impute to religion. Such a conception assumes that religion is a superficial and artificial and therein false façade or screen, covering over and obscuring an authentic nonreligious core, which reason can thus peel or burn away or unmask until the true, nonreligious, secular, universal, humanist essence remains. But by defining the secular *via negativa*, we not only fail to articulate positively what it is, but, linking back to Asad, we simply stop noticing it. For if secularity can be present only when religion is absent, or rather *as* the absence of religion, then, in this perspective, secularity is not some thing, is an absence, and is thus nothing to be seen. Religion, like a hijab in a white public square full of jeans and baseball caps, is the conspicuous and problematic phenomenon and concept that needs accounting, whereas the secular is so visible, it is invisible.

It is this inconspicuousness of the secular, its simultaneous pervasiveness and invisibility, that begins to explain why contemporary scholars of film consistently note the presence of religiosity in film—whether this is to leave it aside (as in film studies) or to focus on it (as in religious studies)—but consistently overlook the secular.

Linking Cinema and Secularism

However secularism should be conceived, and whatever its particular relationship to cinema, secularism would seem necessarily to have *some* connection to cinema, determining in some way what it can be and how it functions, how spectators can view it, how theorists can conceive it and critics analyze it. Even Charles Taylor, who has been formative to the revitalization of secular studies, but who almost never mentions cinema, discerns a connection between them. After arguing that the secular age is constituted not by the waning of religion but by a change in the relationship between immanence and transcendence, he suggests on three separate occasions that this change is the very condition of our experience of cinema, or at least of a certain form of it. He writes in one instance:

> Perhaps the clearest sign of the transformation of our world is that today many people look back to the world of the [pre-secular] porous self with nostalgia. As though the creation of a thick emotional boundary between us and the cosmos were now lived as a loss. The aim is to try to recover some measure of this lost feeling. So people go to the movies about the uncanny in order to experience a frisson. Our [pre-secular] peasant ancestors would have thought us insane. You can't get a frisson from what is really in fact terrifying you.[50] (38; see also 337 and 741)

Taylor's brief comments here, only slightly expanded on in his other references, are admittedly very thin and ultimately inadequate for considering the full complexity of cinema and secularity and would need ample elaboration to be convincing, but they are suggestive and at least point to a connection worth pursuing. What might probing this relation further and deeper look like? What other issues beyond immanence, transcendence, and the uncanny might be relevant (as interesting and underexplored as those are)?

While on first approach the goal of investigating the relationship between cinema and secularism might appear straightforward enough, a moment's reflection reveals just how in the dark we are. Before even considering *how* we might make the secular in cinema visible, do we even know *what is the secular* that is going to be made visible? Does secular simply mean nonreligious? Or atheistic? Or disenchanted? Worldly, modern, democratic, pluralistic, or neutral? How do these relate? For if secular means disenchanted, for example, then it cannot simply mean nonreligious, since, as Max Weber himself argued, biblical monotheism contributed to Western disenchantment.[51] Let's say, for argument's sake, that the secular means nonreligious: What does *that* mean? Does it refer to something that does not belong to a *specific religion* (like Judaism or Buddhism, if those are religions)? Or does it refer to the absence of things associated with religion in a more general sense, like not being theistic, or ritualistic, or devout?

Would it preclude or include what some people call "spirituality"? Does being nonreligious require a *total* absence of religiosity (whatever it is), or can something or someone be *partially* nonreligious (and would that entail being partially or wholly secular?)? Or, rather, does something or someone's secularity consist in *how* they are religious or nonreligious, or how *intensely* they are religious or nonreligious?

In one last thread of questions, if, as is often the case, film is assumed *to be* secular, which is an ontological determination, would "religious films," as scholars sometimes blithely call them, even be possible? Are all supposedly religious films—say, Rossellini's *The Flowers of St. Francis* (1950), Vijay Sharma's *Jai Santoshi Maa* (1975), and Apichatpong Weerasethakul's *Uncle Boonmee Who Can Remember His Past Lives* (2011)—in their essence actually secular? Is their seeming religiosity, then, a mere façade, pretense, or maybe an instrumental device betraying their secular essence? Or, rather, is cinema ontologically neutral, as is sometimes asserted about technology, and so would be, in itself, neither secular nor religious ("neutral" derives from the Latin *ne* and *uter*, meaning "neither/nor")? That definition, unfortunately, is precisely one of the main ways that political secularism is commonly defined (neither this religion nor that one). This point almost pushes us to return to the first questions above about what is secularity and what is religion, suggesting that we do not yet have a viable way through this thicket of problems.

These questions, and others still we have not broached or have not had the acuity to perceive, will not all be answered in this introduction or in the chapters that follow. But they give us a broad sense of what is at stake in this topic and the scope of the lacuna in film scholarship.

Approaching Cinema and Secularism

Individually, the chapters in this volume contribute to making the secular in cinema visible by responding in different ways to various of the issues raised above and to others they generate themselves. This variety is unsurprising and, I believe, desirable in an early attempt to address these issues. Before arguing for definitive understandings of the relationship between cinema and secularism, it is helpful to have a broad and diverse range of different issues and possible approaches. The contributors themselves come from diverse disciplines—film studies, religious studies, philosophy, political theory, and literary studies—and, moreover, tend to be quite interdisciplinary within their fields. In addition to this diversity of approaches, the issues are explored in different film and intellectual cultures: North America, Europe, the Middle East, Africa, South Asia, and East Asia.[52] As such, the chapters included here do not all share the same conceptions of secularism and secularization, do not focus on the same issues, do not all theorize the relationship between cinema and secularism in the same way, and do not adopt the same methodologies.

The book is divided into three parts. Part I: Is Cinema Secular? Genealogy, Theory, Philosophy, comprises theoretical chapters focused on challenging the assumed secularism of cinema. The chapters here set out in different ways and do not necessarily end up with the same position on the relationship between our main concepts. Cumulatively, however, the chapters help us to see that the notion that cinema is secular *is* an assumption, to see how that assumption evolved, and to think about what might make cinema secular or non-secular in differing cultural traditions.

This part begins with my own chapter, "Secularist Film Studies and the Occlusion of the Secular," because it extends the issues raised in this introduction and provides further background for why the topic of cinema and secularism is largely absent in the study of film and so can appear novel today, which is the problem to which most of the other chapters are responding. The chapter adapts Bruno Latour's theory of modernity to think about the relationship between religion and secularity. It argues that, on the one hand, modern thinkers progressively undertake to separate and purify the secular and the religious, while, on the other, their efforts at separation cause the two categories to grow ever more intertwined, leading to an unacknowledged hybridization of them in various phenomena. Moving images, I argue, especially in their early days, are one such secular-religious hybrid phenomenon. While pre-academic film theorists (Epstein, Eisenstein, Benjamin, Krakauer, Bazin, Ayfre, among numerous others) were attuned to this hybridity and thereby self-consciously cognizant of cinema's relation to secularism (and religion), the emergence in the university of academic film studies and religious studies in the 1970s led, ironically, but in keeping with Asad's observations, to the progressive decline of critical attention to the relationship between secularity and cinema.

In Chapter 2, "Deleuze's 'Conversion of Belief': The Time-Image and the Disruption of the Secularist Origin of Cinema," John Caruana treads over some of the same questions as pursued in Chapter 1 about cinema's origins and the shift from epistemological registers to more existential and ethical ones, except that he does so by engaging in an innovative reading of Gilles Deleuze's film-philosophy. Through Deleuze, he undertakes to show doubly how the emergence of cinema cannot be separated from the dynamics of secularism and how what Caruana calls a "critical cinema," linked to Deleuze's time-image, can break from "ideological secularism." Caruana first turns to one of Deleuze's major sources, Nietzsche, and outlines the latter's untimely critique of secularism—that the dogmatic conceptions of transcendence in religion have not disappeared with the death of God but have merely been displaced into various manifestations of humanism (particularly, concepts of subjectivity and history). Caruana then reflects on the evolution of cinema to show that it emerges into the world Nietzsche was describing and argues that Deleuze's concept of the "action-image" in many ways diagnoses in "classical cinema" many of the same issues Nietzsche was critiquing in secularism: an agent in full control of its abilities able to respond to his situation and willfully change history. But just as Nietzsche envisioned alternate forms of religiosity and secularity, so Caruana provocatively suggests that Deleuze's "*Cinema* books . . . become the occasion to imagine a different way of being secular." In particular, Caruana examines the links between Deleuze's concept of the "time-image" and his long-standing concern with belief in the world, which Caruana reads with extraordinary depth and richness, and then concretizes these with a discussion both of Roberto Rossellini's *Europa '51* (1952) and of Deleuze's reading of it. Deleuze's notion of belief, and its presence in Rossellini's film, Caruana argues, eschews the easy opposition between secularism and religion endemic to the post-Enlightenment world, opening up the possibility of a different form of secularism.

Modern Western assumptions about secularism and its link to cinema are challenged in a different way by Francisca Cho in Chapter 3, "The Secular as Sacred: Cinema and Buddhist Ritual." Provocatively rejecting the idea, fairly common in contemporary religious studies, that the concepts of "religion" and "secularism" are legacies of Christianity in modernity and colonially imposed elsewhere, Cho instead argues that the distinction is endemically present in both Christianity and Buddhism, although their relationships function differently. This is important for Cho because it means that "[s]ecularism is not a single universal historical dynamic," and therefore the consideration of secularism's relation to cinema must be considered in specific religious contexts. Offering an account of the cross-pollination of Asian and Western conceptions of secularity and religion in the nineteenth and twentieth centuries, and of this encounter's engendering of "secular spirituality" in both contexts, Cho focuses on how the latter was adopted within various traditions of Buddhism, particularly Mahāyāna Buddhism, allowing the mundane to be conceived as a viable vehicle for nirvana (liberation from the cycle of samsara). From there, Cho goes into a deeply learned discussion of Buddhist philosophy/theology with an eye to demonstrating the blurring of religiosity and secularity (eternity and temporality, non-worldliness and materiality, mystery, and phenomenology) in this discourse and practice, and its consequences for the status of images within it. As Cho shows, despite the fact that the Buddha has been liberated from samsara and that the material world is held to be illusory, certain objects and images are nevertheless understood in Mahāyāna Buddhism as incarnations of the Buddha and therefore as suitable for veneration. Indeed, as she explains, images are understood here as central to Buddhist ritual practices, including meditation. This background is what allows her to propose what she calls a "Buddhist theory of cinema," in which the "cinematic imagination" and its "aesthetic rituals" are used to cultivate "better imaginings" of personhood rather than our usual "maladaptive fantasies." In such a theory, she writes, "the distinction between religious and secular is disposable."

The chapters in Part II: Situating Secularism: Culture, Politics, and Cinema all share the insight of Cho's chapter: that secularism is not a universal category, that how it relates to religion is different in different social and cultural contexts, and therefore that its relationship to cinema will be different in distinct social, cultural, and cinematic contexts. Part II is different from Cho's chapter in that, unlike her mostly theoretical articulation and her central point that the secular and the religious are blurred, the chapters here are substantially engaged in readings of particular films or cinematic traditions. These readings, however, all treat the particular relationships between cinema and secularism they engage with as bound to the places and cultural and political milieu in which they exist: West Africa, the Middle East, India, and the United States.

Earlier in the chapter I had claimed that, to an Anglo-European secularist gaze, religion stands out, particularly if it reinforces the secularist perception that religion is inferior. In Chapter 4, "Ousmane Sembène's *Moolaadé*: Sacred Space as Refuge and Political Agency," Nikolas Kompridis offers a richly detailed and philosophical reading of *Moolaadé* that works against such a secularist view. Thus, rather than concentrate on the issue in the film that stands out most starkly to Anglo and European secular viewers—the critique of female genital cutting, which is often taken to illustrate the alleged barbarity of (non-white) religious traditions—Kompridis concentrates on the film's titular concept, *moolaadé* (the sacred space of refuge and asylum), and draws out from it the role that sacrality plays in the film's internal religious critique. For Kompridis, the film provides "a syncretic vision of politics in which long-standing traditions and practices confront one another, staging a process of reflection on the question of which should be critically exposed and abandoned, and which reflectively renewed and passed on." To demonstrate this "process of reflection," Kompridis attends to how rigorously Sembène has constructed space in the film, particularly that of *moolaadé*, and how his filmic thinking overlaps with dimensions of Fanon, Foucault, Durkheim, and others. Ultimately, Kompridis wants to show that Sembène is not simply attempting to revitalize a precolonial, indigenous tradition of sacrality (*moolaadé*), but to renew and transform the sacred and the contemporary condition. But since it is the sacred that is being drawn upon, this means, Kompridis contends, that "the sacred cannot be desacralized." If the sacred as sacred can be a source for contemporary social forms, then Sembène's sacred is irreducible to our modern conceptions of religion and secularism. Through his engagement with Sembène's film, Kompridis's chapter thus challenges several secularist assumptions—that critique is purely secular, that religious pluralism requires secularism, and that the cinematic configuration of space and time is purely secular.

In Chapter 5, Walid El Khachab shifts our attention to another region of Africa and neighboring territories, namely, the Middle East, and takes up a number of issues that overlap with those identified by Kompridis: religious pluralism, patriarchy, and the critique of religion. However, unlike Kompridis's argument that Sembène's *Moolaadé* renews religious heritage in order to cultivate a democratic politics, El Khachab's chapter considers, theoretically and through readings of particular films, how the traditions of Middle Eastern filmmaking for the most part play a secularizing role that is, in part, due to features of the medium itself and its traditions of filmmaking. To explain this, El Khachab observes that, while there are almost no Middle Eastern films that adopt an anti-religious viewpoint and that cinema is not a "full-fledged agent of secularism" in the Middle East, there are nevertheless two traditions of secular filmmaking that he calls a "cinema of disenchantment" and a "cinema of multiple enchantments." The former, of which El Khachab says there are only a few examples in Middle Eastern cinema, advocates for a rationalist vision of the world, but without completely removing religion from the public sphere. The latter form of cinema is one that also does not wholly evacuate religion, but recognizes a pluralism of religions, particularly of the three Abrahamic faiths. El Khachab then explores the cinema of multiple enchantments by engaging in readings of two Egyptian comedies—*Fatima, Marika and Rachel* (1949) and *Hassan, Marcus and Cohen* (1954) (one name for each of the Abrahamic religions). In the former, El Khachab shows, a religious pluralism is intersected with capitalism and sexism, while in the latter film, secularism works through establishing a series of compromises between different aspects of the faith communities and modernity.

The role of cinema in negotiating secularism is taken up in a different context by Sheila Nayar in Chapter 6, "The Impossible Possible: Secularism and Hindi Popular Cinema." Through readings of numerous popular Hindi films, Nayar examines the different patterns of the treatments of secularism in Indian cinema. She restricts her analysis to popular films because she aims to disclose "what, when it comes to secularism, spectators are willing to ideologically submit or consent to, not to mention what they insist upon and also . . . reject." After a brief, informative discussion of the history and main ideas behind Indian secularism, Nayar generalizes secularism in India by noting that, unlike, say, French *laïcité*, it is not anti-religious and is never "without religion." In fact, the central aspiration of secularism in popular cinema, summarized in Nayar's title (the impossible possible), is that harmony is achievable among religions. This is most clearly evident in the form of cinema she calls AAA, based on the model of secularism projected in the classic, popular film, *Amar Akbar Anthony* (1977), which, like the films discussed by El Khachab, refers to the coexistence of three religions in India (Hindu, Muslim, Christian). This somewhat idealistic form of popular Hindi cinema is nuanced by Nayar, however, when she attends to other sorts of films, or dimensions of films, and the ways they represent or don't represent minority groups, like Muslims, Dalits, or foreigners. Bearing those complexities in mind, the overall image of secularism in popular Hindi cinema that emerges from Nayar's analysis is one that combines religious pluralism and Indian nationalism; as Nayar writes, the view of secularism promulgated in these films is that "any 'real' Hindu, any 'real' Muslim—or Parsi, or Christian, or Buddhist, or Jain—is always one who, in the name of their religion, ethically puts *India first.*"

Where both El Khachab and Nayar show in their respective contexts that cinematic secularism is not nonreligious but a way in which religion is negotiated, Kathryn Lofton makes the even stronger claim in Chapter 7, "Observational Secular: Religion and Documentary Film in the United States," that in the tradition of American Direct Cinema (or Observational Cinema) secularism is "associated not with irreligion but rather with control over the absence or presence of religion." Contextualizing this tradition by noting the link between documentary filmmaking and the discipline and history of anthropology, including its entanglements with colonialism and the religiosity of the other, Lofton observes that, in general, "Documentary film addresses religion poorly." Part of that has to do, she astutely argues, with the particular secularity of its gaze. Indeed, in much thought about documentary, the "documentarian is cast as the nonsectarian broker of subjects imagined to be less neutral than the filmmaker because the filmed subjects are sectarian"; aiming at such neutrality, the documentarian is secular, and the documentary film is thereby secularizing. While Direct Cinema evolves out of this background and bears many of these features, too, Lofton also notes that it "was an explicit reformation of documentary to improve upon its didacticism and legacy of colonial anthropology," a reformation which allowed Direct Cinema to be more self-critical in its secularity and thereby more generously disposed toward religion—forging what she calls an "observational secular." To support these claims, Lofton engages in nuanced readings of three works of Direct Cinema: *A Time for Burning* (1966, dir. William C. Jersey), *Holy Ghost People* (1967, dir. Peter Adair), and *Salesman* (1969, dir. Albert and David Maysles). In these films, "we find filmmakers who are, indeed, self-identified secular subjects," as in most documentary film, but who also "worked to see inside the space of religion rather than decide its oppressions at the outset."

Turning to an issue that recurs in and hovers throughout a number of chapters in the book, Part III: The Dis/Enchantment of the World in Moving Images focuses on an issue that is often central to debates around both secularism and cinema, namely, enchantment. Ever since the early twentieth century, the status of cinema's enchantment has been in question. While Weber and his followers characterized modernity as carrying out a progressive "disenchantment of the world," film promoters simultaneously trumpeted "the magic of the movies." Is cinema fundamentally disenchanted, as Musser and Gunning argue, or enchanted, as does Rachel Moore and Thomas Elssaeser?[53] The three essays that comprise this part explore this entanglement.

Catherine Wheatley delves into some of these theoretical issues in Chapter 8, "The Wonder of Film: Science, Magic, and the Endurance of Enchantment," where she innovatively examines what she calls "the hidden history of wonder in film theory." Adopting both a historical and theoretical approach, interwoven with illuminating reflections on Steven Spielberg's *Jurassic Park* (1993), her chapter undertakes to shift the concern with epistemological and metaphysical questions about cinema's believability (does the spectator believe the image is real?) to the more ontological, existential and ethical issue of wonder. After probing the meaning of wonder in general through attention to its etymology and to its place in the philosophies of Plato, Aristotle, Descartes, and Wittgenstein, Wheatley proceeds through three main steps. First, she shows in dialogue with Fulgence Marion and Tom Gunning that early cinema, while contemporary with a secularizing tendency, takes hold of its publics because of its capacity to make audiences wonder about what they see on screen and in the world, regardless of whether they cognitively understand (believe or don't believe in the reality of) what they are seeing. Next, Wheatley focuses on science fiction, a genre that Gunning had argued evolved out of the early cinema of attractions and is particularly bound up with capitalism, science, and technology—all putatively secular—in order to show that, despite these facts, the central feature of the genre is its capacity to prompt the spectator to wonder: at how these images can be produced, about the possibilities of the world becoming true, and about their insights into the current world. Finally, through attending to the different ways that André Bazin's and Lutz Koepnick's interpretations of specific cinematic means (realism and the long take, respectively) are responses to modern disenchantment, Wheatly argues that cinema's capacity to make the spectator wonder should be conceived as a "secular enchantment." Richly amplifying this point by way of Jane Bennett, Charles Taylor, Paolo Costa, and Sarah Ahmed, she argues that, despite the secularizing drive to knowledge and materialism, "film is able to emphasize and condense the experience of wonder as a visual relationship between the wonderer and the world, a relationship that opens up a space of thought and action and which relates to questions of ontology and ethics."

While Sarah Cooper does not use the words enchantment or disenchantment in Chapter 9, "Vegetal Life, Plant-Soul: Early British Film Flowers," the issues under examination nevertheless reflect those concerns and add to the discussion of wonder raised by Wheatley. Cooper, with a highly original intervention, is focused on the early twentieth-century films of plants and flowers by F. Percy Smith and the contemporary assessments of them. Smith's films, she shows, were originally often perceived as either secularist or sacred. Cooper undertakes to re-read Smith's films, as well as his own writings on them, by drawing on contemporary thinkers like Jane Bennet, Donna Haraway, Bruno Latour, and, especially, Michael Marder's notion of "plant-soul," which is an articulation of the plant as plant (not as divinized or anthropomorphized) and regards "the vegetal [as] fundamental to a web of relations to other life forms with which it is energetically entwined." Applying this thinking to Smith's films, she writes,

> Viewed by their initial respondents in religious and secular terms, Smith's films imbue the plant with qualities that are neither wholly religious (they have been said to possess a secular soul or life principle, to be animated by science, to use naturalistic depiction, and to exhibit human/animal sentience) nor wholly secular (they have been understood to connect with a spiritual soul, to divinize nature, to convey wonder, and to make the invisible visible).

Those other qualities are its plant-soul, which is "no more religious than it is secular in its entwinement with other forms of life." In this way, Cooper shows how a certain discourse about secularism, or resistance to it, shapes the thinking about these films and plants (and, by contrast, animals and humans) and how, following critical plant studies, Smith's films open to a more radical thinking of plant-being that may require stepping beyond this secularist or contra-secularist discourse.

Chapter 10 departs from early cinema and non-fiction and enters into the surreal fictional representation of contemporary America, but it continues to dwell in a space that both acknowledges secularism and challenges it by way of troubling any easy distinction between enchantment and disenchantment. Robert Sinnerbrink's "'There's a sort of evil out there': Uncanny Secularity in Lynch's *Twin Peaks: The Return*" gives its attention to American secularity in David Lynch's acclaimed and utterly singular post-cinematic television series. Sinnerbrink undertakes an insightful analysis of the series that explores "the tension between secularist and post-secularist dimensions of postwar American culture." The secular dimension includes America's liberal democratic politics, government institutions, media, military technology, as well as the secular aesthetics of television and cinema; the postsecular dimension includes its incorporation of and/or references to a Manichean and Gnostic moral framework, surrealism, the Kafkaesque, "Vedic and Hindu mythology, Jungian archetypes, transcendental meditation, Greek mythology, esoteric and occult traditions, theosophy, and so on." It's the fusion or tension between these that constitutes what Sinnerbrink calls "uncanny secularity." He expands on this notion by examining the series' references to Kafka and its Kafkaesque features, which he reads as staging a dialectic of the secular and the postsecular. Following this, Sinnerbrink engages in a detailed reading of three sequences from Season 3, Part 8. "Gotta Light?" Through these, he shows that "Lynch and Frost subject the secular/materialist medium of television to a post-secular/surrealist treatment, transforming the televisual/ cinematic medium into a mode of 'expanded consciousness' via the dialectic between secular and post-secular perspectives, the syncretic combination of mundane and supernatural domains."

Notes

1 Three other scenes in *PlayTime* make reference to religion and deploy the same logic of cloistered visibility, even if manifesting differently in each scene. Shortly after this opening, we will see a priest wandering aimlessly around an airport, as if not at home in the modern, transient world; in the penultimate scene, another disoriented priest will stand in a store with a green neon pharmacy cross displayed prominently, before a worker fixing a different neon sign suddenly causes the letter "O" to illuminate directly above the priest's head like a halo, irreverently mocking the very idea of a real halo; in one of the last scenes, a tourist, Barbara, will be given a scarf and a sprig of lily of the valley by Tati regular, M. Hulot, with which she will wrap her head, making her resemble the virgin Mary. In each of these instances, religion stands out and thus does not fit in to the modernist world around it and so cannot be taken seriously by the enthusiastic participants in that world—but also, apparently, not by film critics.

2 On the role of modernism in *PlayTime*, see Malcolm Turvey, *PlayTime: Jacques Tati and Comedic Modernism* (New York: Columbia University Press, 2020). Turvey argues that the root of Tati's comedy and view of modernism in *Playtime* and elsewhere is that his recurring character Monsieur Hulot is "alienated from modernity in the sense that he is struggling to adapt to the rapid changes of modern life rather than being necessarily opposed to them" (179). Turvey never considers modernity's relation to religion and secularism and how those may relate to Tati's cinema; the same may also be said about Greg Hainge, "Three Non-Places of Supermodernity in the History of French Cinema: 1967, 1985, 2000 *PlayTime*, *Subway*, and *Stand-by*," *Australian Journal of French Studies* 51, no. 2/3 (2014): 234; Yelena McLane, "New, But Not Improved: Defective Domesticity in Jacques Tati's *Mon Oncle* and *PlayTime*," *Interiors: Design, Architecture, and Culture* 1, no. 1 (2010): 61–74.

3 For a more comprehensive list and discussion of such films, see David Shepherd (ed.), *The Silents of Jesus (1897–1927)* (New York and Abingdon: Routledge, 2016).

4 Jolyon Mitchell and S. Brent Plate, *The Religion and Film Reader* (London and New York: Routledge 2007), "General Introduction" and "Part I. Introduction." For examples of these early various positions, see the texts collected in "Part 1: The Dawn of Cinema: Advocates and Detractors," in Mitchell and Plate, *The Religion and Film Reader*.

5 On the history of the religious studies treatment of film, see S. Brent Plate, *Film and Religion: Cinema and the Re-Creation of the World*, 2nd ed. (New York: Columbia University Press, [2008] 2017), xiv–xvi.

6   Mary Lea Bandy and Antonio Monday (eds.), *The Hidden God: Film and Faith* (New York: Museum of Modern Art, 2003); Mitchell and Plate (eds.), *Religion and Film Reader*; John Lydon (ed.), *The Routledge Companion to Religion and Film* (New York: Routledge, 2009); William Blizek (ed.), *The Continuum Companion to Religion and Film* (London: Continuum Books, 2009); and Eric Michael Mazur (ed.), *Encyclopedia of Religion and Film* (Santa Barbara, CA: ABC-CLIO, 2011).

7   See, for instance: Diana Dimitrova (ed.), *Religion in Literature and Film in South Asia* (New York: Palgrave, 2010); Kristian Petersen (ed.), *New Approaches to Islam in Film* (New York: Routledge, 2023); Shephard, *The Silents of Jesus in the Cinema (1897–1927)* (New York: Routledge, 2016); Eric S. Christianson, Peter Francis, and William Telford (eds.), *Cinéma Divinité: Religion, Theology, and Bible in Film* (London: SCM Press, 2005); Elijah Siegler (ed.), *Coen: Framing Religion in Amoral Order* (Waco: Baylor University Press, 2016).

8   To name some of the most well-known and most general, excluding again the more specialized ones: John C. Lyden, *Film as Religion: Myths, Morals, Rituals* (New York: New York University Press, 2003); Robert K. Johnston, *Reel Spirituality: Theology and Film in Dialogue*, 2nd ed. (Grand Rapids: Baker Academic, 2006); Melanie J. Wright, *Religion and Film: An Introduction* (New York: I. B. Taurus, 2007); Judith Weisenfeld, *Hollywood Be Thy Name: African American Religion in American Film, 1929–1949* (Berkeley, CA: University of California Press, 2007); Plate, *Film and Religion*; M. Gail Hamner, *Imagining Religion in Film: The Politics of Nostalgia* (New York: Palgrave Macmillan, 2011).

9   For works on secularism in Indian cinema, see the foundational essay by Indian filmmaker Shyam Benegal, "Secularism and Indian Popular Cinema," in *The Crisis of Secularism in India*, ed. Anuradha Dingwaney Needham and Rajeswari Sunder Rajan (Durham, NC: Duke University Press, 2007); Priya Kumar, *Limiting Secularism: The Ethics of Coexistence in Indian Literature and Film* (Minneapolis: University of Minnesota Press, 2008). For a work that addresses issues in Indian cinema beyond representation and pluralism, see Rachel Dwyer, "The Religious and the Secular in the Hindi Film," in *Filming the Gods: Religion and Indian Cinema* (New York: Routledge, 2006): 132–61.

10 The two major exceptions are Conrad Ostwalt, *Secular Steeples: Popular Culture and the Religious Imagination*, second edition (London: Bloomsbury, 2012); and Phillip Maciak, *The Disappearance of Christ: Secularism in the Silent Era* (New York: Columbia University Press, 2019). Other works in which secularism plays an important role but is not the focus include: Miriam Bratu Hansen, *Cinema and Experience: Siegfried Krakauer, Walter Benjamin, Theodor W. Adorno* (Berkeley, CA: University of California Press 2012); Bliss Cua Lim, *Translating Time: Cinema, the Fantastic, and Temporal Critique* (Durham, NC: Duke University Press, 2009), esp. Introduction; Brian Price, *Neither God Nor Master: Robert Bresson and Radical Politics* (Minneapolis: University of Minnesota Press, 2011).

11 For articles on cinema and secularism, see Sophie Sunderland, "Grieving Secularism: Jane Campion's Secular Daughters in Spiritual Spaces," *Studies in Australasian Cinema* 6, no. 1 (2012): 73–85; Bliss Cua Lim and Lara K. Giordano, "Cavell, Secularism, Cinema: The Politics of *The World Viewed*," *Constellations* 23, no. 4 (December 2016): 536–647; Kaya Davies Hayon, "Faiza Ambah's *Mariam* and the Embodied Politics of Veiling in France," *Paragraph* 42, no. 3 (November 2019): 333–50; Fiona Handyside, "The Politics of Hair: Girls, Secularism, and (Not) the Veil in *Mustang* and Other Recent French Films," *Paragraph* 42, no. 3 (November 2019): 351–63; Constance Balides, "Sociological Film, Reform Publicity, and the Secular Spectator: Social Problems and the Transitional Era," *Feminist Media Histories* 3, no. 4 (Fall 2017): 10–45.

12 Sunderland, "Grieving Secularism," 76.

13 Leo Braudy, *The World in a Frame: What We See in Films*, 25th Anniversary ed. (Chicago, IL: University of Chicago Press, [1976] 2002), 69.

14 Maciak, *Disappearance of Christ*, 17–18.

15 Charles Musser, *The Emergence of Cinema: The American Screen to 1907* (Berkeley, CA: University of California Press, 1990), 19.

16 Ibid., 17; see also all of chap. 1.

17 Laura Mulvey, "Visual Pleasure and Narrative Cinema," *Screen* 16, no. 3 (Autumn 1975): 6–18.

18 This point about Mulvey's unacknowledged reliance on a Christian sensibility was suggested to me by Catherine Wheatley.

19 On the secularization of European art, see Hans Belting, *Likeness and Presence: A History of the Image before the Era of Art*, trans. Edmund Jephcott (Chicago, IL: University of Chicago Press, 1994), esp. Introduction and chap. 20.

20 Laura Mulvey, *Death 24x a Second: Stillness and the Moving Image* (London: Reaktion, 2006), 139–40.

21 Christian Metz, *Imaginary Signifier: Psychoanalysis and Cinema*, trans. Celia Britton et al., (London: MacMillan Press, 1982); the discussion of phenomenology is on 52–3; quotations from 52, 72, and 73.

22 See Metz, *Imaginary Signifier*, chap. 5.

23 David Bordwell, *Making Meaning: Inference and rhetoric in the Interpretation of Cinema* (Cambridge, MA: Harvard University Press, 1989), 24; the same general idea is repeated elsewhere: 13–14, 18, 66, 169, and 259.

24 Bordwell, *Making Meaning*, 259.

25 Ibid., 266–74.

26 David Bordwell, *Figures Traced in Light: On Cinematic Staging* (Berkeley, CA: University of California Press, 2005), 258–60, 265.

27 Joel Martin, "Introduction: Screening the Sacred on the Screen," in *Screening the Sacred: Religion, Myth, and Ideology in Popular American Film*, ed. Joel Martin and Conrad Ostwalt (Boulder, CO: Westview Press, 1995), 2.

28 Lyden, *Film as Religion*, chap. 2.
29 Ibid., 12.
30 Ibid., 104–7.
31 Ostwalt, *Secular Steeples*, 26–7.
32 Ibid., 157, 161.
33 Ibid., 151, 166, 167, 169, 171, 173, 174.
34 For a critical response to this development, see Niels Niessen, *Miraculous Realism: The French-Walloon Cinéma du Nord* (Albany, NY: SUNY Press, 2020), esp. Introduction and Epilogue.
35 Evidence of the emergence of secular studies as an area are the two dedicated journals, *Secular Studies* (https://brill.com/view/journals/secu/secu-overview.xml) and *Secularism and Nonreligion* (https://secularismandnonreligion.org), a Secular Studies book series at NYU Press, dedicated academic societies (Secular Studies Association of Brussels, Secularism and Secularity Unit in the AAR), and a new department and degree in Secular Studies offered at Pitzer College in California.
36 Jurgen Habermas, "What is Meant by a 'Post-Secular Society'? A Discussion on Islam in Europe," in *Europe: The Faltering Project*, trans. Ciaran Cronin (Malden, MA: Polity, 2009), 59, 75; Hent de Vries, "Global Religion and the Postsecular Challenge," in *Habermas and Religion*, ed. Craig Calhoun, Eduardo Mendieta, and Jonathan VanAntwerpen (Malden, MA: Polity, 2013), 203–4.
37 Costica Bradatan and Camil Ungureanu, *Religion in Contemporary European Cinema: The Postsecular Constellation* (New York: Routledge, 2014); John Caruana and Mark Cauchi, *Immanent Frames: Postsecular Cinema between Malick and von Trier* (Albany, NY: SUNY Press, 2018); Maciak, *The Disappearing Christ*. Catherine Wheatley: For a critique of the approach to postsecular cinema, see Niessen, *Miraculous Realism*.
38 Maciak, *Disappearance of Christ*, 17.
39 Ibid., 107.
40 Talal Asad, *Formations of the Secular: Christianity, Islam, Modernity* (Stanford, CA: Stanford University Press, 2003), 1.
41 See Bruno Latour, *We Have Never Been Modern*, trans. Catherine Porter (Cambridge, MA: Harvard University Press, 1993), esp. chap. 4.
42 Asad, *Formations of the Secular*, 16.
43 While the idea of a "sacred gaze" has been developed by David Morgan in *The Sacred Gaze: Religious Visual Culture in Theory and Practice* (Berkeley, CA: University of California Press, 2005), the idea of a "secular gaze" has not, to my knowledge, received any attention.
44 Richard Dyer, *White*, 20th Anniversary ed. (Abingdon and New York: Routledge, [1997] 2017), 1.
45 Ibid., 1.
46 On imputing "religion" to non-white peoples, see Tomoko Masuzawa, *The Invention of World Religions: Or, How European Universalism was Preserved*

in the Language of Pluralism (Chicago, IL: University of Chicago Press, 2005); on "evangelical secularism," see John Lardas Modern, *Secularism in Antebellum America* (Chicago, IL: University of Chicago Press, 2011), esp. chap. 1; on the racialization of Irish and Jewish people, see Dyer, *White*, 51–7, and the classic work, Noel Ignatiev, *How the Irish Became White* (Abingdon and New York: Routledge, 2009 [orig. 1995]).

47 Vincent W. Lloyd, "Introduction: Managing Race, Managing Religion," in *Race and Secularism in America*, ed. Jonathan S. Kahn and Vincent W. Lloyd (New York, NY: Columbia University Press, 2016), 5.

48 Charles Taylor, *A Secular Age* (Cambridge, MA: Belknap Press, 2007), 22.

49 Craig Calhoun, Mark Juergensmeyer, and Jonathan VanAntwerpen (eds.), "Introduction," in *Rethinking Secularism* (Oxford: Oxford University Press, 2011), 5.

50 Taylor, *Secular Age*, 38; see also 337 and 741.

51 Max Weber, *Ancient Judaism*, trans. Hans Gerth and Don Martindale (New York: The Free Press, 1952). Although Weber never uses the term "disenchantment" in this work, he does use "rationalization" and discusses the rejection of magic in several facets of Israelite religion; see esp. Pt. VII, chap. 3, all of Pt. VIII, and Pt. IX, chap. 1.

52 As greatly pleased as I am with the chapters included in this collection, I am regretful for the absence of chapters connecting these issues to Black American, Jewish-Israeli, and Indigenous cinemas. I did have at various points commitments from different scholars to address the former two topics (who, unfortunately, had to withdraw for various reasons), but I never managed to find a suitable contributor to address the latter. In general, the intersections of secular studies with Black studies and with Indigenous studies are underexplored; on the former, see note 45; on the latter, Vincent Lloyd, again, is one of the few to explore it: see his forum *Indigeneity and Secularity* on the *Immanent Frame* blog, https://tif.ssrc.org/category/exchanges/indigeneity-and-secularity/ (accessed July 30, 2022); as well as Ryan Carr, "Indigenous Secularism and the Secular-Colonial," *Critical Research on Religion* 10, no. 1 (March 2022): 24–40.

53 Rachel Moore, *Savage Theory: Cinema as Modern Magic* (Durham, NC: Duke University Press, 2000); Thomas Elssaeser, "Cinephilia or the Uses of Disenchantment," in *Cinephilia: Movies, Love and Memory*, ed. Marijke de Valck and Malte Hagener (Amsterdam: Amsterdam University Press, 2005).

PART I

Is Cinema Secular? Genealogy, Theory, Philosophy

1

Secularist Film Studies and the Occlusion of the Secular

Mark Cauchi

One would think that secularism—defined in a provisionally broad and generic sense, encompassing the separation of religion and political power, the categorization of something as nonreligious, and the ontological condition of things being worldly or immanent—is fundamental in every respect to cinema. Yet a quick canvas of the field of professional film studies in the Anglo and Western European worlds will reveal that secularism has, in fact, rarely been given substantive consideration by scholars (see my introduction). This absence of attention to the secular in film studies mirrors, and, in fact, is derivative of, the long-standing invisibility of the secular in the humanities and the social sciences more generally.[1] In this chapter, I would like to sketch in very general outlines how this pervasive invisibility of the secular came to be and how the study of film unwittingly came to inherit it. Indeed, I want to argue that it is the unquestioned secularism of film studies that renders invisible to film studies the question of secularism in cinema.

In my account, I turn to Bruno Latour's theory of modernity because it helps to explain this discrepancy between film studies' secularism and its blindness toward secularism's relation to cinema. Through Latour, we can see how, on the one hand, modernity engages in a process of separating and purifying the secular and the religious, while, on the other, through this process, the two grow more entangled and produce a series of secular-religious hybrid phenomena. Following the Enlightenment, universities and their growing number of disciplines in the Anglo and European worlds gradually but progressively secularized along the lines of the former (separation and purification), while outside of these institutions and discourses religion and secularity continued to hybridize. Cinema, I will show, is one such hybrid phenomenon. But, as I will further argue, where pre-academic film critics and theorists were attuned to this hybridity and alive to the peculiar secularity (and religiosity) of cinema, academic film scholars in secularized universities almost completely ignored these issues. To take account of these developments requires a genealogy of secular invisibility. My account will be sweeping and therefore full of lacunae, but nonetheless essential in order to see that and how secularity in cinema and its study became invisible. To do the latter, I will trace the links between the pervasive invisibility of the secular in the contemporary study of the film and the emergence of secularity and secularism as a condition and ideology.

The chapter is focused primarily on film studies in the English world, and also as this is connected to France and Germany. This context is the one I know best, but it is also a uniquely important one insofar as film studies as a professional academic discipline is forged there and because that region of film studies still exerts, for better or for worse, an asymmetrical influence on many other cultures of film study and how those cultures are, in turn, taken up in English film studies. This delimitation does not mean, however, that I will not pay any attention to the role played in these discourses and practices by colonialism and racism, which are together interdependently forged with the formation of secularism in the Anglo and Western European worlds. Engaging in a comparative analysis of more than one tradition of secularism and film culture would go beyond what I could reasonably accomplish well in a single chapter.

The Separation and Hybridization of Religion and Secularity in Modernity

By the time moving pictures and the first ventures in film writing emerge at the turn of the nineteenth and twentieth centuries, there is forming among intellectuals and within institutions of higher learning in Europe and North America, where film studies will eventually emerge as an academic discipline, a loose and rather thin conception of secularity. We can understand the process of this emergence, the shape this conception takes, and the effect it has on the study of film, if we turn to the work of Bruno Latour. In *We Have Never Been Modern* (1991), Latour argues that modernity is constituted by a twofold or bi-level process.[2] At one level, there is first an effort by self-identified moderns to distinguish and purify from each other *culture* and *nature*, the *human* and the *nonhuman*, *subject* and *object*; at another level, and usually unregistered by the discourse of moderns, these paired categories and their corresponding phenomena, in reality, interact and become entangled with each other, generating hybrid phenomena (an example of which, for Latour, would be something like climate change or the Anthropocene, which he claims are simultaneously natural and cultural).

If we transfer Latour's theory of modernity to the relationship between religion and secularity, as he does in a more limited way with religion and science elsewhere, then it becomes possible to conceive how, on the one hand, modernity seeks to separate and purify from each other the secular and the religious, while, on the other hand, the two grow, precisely through this effort to separate them, ever more entangled, producing ever more hybrid secular-religious phenomena.[3] Latour calls one type of these hybrids *factishes*—part-fact/part-fetish, part-disenchanted/part-enchanted—one example of which, I shall argue, is cinema.[4] The fact that religion and secularity hybridize means that the purifying, secularizing discourse and point of view is, in fact, inadequate for describing what is actually happening in society and culture. Secularist discourse tells us that society and culture *are* and/or *should be* secularizing, becoming more purely secular, more purely nonreligious, when, in fact, that is not happening or is not happening in the way this discourse suggests. Unlike Latour, however, who concludes that "we have never been modern," I do not think we have simply never been secular. Instead, we have never been secular *as secularist discourse conceives secularity*.[5] It is for this reason that it may be helpful to speak, as some theorists have, of postsecularism, or of a "secularism otherwise."[6]

Both processes—purifying and hybridizing—are initiated in the Enlightenment. The general Enlightenment project identified by Latour of separating and purifying nature and culture had effects on the conceptualization—which is ultimately the construction—of the concepts of religion and secularity. The attempt to purify and separate religion was carried out primarily by philologists and (non-Scholastic) philosophers who eventually entered the European and American university at the end of the eighteenth century and brought with them this new approach to thinking about religion. This shift into higher education set off the production of a vast amount of scholarly work on religion throughout the nineteenth century, which led, ultimately, to the formation of the academic disciplines of biblical studies, comparative religion, and anthropology, forerunners of modern religious studies.[7] By approaching religion in this way, Enlightenment and post-Enlightenment scholars and intellectuals were actively configuring religion both as a universal phenomenon and category ("Religion") and as an object to be analyzed. In doing so, however, they were thereby also distinguishing *it* from *themselves* and their as-yet-unnamed secular point of view. In other words, their own point of view, or the unnamed category to which it belonged, was not the intent or focus of their concern, which is why this point of view and category did not begin to be named "secularism" in English (*laïcité* in French, *Weltlichkeit* in German[8]) until the middle of the nineteenth century (unlike "religion," whose modern meaning stabilized in the early eighteenth century).[9] The proto-secular point of view was thus being formed *indirectly* as a *by-product* of the process of naming and reducing religion. Whatever was said about unnatural or cultural religion—that it was irrational, superstitious, enthusiastic, intolerant, and tyrannical—could therefore not be applied to this proto-secular point of view or gaze (often figured as naturally religious or nonreligious), which was what it was precisely because it was *not those things*. If secularity is being formed as the negation of and absence of religion, then this also means that religion and secularity were being formed as a "binary pair."[10]

Perhaps the clearest and most well-known illustration of this purifying secularity is to be found in Max Weber's concept and account of disenchantment. Disenchantment and secularity are not equivalent concepts, but the former is often thought to be a key part of the latter, and religion is often thought to possess elements of magical thinking, especially at the time Weber developed the idea. Weber introduces the idea approximately twenty years after the emergence of moving images, in his 1917 lecture, "Science as Vocation." As he had argued about capitalism thirteen years earlier in *The Protestant Ethic and the Spirit of Capitalism* (1904), he argues here that science is made possible by a process he calls "intellectualization" or "rationalization" [*Rationalisierung*]. For the modern Westerners, intellectualization means that

> there are no mysterious incalculable forces that come into play, but rather that one can, in principle, master all things by calculation. This means that the world is disenchanted. One need no longer have recourse to magical means in order to master or implore the spirits, as did the savage, for whom such mysterious powers existed. Technical means and calculations perform the service. This above all is what intellectualization means.[11]

The process of intellectualization is thus a process of removing magic, of de-magic-ing the world, which is what Weber's term *Entzauberung* (usually more ambiguously translated as "disenchantment") literally means. Now, if "our times [are] characterized . . . above all, by the 'disenchantment of the world,'"[12] as Weber writes later, then our modern times are being characterized negatively as the purging of a certain form of religiosity. This negative, purgative sense of modernity is congruent with Weber's general lament that modern science and modern life *lack* meaning. Modernity's secularity, then, is conceived primarily as religiosity's removal.

As one can further glean from Weber's reference to "savages," a central element of the separation of religion and secularity in the Enlightenment and post-Enlightenment eras is racialization. As Enlightened Europeans began in the seventeenth century to see religion universally as a distinct dimension and category of life,[13] and thus as part of non-European cultures, too, they simultaneously intensified their critique of religion and so began to separate themselves from it. But in separating themselves from religion,

Enlightenment thinkers thereby began conceptually to separate themselves from the non-Europeans who were regarded as not equally capable of making such a separation and thus as indelibly religious.[14] This racialized framework is the source of so much of nineteenth- and twentieth-century Western thought about religion: the idea of primitive animistic religions of African, Indigenous, and pre-historic Western traditions; the emergence of the concepts of Aryan and Semite in philology; Weber's ideas about monotheism disenchanting religion; nineteenth-century American white Protestants viewing themselves as secular (in distinction to Catholics, the Irish, or African Americans), and so forth. This framework influences aesthetics as well, with the emergence of Orientalism in nineteenth-century painting, primitivism in twentieth-century art, and even the representation of African Americans as naively religious in early white American film.[15]

At the same time as intellectuals were purifying the secular and the religious, we can also see, consistent with Latour's theory, that their discourse was unwittingly causing the two to grow ever more entangled. The process is evident in Charles Taylor's argument that the secular age does not lead to a simple waning of religiosity, as the secularization thesis holds. Rather, reflecting on the aftermath of the Enlightenment, he writes, "It's as though the original [Enlightenment] duality, the positing of a viable humanist alternative [to religion], set in train a dynamic, something like a nova effect, spawning an ever-widening variety of moral/spiritual options."[16] These growing options emerge because of the confluence of things associated with secularity (reason, critique, disenchantment, democracy, modernization) and religion. With this nova effect, Taylor is thinking not only of the proliferation between the eighteenth and twentieth centuries of more "official" religious positions in Christian denominations and schools of theology (Deism, Pietism, liberal Christianity, Evangelicalism, Pentecostalism, the Black Church, Social Gospel, Prosperity Gospel, Christian Nationalism, etc.), to which we can add analogous splinterings in Judaism (Ultra-Orthodox, Orthodox, Reform, Conservative) and Islam (*Atatürkian* secularism, Arab nationalism, Wahhabism, Islamic modernism), as well as the designations and unifications of Buddhism and Hinduism as "world religions"; he is also thinking of the emergence in the West of movements like "spirituality" and "new age-ism," which themselves begin back in the Enlightenment itself with the advent of Mesmerism and Phrenology. But even beyond what Taylor says here, we should also understand this hybridizing nova effect to include the academic study of religion and culture itself, for, in the late nineteenth century, these were often thought to possess a "religious" quality (think of *Bildung* in the German university, and the work of Max Müller, Matthew Arnold, Charles Eliot Norton, or even Friedrich Nietzsche), as well as the artistic, intellectual, and academic attention paid to phenomena and ideas like the Romantic sublime and apocalypse, the gothic, melancholia, angst, and the uncanny.[17] All of these phenomena retain some element of what intellectual secularists would consider the "religious" and combine it with what they would think of as the nonreligious. Such studies may thus be thought in a Latourian sense as secular-religious hybrids.

The fact of this hybridity demonstrates that the idea of secularity that was emerging at the turn of the century—that it was purified of religion—was inadequate; as Jason Josephson-Storm puts it, the presence of the mythological and the magical within modernity demonstrates that demythologization and disenchantment are themselves myths.[18] Indeed, if we return to Weber for a moment (to his new 1920 Introduction to *Protestant Ethic* and other works), we can see his negative conception of the modern as disenchanted is threatened, if not contradicted, by other observations he repeatedly makes about the times, particularly the observation that motivates "Science as Vocation," namely, the spiritual yearning that he perceives in the emerging intellectual movements of his era, in relation to which he makes a startling connection:

> Fashion and the zeal of the *literati* would have us think that the [academic] specialist can today be spared, or degraded to a position subordinate to that of the seer. Almost all sciences owe something to dilettantes [like seers], often very valuable view-points. But dilettantism as a leading principle would be the end of science. *He who yearns for seeing should go to the cinema* . . . . Nothing is farther from the intent of these [i.e., Weber's] thoroughly serious studies than such an attitude. And I might add, *whoever wants a sermon should go to the conventicle.*[19]

Although he does not use the words enchantment and disenchantment in this passage (as he will in the revisions he makes to *The Protestant Ethic*), they are clearly at work organizing his thought here. Remarkable but not surprisingly, he places religion and cinema on the side of enchantment. To Weber's purifying, secularist thinking, cinema is a kind of religiosity and enchantment that stubbornly persists in and threatens the supposed age of disenchantment. This persistence leads us to ask with Latour, "How could we be capable of disenchanting the world, when every day our laboratories and our factories populate the world with hundreds of hybrids stranger than those of the day before?"[20] To Latour's laboratories and factories of undisenchanted hybridity, we should probably now also add what has been called the "dream factory"—cinema.

Secular-Religious Hybridity and Early Moving Images

This tension between the purely secular, on the one hand, and the hybridly secular-religious, on the other, marks the intellectual and cultural milieu into which—*and out of which*—cinema and film culture evolved. Indeed, early film and film culture, I suggest, should be seen precisely *as* secular-religious hybrids. On the one hand, the technical dimensions of film are clearly dependent on advances in the physics of light, chemistry, mechanics, and technology.[21] Moreover, filmmaking, distribution, and exhibition are dependent, as thinkers from Benjamin to Metz recognized, on a capitalist and industrial economy, given the vast sums of capital and complex production and logistical systems needed to undertake these activities. If we grant that these dimensions of film could acceptably be conceived as secular, this interpretation would still have to be squared with the fact that cinema could only be intelligible to and desirable for its publics because it came into being in an already-existent social and cultural milieu that was not itself necessarily purely secular, as we saw earlier. As Tom Gunning explains about the anterior phenomenon of photography, "While the process of photography could be thoroughly explained by chemical and physical operations, the cultural reception of the process frequently associated it with the occult and the supernatural."[22]

Indeed, we get a sense of this hybrid milieu in Gunning's pioneering work on early cinema and photography, although his uncovering of this hybridity has to be read against the grain of his own sometimes secularizing interpretation of it. The tension between this hybridity and secularization is most evident in his landmark article, "An Aesthetic of Astonishment: Early Film and the (In)Credulous Spectator" (1989).[23] On the one hand, the stated goal of the article, articulated in nineteenth- and twentieth-century secularist language, is to "demythologize" the "founding myth" of cinema and film studies—namely, "the terrified reaction of spectators to Lumiere's *Arrival of a Train at the Station*" (1895)[24]—a myth which, Gunning claims, falsely reduces early film spectators to being naïve, defenseless, and credulous. It is for this reason that, even though Gunning never uses the terms "secular" or "religious" in the article, Phillip Maciak is not wrong to claim that the article is "perhaps the foundational essay on secularization in early cinema studies."[25] Consistent with this secularizing goal, Gunning asserts that in the nineteenth-century context of early cinema, there was a "widespread decline in belief in the marvelous" which created for film "a fundamental rationalist context."[26] Indeed, within this putatively secularized context, "the first spectators' experience [of moving images] reveals not a childlike belief, but an undisguised awareness of (and delight in) film's illusionist capabilities."[27] In framing the early film spectator this way, Gunning makes the spectator sound like a neo-Enlightenment unmasker or a proto-Christian Metz.

Gunning, with his mastery of the sources, is very convincing that early spectators knew film images were illusions and that the myth is thus mistaken, but he places perhaps too much emphasis in this early article on this secular dimension of the cinematic experience. For he also somewhat recognizes, on the other hand, that, despite their savviness, early spectators experienced "contradictory stages of involvement with the image," specifically, a "vacillation between belief and incredulity."[28] They knew the cinematic image was an illusion, but they were still, in another level of their experience, taken in by "the *seeming* transcendence of the laws of the material universe" and experienced a "*type* of terror [emphasis added]."[29] This is not *literal* transcendence or *actual* terror, granted, but in qualifying transcendence and terror in this way he reveals it is also not wholly non-transcendence or wholly non-terror. A type of transcendence and terror, albeit qualified, remain part of the film experience. As he suggests in one passing moment, the realism of the cinema of attractions gave viewers an experience of the "uncanny."[30] In Freud's famous essay on the latter, written in 1919 (roughly Gunning's cut-off date for the cinema of attractions), he is acutely alive to the secular-religious hybridity of the experience. "Nowadays we no longer believe," he writes, in the "realities" of various superstitious ideas; "we have *surmounted* these modes of thought," he adds. But, Freud goes on, "the old [beliefs] still exist within us ready to seize upon any confirmation," so that "[a]s soon as something *actually happens* in our lives which seems to confirm the old, discarded beliefs we get a feeling of the uncanny." Secularization is *necessary* for the uncanny (we must have given up our old beliefs), but the secularization cannot be total or pure: as Freud writes, "anyone who has completely and finally rid himself of animistic beliefs will be insensible to this type of the uncanny."[31] The uncanny thus testifies to the absence/presence of *belief* in us, to our secular-religious hybridity.

In later work, Gunning more unreservedly discusses this hybridity, particularly when he turns to the study of the relationship between photography and Spiritualism in the decades preceding the emergence of cinema, and draws out of this encounter implications for thinking about early film.[32] Spiritualism was a controversial secular-religious movement that emerged in the United States in the 1840s, as part of the "nova effect" described by Taylor, and subsequently spread around the world. It held that the spirits of the dead try to communicate with the living via human "mediums" through seances, Ouija boards, knocking cabinets, levitating tables, and ectoplasmic extrusions, as well as through image technologies like magic lanterns, photography, and x-rays (film pioneer Thomas Edison even worked on a machine to "hear" spirits[33]). Spiritualism naturally provoked much skepticism, and a number of groups emerged to debunk it, including academics like Hugo Münsterberg, who would go on to write one of the first theoretically robust accounts of film, but also magicians, photographers, and phantasmagoria exhibitors trying to demonstrate that they could generate the same "spiritual" phenomena without supernatural means. Erik Barnouw showed that many early film practitioners, like Georges Méliès and George Albert Smith among others, have their origins in these shows.[34]

When Gunning turns his attention to the use of photography in spirit photographs—popular photographs in the late nineteenth century, produced through double exposures and other tricks, allegedly showing spirits in them—it is to reveal that there is something about the nature of the photographic medium itself, as well as that of film, that makes it constitutively open to this use. "The spiritualist encounter with photography reveals the uncanny aspect of this technological process, as one is confronted with doubles that can be endlessly scrutinized for their recognizable features, but whose origins remain obscure."[35] While a viewer knows that photographic images (say, an image of a loved one) retain a causal link to reality, the reception and significance of the images themselves by and for the viewer belong to a different register, one less about the link to reality and more about the presencing of the loved one that the image produces, even while the presence of the loved one in a photo immediately tells one about the loved one's absence. The doubling of reality in photographic and filmic images—images that appear, because of this doubling, to be both real and not real, believable and unbelievable—results in a feeling of the "uncanny." In a later essay, he articulates this uncanny nature of photographic and filmic images through the figures of the phantasm and haunting. He writes that, "[s]uch phantasms with their haunting blend of presence/absence, not only formed the subject of Spirit Photography but cast a continued, if occluded, influence over our experience of mediated visual images and photographs."[36] So while it is true that, literally speaking, "there was never a spirit-cinema parallel to the practices of spirit photography,"[37] as Mathew Solomon writes, the implication of Gunning's work is that, in a certain sense, *all* photography and film is spirit photography/film. Thus, even though Gunning claims to be "far from proposing . . . a project of reenchantment of technology,"[38] he regards Spiritualism as "in effect reenchanting the disenchanted world";[39] and since he sees both photography and film as producing, like Spiritualism, phantasmatic images, it would seem that he would have to regard early photography and film as re-enchantments of the world. What we begin to see here is that early film was not a purely secular medium, which is not to say it was a purely religious medium, either.

In his book, *The Disappearing Christ: Secularism in the Silent Era*, Phillip Maciak arrives at a similar or at least overlapping characterization of early film and its aesthetics. Analyzing the cinema of attractions, filmed Passion Plays, and the early distinction between tricks and actualities, as well as the early films of Griffith and De Mille, he argues that

> the question that film as a medium is set up to answer is a question about the relationship between observable reality and what William James would later call the "reality of the unseen." . . . Every frame of every film from 1895 to the present, whether it contains a baby's breakfast or a vanishing lady, is occupied with visually adjudicating this relationship.[40]

This quality of the filmic medium enables, according to Maciak, a particular aesthetic of early cinema that he calls "spectacular realism." Describing the latter, he writes that it is "the aesthetic of the contact zone between realism and fantasy, the uncanny superimposition of disbelief and its suspension, the seamless balancing of the naïve pleasure of credulity with the smug pleasure of incredulity."[41] More than "a free space in which realism and fantasy, reason and irrationality bump up against each other," he goes on, the contact zone of cinema is "a space in which these orientations are forcibly combined, in which a vision of reality is presented to authorize a particular fantasy and vice versa."[42] Because of this ability of cinema to make compatible the seen and the unseen, Maciak regards the cinema as "a training ground for belief in a secular age."[43]

Given the ambiguous entanglement of religion and secularity throughout society and culture at the turn of the century, it should not be surprising that cinema reflected this milieu. If early film's publics and spectators were not homogenously and purely secular, then their reception of film—film's intelligibility to them, its import for them, how it affected them—could not be homogenously and purely secular either. Without question, there were filmmakers, exhibitors, and spectators, as well as particular filmic works, that were closer to the pole of secularist purification, but that did not exhaust the playing field and should not be assumed to be definitive of the medium, the institution, and its spectator.

Secular-Religious Hybridity and Pre-academic Film Theory

Among the publics and spectators of early moving pictures must be counted, of course, intellectual viewers: critics and theorists. Just like the broad response to moving pictures discussed earlier via Gunning, the early intellectual response to moving pictures among critics and theorists was not, in its avowed stance, purely secular and did not take cinema to be purely secular. But the attention to secular-religious fluidity clearly includes an attention to secularity.

In order to understand this point, it is important to recognize that, prior to the 1960s and 1970s, the study of film was not a professional discipline in the university.[44] Some scholars have pointed out recently, in an effort to dispute this thesis, that there were, before the 1960s, scattered efforts in North America and Europe to study and teach various dimensions of cinema in universities (production, business, social impact, aesthetic appreciation) and to establish academic disciplines for the study of film, the most well-known and consequential of these being the Filmology movement in France.[45] But, as Dana Polan has argued, "the efforts of these early figures failed to coalesce into a disciplinary tradition of film studies,"[46] and consequently "the 1960s are indeed the period when film studies as an academic field did begin to take on disciplinary solidity and regularity."[47] Moreover, consistent with my overall point that the university secularized the study of film, these pre-film-studies academic approaches to film largely adopted the methods of social science (empiricism, positivism, and social utility), which at the time, as Dana Polan himself glimpses, had a secularist slant.[48] The most impactful and vital study of film in the early twentieth century—the form that is usually taught in film studies programs today as central to the discipline's provenance—mostly took place outside the academy.[49] As outside of academia, these writers were less captive to the notion of a purified secularism and thus could possess a more fluid secular-religious sensibility.

To be sure, there were theorists and critics of film in this pre-academic era who were, in their declared positions, closer to the pole or ideal of purified secularism. One thinks, for instance, of Béla Balász, Dziga Vertov, or Hugo Münsterberg. To focus on the latter, because he connects to many threads already established here, Münsterberg was a professor of psychology at Harvard (and one-time collaborator with Max Weber, as well as briefly friends with William James). Münsterberg was a critic of Spiritualism at the turn of the century, famously unmasking as a fraud the renowned Spiritualist medium, Eusapia Palladino.[50] No less important to his secularist credentials was his involvement with university reform in America, which he undertook with a decidedly rationalizing (disenchanting) approach.[51] Münsterberg's film theory in *The Photoplay: A Psychological Study* (1916) reflects this secularity. With the exception of the words "soul" and "spirit," which Sarah Cooper has brilliantly analyzed in previous work, his discussion of film almost entirely eschews religious imagery, language, and concepts, and does not even situate film in relation to religion historically or philosophically, as many other early theorists did.[52]

Beyond this kind of secularist approach to film, a great many of the major film theorists and critics in the pre-academic era occupied a more secular-religious hybrid position. Without question, they noticed—or, better, marveled at—factors we might think of as secular: the glaring scientificness of film, its brazen modernity, its feel and tone, and its distinctive attentiveness to the material and interpersonal world around them. But, at the same time, many (although not all) experienced film, and tried to explain this experience, as a kind of "revelation," to use Malcolm Turvey's word, of aspects of reality not usually experienced. While such "hidden" dimensions are not necessarily religious or spiritual (after all, microscopes naturally reveal unseen entities, too), Turvey nevertheless explains that even seemingly nonreligious revelationist theorists like Balázs and Vertov "express near-religious extremes of euphoria about [cinema's] revelatory capacity," conceiving it "as an awesome, even miraculous power."[53] Indeed, very often (but not always) pre-academic theorists draw upon religious language and thought to help construe and express this experience. In doing so, they operated with a hybrid secular-religious conceptual framework and thereby conceived film as a secular-religious hybrid. There are broadly three forms of religiosity these thinkers draw upon—animist, messianic, and Christian—which we can sketch now.

Animism

The deployment of animism in the study of film stretches from Ricciotto Canudo in the teens, the French Impressionists in the twenties (particularly Jean Epstein, René Clair, Louise Delluc, Élie Faure, Abel Gance, Emile Vuillermoz), Sergei Eisenstein in the thirties and forties, and Edgar Morin in the fifties, and has been revived in recent discussions of posthumanism and Indigeneity.[54] The term "animism" was coined by one of the founders of cultural anthropology, Edward Tylor, in his book *Primitive Culture* (1871), was taken up by James George Frazer and Lucien Lévy-Bruhl, and through the latter entered a wider intellectual circulation. For Tylor, animism referred to a thought system in which, contrary to the purifying drive of modernity described by Latour, nature was personified and suffused with life, sentience, and agency.[55] It is important to bear in mind the emergence of cultural anthropology out of philology and the post-Enlightenment analysis and construction of "religion," discussed earlier, for the very approach adopted by Tylor belongs to the formation of the secularist ideal. Indeed, Tylor constructed an evolutionary or stadial model according to which the most primitive cultures were animistic, with subsequent stages becoming more and more rationalistic (as in the newly named "world religions" like Judaism, Christianity, Hinduism, etc.[56]), leading ultimately to a wholly rational and scientific modern culture that would fully leave animism behind (*a la* Weber's disenchantment). It was not long after the emergence of this idea that critics of modernity began to appeal to animistic thinking as a way to imagine alternatives to modernity and its supposedly deleterious effects, as is evidenced, for example, in Nietzschean Dionysianism, Theosophy, Bergson's vitalism, Process Philosophy, Jungian psychology, and Primitivism in visual art.

It is out of this line of thought that the first film theorists begin to think about cinema in terms of animism. I will briefly focus here on Epstein, since he gives the first substantial and most sustained articulation of it. In a 1921 essay, Epstein sees projected moving images hybridly, on the one hand, as modern and technological, but, on the other, as making objects on screen "quiver with bewitchment," leading him to conclude that "cinema is essentially supernatural."[57] Three years later, seemingly under the influence of anthropologist Lévy-Bruhl's 1910 work *How Natives Think*, which, among other things, rejected Tylor's view that animism was only a feature of primitive thought, Epstein actually specifies that cinema is "animistic" because it "endow[s] the objects it is called upon to depict with such intense life."[58] Endowed with life, the multiple objects cinema creates on screen are "godlike," which makes cinema "polytheistic and theogonic."[59] Less than a decade after Weber lectured about the disenchantment of the world, Epstein strikingly writes,

> These lives [on screen] are like the life in charms and amulets, the ominous, tabooed objects of certain primitive religions. If we wish to understand how an animal, a plant, or a stone can inspire respect, fear, or horror, those three most sacred sentiments, I think we must watch them on the screen, living their mysterious, silent lives, alien to the human sensibility.[60]

As time goes on, Epstein will lose the term animism, but the position remains and is, in fact, deepened, as is evident in his 1946 work on cinema, *The Intelligence of the Machine*: through the cinematograph, he writes, "The whole universe becomes a giant beast whose stones, flowers, and birds are so many organs that cohere with precision in their participation as single common soul."[61] The fact that Epstein states earlier that cinema is *like* magic and religion, and, later, that cinema's animism is produced by a machine, suggests that, for him cinema is not identical to (purely) animistic religion and that cinema hybridly retains some secularity.

Messianism

A second form of secular-religious hybridity in the pre-academic study of film emerges in what we may call, following Miriam Hansen, messianic theory and criticism.[62] This version is evident in a number of the Jewish-German thinkers associated with the Frankfurt school who wrote on film: Siegfried Kracauer, Walter Benjamin, Max Horkheimer, Theodor Adorno, and Ernst Bloch. All were deeply influenced by secularizing strains of European thought, particularly Marx and Weber. But they must also be understood, as Hansen hybridly puts it, "in the context of modern, secular Jewish messianism."[63] The latter idea helped them to articulate how the world in its present condition—most saliently, for them, under liberal capitalism and threatened by fascism—was in need of redemption. None of them actually believed a real messiah would come, of course, but they held in various ways that adopting the perspective of one enabled the critic to penetrate to the true conditions of the world and to reveal thereby the possibilities for its transformation.

The approach is most succinctly and explicitly articulated in Benjamin. In his "Theses on the Philosophy of History" (1940), Benjamin contrasts two forms of historical interpretation. First, the progressivist historian understands history as forming a single linear chain of causality culminating in the present, but therein fails to register any countervailing or anomalous historical forces in any specific era (like oppressed classes) and thus treats history as "homogenous, empty time."[64] By contrast, the messianic Marxian historian "blast[s] open the continuum of history" by forming a non-linear temporal relationship (a "constellation"[65]) between the overlooked, oppressed past and the present, in which the hopes and forces of the past are suddenly alive again. The messianic historian thus *sees more* of the past and the present than does the progressivist historian. As much as Benjamin figures this form of history in religious terms (messianic), it is not purely religious, for Benjamin is also clear, now in a Weberian mode, that it is "stripped" of "magic."[66]

This distinction between a kind of pure religiosity (literal messianism) and a hybrid secular-religiousness ("weak messianism") recurs in Benjamin's well-known distinction between pure "religious illumination" (which he directly associates with Spiritualism) and hybrid "profane illumination" (which reveals "mystery . . . in the everyday world").[67] This distinction also carries over into his thinking on film. In "The Work of Art in the Age of Mechanical Reproduction" (1936), he accuses "early theories of the film" (namely, those of the animistic French Impressionists) of possessing an "insensitive and forced character" for trying to "read ritual elements into" film, falsely ascribing to it a significance that is, "if not an outright sacred one, then at least supernatural."[68] What these mistaken early theorists fail to see, according to Benjamin, is how the age of mechanical reproduction leads to "the secularization of art."[69] Benjamin explains the latter through his Weberian ideas of the decline of *aura* (a term, incidentally, popularized by Spiritualism in the nineteenth century[70]) and the loss of the cult value of art precipitated by mechanical reproduction. Given this disenchantment of film and film theory, according to Benjamin, it is striking that when he then turns to discuss cinema's unique contribution and "revolutionary functions"[71]—specifically, its "enrich[ment] [of] our field of perception"[72]—he focuses on what he calls its "unconscious optics,"[73] which it turns out is essentially another name for hybrid "profane illumination." Cinema allows us to see more than what we can consciously see, a viewpoint that presumes there is more to the world than meets the eye. Through its various techniques of presenting everyday life, film "reveals entirely new structural formations" and "assure[s] us of an immense and unexpected field of action." "Evidently a different nature opens itself to the camera," Benjamin writes, "than opens to the naked eye." Then, approvingly quoting Rudolf Arnheim, and now directly contradicting his earlier criticism of early animistic film theorists, Benjamin comments on the example of the movements of objects in slow motion: "far from looking like retarded rapid movements, [they instead] give the effect of singularly gliding, floating, *supernatural* motions[emphasis added]."⁷⁴ In slow motion, what one sees is not actually supernatural, of course, since it is produced naturally through the interaction of mechanics and human perception, but the "effect" of the experience is one of the supernatural. Film does not show us, we might say, homogenous, empty time (or homogenous, empty space); it reveals to us, instead, a space and time full of previously unseen significance. Again, this does not mean it is wholly religious, for it does so through its attention to space and time. But by eschewing both a purely religious interpretation and a purely secular one—both of which would inhibit the positive thematization of the secular—Benjamin is able to remain attuned to, to discern, the secularity of cinema.

Christian

The final form of secular-religious hybridity in the pre-academic Anglo and European study of film is evident in the distinctly Christian inflection of theorists and critics like André Bazin, Amédée Ayfre, Henri Agel, and Americans like Vachel Lindsay, Paul Schrader, and James Baldwin. All of these thinkers are variously concerned with film content, and/or deploy concepts, and/or have a sensibility that derive in part from Christianity, and that provenance is often consciously drawn upon in their thinking. That said, none of their most significant work is doctrinely Christian (the closest to that position would be Ayfre and Agel, but even their work is not reducible purely to Christianity). That is, they address films, use concepts, and are sensitive to issues that are not exclusively Christian, but hybridly secular and religious.

The most influential of them is certainly Bazin, and we can see this secular-religious hybridity in his work very clearly. As Dudley Andrew has written, Bazin was long interested in attempting "to wed science and religion."⁷⁵ This interest drew him to the work of other contemporary French thinkers who adopted a secular-religious hybridity, like Pierre Teilhard de Chardin, Charles Péguy, and Emmanuel Mounier.⁷⁶ Bazin's film theory and criticism were not strictly derivative of these thinkers, but he was likewise drawn to secular-religious hybridity. This hybridity is evident both in Bazin's accounts of seemingly nonreligious realist filmmaking, but also in his critique of non-realist religious filmmaking.

Consider the latter first. In his early essay, "The Life and Death of Superimposition" (1946), Bazin criticizes the conventional opposition between the two alleged modes of cinema—realism and fantasy (actuality and trick). Instead of this opposition and their various corresponding techniques, Bazin dialectically argues that "supernatural phenomena are essential to verisimilitude" and that recent Hollywood films are praiseworthy for "creating the supernatural in a more purely psychological manner."⁷⁷ For Bazin, there can be no realism without the supernatural, and no supernatural without realism. This dialectical perspective is taken up again and expanded upon in his later essay, "Cinema and Theology: The Case of *Heaven Over the Marshes*" (1951), in which he offers a taxonomy of religious films and advocates for the kind of film exemplified by Augusto Genina's *Heaven Over the Marshes* (1949).[78] According to Bazin, the great virtue of Genina's film, about the life of a girl before being canonized by the Church, is that it eschews the overt "religious symbolism" and "supernatural element" of most conventionally religious films.[79] Instead, the film offers a "phenomenology of sainthood" by depicting the latter as "an event occurring in the world."[80] "Divine grace," Bazin explains, "doesn't manifest itself in nature as the product of tangible causality"—that is, like a literal magical miracle zapped into being by God—but through "ambiguous signs that can all be explained in quite natural terms."[81] Eschewing both pure supernaturalism and pure realism, this type of hybrid film alienates and draws the ire of both conventionally religious and conventionally secular viewers and critics, making it what Bazin hybridly calls an "accursed film."[82]

This hybrid, accursed sensibility lies behind much of Bazin's influential ideas about the cinematic medium. On the one hand, as Bazin argues in "Ontology of the Photographic Image," by circumventing human agency, the mechanical nature of the photographic and cinematic medium allows its images to get closer to reality than previous art media. This unmasking capacity to "reveal reality" gives to photography and cinema a disenchanting quality, since it "strip[s] the objects of habits and preconceived notions, of all the spiritual detritus that my perception has wrapped it in." If cinematic images do not appear to us as *wholly* disenchanted, however, that is because, on the other hand, reality itself is not, according to Bazin, wholly disenchanted. The natural world, he holds, "surpasses even the artist in creative power," so that in getting us closer to this "natural creation," photography and film actually "play a real part" in the latter. Cinema co-creates the world, which is why, as Bazin says elsewhere, "cinema is in itself already a kind of miracle."[83] This is not to say it *is* a miracle; it is, he says, a *kind* of miracle. It is a mechanical, natural phenomenon that nevertheless has something of the religious about it. By attending to the ways that both the filmic medium and its language allow us to project reality, Bazin contributes to theorizing the secularity of cinema; but because, for him, reality *is* mysterious, true cinematic realism is inseparable from a cinematic religiosity, so to speak.

Again, to claim that these early theorists were hybridly secular-religious is not to claim that they failed to address the secular. On the contrary, they *were* addressing the secular, just not in a manner divorced from the religious. Benjamin clearly felt the need to criticize the animism of early French theorists because he *saw* and *felt* acutely the novelty of the mechanistic nature of film and of the everydayness it projected on screen, even if he simultaneously experienced something else in it that he felt he needed religious thought to explain. Benjamin, Epstein, Bazin, and the others I mentioned did not take the secular for granted, either in their own discourses or in the object they studied (film), the way academic film scholars will begin to do. Religion was not so dead for them, secularity not so obvious, that they could afford to be oblivious to them. The secularity of cinema, like its religiosity, had to be attended to and explained.

Academic Film Studies and Secular Purification

The hybridization of secularity and religiosity continues in our contemporary world, including in cinema and some film writing. But with the advent of academic film studies in the 1960s and 1970s, the secular-religious hybridity of film theory and criticism will rather rapidly dissolve, and professional film studies will come to adopt an almost exclusively secularist point of view. With this development, the self-conscious and critical consideration of a perennial element in cinema—religion—will for the most part be pushed out of film studies and into religious studies, while the capacity and the desire to discern and to study the secularity of both cinema and film studies itself will mostly disappear from both film studies and religious studies.

The argument of this section thus runs adjacent to the argument of Sarah Cooper's *The Soul of Film Theory*, which investigates the pervasive presence of the language of "soul" and "spirit" in pre-academic film theory and its almost complete disappearance in what she calls the "secular contemporary film theory" of academia.[84] But rather than chalk this disappearance up to the effect of secularization, she imputes it to the development of postwar anti-humanism: in the early twentieth century, soul and spirit had become metaphors for humanistic conceptions of subjectivity, and with the discourses of the "death of man" and anti-humanism in structuralism and post-structuralism, the humanist language of soul and spirit was abandoned. Cooper is no doubt correct here, but as we shall see through Geroulanos below, anti-humanist discourses were, at the same time, secularist/secularizing discourses. According to the anti-humanists, part of the problem with humanist ideas and ideals, like Sartre's radical freedom, say, is that they were merely secularized theological ideas which needed a more thorough secularization.

The secularizing of the study of film in film studies, and the latter's uncriticalness toward secularity, happens for three reasons, which I will trace now.

1. *Secularization of the University*
By the time the study of film fully enters the academy in France, Germany, the UK, and North America beginning in the 1960s and 1970s, the university itself, and especially the humanities, is for all intents and purposes secular.[85] Secular means here mostly no longer under the control of religious institutions (i.e., Christian churches) or under the sway of overtly Christian

ideas and values (although some may credibly argue they are latently so). While the process and pace of secularization is different in all of these different national university systems, the 1960s cultural revolution and accompanying "religious crisis of the 1960s," as Hugh McLeod calls it, eventually mostly equalizes them by the beginning of the 1970s,[86] including in the United States.[87] For, even though sociologist Peter Berger revised his famous secularization thesis on the evidence of the resurgence of religion in the 1980s and 1990s, referring to it in a counter-Weberian fashion as a "desecularization of the world," he nevertheless also observed:

> There exists an international subculture composed of people with Western-type higher education, especially in the humanities and social sciences, that is indeed secularized. This subculture is the principal "carrier" of progressive, Enlightened beliefs and values. While its members are relatively thin on the ground, they are very influential, as they control the institutions that provide the "official" definitions of reality, notably the educational system, the media of mass communication, and the higher reaches of the legal system.[88]

The significance for us of this whole development is that, by the time film studies becomes an established academic discipline in the Western world (with several departments, journals, societies, theories and methodologies, and a cohort of graduates who in turn become professors), the university was now dominated by, in Latourian terms, a purifying secularism.

2. Secularist French Thought

The second factor to consider in the secularization of film studies is the more specific one of the intellectual climate and film culture in France from the First World War onward. France will come to exert an enormous influence on the eventual formation of academic film studies throughout the West (as on the humanities more generally). Stefanos Geroulanos characterizes the main thrust of French thought after the First World War as the development of what he calls, borrowing from Levinas, "an atheism that is not humanist."[89] French thought had, of course, been secularizing since the Enlightenment. But beginning around the First World War, and intensifying after the Second World War, many French thinkers across numerous disciplines—philosophy, linguistics, anthropology, literature, politics, and even theology—came to see this tradition of secularization as insufficiently secular. Geroulanos writes that, for these postwar thinkers, "theological shadows lurked in the history of modern thought, in concepts and ontological arrangements that grounded notions of man, and even in political movements that flaunted their secular credentials."[90] Current secularity, for them, was not pure enough, was still too hybrid, maintaining what Raymond Aron called in 1944 "secular religions" (movements that appear secular but are latently religious).[91] To escape this covert religiosity, these and subsequent thinkers—specifically, those associated with structuralism and post-structuralism, which Geroulanos describes as "the most influential inheritor[s] of early antihumanism"[92]—thus adopted a non-humanist and increasingly anti-humanist point of view. This move rejected the idea that the human being, like a putative God, had an essence or that systems of meaning were grounded in humanity's divine-like subjectivity. While this anti-humanism was, as Geroulanos shows, both critical of classical atheism's and classical secularism's efforts at "pushing under the rug religious problems and questions" and more alert to the ways that it itself possessed a "dependency on Christian and theological motifs,"[93] it was nevertheless aiming at a more rigorous—in Latourian terms, more pure—atheism and secularism.

This intellectual development dovetailed in France with 1960s political radicalism, culminating in May 1968, which would have an enormous influence on French and then English film theory in the era, as Sylvia Harvey, Colin McCabe, and D. N. Rodowick have outlined.[94] The most important and influential figure who served as a bridge between anti-humanist thought, political radicalism, and film theory is Louis Althusser. Althusser gave to the era a language, set of concepts, and theoretical apparatus that pitted critique against ideology and which was combined with other disciplines—semiotics, psychoanalysis, and anthropology—to produce a radical politico-cultural critical discourse. As we shall see, implicit in Althusser's explicit association of science with anti-humanism is a deliberate but uncritical secularism. Indeed, even though Althusser later acknowledged the formative influence of Catholicism on his thinking and in fact wrote about it in his early writings, the substantive discussion of religion and secularity significantly wanes in his major works from the 1960s and 1970s, except to use religion as an example, indeed, the archetype, of ideology.[95]

In order to understand Althusser's (secularist) thinking about religion and its impact on his thinking more broadly, we have to grasp how he conceives the relationship between science and ideology through an oppositional frame. While the finer points of his idea of ideology change over this period, the kernel remains roughly the same: ideology is an unconsciously held imaginary, illusory, and distorting representation of the real economic and political conditions of the world that serves the purpose of legitimating and reinforcing those economic and political conditions so as to facilitate the proletariat's complicity with its own exploitation. In contrast to distorting ideology, Althusser posits what he calls "science" (which refers not simply to natural science, but to any putatively rational, analytical discipline)—but also "theory" and "genuine philosophy," what his later readers will simply call "critique"—which penetrates through mystifying ideology and articulates the real economic and political conditions. Now, ideology and science are not simply *different*, according to Althusser; instead, there is an "*opposition* of science and ideology."[96] Oppositions, by positioning their poles *via negativa*, posit each of their poles as purely devoid of the other and thereby foreclose the acknowledgment of any hybridity between them, even if, in fact, they are determined by, and so incorporate, their opposites. This oppositional thinking is the source of Althusser's deployment of the idea of "epistemological break": science does not *evolve* out of ideology, which would suggest ideologies hybridly bear within themselves the conditions for science, but radically breaks—in Latourian terms, *separates* itself, *purifies* itself—from ideology (consider here Althusser's obsessive and painstaking parsing of the early humanist Marx and the mature scientific Marx). Whence it follows that, if ideology is purely distorting, false, and mythological, then science is purely clarifying, true, and demythologizing, and never the twain shall meet.

Althusser's oppositional framework of conceiving ideology and science is, as I stated above, secularist, which is to say, it uncritically (unscientifically) privileges and identifies with secularity on the basis of uncritical assumptions about religion and secularity. These assumptions arise from his alignment of the distinction between secularity and religion with the opposition between science and ideology, respectively, on the grounds that "the formal structure of all ideology is always the same."[97] It is this alignment that allows him frequently to name religion as an example of ideology and then to perform a supposedly scientific analysis of it as the privileged example of ideology in the final section of his best-known work, "Ideology and Ideological State Apparatuses." This alignment entails that religion is purely ideological, and thus itself incapable of being scientific, and that secularity itself need not (indeed, *cannot*) be subject to scientific critique (if secularity could be critiqued, it would demonstrate that it was ideological, which is to say, not scientific). The stringency of this opposition is evident, for instance, in Althusser's comments on Pascal. Unlike, say, Nietzsche, who argued that Christian dogma was overthrown by Christian morality and thereby regarded modern atheism as the outcome of an internal Christian self-critique, Althusser oppositionally reads Pascal's "scientific genius" as breaking from what he calls Pascal's "religious philosophy" (i.e., ideology).[98]

In holding that religion is purely ideological and that secularity cannot be subject to critique, Althusser's secular gaze is unable to see, is uncritical of, the problems into which this gaze and its oppositional thinking pushes him. For example, after arguing, like the young Marx he normally calls a humanist, that anti-ideological struggles (science) first took the form of anti-religious struggles, and thus that science is secular and secularizing, he then argues that, later, "the bourgeoisie . . . installed as its number-one, i.e. as its dominant Ideological State Apparatus, . . . the educational apparatus, which has in fact replaced in its functions the previously dominant Ideological State Apparatus, the Church."[99] While Althusser is no doubt correct here that secular culture, like religious culture, is also ideological, he somehow does not notice or explain how and why the scientific secularization of society simply leads to a secular ideology (education apparatus). If secularity is not a guarantee of science or critique (non-ideology), that is, if secularity is not inherently non-ideological, then why assume, first, that secularization (anti-religious struggle) is an instance of anti-ideological struggle, that is, science? Perhaps anti-religious struggle is itself merely one of many competing ideologies. And if secularity can be either ideological or scientific, then why can religion not be? What exactly is religion, and what exactly is secularity, in this conception of science and ideology? My interest in these questions, at this moment anyway, is not in the answers they may generate (although I do think those would be interesting), but in the fact that such questioning, such parsing, seems to have escaped Althusser and to go beyond what his oppositional framework allows him and us to think. That these questions remain unasked by Althusser indicates that he has not reflected adequately, critically, scientifically on the secularity that he assumes is a condition of science. That is to say, his conception of science as secular is itself ideological.

As I indicated, Althusser's thought would come to play a major role in the development of politico-cultural analysis in the 1960s, 1970s, and 1980s, including in the study of film. Not everyone was strictly Althusserian, of course, and Althusser was certainly not the only theoretical resource (Lacan, Barthes, Foucault, Deleuze, Derrida, and Kristeva would all be resources). Nonetheless, the basic contours of his theory of the critique of ideology could be felt widely. His presence is most overt in the study of film in the explicitly Althusserian turn in the late 1960s, most visibly in the two most important journals of the era, *Cahiers du Cinéma* and *Cinéthique*, in which Althusser was often quoted.[100] But his thinking could be felt in more subtle ways too, as Colin MacCabe explains:

> Marxism's abiding problem has always been to explain the way in which capitalist relations reproduce themselves in non-coercive ways [Althusser's answer to which is ideology]. Throughout the seventies there were many who felt that the key to such an understanding lay in an analysis of culture which would not simply read it off as an effect of the economic base but would understand its ability to reproduce subjectivities, a reproduction finally determined by the economic relations but the mechanisms of which had to be comprehended in their own right.[101]

As I have suggested, Althusserian thought could thus be modified or coupled with other theories[102] and the new discourses could be deployed to help articulate how subjects are constituted by the ideological framework of cultural works. But implanted in these new discourses is the Althusserian assumption that the theoretical or "scientific" gaze itself is outside ideology and therefore that the putatively critical gaze itself is not subject to critical interrogation. Within that gaze, religion is simply assumed to be uncritically ideological and so not worthy of sustained attention, and secularity so aligned with critique that it, too, did not require critical attention.

One can see this more subtle Althusserianism in the work of Christian Metz, who is notably often described as the first academic film theorist.[103] In his epoch-making work on psychoanalysis and cinema, *The Imaginary Signifier* (1977), Althusser is never once directly mentioned, but his presence is nevertheless felt. Here I am less interested in Metz's framing of his discussion according to the Althusserian problematic of the reproduction of capitalism, as Rodowick has shown,[104] than to the ways in which Metz incorporates into the very ground of his theory an Althusserian distinction between (1) the mythic illusoriness of cinema and some forms of unscientific intellectual engagement with it and (2) the scientific unmasking that his theory supposedly brings to it.

To be fair, at face value, Metz does articulate a complex, almost dialectical relation between these two sides. While the casual film viewer and the cinephile will both be charged by him with maintaining an unreflexive, fetishistic relation to the cinema ("it does not know what it is saying"[105]), the scientific viewer who aims to arrive at "true theory"[106] and "true knowledge"[107] (as opposed to pseudo-theory and pseudo-knowledge) must *simultaneously* maintain their fetishism *and*, just as Althusser says, "break" from it.[108] Metz explains:

> To be a theoretician of the cinema, one should ideally no longer love the cinema and yet still love it: have loved it a lot and only have detached oneself from it by taking it up again from the other end, taking it as the target for the very same scopic drive which had made one love it. Have broken with it, as certain relationships are broken, not in order to move on to something else, but in order to return to it at the next bend in the spiral.[109]

True theory must in a way preserve within itself cinephilia because, as with the transference in psychoanalysis, in order to understand film the theorist must reflexively study the unreflexive attachment induced by cinema, and to do that, they must (also) be attached to it. That one of the two terms maintain within itself a version of its other troubles any simple opposition between them.

Despite this almost dialectical relationship between fetishism and science, Metz nevertheless still holds to a strict distinction between unscientific cinema and viewing, on the one hand, and scientific theory, on the other. And, as we have seen several times now with others, this distinction is uncritically aligned by Metz, too, with an implicit distinction between the religious and the secular, respectively, which plays a role in determining what he is able to think and not think. This alignment makes its most visible appearance in Metz's use, following Marx, Freud, and Lacan, of the concept of fetishism. All of his predecessors knew they were drawing on the study of religion when they adopted the concept of the fetish to name problematic economic and psychical phenomena. The word fetish, which derives from the Portuguese *feitiço* meaning "charm, sorcery, allurement"[110]—that is, enchantment—originates in the colonial history traced earlier, and was used by Europeans (first Portuguese sailors, then anthropologists of "primitive culture") to name and denigrate the venerated objects of non-Europeans (totems, masks, idols, etc.). For the putatively rational, secular European, the fetish is an object that is mistakenly assumed to have mystical power, to be enchanted. Thus, when Marx, Freud, and Lacan draw on the concept of the fetish, it is always to name something that has been improperly (perversely) imbued with power it does not (should not) have. When Metz, in turn, applies the concept of fetishism to film spectatorship, it is to designate a type of relationship to cinema that, while inevitable, is nevertheless for the aspiring theorist improper because reflective of an *irrational power* the cinema holds over them: "The cinema fetishist is the person who is *enchanted* at what the machine is capable of [emphasis added]."[111]

By framing cinema and the unscientific viewing of it in quasi-religious terms (fetishism)—more specifically, a term utilized in secular discourse to designate *bad* religion—Metz inevitably, if implicitly, sets up scientific film theory's epistemic break from such religiosity as a kind of secularization of spectatorship and theory. We can see this secularization again in his recurrent treatments of the "structure of belief" in cinema. It should be noted that Metz appears to hold the standard post-Enlightenment epistemic meaning of belief as a holding something as true without logical or empirical evidence, which Enlightenment thinkers increasingly aligned with religion or primitive cultures (which were also associated together).[112] Adapting and expanding upon both Lacan's treatment of fetishism as a structure of disavowal and Octave Mannoni's work on theatrical illusion, Metz claims that in viewing films there is a threefold structure of belief: at the *first* level, it is known by the viewer that "the diegetic events are fictional" and so the viewer is "not duped" and "doesn't believe it"; yet, *second*, there is a suspension of disbelief, that is, "everyone pretends to believe that [the diegetic events] are true," and so it is "as if . . . someone really would 'believe in it'"; but, similar to Freud on the uncanny, Metz adds that behind or below this disbelief and feigned belief, there is a *third*, deeper level: "somewhere in oneself one believes they are genuinely true."[113] Thus, even though (one claims that) one doesn't truly believe in the film image, and then suspends that disbelief, somewhere in oneself one also truly believes. The secular and religious undertones of this language become more clearly audible when Metz points out that Mannoni connects these "switches of belief" to how "the ethnologist observes in certain populations"—that is, non-European populations—that the latter will claim about their masks (i.e., fetishes in the original sense) that "long ago we used to believe in the masks."[114] This relegation of belief to the past—a move, we have seen, also central to Enlightenment progressivism and its offspring, the secularization thesis—is a way, Metz claims, to disavow their current belief, to say that they no longer believed, that is, to feign a kind of secularism. Taken together, it as if Metz is showing that, just as the secularization thesis claims to have moved past religion, but has not really, so the film spectator and pseudo-theorist claim to have moved past belief but have not really. Despite the fact that Metz thus imputes to the casual viewer, the cinephile, and the pseudo-theorist a kind of Latourian hybrid secular-religious position, it is critical to stress that, for Metz, scientific viewing and theorizing must break from this secular-religious hybridity. True scientific film theory would thus be secularizing. What Geroulanos had argued about postwar French thought—that it regarded earlier secular humanist thought as latently religious, as still too hybrid, as not purely secular enough, and therein requiring a radical, anti-humanist break from it—is thus visible here in Metz, too.

Nowhere is Metz's anti-hybridity position clearer than in his treatment of phenomenological film theory, best exemplified, according to him, in the work of Bazin. Consistent with the long line of thought we have traced back to the Enlightenment which associates religiosity with what is not scientific, Metz draws upon a religious lexicon to cast Bazin's thought as unscientific (beyond Bazin's own intentionally religious concepts). Bazinian theory, Metz argues, offers "excellent descriptions" of the ways in which cinema is a "mystical revelation" and "epiphany" that puts its viewers into "prophetic trances."[115] Metz even grants that these quasi-religious descriptions have "something scientific about them,"[116] a backhanded compliment which, of course, implies that there is much that is non-scientific about them, too. To be precise, what is nonscientific is what he calls "the *lure of the ego*" which, he says, constitutes this theory's "blind spot."[117] The ego is lured, seduced, tricked into desiring—"duped," Metz will say later[118]—the cinema. If the ego is lured, if cinema is entrancing or enchanting, if there is magic in the movies, "it can only be so," declares Metz the disenchanter, "because its objective determinations make it so."[119] In other words, cinema and the ego/spectator are (over)determined by objective forces beyond them that phenomenology is allegedly incapable of disclosing, but which Metz's scientific theory, fortunately, can unmask: "it is on cinema and phenomenology in their common *illusion* of perceptual mastery that light must be cast by the *real conditions* of society and man [emphases altered]."[120] If phenomenological film theory, in its fetishistic unscientificness, is latently religious, then Metz's scientific film theory clearly is not. Film theory, properly speaking, without ever critically attending to secularity in any substantive sense, is nevertheless secular and secularizing.

3. *The Dissemination of French Thought*

The third factor in the secularist formation of film studies is simply the transfer of this secularist French thought (and through its backdoor, German and Russian film theory) to the rest of the Anglo and European academic humanities and the burgeoning film departments of the 1970s. Here we must note the pivotal role played by the British journal, *Screen*, which arguably becomes the single most important site at the time in the English world for the cultivation of professional film theory. It begins in 1971 to fall under the sway of the particular French amalgamation (forged by *Tel Quel*) of Marxism, semiology, deconstruction, and psychoanalysis.[121] It publishes for the first time in English translation works by Russian formalists, Benjamin, French thought from the 1960s, and essays from *Cahiers* and *Cinéthique*, including essays by Metz and Mulvey. Colin MacCabe, a precocious graduate student in the early 1970s and attending the classes of Althusser and Derrida in Paris, would join the editorial board of *Screen* in 1973.[122] As he explains, "There was never any engagement with Althusser's thought in the pages of *Screen* and his work was rarely quoted but he provided the intellectual space in which a specific analysis of a cultural form, in this case film and cinema, could be carried out."[123] A similar transfer occurred in the United States. Robert Stam explains how a number of American film scholars (Janet Bergstrom, Dana Polan, David Rodowick, Stam himself, and many others he lists) studied in Paris at *Le Centre Americain d'Etudes du Cinema* (later *Le Centre Parisien d'Etudes Critiques*) where they worked with Christian Metz, Raymond Bellour, and Thierry Kuntzel, among other influential French theorists.[124] With these importations of French thought, the world of academic English film studies absorbed an Althusserian, secularist framework for the study of film.

Of course, film studies continued to evolve following the 1970s, in tandem with cultural studies and the emergence of postmodernism. But as Stam and Rodowick have both argued, these theoretical developments remained tacitly very influenced by the Althusserian frame. Stam explains that "1960s radical film theory and semiotics anticipated and came to form part of the Cultural Studies that came later,"[125] while Rodowick explains about later film theories that "Althusser's concept of Theory remains strongly present, if often unrecognized as such, in almost every instance of contemporary theory."[126] In retaining a fundamentally Althusserian framework, cultural studies and postmodernism leave the door open to its ideological secularism, even if the latter remains present in a more infrastructural and so harder to perceive form. In *Culture and the Death of God*, Terry Eagleton evocatively explains the difference between modernism and postmodernism on this point when he observes, "Whereas modernism experiences the death of God as a trauma, an affront, a source of anguish as well as a cause for celebration, postmodernism does not experience it at all. There is no God-shaped hole at the centre of its universe."[127] Unlike in the pre-War period when, as Geroulanos showed, modernist thinkers and artists thought that religion's absence or latent presence mattered (think of Munch, Beckett, Weber, Sartre), in postmodernism God is so dead that its absence is a non-issue. Postmodernism is thus secular, but it is perfunctorily so and therefore indifferently, unthinkingly, and necessarily uncritically secular.

Even though the origins of film studies can thus be linked to an Althusserian secularism, it is important to acknowledge that film studies underwent major changes in the 1980s and 1990s with the introduction of post-theoretical, cognitivist, neo-formalist, and historicist approaches to film cultivated in the works of David Bordwell, Noël Carroll, Janet Staiger, Tom Gunning, Miriam Hansen, and others. Some of Gunning's, Hansen's, and Bordwell's works grapple with issues of secularism, as I have briefly indicated above and in the introduction to this volume, but for the most part attention to it is quite rare and usually not very thorough or critical (Hansen excluded). As a result, the secularist framework that marked the origins of film studies as a discipline in the universities of Europe, the UK, and North America persists. Because the universities, journals, and scholars which constitute the discipline reinforce each other—journals publishing articles by professors that students must read in order to become professors who publish in these journals—the framework becomes self-perpetuating. And because this framework is secularist, what we witness is a reproduction of secularism. Kevin Flatt is not wrong, even if heavy-handed, when he writes that the Western university in general is "controlled by and reproduces a self-governing academic guild that is—by design—insulated from religious orthodoxy," and thereby possesses an "inherent secularizing power."[128] As the history of the academic study of film continues within this reproductive system, we do in fact witness in film studies declining attention to religion in cinema, its relegation to, and sequestration in, religious studies, the almost complete absence of attention to secularity in either film studies or religious studies, and the absence of any meta-awareness that any of this is happening, why and how it is happening, or that it matters. The paradox of film studies, which is a version of the paradox of secularity more broadly, is that as it secularizes it becomes less conscious of secularity and therefore less conscious of the grip secularity has on itself.

Notes

1 Outside of specialized work on secularization in the social sciences, the topic of the secular has not had widespread general relevance in the humanities and social sciences for many decades until the "secular turn" of the last two decades. Talal Asad notes that "anthropologists have paid scarcely any attention to the idea of the secular" (21), while Michael Kauffman, writing about literary studies, discusses how the long-standing "assumed fact of secularization" (609) underwriting the discipline renders the secular and the religious "so normative that we no longer even notice them" (614). One could find similar facts across the academy. Talal Asad, *Formations of the Secular: Christianity, Islam, Modernity* (Stanford, CA: Stanford University Press,

2003); Michael Kaufman, "The Religious, the Secular, and Literary Studies: Rethinking the Secularization Narrative in Histories of the Profession," *New Literary History* 38, no. 4 (Autumn 2007): 607–27.

2 Bruno Latour, *We Have Never Been Modern*, trans. Catherine Porter (Cambridge, MA: Harvard University Press, 1993), chap. 2.

3 For Latour's discussions of the relationship between science and religion, see *We Have Never Been Modern*, 32–5, 38, 127–9, as well as his *On the Modern Cult of the Factish Gods* (Durham, NC: Duke University Press, 2010).

4 Latour, *On the Modern Cult of Factish Gods*, 22.

5 Latour is ambiguous on the question of whether we are, in fact, modern. At times, he states it clearly, and obviously names his book after the idea (*We Have Never Been Modern*, 46–8). At others, he appears to recognize that the blindness to our modernity is part of what makes us distinct from other societies and hence modern and that elements of modernity may be retained (ibid., chap. 5).

6 See my discussions of postsecularism in Introduction to the present volume and in my coauthored chapter with John Caruana, "What Is Postsecular Cinema?" in *Immanent Frames: Postsecular Cinema Between Malick and von Trier*, ed. John Caruana and Mark Cauchi (Albany: SUNY Press, 2018).

7 See James Turner, *Philology: The Forgotten Origins of the Modern Humanities* (Princeton, NJ: Princeton University Press, 2014); Tomoko Masuzawa, *The Invention of World Religions: Or, How European Universalism was Preserved in the Language Pluralism* (Chicago, IL: University of Chicago Press, 2005); Guy G. Stroumsa, *A New Science: The Discovery of Religion in the Age of Reason* (Cambridge, MA: Harvard University Press, 2010).

8 The English term "secularism" is usually attributed to the English Freethinker George Holyoake in 1851. On *laïcité*, see Sylvie Le Grand, "The Origin of the Concept of *Laïcité* in Nineteenth Century France," in *Religion and Secularity: Transformations and Transfers of Religious Discourses in Europe and Asia*, ed. Martin Eggert and Lucian Hölscher (Leiden: Brill, 2013); on *Weltlichkeit*, see Lucian Hölscher, "The Religious and the Secular: Semantic Reconfigurations of the Religious Field in Germany from the Eighteenth to the Twentieth Centuries," in Eggert and Hölscher, *Religion and Secularity*.

9 On the history of the concept of "religion," see the classic work by Wilfred Cantwell Smith, *The Meaning and End of Religion: A Revolutionary Approach to the Great Religious Traditions* (New York: Harper & Row Publishers, 1978); Daniel Dubuisson, *The Western Construction of Religion: Myths, Knowledge, and Ideology*, trans. William Sayers (Baltimore, MD: The Johns Hopkins University Press, 2003); Brent Nongbri, *Before Religion: A History of a Modern Concept* (New Haven, CT: Yale University Press, 2013).

10 William E. Arnal and Russell T. McCutcheon, *The Sacred is the Profane: The Political Nature of "Religion"* (New York: Oxford University Press, 2013), 119.

11 Max Weber, "Science as Vocation," *From Max Weber: Essays in Sociology*, ed. H. H. Gerth and C. Wright Mills (Abingdon: Routledge, 1991 [orig. 1948]), 139.
12 Ibid., 155.
13 Stroumsa, *A New Science*, chap. 1.
14 Masuzawa, *Invention of World Religion*, 19.
15 As examples of the white American representation of Black religious subjects as naïve, Judith Weisenfeld points to King Vidor's first sound film, *Hallelujah* (1929), and Connelly and Keighley's *The Green Pastures* (1936); see her *Hollywood Be Thy Name: African American Religion in Film, 1929–1949* (Berkeley, CA: University of California Press, 2007), chaps. 1 and 2.
16 Charles Taylor, *A Secular Age* (Cambridge, MA: Belknap Press, 2007), 299.
17 In his classic study, M. H. Abrams argued that many tropes of Romantic poetry are secularized versions of Christian ideas; see his *Natural Supernaturalism: Tradition and Revolution in Romantic Literature* (New York: W. W. Norton & Company, 1971). Similarly, in *Gothic Riffs: Secularizing the Uncanny in the European Imaginary, 1780–1820* (Columbus, OH: Ohio State University Press, 2010), Diane Long Hoeveler argues that in Romantic literature the uncanny emerges as a way to resist the pressure within the Enlightenment to "secularize," and that the transcendent takes on various "secular" uncanny avatars in literature. On the "religiousness" of humanities education, see Turner, *Philology*, 269–70, and Jon H. Roberts and James Turner, *The Sacred and Secular University* (Princeton, NJ: Princeton University Press, 2000), 108–17.
18 Jason A. Josephson-Storm, *The Myth of Disenchantment: Magic, Modernity, and the Birth of the Human Sciences* (Chicago, IL: University of Chicago Press, 2017), 300–1.
19 Max Weber, *The Protestant Ethic and the Spirit of Capitalism*, trans. Talcott Parsons (New York: Routledge, 2001 [orig. 1930]), xli.
20 Latour, *We Have Never Been Modern*, 115.
21 Many early theorists paid significant attention to the technological development necessary to the emergence of moving images. See, e.g., Hugo Münsterberg, "The Photoplay," chapter 1 in *Hugo Münsterberg on Film: The Photoplay: A Psychological Study and Other Writings*, ed. Allan Longdale (New York: Routledge, 2001).
22 Tom Gunning, "Phantom Images and Modern Manifestations: Spirit Photography, Magic Theatre, Trick Films, and Photography's Uncanny," in *Cinematic Ghosts: Haunting and Spectrality from Silent Cinema to the Digital Era*, ed. Murray Leeder (London: Bloomsbury, 2015), 18.
23 Tom Gunning, "An Aesthetic of Astonishment: Early Film and the (In) Credulous Spectator," in *Viewing Positions: Ways of Seeing Film*, ed. Linda Williams (New Brunswick, NJ: Rutgers University Press, 1995).
24 Gunning, "An Aesthetic of Astonishment," 115, 114.

25 Phillip Maciak, *The Disappearing Christ: Secularism in the Silent Era* (New York: Columbia University Press, 2019), 18.
26 Gunning, "An Aesthetic of Astonishment," 117.
27 Ibid.,129.
28 Ibid., 119; see also 117.
29 Ibid., 116.
30 Ibid.
31 Sigmund Freud, "The Uncanny," in *Standard Edition of the Complete Psychological Works of Sigmund Freud*, trans. James Strachey (Hogarth Press, 1953–74), 247–8.
32 See Tom Gunning, "To Scan a Ghost: The Ontology of the Mediated Vision," *Grey Room*, no. 26 (Winter 2007): 94–127; Gunning, "Phantom Images and Modern Manifestations."
33 Austin C. Lescarboura, "Edison's Views on Life and Death: An Interview with the Famous Inventor Regarding His Attempt to Communicate with the Next World," *Scientific American* 123, no. 18 (October 30, 1920): 446–60.
34 Erik Barnouw, *The Magician and the Cinema* (New York: Oxford University Press, 1981).
35 Gunning, "Phantom Images and Modern Manifestations," 38.
36 Gunning, "To Scan a Ghost," 100.
37 Quoted in Maciak, *The Disappearing Christ*, 158.
38 Gunning, "To Scan a ghost," 100.
39 Ibid., 114–15.
40 Maciak, *The Disappearing Christ*, 106.
41 Ibid., 17.
42 Ibid.,106.
43 Ibid. A key difference between our two readings is that, for Maciak, this contact zone does not demonstrate that "religion and the secular freely intermixed and improvised with each other," but instead takes place within secularism, which he defines, following John Lardas Modern, "be[ing] religious in a particular way" (ibid.,15). There are, in my view, two problems with this view. First, within Modern's book and Maciak's use of it, the "particular" religions specified are Protestant denominations, which again does not account for the forms of secularity that emerge outside the United States. Second, this position leaves out the development of a purified secularist ideology or what Taylor calls a "closed world system" (anti-transcendental positions), which do, in fact, evolve in modernity.
44 For a classic discussion of this narrative, see Dudley Andrew, "The 'Three Ages' of Cinema Studies and the Age to Come," *PMLA* 115, no. 3 (May 2000): 341–51. The first two ages are the pre-academic age and the early academic age (1960s–1980s).

45 On challenges to this narrative, see the two collections: *Looking Past the Screen: Case Studies in American Film History*, ed. Jon Lewis and Eric Smoodin (Durham, NC: Duke University Press, 2007); *Inventing Film Studies*, ed. Lee Grieveson and Haidee Wasson (Durham, NC: Duke University Press, 2008). Filmology was operative from the late 1940s to the late 1950s, but it is telling that it had only one journal in France (eventually a second in Italy), granted degrees at only one institution (Sorbonne), lasted only a decade, and has mostly been neglected by subsequent film scholars (the persistence of concepts like "diegetic" and Metz's references to it notwithstanding). For more on the filmology movement, see Edward Lowry, *The Filmology Movement and Film Study in France* (Ann Arbor, MI: UMI Research Press, 1985) and D. N. Rodowick, *Elegy for Theory* (Cambridge, MA: Harvard University Press, 2014), chap. 14. On the early study of film in America, see Dana Polan, *Scenes of Instruction: The Beginnings of the U.S. Study of Film* (Berkeley, CA: University of California Press, 2007).

46 Polan, *Scenes of Instruction*, 7.

47 Ibid., 5.

48 Although he does not pursue it, Dana Polan discerns a parallel between the early history of film in the academy and the history of the university's secularization (ibid., 13–14).

49 There were, of course, a few university academics who wrote on film as an art form (some well-known ones include Hugo Münsterberg, Mortimer Adler, Erwin Panofksy, Rudolf Arnheim, and Max Horkheimer and Theodor Adorno), but these were all located, obviously, in disciplines other than film studies.

50 For a discussion of this episode, recounted in Münsterberg's own writings, see Andreas Sommer, "Psychical Research and the Origins of American Psychology: Hugo Münsterberg, William James, and Eusapia Palladino," *History of the Human Sciences* 25, no. 2 (2012): 23–44.

51 See the discussion of his plan for university reform, which very much follows what Weber would call rationalization, in Julie A. Reuben, *The Making of the Modern University: Intellectual Transformation and the Marginalization of Morality* (Chicago, IL: University of Chicago Press, 1996), 176–9.

52 On Münsterberg's use of the terms soul and spirit, see Sarah Cooper, *The Soul of Film Theory* (New York: Palgrave Macmillan, 2013), 24–38.

53 Malcolm Turvey, *Doubting Vision: Film and the Revelationist Tradition* (New York: Oxford University Press, 2008), 6.

54 On the hybridity of Canudo's thinking, see Rodowick, *Elegy for Theory*, where he describes Canudo as conceiving of the aesthetic as "the new secular religion of modernity" (82). For more on the animism of the French Impressionists and especially Eisenstein, see Rachel O. Moore, *Savage Theory: Cinema as Modern Magic* (Durham, NC: Duke University Press, 2000). Edgar Morin's own work makes constant reference to his predecessors's works that reflect an animistic thinking about cinema; see Edgar Morin, *The Cinema, or The Imaginary Man* (Minneapolis: University of Minnesota Press,

[orig. 1956/1978] 2005). On the link between animism and Indigeneity in cinema, see May Adadol Ingawanij, "Animism and the Performative Realist Cinema of Apichatpong Weerasethakul," in *Screening Nature: Cinema Beyond the Human*, ed. Anat Pick and Guinevere Narraway (New York: Berghan Books, 2022) and Rosalind Galt, *Alluring Monsters: The Pontianak and Cinemas of Decolonization* (New York: Columbia University Press, 2021).

55 Edward Tylor, *Primitive Religion: Researches into the Development of Mythology, Philosophy, Religion, Language, Art, and Custom* (London: John Murray, 1920), 287, https://archive.org/details/in.ernet.dli.2015.42334/page/n5/mode/2up (accessed August 1, 2020).

56 See Masuzawa, *The Invention of World Religions*, esp. chap. 3.

57 Jean Epstein, "The Senses I (b)," in *French Film Theory and Criticism: A History/Anthology, 1907–1939*, vol. I, ed. Richard Abel (Princeton, NJ: Princeton University Press, 1988), 243, 246. Recognizing Epstein's theory as developing a secular-religious hybridity, Rachel Moore writes, "Epstein's writing often stages the encounter between the primitive and the technological, between science and poetry, between objective reality and the world the film creates—to put it more generally, between nature and second nature. Second nature is the nature that culture makes.'" See Rachel Moore, "A Different Nature," in *Jean Epstein: Critical Essays and New Translations*, ed. Sarah Keller and Jason N. Paul (Amsterdam: Amsterdam University Press, 2012), 180.

58 Jean Epstein, "On Certain Characteristics of *Photogénie*," in Abel, *French Film Theory*, 316. Lévy-Bruhl does not accept that moderns simply leave behind animist impulses: "When they ['partisans of animism'] describe a world peopled by ghosts and spirits and phantoms for primitives, we realize at once that beliefs of this kind have not wholly disappeared even in civilized countries" (53). Lucien Lévy-Bruhl, *How Natives Think*, trans. Lilian A. Clare (New York: Washington Square Press, [orig. 1910] 1966).

59 Epstein, "On Certain Characteristics of *Photogénie*," 316, 317.

60 Ibid., 316.

61 Jean Epstein, *The Intelligence of the Machine*, trans. Christophe Wall-Romana (Minneapolis: Univocal Publishing, 2014), 3.

62 Miriam Bratu Hansen, *Cinema and Experience: Siegfried Kracauer, Walter Benjamin, and Theodor W. Adorno* (Berkeley, CA: University of California Press, 2012), esp. chap. 1.

63 Ibid., 20.

64 Walter Benjamin, "Theses on the Philosophy of History," in *Illuminations*, by Walter Benjamin, ed. Hannah Arendt, trans. Harry Zohn (New York: Schocken Books, 1969), 264.

65 Ibid., 262, 263.

66 Ibid., 264.

67 See Walter Benjamin, *Reflections*, ed. Peter Demetz and trans. Edmund Jephcott (New York: Schocken Books, 1978), 179 and 190. I have discussed

Benjamin's thought in more depth in Mark Cauchi, "Infinite Spaces: Walter Benjamin and the Spurious Creations of Capitalism," *Angelaki* 8, no. 3 (2003): 23–39.
68. Walter Benjamin, "The Work of Art in the Age of Mechanical Reproduction," in *Illuminations*, 227–8.
69. Ibid., 244, n6.
70. "Aura (n)," *Online Etymology Dictionary*, https://www.etymonline.com/search?q=aura (accessed July 16, 2020).
71. Benjamin, "The Work of Art in the Age of Mechanical Reproduction," 236.
72. Ibid., 235.
73. Ibid., 237.
74. Ibid., 236.
75. Dudley Andrew, *André Bazin*, ed. rev. (New York: Oxford University Press, 1978), 57.
76. For a discussion of Bazin's relation to Peguy and Mournier, see John Caruana, "'My Sister Reality': The Franciscan Sources of Bazin's Philosophy of Cinema," in *Explorations on Film and Christianity*, ed. Rita Benis and Sérgio Dias Branco (Routledge, 2023).
77. André Bazin, "The Life and Death of Superimposition," trans. Bert Cardullo, *Film-Philosophy Journal* 6, no. 1 (January 2002), http://www.film-philosophy.com/vol6-2002/n1bazin (accessed September 2020).
78. Bert Cardullo and André Bazin, "Cinema and Theology: The Case of Heaven Over the Marshes," *Journal of Religion & Film* 6, no. 2 (2002): Article 15. For a discussion of *Heaven Over the Marshes* in relation to questions of religion and secularism, see Russell J. A. Killbourn, "The Immortal Thighs of Ines Orsini: The Transcendence of Grace in Denys Arcand's *The Barbarian Invasions*," in Caruana and Cauchi, *Immanent Frames*.
79. Cardullo and Bazin, "Cinema and Theology," 6.
80. Ibid.
81. Ibid., 9.
82. Ibid. See also Caruana, "What is Postsecular Cinema?".
83. Cardullo and Bazin, "Cinema and Theology," 3.
84. Cooper, *Soul of Film Theory*, 11.
85. See Kevin N. Flatt, "The Secularization of Western Universities in International Perspective: Toward a Historicist Account," *The Review of Faith & International Affairs* 18, no. 2 (2020): 30–43.
86. Hugh McLeod, *The Religious Crisis of the 1960s* (Oxford: Oxford University Press, 2007).
87. George M. Marsden, *The Soul of the American University: From Protestant Establishment to Established Nonbelief* (New York: Oxford University Press,

1994), chap. 22; Reuben, *The Making of the Modern University*; and Roberts and Turner, *The Sacred and the Secular University*.

88 Peter L. Berger, "The Desecularization of the World: A Global Overview," in *The Desecularization of the World: Resurgent Religion and World Politics*, ed. Peter Berger (Grand Rapids, MI: William B. Eerdmans Publishing Company, 1999), 10.

89 Stefanos Geroulanos, *An Atheism that is Not Humanist Emerges in French Thought* (Stanford, CA: Stanford University Press, 2010).

90 Ibid., 6.

91 The idea was first proposed in Raymond Aron, "The Future of Secular Religions" [1944] in *The Dawn of Universal History: Selected Essays from a Witness to the Twentieth Century*, trans. Barbara Bray (New York: Basic Books, 2002). He deploys the concept again in his *The Opium of the Intellectuals* [1955] (New York: Routledge, 2007).

92 Geroulanos, *Atheism that is Not Humanist*, 307.

93 Ibid., 6, 7.

94 Sylvia Harvey, *May '68 and Film Culture* (London: British Film Institute Publishing, 1980); Colin McCabe, "Class of '68: Elements of an Intellectual Autobiography 1967–81," in *Tracking the Signifier: Theoretical Essays: Film, Linguistics, Literature* (Minneapolis: University of Minnesota Press, 1985); D. N. Rodowick, *The Crisis of Political Modernism: Criticism and Ideology in Contemporary Film Theory* (Berkeley, CA: University of California Press, 1994).

95 See the pieces gathered in *Althusser and Theology: Religion, Politics, and Philosophy*, ed. Agon Hamza (Chicago, IL: Haymarket Books, 2018). Althusser makes some provocative claims in a late interview identifying himself with Catholicism, but it is hard to gauge how seriously these comments should be taken; see "An Interview with Louis Althusser: The Crisis of Marxism," trans. Ron Salaj, in *Crisis and Critique*, http://crisiscritique.org/blog.html (accessed March 12, 2021).

96 Louis Althusser, *For Marx* (London: Verso, 2005), 13.

97 Louis Althusser, "Ideology and Ideological State Apparatuses," in Althusser's *On the Reproduction of Capitalism: Ideology and Ideological State Apparatuses*, trans. G. M. Goshgarian (London: Verso, 2014), 266.

98 Louis Althusser, *Philosophy, and the Spontaneous Philosophy of the Scientists & Other Essays*, ed. Gregory Elliott, trans. Ben Brewster (London: Verso, 1990),112, 121.

99 Althusser, "Ideology and Ideological State Apparatuses," 250.

100 There were differences between the two. While *Cahiers* generally held the position that revolutionary potential could be found in the subtle formal properties of otherwise ideological works (most famously in John Ford's *Young Mr. Lincoln*), *Cinethique* generally rejected this and instead insisted that only formally radical works, such as in Godard's militant period (late 1960s to mid-1970s), could actually critique ideology. For a discussion of

Althusser's role in the formation of French film theory in this period, see Harvey, *May '68 and Film Culture*, chap. 3.
101 MacCabe, "Class of '68," 7.
102 See MacCabe, "Class of '68"; Rodowick, *The Crisis of Political Modernism*, chap. 3.
103 See Richard Rushton, "Christian Metz," in *Film, Theory, and Philosophy: The Key Thinkers*, ed. Felicity Colman (London : Routledge, 2014), 266, and Robert Stam, *Film Theory: An Introduction* (Blackwell Publishers, 2000), 109.
104 Rodowick, *Elegy for Theory*, 252.
105 Christian Metz, *The Imaginary Signifier: Psychoanalysis and the Cinema*, trans. Celia Britton et al., (Bloomington: Indiana University Press, 1981), 14.
106 Ibid., 12.
107 Ibid., 18.
108 Ibid., 15, 79.
109 Ibid., 15; see also 79–80.
110 My discussion of the etymology follows the entry on "fetish" in the *Online Etymology Dictionary*, https://www.etymonline.com/search?q=fetish (accessed October 7, 2022). The definitive critical analysis of the concept of fetishism is William Pietz, *The Problem of the Fetish*, ed. Francesco Pellizzi et al. (Chicago, IL: University of Chicago Press, 2022). For more on the colonial and religious history of the concept of fetishism and its link to Marx and Freud, see J. Lorand Matory, *The Fetish Revisited: Marx, Freud, and the Gods Black People Make* (Durham, NC: Duke University Press, 2018). For how the concept of the fetish connects to my earlier discussion of purification and hybridity, see Latour, *On the Modern Cult of the Factish Gods*.
111 Metz, *The Imaginary Signifier*, 74.
112 On the shift of the meanings of "belief" and "faith" in modernity, see Wilfred Cantwell Smith, *Believing: An Historical Perspective* (Oxford: Oneworld Publications, [orig. 1977] 1998), Chapter II, "The Modern History of 'Believing': The Drift away from Faith."
113 Metz, *The Imaginary Signifier*, 72.
114 Ibid., 73.
115 Ibid., 52.
116 Ibid.
117 Ibid.
118 Ibid., 72, 73.
119 Ibid., 53.
120 Ibid.

121 For an account of this history, see Terry Bolas, *Screen Education: From Film Appreciation to Media Studies* (Bristol: Intellect Books, 2009), esp. chaps. 6 and 7.
122 MacCabe, "Class of '68," 7.
123 Ibid., 13.
124 Robert Stam, *World Literature, Transnational Cinema, and Global Media: Towards a Transartistic Commons* (Abingdon, Oxon: Routledge, 2019), 60.
125 Ibid., 59.
126 Rodowick, *Elegy for Theory*, 246.
127 Terry Eagleton, *Culture and the Death of God* (New Haven, CT: Yale University Press, 2014), 186.
128 Flatt, "The Secularization of Western Universities in International Perspective," 39.

2

Deleuze's "Conversion of Belief"

The Time-Image and the Disruption of Cinema's Secularist Origins

John Caruana

Introduction

Over the last quarter century, a vibrant discussion has opened up about the meaning, significance, and legitimacy of the secularist underpinnings of our modern era. This conversation has attracted some of the most important thinkers of our times, including Charles Taylor and Jürgen Habermas. The discussion has not been limited to philosophers, however. Questions relating to the problem of secularism have also garnered considerable attention from sociologists, anthropologists, and literary scholars, among others.[1] Yet, with a few exceptions, these concerns have not found much traction among scholars who write on film.[2] There could be a number of reasons for this. As Carl Schmitt and others have reminded us, secularism is inextricably linked to religion. It is probably safe to assume that religion does not sit well with a significant swathe of the academy. As Taylor observes: "the exclusion/irrelevance of religion is often part of the unnoticed background" for many academics today.[3] This aversion for anything related to religion—which expresses itself as disinterest at best and dismissiveness at worst—is particularly noticeable in those parts of the academy that are more strongly connected to modernist aesthetics and theory. What James Elkins observes in his study of the omission of religion in modern and contemporary art theory and criticism likely applies just as well to the academic study of cinema. Elkins notes that "[m]odernism was predicated on a series of rejections and refusals."[4] One of its defining refusals is the requirement to keep religion at a distance—ideally, out of sight and out of mind. If religion has to be treated at all, then the modernist intellectual will dutifully follow the Kantian dictum of "religion within the bounds of reason alone." In its crassest terms today, that typically means that religion is deemed worthy of our consideration only when it serves some useful objective. Thus, in the context of film scholarship, "Religion and Film" courses pass the test because of what is deemed to be the *reasonable* need to discuss, catalogue, and classify films with religious content. *But* this same attitude discourages the otherwise interesting question of how cinema might itself be imbricated with religious phenomena.[5] The blind spot here likely involves a scornful pride that many late modern intellectuals feel, especially in contrast to our more religiously minded ancestors and co-citizens today. Nietzsche warned us a while ago that secularization is a complex phenomenon that cannot be disentangled entirely from religion. But more than that, he bluntly chastises those who adopt a triumphalist stance in relation to their secularist identity: "The educated classes are no longer lighthouses or refuges in the midst of this turmoil of secularization. . . . They would dearly like to make us believe that of all the centuries theirs has borne the prize away, and they shake with artificial merriment."[6] An honest appraisal of our current situation requires us to think more carefully about the interlacing of religion with our modern secular institutions and practices. Ironically, Nietzsche is often appealed to in an effort to justify the refusal to take religion seriously, even though he alerted us against the dangers of such a dismissive attitude.[7] But if we take Nietzsche seriously, we would see that religious assumptions and ideals, for better or worse, and whether we are conscious of them or not, are woven into the fabric of our modern reality—much more so than we dare to admit.

One would think that there is a very interesting story to be told here about cinema, born, as it was, a mere number of years after Nietzsche's famous declaration of the "death of God." As a product of late modernity, one would think that cinema has surely inherited and been marked by—both as a practice and as an object of study—the many hidden presuppositions of its epoch. If, as it was indeed the case, cinema emerged just as the processes of secularization were in full bloom, then we might have good reasons for suspecting that secularism, with all its religious undercurrents, constitutes one of the inconspicuous cloaks that it wears.[8]

The relative silence concerning this topic makes locating the connections between secularism and cinema a daunting task. Where do we begin? One way forward might involve building on an existing work that situates cinema against a broad historical and philosophical backdrop. Such a work could point us in the right direction concerning this question. William Connolly proposes something like this in turning to Gilles Deleuze's philosophy, particularly his influential study of cinema.[9] Connolly's strategy is effective because he places Deleuze's reflections in dialogue with others who have foregrounded the problem of secularism, Charles Taylor, in particular. My objective here, however, differs somewhat from Connolly's. For my purposes, I want to focus less on the problem of postsecularism—which is Connolly's primary concern—and more on how Deleuze's thought helps us to see in what ways secularism has shaped cinema itself.

It is true that Deleuze does not explicitly use terms like "secularism" and "secularist" in the critical fashion that we find in today's literature. However, if we read him with those questions in mind, we can see that Deleuze is quite sensitive to the problems that have been raised about the dominant secular narrative—which I denote here as "secular*ism*" and "secular*ist*," while generally reserving the term "secular" to denote something like *this-worldliness*[10]—that is at the heart of late modern experience. Given the specific contexts in which he raises important questions about the nature of belief and subjectivity, it becomes apparent that Deleuze, like Nietzsche before him, understands that secularism harbors knotty, stifling presuppositions. He understands, furthermore—and this is my primary reason for focusing on Deleuze here—that cinema has played a not insignificant part in this ongoing problem. In charting out this territory, my goal in this chapter is twofold: first, to make the case that Deleuze can be read in such a way as to help us see that the development and trajectory of cinema cannot be dissociated from the broader secularist dynamics of late modern life; and, second, to show, that a critical cinema, what Deleuze famously calls the "time-image," offers us an alternative take on what it means to be secular, one that has the potential to free us from the straitjacket of ideological secularism.

Secularism as the Dominant Image of Thought of Our Age

As Taylor, Connolly, and others remind us, our secular age is blinded by certain conceits.[11] As a consequence of the reigning secular discourse that shapes our epoch, we imagine ourselves liberated from what we take to be the superstitious trappings of both past and current religious forms of life. Inheritors of the Enlightenment legacy, we are confident that our unconditional allegiance to disenchanted reason makes us immune to the religious and metaphysical ills that afflicted our ancestors. But that self-narrative does not hold up well upon closer scrutiny. When we widen the lens of observation to allow us to see more clearly the antecedents to our current worldview, we become aware of the shortcomings and blind spots of this story. One thing that becomes quite apparent about this storyline is how it is structured around a series of binary—and, it should be noted, self-serving—oppositions. On the side of enlightened secularism, we find a set of positive features and values that we associate, among others, with unprejudiced reason, knowledge, and the communicative transparency of the public sphere. On the other side of that ledger, which we align with the regressive forces of religion and superstitious thinking in general, fall a host of different contrasting, negative associations: unchallenged faith, opinion, and the inscrutable opaqueness of the private sphere of interiority and family life. These structuring oppositions conceal the extent to which our modern, liberal worldview is underpinned by its own metaphysical prejudices. Nietzsche, as we know, developed a very powerful genealogy of modernity. It is impossible to do justice to his account in a few paragraphs. For our purposes, it suffices to highlight a few key features. According to Nietzsche, it is difficult to recognize these prejudices because they are displacements of older drives and impulses, now dressed up in modern garb. Nietzsche traces what he calls the ascetic ideal to ancient Athens (Platonism) and Jerusalem (Paul's Christianity). For Nietzsche, these two traditions, which eventually melded into one distinct worldview, express an aversion to life and are at the root of the western ascetic ideal. He names that ideal the "will to truth"— the conviction that there is a timeless reality "out there," which we can know in the most robust sense of that term. Nietzsche's counter-narrative has been rightly contested for the way it sometimes caricatures the complex history of Christianity[12]—a problem that also shows up in some of Deleuze's indiscriminate swipes at Christianity (especially in his early work). For my purposes, however, I want to underscore the point that Nietzsche provides Deleuze with the means to understand secularism critically.

Too often, we take Nietzsche's parable of the death of God to be about the incredulity of religion in general, Christianity in particular. But for Nietzsche, the madman's proclamation of the demise of God has its most significant bearing on *our time*, that is, *our secular age*. As Nietzsche puts it, the supposed lucidity of our secularized Enlightenment culture is obscured by the "shadow" of earlier metaphysical ideals that continue to cast its pall over the modern world. Nietzsche powerfully conveys the conceit of our time in the passage from the *Untimely Meditations* that I cited in an abbreviated form above. The extended passage reads:

> The educated classes are no longer lighthouses or refuges in the midst of this turmoil of secularization; they themselves grow daily more restless, thoughtless and loveless. Everything, contemporary art and science included, serves the coming barbarism. The cultured man has degenerated to the greatest enemy of culture, for he wants lyingly to deny the existence of the universal sickness and thus obstructs the physicians. They become

incensed, these poor wretches, whenever one speaks of their weakness and resists their pernicious lying spirit. They would dearly like to make us believe that of all the centuries, theirs has borne the prize away, and they shake with artificial merriment.[13]

Here, Nietzsche spells out the conceit of our secular era—an age he explicitly characterizes in terms of the "turmoil of secularization." The "cultured man," this member of the "educated classes," champion of secular reason, would "make us believe" that we now live at a time like no other, liberated from the shackles of outdated beliefs. In this and related passages, Nietzsche makes it a point to single out the most prestigious avatars of the modern world: "contemporary art and science included." In doing so, he is not merely pointing to the fact that art and science enjoy a special kind of reverence in the eyes of the "educated." He is also endeavoring to make us see how these signature modern institutions deflect attention away from themselves—lest we catch a glimpse of "their weakness"—by setting themselves entirely apart from the past. How? By a sort of epistemological sleight of hand. Unlike their superstitious predecessors, these proud moderns want us to believe they can *see through* the veils of religious ignorance. By contrast, the cultured classes *know* reality as it truly is. They wave this "prize" triumphantly, lording it over others, past and present. But they do so despite the specter of the "coming barbarism," which their worldview "serves," as Nietzsche cannot help to punctuate. This is all to say that far from breaking with the ascetic ideal, the modern project—with its co-opted institutions of art and science—surreptitiously incorporates and extends several of its essential features.

One of Deleuze's names for that ideal is the "dominant image of thought." That image has transfixed western culture, at least since the birth of philosophy. Its spell makes us imagine we have access to timeless ideals that permit us to remake our reality accordingly. But as Nietzsche shows—followed by Heidegger—our unquestioned attachment to these ideals drives us to remake the world *at all costs*. To make reality conform to these imagined ideals, we have unleashed terrible forces of domination and exploitation on the natural world and other human beings. In his prognosis, Nietzsche names this malady nihilism. What makes the image of thought so difficult to discern is that it operates as the unthought of an age. The postulates of the image of thought "need not be spoken: they function all the more effectively in silence" (DR 167).

Both Nietzsche and his intellectual heir, Deleuze, are wary of the secularist's claim that modernity represents a break with the past. They see in such claims the return, this time more furtive, of earlier specious dynamics, dispositions, and reactive expressions of the will-to-power. In addition to the religious dogmatist, both philosophers have the secularist counterpart in their crosshairs. Thus, in his "Preface to the English Translation" of

Nietzsche and Philosophy, Deleuze notes, in good Nietzschean fashion, that we must also be apprehensive of our modern-day "secular priest" who is no less mired in *ressentiment* (NP x). This modern priest, if we are to be more precise, is a secularist, who, armed with his or her conceptual a priori truths, is firmly convinced that an utterly denatured reason and disenchanted reality will bring about, through the mediation of a secularized aesthetics, science, and technology, a complete, progressive transformation of this world.

Cinema's Secularist Origins

One of the claims I want to make here is that our understanding of cinema as a historical phenomenon is enriched if we pay attention to the specific ways cinema's origins are bound up with secularist assumptions. To better understand those origins, we would do well to pay attention to a theme that Deleuze introduces in the opening pages of *Cinema 1*. Since its earliest days, the origins of cinema appear inseparable from the scientific and industrial processes that define the late modern period. Consequently, cinema, from its earliest days onward, has been conceived as the "industrial art" par excellence—an expression that gets to "the very heart of cinema's ambiguous position" (C1 6). It is difficult to disagree with film historian Geoffrey Nowell-Smith when he concludes that "cinema is industrial almost by definition."[14] The "almost" here is meant to capture the same ambiguity that interests Deleuze, namely, that while cinema is inextricably linked to industrialization, it is not reducible to it. In this section, I want to focus on the industrial side of that ambiguity before saying a few things about cinema as art in the next section.

While André Bazin was no doubt correct to argue that the mythical (what he describes as the spiritual or psychological) *desire* for cinema predates the technological achievements of the modern world,[15] its practical actualization would not have been possible, of course, without the fulfillment of specific material and technical conditions. Emerging at the end of the nineteenth century, cinema was forged during the heart of the Second Industrial Revolution. One of the consummate achievements of our modern technological age, it was made possible by advancements in machinery, optics, the harnessing of electricity, and the invention of synthetic plastic materials—all of which had been facilitated by the remarkable achievements of the scientific revolution that was initiated in the seventeenth century. As Deleuze notes, commenting on Bergson's reflections, cinema "seems to be the last descendent of [a] lineage" that goes back to the "modern scientific revolution" (C1, p. 4). Therefore, cinema as we know it is unthinkable outside of this scientific and industrial context. Cinema's unparalleled technical capacities have made it amenable to the large-scale ambitions of modern societies, and from the vital part it has played in the development of mass culture—

the entertainment industry, in particular—to the propagandistic efforts of various state actors. Commenting on Paul Virilio's work, Deleuze connects the capacities of the cinematic apparatus with the dramatic deployment of an unprecedented war machine in the first half of the twentieth century. As Walter Benjamin also warned, it is not by chance that totalitarian forces seized on cinema's technical powers. Fashioned under the conditions that reigned during the height of the industrial era, cinema could, and, indeed, did have the power to summon vast numbers of people for the war effort as well as for commercial exploitation. In this manner, cinema played an essential part in the development of a new large-scale, truly, global stage of technological control and weaponry. "The system of war," Deleuze observes, "mobilizes perception as much as arms and actions: thus photography and cinema pass through war, and are coupled together with arms . . . . But it is the whole of civil life which passes into the mode of the *mise-en-scène*, in the fascist system: real power is henceforth shared between the logistics of arms and that of images and sounds" (C2, 309n16; trans. slightly modified, see *Cinéma 2: L'image-temps* [Paris: Minuit, 1985], 214n16).

But what is it about modern industrialization and science, as they have developed in late modernity, that makes them such potent global forces? And what has this meant for cinema specifically? Deleuze tackles these questions by shining a light on two features of the ascetic ideal that are intricately bound up with industrialization and science, and which are vividly reflected in normative cinema, or what Deleuze refers to as "classical cinema."[16] In *Cinema 1*, in particular, he highlights the following two dynamics of the dominant image of thought: (1) a certain conception of subjectivity, along with (2) a distinctive philosophy of history. These two features of cinema's cultural and social backdrop play an essential part in Deleuze's genealogy of cinema. A significant portion of the first volume concerns itself with the three primary forms of the movement-image—affect, perception, and action, along with their various permutations—that define classical cinema. Of these three types, it is evident that the action-image features most conspicuously in his account of mass culture cinema. That is not an accident. The action-image captures the culmination of an agent's efforts to take full measure of a situation in order to alter it and, in so doing, produce a more amenable situation. Deleuze, as his readers know, helpfully abbreviates this process as SAS': *situation* [S] (the circumstances or problem that requires solving), *action* [A] (the intervention that is carried out by a protagonist or hero), and a *new situation* [S'] (the resolution made possible by the hero's determinate efforts). The overwhelming focus on the action-image in classical cinema perpetuates the image of a subject in complete control of itself and its environment. In this manner, it powerfully echoes the founding moment of the modern period, the inauguration of the distinctively Cartesian view of the human subject as the center of its reality.

Classical cinema is also a reflection of a particular view of history, one that is intimately bound up with the conception of modern subjectivity. Adopting the categories that Nietzsche deploys in "The Uses and Disadvantages of History for Life" for understanding the modern philosophy of history, Deleuze characterizes the action-image in terms of its monumental, antiquarian, and critical aspects. The action-image—in combination with these aspects of a nineteenth-century philosophy of history, which advance a picture of history as destiny and universality (C1 148–151)—plays a vital part in underwriting a secularist worldview.[17] These motifs are particularly conspicuous in American classical cinema. In his effort to sketch America's infatuation with the action-image, from Griffith's landmark productions to the westerns of John Wayne, Deleuze concludes—rhetorically, of course—that classical American cinema "constantly shoots and reshoots a single fundamental film," namely, the rise of a salvific civilization. Appearances to the contrary, the individualist ethos of American culture shares the same faith in reason and action that one finds in the collectivist aspirations of Soviet cinema: their respective cinemas reveal and reinforce the idea of the human being's power to conquer new frontiers and control its own destiny (C1 148). While on the surface of things, Griffith seems far removed from Eisenstein's avant-garde cinema, in other respects, their shared faith in human agency indicates a much deeper affinity than their differences might otherwise suggest.

Undoubtedly, the action-oriented view of the subject and the monumental outlook described above are conspicuously present in the first few decades of cinema. But these dynamics also exert a powerful influence well into the second half of the twentieth century and undoubtedly into the early decades of the twenty-first century. Thus, despite the revolutionary innovations of art-house films, normative cinema, in keeping with the colossal scale of mass production, continues to bolster a particular view of reality and an image of the subject as a powerful agent exerting itself in the face of hostile forces. As Deleuze points out, under "the conditions of an industrial art, where the proportion of disgraceful works calls the most basic goals and capacities directly into question," commercial and exploitative cinema will continue to prevail. Consequently, if cinema is supposed to be "dying," as some maintain, "then [it is] from its quantitative mediocrity. But there is a still more important reason: the mass-art, the treatment of masses, which should not have been separable from an accession of the masses to the status of true subject, has degenerated into state propaganda and manipulation" (C2 164).

Another way of expressing what I have just outlined is in terms of the prevailing secularist story that holds sway to our day.[18] As we moved from a God-centered view of the world to a humanist one, a number of the more problematic conceptions that were previously identified with a metaphysical God—in particular, the view of the divine as absolutely sovereign and radically removed from the transient character of terrestrial life—were transferred to a humanist register. This particular theological view underwent a crisis at the start of the modern period, culminating in Nietzsche's declaration of the death of God. But as I discussed in the previous section, the underlying assumptions remained intact and were simply displaced to the domain of humanism and secular rationality. The problem is that we have yet to catch up with that ongoing crisis; we continue to act as if we were not fully aware of the metaphysical baggage carried over to our secular discourses and institutions. Deleuze's originality here is to suggest that a powerful expression of cinema has been a major contributor to this problem.

Far from offering a viable alternative to the death of a metaphysical God—the "God" of the three O's, that is, *omnipotence, omniscience, omnipresence*—classical cinema contributes to the problem of nihilism by sustaining the various illusions that undergird the modern ideal of a sovereign subject and its corresponding view of history. No matter what level of adversity it might face, the modern subject inevitably triumphs. The self-confidence of classical cinema's protagonist heroes, and the viewers who identify with them, should remind us of those in the marketplace who ridicule the madman's annunciation of the death of God. They do not understand the implications of the madman's parable. They think it concerns religious faith, in this case, a Christian belief in God. It must be emphasized that they laugh at the madman because, as it turns out, "many of those who did not believe in God were standing around just then."[19] These all-too-modern people do not understand because, as Heidegger points out, the "death of God" has nothing to do with the "external and paltry façades of nihilism," that is, the superficial debates about the existence or non-existence of God. The madman's announcement concerns the end of the *metaphysical* God, the "truth of the suprasensory world," the belief in a fixed, objective reality that we can know perfectly. The death of *this* version of God has yet to register for these moderns. They continue to act and behave as if it were still the case that we can access and realize the higher values of a perfect world. The proud modern epoch reflects the very thing that it claims to reject. Heidegger expresses this succinctly in his attempt to interpret Nietzsche's parable: "Those who fancy themselves free of nihilism"—especially those who express an unquestioned confidence in the power of reason—"perhaps push forward its development most fundamentally."[20] In a way, what Heidegger says next, repeating in large part Nietzsche's own words, applies just as well to normative cinema: "it belongs to the uncanniness of this uncanny guest that it cannot name its own origin."[21] That uncanny guest in this particular context can be identified with the secularist myth that strongly informs the action-image orientation of classical cinema, along with many of the other major institutions of the modern period.

The Time-Image and the Subversion of Secularism

In the previous section, I deliberately focused on cinema as an industrial form to tease out some of the broader secularist underpinnings of cinema's origins. While acknowledging some of the obvious ways cinema has been imbricated with the broader modern history of industrialization, Deleuze, nevertheless, refuses to identify cinema as a mere organ of nineteenth- and twentieth-century industry. As industrial as it might be, cinema, as the ambiguity of the nomenclature "industrial *art*" suggests, always remains more than just that. As an art form, and a remarkably distinct one at that, its creative promise should not be understated, even if it is undeniable that the story of mainstream cinema has been one of "unparalleled economic and industrial consequences," according to Deleuze. It is true that, seen from a perspective that emphasizes its industrial character, "[t]he history of the cinema is a long martyrology." What has been sacrificed is the potential of cinema to be an art form in the fullest sense of that term, that is, as a mode of expressing and creating something genuinely new. But that is not the whole story. Despite the forces that work to undermine its creativity, "cinema still forms part of art and part of thought, in the irreplaceable, autonomous forms which these directors were able to invent and get screened, in spite of everything" (C1 xiv). Cinema has always had the potential to produce new ways of seeing, novel ways to configure reality, and the capacity to subvert the conditioned responses of modern subjects. It is this relatively untapped potentiality, frequently neglected in classical cinema, that Deleuze attempts to adumbrate in the second *Cinema* volume. For Deleuze, cinema's most radical potential lies in what he describes as the time-image, that is, cinema in the service of the becoming of life. More to the point, the time-image is significant, especially in the context of this chapter, because (1) it undermines the metaphysical pillars of secularism, while, at the same time (2) it entails a renewal of a legitimate form of the secular, a return to a much-needed this-worldly orientation.

Very much in the spirit of Nietzsche, Deleuze understands that there is a secularist position that is, in some crucial respects, cut from the same cloth as certain escapist religious discourses. A dominant strand of classical cinema is tinged by that particular secular ideology. But the *Cinema* books also become the occasion to imagine a different way of being secular. It is in that context that Deleuze brings up what is no doubt one of the most memorable lines from the two volumes: the "need to believe in this world" (C2 173). Deleuze recognizes that our current age is diminished by a profound loss of faith, though not in a transcendent Being beyond this world, but a belief *in* the world.[22] It may be the case, Deleuze and Guattari write shortly after the publication of the second *Cinema* volume, that "believing in this world, in this life, becomes our most difficult task, or the task of a mode of existence still to be discovered on our plane of immanence today." They name this most difficult of challenges the "empiricist conversion" (WP 75).

We find Deleuze engaging in the problem of belief in his earliest writings. It was a central theme of his first book, *Empirisme et subjectivité* (1953), which was devoted to the thought of David Hume. For the 1989 Preface to the English-language edition, Deleuze returns to the centrality of belief, noting that "[Hume] established the concept of belief and put it in the place of knowledge. He laicized belief, turning knowledge into a legitimate belief." (ES, ix) What does it mean that Hume "laicized belief" [*a laïcisé la croyance*] (DRF 341)? We might be tempted initially to understand that to mean nothing more than what secularization implies, namely, the transformation of religious beliefs into secular ones. What might nudge us in that interpretive direction is the explicit reference to Hume, whose proper name is virtually synonymous with religious skepticism. That might lead us to think that what Deleuze has in mind is a straightforward opposition to religion. My concern with that reading is that it entangles Deleuze's thought with the detrimental binarism of a secularist worldview. That would be to betray the spirit of his thought. Secularism is a vehicle for the passive nihilism that Deleuze—like Nietzsche before him—wishes to overcome.[23]

It is worth noting that even Deleuze, early on, was not immune from certain secularist assumptions. For example, while acknowledging the novelty and usefulness of Kierkegaard's notion of repetition, Deleuze, in 1968, nevertheless felt compelled to contrast Kierkegaard's "theatre of faith" with Nietzsche's "theatre of unbelief" (DR 11). As Deleuze saw it then, the truth about faith is that it remains, at the end of the day, a "simulacrum" (DR 95). By contrast, Nietzsche's doctrine of eternal return, Deleuze goes on to say, is "not a belief but the parody of every belief" (DR 95-96). To his credit, he drops this language a little more than a decade after the publication of *Difference and Repetition*. Now, instead, Deleuze regards Kierkegaard as someone who rehabilitates belief over and against those who presume that we can have real knowledge of the world. In his later work, Deleuze, as far as I know, no longer contrasts faith with unbelief. Instead, in a notable footnote in the second cinema volume, he pairs Kierkegaard and Nietzsche as a "real couple" who together circumvent the superficial distinctions between belief and unbelief, believer and unbeliever (C2 311n30). In the *Cinema* volumes, there are *only* beliefs, some more life-enhancing than others; "unbelief" turns out to be just another kind of belief.

By the time we get to the *Cinema* project, we begin to appreciate that Deleuze's concern when he speaks of laicizing belief is not religion as such but rather a certain metaphysical stance that finds expression in both religious and nonreligious forms. That belief is "laicized" means that it is detached from all forms of conceptual transcendence. All efforts to hitch belief to some otherworldly grounding—be it Being, the One, Reason, a metaphysical God, or some other similar idea—are deemed illegitimate. In *What Is Philosophy?* Deleuze and Guattari ask: "Under what conditions can belief be legitimate when it has become secular?" (WP 53). Beliefs remain illegitimate when staked to a desire for a perfect plane of reality. Such a belief can just as well find a home in a nonreligious context as it can within a religious worldview. Beliefs have to undergo a further "conversion"—away from the escapism of otherworldly thinking to one oriented to this world, these bodies, this reality. Knowledge does not involve a direct and immediate form of knowing separate from belief. There is a dominant form of religion and philosophy that would have us imagine that we can possess a privileged form of knowing, a knowledge of true reality, as opposed to what it takes to be those beliefs generated by our deception-prone bodies and senses. In the *Cinema* books, it becomes clear that what is at issue here is not the secular *vs* the religious or unbeliever *vs* believer distinction. Indeed, the great "unbelievers" (of theistic religion), Hume and Nietzsche, no longer exclusively hold center-stage in this discussion. Both Hume and Nietzsche are, in the context of the *Cinema* volumes, but two points of reference among others, including religiously minded thinkers and artists: "It was already a great turning-point in philosophy, from Pascal to Nietzsche: to replace the model of knowledge with belief" (C2 172). Three decades after the Hume book, it is Pascal and Kierkegaard, along with a group of Christian filmmakers—in particular, Dreyer, Bresson, Rossellini, and Rohmer—that Deleuze foregrounds in his discussion of the need to believe anew. "Belief replaces knowledge only when it becomes belief in this world, as it is. With Dreyer, then Rossellini, cinema takes the same turn" (C2 172). In significant ways, all of these figures have contributed to the laicizing of belief, or what Deleuze names the "conversion of belief"—a phrase that is blunted in the English translation of the *Time-Image* book as the "transformation of belief" (C2 172).[24] In a university lecture, Deleuze makes these connections even more explicit. He describes here what it means to undergo this conversion:

> Hence, it's when Rossellini says no: "I call infantile any position which derives its joy from the rupture of man and the world." . . . I'm claiming a belief (not in the name of Catholicism); it was already in Kierkegaard. With Kierkegaard, belief consisted of "give me back the world," "give me back the world, this world." With Pascal the wager is "give me back the world, this world." So much so that at the same time that belief replaces knowledge, belief undergoes a conversion, a fundamental conversion that, in my opinion, one finds in all the authors who participate in this substitution of belief for knowledge—all of whom undergo conversion in very different ways. They all convert belief, which ceases to be belief in another world, to belief in this world, that is to say, restoration of a relationship between man and the world.[25]

It is important to take note of Deleuze's recognition of the "very different ways" in which the conversion of belief is undergone. Those who wish to downplay Deleuze's references to religious thinkers and filmmakers in the expression of the time-image risk missing an important point.[26] The laicizing or conversion of belief does not concern some facile distinction between the secular and the religious—but one that cuts through the heart of both. If we keep that in mind, then we are in a better position to grasp Deleuze's observation that

> a certain Catholic quality has continued to inspire a great number of authors, and revolutionary passion has passed into third world cinema. What has changed is, however, the crucial point, and there is as much difference between the Catholicism of Rossellini or Bresson, and that of Ford, as between the revolutionary qualities of Rocha or Güney, and those of Eisenstein. (C2 171)

From Deleuze's perspective, Ford's Catholicism is perfectly compatible with the assuredness of action-focused classical cinema. In that respect, Ford has more in common with Eisenstein—whose cinema is also underwritten by an adherence to the model of knowledge—than he does with his fellow Catholic filmmakers, in this case, Rossellini and Bresson. Whereas Ford's faith participates in the illusions of uncritical secularism, placing the human subject at the center of reality, the more radical faith expressed in the work of Rossellini and Bresson represents an actual threat to both the guardians of secularism as well as the institutional Church. The suggestion here is that the revolutionary cinema of Rocha or Güney also demonstrates a similar conversion. Whereas their revolutionary predecessor, Eisenstein, remains mired in a view of subjectivity and action that reflects the displacement of a sovereign conception of God onto the human agent.

I would venture that Deleuze's turn to these religiously minded figures has to do with his awareness that certain Christians have had to deal with the uncertainty of their faith in a way that nonreligious philosophers have not had to—at least not until quite recently. Christian thinkers have been required to justify their beliefs before the tribunal of the Enlightenment. But that also means that, as the dominant bearer of Truth, the Enlightenment sheltered itself from more careful scrutiny. That would change dramatically, especially in the first half of the twentieth century. "These days," Deleuze avers, "it's no longer theological reason but human reason, Enlightenment reason, that's entering a crisis and breaking down" (N 162). Thus, it is only relatively recently that the nonreligious defenders of secularity have had to think seriously about the nonfoundational character of their beliefs. By contrast, the Christian authors and filmmakers Deleuze discusses in *Cinema 2* have been compelled to take stock of the crisis that befell Christendom. Beginning with Pascal, these figures readily relinquish the idea that their

Christian faith can be secured by knowledge. Pascal's existential response to the crisis involves a wager, a recognition of the gamble of faith—even if he puts this in terms of rational probabilities (a rhetorical strategy that is mainly due to the fact that his feigned interlocutor in that section of the *Pensées*, where he inserts his famous argument for God, is a gambler).[27] Kierkegaard amplifies the risk-taking character of faith, which cannot rest on any preconceived knowledge. For that reason, he famously declares that one is not born a Christian but strives to become one if she so ventures. A new generation of Christian-inspired filmmakers takes their cue from this reconfiguring of religious belief. With a filmmaker like Rossellini, there is a "return of Christian belief . . . which is the highest paradox" (C2 172). Much revolves around this "return." This is not a self-assured Christian belief grounded in the certainty of knowing the idea of God. On the contrary, it stakes everything on the moment of decision that one is called to take precisely when everything remains uncertain. Nothing could be further removed from a more conventional, self-assured Christian outlook, or for that matter, the overly confident secularist outlook that so permeates modern life.

As conceived by Deleuze, the notion of laicizing belief is not simply directed at a certain kind of theological outlook. It is equally subversive toward that form of secularism that became Europe's de facto modern credo. The trap today is to think that one is born a secularist as if that is the obvious default position for the modern individual. That way of thinking assumes one is sheltered from the need to believe. For too many, the reigning—"illegitimate," Deleuze might say—belief is that secular reason acts as a foundational warrant. It is precisely that level of certainty, that unquestioned confidence in the powers of reason, that is completely dissonant with the traumatic realities brought on by the murderous war machines that engulfed the entire planet in the first half of the twentieth century. Just as one is not born a Christian but must *become* a Christian, so Deleuze, or at least the view of Deleuze that I am defending here, might say that one is not born an atheist, an agnostic, or a secular individual but instead, one risks or wagers that subjectivity; a bet that requires indefinite repetitions lest its associated worldview becomes rigid and closed.

Following Pascal and Kierkegaard, Deleuze recognizes that no philosophy or worldview can escape the need to wager. The militant secular atheist, no less than the undoubting rigid believer, must undertake the task of letting go of their metaphysical idols. But this is no easy task. In a lecture he gave just before the publication of the second *Cinema* volume, Deleuze confesses: "A question that tortures me: why has there never been any atheist cinema? . . . Godard nearly did; he circled around it. But no one is safe from faith."[28] Putting it this way, Deleuze attests to the daunting challenge of the sort of "conversion" he has in mind in an age of uncritical secularism. A secularism that imagines itself immune from having to make and repeat such a wager—because it has convinced itself that it possesses actual knowledge of reality—risks becoming a dead worldview in no time. Christianity has produced thinkers like Pascal and Kierkegaard, who recognize those stakes. They, in turn, have inspired certain filmmakers to do the same with their cinema: Dreyer, Rossellini, and Rohmer, among others. Perhaps it is a greater challenge today—the question that "tortures" Deleuze—for those without religious faith. They might not feel the existential pressure for wagering. They might be tempted to ride the coattails of the unreflective secularism that permeates late modern culture, including the world of normative cinema.

Unlearning Secularism: Rossellini's Seer

There are, of course, thoughtful atheist filmmakers, like Jean-Luc Godard and Philippe Garrel, to whom Deleuze draws much attention in the second *Cinema* volume. There are even some who, like Pasolini, are even more challenging to pin down. Of *Theorem* (*Teorema*, 1968), Deleuze notes: "Was this Pasolini's way of still being Catholic? Was it on the contrary his way of being a radical atheist?" (C2 175–6). These filmmakers represent a motley crew of unconventional views—definitely outside the secularist and institutionalized religious folds. They defy the narrow conceptual boxes of "believers" and "unbelievers." Of this group, Rossellini is one of the more intriguing artists of the time-image cinema, a notable standout within that strand of paradoxical Christianity that intrigues Deleuze. The Italian neorealist filmmaker comes up at a critical moment in Deleuze's analysis, early on in *Cinema 2*, when he introduces the theme of the seer. Deleuze mentions a few films by Rossellini, but he dedicates special attention to *Europa '51* (1952). It is not difficult to appreciate why this film would be of tremendous interest to him. The film presents us with a dramatic contrast of two competing stances, between the model of knowledge that is operative in the movement-image of classical cinema and the conversion of belief that one discerns in the time-image of the new cinema that begins to take focus toward the end of the Second World War. The protagonist of *Europa '51* is a middle-aged bourgeois woman, Irene Girard (Ingrid Bergman), who becomes intensely unsettled after the suicide of her son. That personal tragedy becomes the catalyst for a radical spiritual conversion that she undergoes. Her waywardness inevitably draws her to some of Rome's most destitute quarters. Irene represents for Deleuze an exemplary instance of the seer, the one who finds herself decoupled from the sensory-motor apparatus that defines normative actions and discourse. Immobilized by the incongruity and alien character of her environment, the seer must feel her way through it, unaided, as if in the dark, without the conceptual anticipations of an established scheme. No longer bound to circuits that mindlessly direct her behavior, she is instead made to confront what Deleuze calls the "intolerable" nature of the world—that is, everything that escapes our normative categories or understanding, including the unbearable afflictions endured by others. With no social or moral map to guide her, all she has to go on in this regard is something akin to faith, a leap of trust that is taken without the safety net afforded by a template of predefined options. Compelled to respond to the strangeness of her experiences, Irene binds herself to the unknown through trust and, in so doing, forges deeper connections with the marginalized individuals that she encounters in her daily forays.

Irene's cousin, Andrea (Ettore Giannini), a communist journalist, is the one who initially urges her to step outside her cocooned life to witness the underbelly of Rome. While Andrea's political posture appears to represent a challenge to the status quo, his uncritical appeal to a revolutionary knowledge is rooted in the same epistemic privileging of rationality that informs Enlightenment thought in general. He operates, in other words, with a predetermined conceptual model of the world as it should be. Andrea's confidence in a progressive "knowledge"—in this case, the Marxist dialectic—involves an unshakable optimism in a picture of ideal reality that remains hidden to those who cannot get beyond their ideological blinders. His recourse to knowledge is sanctioned by the secularist age, even if vested economic and political interests might perceive it as "radical" or "revolutionary." Clad in the vernacular of philosophical expertise, Andrea's chosen discourse projects a powerful image of itself as a form of determinate knowing: it *knows* how things truly are, and it *knows* the shape of the future. For Nietzsche, as for Deleuze, this discourse has all the markings of the ascetic ideal. The true radical in Rossellini's film, however, is Irene, whose condition of unknowingness allows her to be open to what others are incapable of registering. This visionary is "given over to something intolerable" in the "everydayness" of her reality (C2 41). Incapable of falling back on the conditioned responses that the dominant ideology requires, it is the seer who stumbles upon the need to believe in this world, to take a leap into an indeterminate reality without the illusory safety net offered by whatever purveyors of knowledge that happen to command attention at that particular point in time.

In one critical scene, Irene expresses to Andrea her feelings of helplessness vis-à-vis the dire circumstances of the workers and their families. Quick to want to suture the powerlessness [*l'impuissance*]—what Deleuze also refers to, nodding in the direction of both Antonin Artaud and Maurice Blanchot, as the "impower" [*l'impouvoir*] (C2 166) nestled at the heart of reality—that Irene both identifies and endures in herself, Andrea responds in a manner that is all too typical of many Marxists of this period, namely, that it is their duty as enlightened, engaged intellectuals to awaken their working-class comrades to a veritable knowledge of the supposed real world. Suspicious of Andrea's hasty assuredness in his appeal to the authority of

FIGURE 2.1 *Irene and Andrea, still from* Europa '51 *(dir. Roberto Rossellini, 1952).*

reason, Irene interjects by offering another virtue, in this case, the Christian virtue of hope—of patience—rather than the foreseen action dictated by the Marxist literature that he hands her (see Figure 2.1). Annoyed by Irene's invocation of hope and her talk of a "different path," the communist Andrea corrects her, not once, but twice, repeating the word "knowledge" as if that word could magically fill the void that her patient response demands. Her suspicion comes to a head in a later scene when she confronts Andrea and exposes his Marxist narrative as an unconfessed faith in apodictic reason. Intuitively, Irene senses that his constant appeal to knowledge is nothing more than the hubris of an ego that craves certainty. Irene is a paradigmatic example of the paradoxical Christianity that Deleuze discerns at work in filmmakers like Rossellini. She, and not the secularist intellectual, Andrea, is the one who expresses a genuine belief in the world.

What makes Irene a paradoxical figure is that her outlook is not simply a rejection of abstract secular reason or an embrace of the ossified faith of institutional religion. After having been committed to a psychiatric ward by her family as a result of having abandoned her leisured upper-class way of life to serve the needs of the poor, the chaplain priest admonishes her for taking Jesus's radical message of self-dispossession to heart and for stepping outside of the prescribed roles set by the Church. If Irene's faith is threatening, it is because she embraces it without the guarantees that religion often promises to its adherents or the unwavering belief in progressive reason offered by revolutionary secularism. We can appreciate why Deleuze singles out Rossellini's character as an exemplary seer who has undergone an actual conversion of belief. Despite its religious inspiration, Rossellini's depiction of the seer, nevertheless, aligns well with Deleuze's description of a belief that is genuinely secular and this-worldly. Once again, we see that for Deleuze, what is distinctive about the time-image cinema is that it simultaneously circumvents the secularist desire to maintain a strict but specious separation between, on the one hand, a pure knowledge that is uncontaminated by assumptions of any kind and, on the other hand, all other belief-based paradigms (religions, in particular). Rossellini's cinema robs us of this self-serving fantasy. Religious or not, atheist or not, we need reasons to believe in this world:

> [F]or [Rossellini], the problem is not to confirm the rupture of man and the world; it is to find the means to give reasons again, whatever they are, to believe in this world. So, he may be Catholic, but it is a Catholicism that has, strictly speaking, no importance except for him. You understand that at that moment, Catholic or atheist, there is absolutely no difference.[29]

Conclusion

Classical cinema has done its part in displacing the notion of a sovereign agency from an earlier theological setting to the human-centered subjectivity of the modern age. Modernity might have lost confidence in the picture of an all-powerful God, but it made up for that loss by substituting the human subject for God. Counteracting this regressive form of the secular, Deleuze's notion of the time-image can be understood as showing us an alternative to the reigning secularist ideology of the modern era. While classical cinema acts to prop up the secularist tenets of an all-powerful agency and its faith in the perpetual progress of scientific innovation and technological advancement, time-image cinema refuses to sustain this modern fantasy of a knowledge that transcends our inescapable need to trust the world. It forces us all to become the ones who must repeatedly believe again and renew our trust in reality. The time-image cinema refuses to be complicit in the displacement that secularism carries out. Instead, it plays a critical role in helping us to undergo a conversion from the fantasy of the one-who-knows to one who, as the medieval mystics would say, must unlearn their knowingness. The implications here apply equally to religious believers and nonbelievers alike. In this respect, I could not agree more with Paola Marrati, who writes that "[t]his conversion of belief is more profound and more significant than conventional rifts between religion and atheism or than debates on secularization or, conversely, on the return of the religious. Indeed, it defines our 'modern condition,' insofar as there is one."[30]

Notes

1 The literature on this topic is already quite significant and growing. Some of the most notable points of reference include Charles Taylor, *A Secular Age*

(Cambridge, MA: Harvard University Press, 2009); Jürgen Habermas and Joseph Ratzinger, *The Dialectics of Secularization: On Reason and Religion*, trans. Brian McNeil (San Francisco: Ignatius Press, 2006), and Talal Asad, *Formations of the Secular: Christianity, Islam, Modernity* (Stanford, CA: Stanford University Press, 2003).

2 See Costica Bradatan and Camil Ungureanu (eds.), *Religion in Contemporary European Cinema: The Postsecular Constellation* (New York and London: Routledge, 2014), and John Caruana and Mark Cauchi (eds.), *Immanent Frames: Postsecular Cinema between Malick and von Trier* (Albany: SUNY Press, 2018).

3 Taylor, *A Secular Age*, 429.

4 James Elkins, *On the Strange Place of Religion in Contemporary Art* (New York and London: Routledge, 2004), ix.

5 There is, of course, a literature that does just that. Two notable examples are Paul Schrader, *Transcendental Style in Film: Ozu, Bresson, Dreyer* (New York: Da Capo Press, 1988), and, more recently, Nathaniel Dorsky, *Devotional Cinema* (Berkeley: Tuumba Press, 2005). But I think it is fair to say that such literature has, until now, remained on the fringes of mainstream scholarship. Though, it might be the case that we are now beginning to see a shift in attitude on that front. Schrader's book, for example, has been recently reissued by the University of California Press with a new introduction by him.

6 Friedrich Nietzsche, *Untimely Meditations*, trans. R. J. Hollingdale (Cambridge and New York: Cambridge University Press, 1983), 148.

7 Far from being, anti-religious, Nietzsche was throughout his career deeply interested and even sympathetic toward religion, notwithstanding the profound aversion he had for a dominant form of Christianity that shared the same other-worldliness found in Platonist philosophy. Despite textual evidence to the contrary, the view that Nietzsche is anti-religious prevails to our day. To counteract this caricature, Julian Young takes readers through the entire span of Nietzsche's corpus in order to show us the German philosopher's nuanced and often positive views on religion. Young goes so far as to describe Nietzsche as a "religious reformer rather than an enemy of religion," *Nietzsche's Philosophy of Religion* (Cambridge and New York: Cambridge University Press, 2006), 2.

8 My comments here are heavily indebted to Mark Cauchi, who more than anyone else has made me aware of the deep connections between the birth of cinema and normative secularism.

9 William E. Connolly, *A World of Becoming* (Durham, NC and London: Duke University Press, 2011).

10 I clearly have both Nietzsche and Deleuze in mind here, but not only them. My use of the term "secular" in this case is meant to be catholic (in the secular sense!) in that it encompasses a plurality of perspectives, such that the idea of the secular as this-worldliness does not exclude certain forms of religiosity. Even Deleuze, as we will see later in this chapter recognized that fact. Taylor reminds us that the seeds of that modern form of secularity that requires us

to be attentive to the materiality and fleshiness of the world are to be found in the monastic reforms that were introduced in the early centuries of the second millennium, most famously with the Franciscans. See, *A Secular Age*, especially, 61–75.

11 See, in particular, Charles Taylor's chapter "The Immanent Frame," in *A Secular Age*, 539–93, and William Connolly's aptly entitled chapter, "The Conceits of Secularism," in *Why I Am Not a Secularist* (Minneapolis: University of Minnesota Press, 1999), 19–46.

12 For example, Taylor looks at some of the ways in which Nietzsche's criticisms (and that of more recent critics, like Martha Nussbaum) do legitimately apply to certain expressions of Christianity, but not to the tradition as a whole; *A Secular Age*, 618–73. This tendency is symptomatic of a broader, uncritical approach that is apt to identify specific historical instances of a complex religion like Christianity with the religion in toto.

13 Nietzsche, *Untimely Meditations*, 148.

14 Geoffrey Nowell-Smith, ed., *The Oxford History of World Cinema* (Oxford: Oxford University Press, 1997), xix.

15 André Bazin, "The Myth of Total Cinema," in *What Is Cinema? Volume 1*, trans. Hugh Gray (Berkeley, CA: University of California Press, 1967).

16 As I hope it will become clearer: what is at issue here is not classical cinema per se. I do not wish to leave the impression that classical cinema is synonymous with secularism. The point that I develop in more detail below concerns *certain* features of what Deleuze names "classical cinema," in particular, the preponderance of the action-image in combination with a nineteenth-century philosophy of history that has shaped normative cinema since its inception. *These* features are strongly implicated in advancing and bolstering secularist assumptions.

17 See Paola Marrati's perceptive remarks in *Gilles Deleuze: Cinema and Philosophy*, trans. Alisa Hartz (Baltimore: Johns Hopkins University Press, 2008), 54–5, 64, and 105.

18 What we have said thus far represents only part of the story that Deleuze weaves for us. For the particular notions of the subject and philosophy of history that subtend classical cinema have deeper roots yet. These roots receive attention in the second *Cinema* volume, chapter 7, in particular. It is in that chapter that we see most forcefully in what way secularism is at issue.

19 Nietzsche, *The Gay Science*, §125.

20 Martin Heidegger, "The Word of Nietzsche," in *The Question Concerning Technology and Other Essays*, trans. William Lovitt (New York and London: Harper Collins, 2013), 63.

21 Ibid. Heidegger is referencing Nietzsche's *The Will to Power*, trans. Walter Arnold Kaufmann and R. J. Hollingdale (New York: Vintage Books, 1968), 8 (§1).

22 That said, we should note that Deleuze does recognize that certain believers, like Kierkegaard, relate to their faith in God as a way to return more intensely to this finite world.

23 See, for example, NP, 150–2.

24 The original is quite clear: "c'est toute une conversion de la croyance," Gilles Deleuze, *Cinema-2: L'image-temps* (Paris: Éditions de Minuit, 1985), 223–4. The entire context of this passage deals with belief in the stronger sense of a deeply affective, existential, even spiritual faith. Even the footnote that follows it speaks of "authors of whom some are still believers, while others carry out an atheistic conversion" (C2 311n30).

25 Gilles Deleuze—"Cinéma /pensée cours 69 du 13/11/1984—3," http://www2.univ-paris8.fr/deleuze/article.php3?id_article=372 [my translation].

26 In an otherwise fine analysis, Joseph Hughes acknowledges the significance of Deleuze's discussion of belief and faith in the *Cinema* volumes, but then feels compelled to downplay the significance of Christian thinkers for the French philosopher. Hughes writes: "Deleuze insists in all of these discussions that Kierkegaard and Pascal do not go far enough. As he puts it in *What Is Philosophy?* the concept of faith needs to undergo an 'empiricist conversion.' . . . This was Hume's 'accomplishment,' and through this empiricist conversion the notion of belief begins to express our relationship not only to God but also to ideas in general," "Believing in the World: Toward an Ethics of Form," in *Deleuze and the Body*, eds. Laura Guillaume and Joe Hughes (Edinburgh: Edinburgh University Press, 2011), 84. I think this way of putting it does not quite do justice to Deleuze's provocative position on the conversion of belief. There are at least two points or issues here: (1) Hughes is right: it is not only religious faith that has to undergo a "conversion," but *all* beliefs—religious or otherwise. I take the "empiricist" qualification to mean a return to "this-worldliness." That said, in several places (including ones that I cite above), Deleuze's language makes it clear that both Kierkegaard and Pascal have undertaken that conversion. (2) Despite that, Deleuze, it is true, continues to have lingering reservations with the likes of Pascal and Kierkegaard. This second issue is complex and beyond the scope of this paper to deal with properly here. But we can at least say the following. Some of Deleuze's later comments about Kierkegaard's thought, for example, express reservations about the Danish philosopher's appeal to the categories of "God" and "transcendence." Undoubtedly, the invocation of these terms makes immanentists like Deleuze, and his followers (Hughes, for instance) nervous. But when we look closer, we discover that these reservations are based on the assumption that Kierkegaard (and others like him) are deploying these words in a manner that is not that much different from their conventional usage in the history of philosophy. To read Kierkegaard in that manner entails ignoring his own stated desire to reimagine these terms. For two excellent attempts to work out of some of these issues, see Steven Shakespeare, *Kierkegaard and the Refusal of Transcendence* (New York: Palgrave Macmillan, 2015), and Andrew Jampol-Petzinger, "Faith and Repetition in Kierkegaard and Deleuze," *Philosophy Today* 63, no. 2 (2019): 383–401. When we read Kierkegaard as he himself wanted to be read, we see a thinker who makes questions of religious faith provocative again, and impossible to pigeon-hole in simplistic category boxes. Regardless of the issue of how Deleuze reads (and sometimes

misreads) Christian thinkers like Kierkegaard, it is worth repeating that his views on these writers evolved with time. Deleuze's characterization of both Pascal and Kierkegaard became increasingly more nuanced and, in some respects, even sympathetic. At minimum, his later views no longer exhibit a tendency toward dismissiveness that is typical of his earlier writing, as when he characterizes Pascal and Kierkegaard as thinkers "ensnared in *ressentiment*" (NP 36).

27   Blaise Pascal, *Pensées*, trans. A. J. Krailsheimer (London: Penguin Books, 2003), §418.
28   Gilles Deleuze, "Cinéma Cours 43 du 31 Mai 1983—2," http://www2.univ-paris8.fr/deleuze/article.php3?id_article=252 [my translation].
29   Deleuze—"Cinéma /pensée cours 69 du 13/11/1984—3."
30   Marrati, *Gilles Deleuze*, 88.

Works Cited

C1   Gilles Deleuze, *Cinema 1: The Movement-Image*, trans. Hugh Tomlinson and Barbara Habberjam (Minneapolis: University of Minnesota Press, 1986).
C2   Gilles Deleuze, *Cinema 2: The Time-Image*, trans. Hugh Tomlinson and Robert Galeta (Minneapolis: University of Minnesota Press, 1989).
DR   Gilles Deleuze, *Difference and Repetition*, trans. Paul Patton (New York: Columbia University Press, 1994).
DRF Gilles Deleuze, *Deux régimes de fous. Textes et entretiens 1975-1995* (Paris: Les Éditions de Minuit, 2003).
ES   Gilles Deleuze, *Empiricism and Subjectivity: An Essay on Hume's Theory of Human Nature*, trans. Constantin Boundas (New York: Columbia University Press, 1991).
N   Gilles Deleuze, *Negotiations, 1972–1990*, trans. Martin Joughin (New York: Columbia University Press, 1995).
NP   Gilles Deleuze, *Nietzsche and Philosophy*, trans. Hugh Tomlinson (New York: Columbia University Press, 1983).
WP   Gilles Deleuze and Félix Guattari, *What Is Philosophy?* trans. Hugh Tomlinson and Graham Burchell (New York: Columbia University Press, 2014).

3

The Secular as Sacred

Cinema and Buddhist Ritual

Francisca Cho

The title of this chapter is an homage to Herbert Fingerette's *Confucius: The Secular as Sacred* (1972).[1] The premise of this diminutive book by the Western philosopher is that Confucius was concerned with the moral (and religious) significance of *all* social actions rather than with a distinct set of behaviors that can be designated as moral. In this reading, the ethical and the sacred are not autonomous realms of activity, and they encompass the performance of social customs such as proper table manners and the rituals of greeting and parting. This non-dichotomizing approach to religion, in which the putatively secular can also become sacred, accentuates how modern Western thought segregates territories that other cultures do not.

But that does not mean that premodern East Asia had no concept of religion as a distinct pursuit, even though the lexical equivalent of the term was not coined until the arrival of Western colonizers and missionaries. In medieval Chinese texts, the term *zongjiao* 宗教 ("teaching of the ancestors") referred to the teachings of a distinct lineage, sect, or school and was used to describe Confucianism, Buddhism, and Daoism. During the early years of the Meiji era (1868–1912), the Japanese used the same term (pronounced *shūkyō*) in the course of formulating trade treaties with American and European powers regarding the free practice and exercise of religion. As a result, the Chinese term was imbued with fresh meaning as a sphere of activity distinct from secular and public state polity. This sense of *zongjiao* eventually circulated back to late Qing China via the writings of influential scholar-officials and reformers like Huang Zunxian (1848–1905) and Liang Qichao (1873–1929).

As Anthony C. Yu observes, the term *zongjiao* was "produced from a context inextricably tied to cultural otherness, to encounter[s] with 'religion' involving non-native cultures."[2] Some observers have made much of this, suggesting that "religion" is a fundamentally Christian idea that Asians were compelled to adopt in response to the demands of global geopolitics. As a result, there is significant skepticism about the category of religion for understanding native East Asian cultures.[3] I believe the more constructive approach is to examine East Asian practices to broaden our understanding of religion as an analytical construct. My approach in this chapter is to use Mahāyāna Buddhism to get past the customary distinction between the religious and the secular, by which I mean the modern Western assumption that "secularism" refers to a post-religious age. I contend that secularism is itself a religious category, but in ways that differ across the modern Western and Buddhist contexts.

Mahāyāna Buddhist traditions reject the distinction between samsara and nirvana, which are analogous to the idea of secular and religious realms. Samsara is the relentless cycle of birth and death, and nirvana is the liberation from samsara that comes after one attains enlightenment. Although this reverses earlier Buddhist thought that treats samsara and nirvana as a mutually exclusive binary, it is significant that from the beginning, nirvana never signified a metaphysically transcendent location. Therefore, Mahāyāna Buddhism's subsequent anti-dualism is almost inevitable, as enlightenment entails the realization that there is no otherworldly place to go. Instead, the original discrimination between the secular and the sacred is declared to be an illusion.

This leads me to two observations. The first is that the distinction between the religious and the secular exists in both Buddhist and Christian discourses, making the distinction itself fundamentally religious. When modern Western institutions proclaim their secularity, consistent with Charles Taylor's "subtraction story" of purging religion from its sphere, they adhere to the Christian religious story about the twofold geography of religious and secular spaces. Similarly, when a Buddhist proclaims that all beings are already possessed of buddha-nature, this adheres to the Buddhist religious story about the identity of samsara and nirvana. Whether the religious and the secular are thought to be segregated or integrated, the notion of the secular cannot shed its religious provenance and logic. Furthermore, given the opposing manner in which Buddhists and Christians have imagined secularism, it is important to recognize its culture-specificity. Secularism is not a single universal historical dynamic.

This then leads to my second observation, which is that the secular or religious nature of cinema must be considered in specific religious contexts rather than in universal terms. I will sketch a Buddhist interpretation of cinematic experience as religious in nature, in spite of the "secularity" (as understood in Christian terms) of its medium, content, and audience reception. I regard the phenomenon of cinema as a whole rather than particular movies that might be interpreted religiously—whether in terms of symbolism, narrative, or style. My position is that cinema is a ritual experience that enables even non-Buddhist and nonreligious viewers to practice what Mahāyāna Buddhism has long advocated—namely, to deliberately manufacture aesthetic and affective experiences in order to shape and transform one's sense of the world. I draw specifically on Mahāyāna ritual theory in order to establish the religious value of *all* cinema, similar to the way that Fingerette sees Confucianism as sacralizing all social interactions rather than distinguishing between religious and secular ones. Although this interpretation of cinema arises from a Buddhist milieu, it might nevertheless have cross-cultural traction, particularly in the post-secular age.

Secularism and Spirituality

In keeping with this cross-cultural focus, it is worth noting that Buddhist and Western versions of secularism are already intertwined, through interactions beginning in the nineteenth century that have led to the current terminology of "spirituality." This history divulges a connection between traditional Buddhist and contemporary Western secularism.

Asian nations modernized in the context of colonial encounters, which resulted in adaptations of Western nation-state secularism. In Republican and Communist China, as well as Taiwan, secularism has meant state control over religious organizations. This secularism has a very different purpose than the separation of church and state in the United States, which has the intent of protecting religious freedom. In contrast, the Chinese concern is over religious movements that might undermine the authority of the state. A famous case in point is the rise of Falungong in China during the 1990s—a syncretic Buddhist-Daoist movement centered on *qigong* practice with overtones of messianism. When the Communist Party suppressed it in 1999, the organization claimed to have more members than the Party itself. The threat of mass religious mobilization goes back to premodern times, and the modern secular nation-state is readily adapted to managing this traditional problem.

There is more to secularism than the formation of the nation-state, of course, and that is the epistemic opposition to religion as a false and outmoded form of knowledge. Although this attitude grew out of the Western Enlightenment and scientific rationalism, Asian modernism has been deeply shaped by the impact of Western military and scientific superiority. This led native intellectuals to campaign against "superstition" (*mixin* 迷信), a neologism used by nationalists, communists, and religious reformers alike as a culprit for Asian backwardness on the global stage. But this critical turn did not mean the wholesale sacrifice of traditional religious activities. Defenders of Confucian, Buddhist, and Daoist traditions responded with reforms that recreated them as secular humanism, in the case of Confucianism, and even as science, in the cases of Daoist-derived body technologies such as *qigong* and the Buddhist doctrine of causality. In tandem with these approaches, ancient traditions were refashioned within the model of the modern Western notion of "spirituality."

As Peter Van der Veer notes, the idea of spirituality was closely mated with scientific secularism in nineteenth-century America and Europe, which belies the idea that secularism automatically entails a reductive, "matter-only" materialist worldview. What the concepts of secularism and spirituality had most in common was their opposition to church Christianity, and an embrace of a universalist and transcultural attitude: "Spiritualism was seen as a secular truth-seeking, experimental in nature and opposed to religious obscurantism and hierarchy."[4] The Secular Societies that began forming in mid-nineteenth-century Britain, for example, were religiously and politically anti-establishment but "hugely interested in connecting to the other spiritual world through do-it-yourself science."[5] The Theosophical Movement, founded in New York City in 1875, disavowed the label of "religion" and claimed to embrace essential truths that were consonant with science.

This secular spirituality did not develop in a cultural vacuum and was in fact shaped by Euro-American access to newly translated Asian religious texts and leaders. As scholars have documented, the image of the "spiritual East" arose as a dialogue between Western Romanticism and reformed versions of Hinduism, Buddhism, and Daoism.[6] In Van der Veer's description, these Asian traditions were translated into a universal spirituality through reform movements such as Vivekananda's (1863–1902) Advaita Vedanta in India, Anagarika Dhammapala's (1864–1933) global Buddhism in Sri Lanka, Taixu's (1890–1947) Humanistic Buddhism in China, and Chen Yingning's (1880–1969) spiritualized Daoism that paralleled the birth of modern yoga in India.[7] Although the categories of religion, secularism, and spirituality originate in Euro-American languages with no original Asian lexical equivalents, "China and India are not only important social arenas for the application of these concepts, but they have been crucial to their development."[8]

Wakoh Shannon Hickey's recent history of the New Thought movements in nineteenth-century America (2019) documents an extensive network of individuals and communities that crafted spiritual practices from a bricolage of Hindu yoga, Buddhist meditation, and Western esotericism. This network brings together extremely diverse entities, with direct links to Mary Baker Eddy's Christian Science and indirect influences on African American movements such as the Nation of Islam, and Marcus Garvey's Universal Negro Improvement Association. Nevertheless, there are common threads that hold them together which are now recognizable as the basic tenets of contemporary spirituality. This includes hostility or indifference to established religions, expressed negatively as skepticism toward supernaturalism and positively through a theology that regards "God or the divine as immanent in the world and revealed through nature, rather than occupying a transcendent position outside the created order."[9] There is also a distaste for modern scientific materialism, particularly when it comes to health and healing. Alternative mind-body medicine began in the late nineteenth century with the idea of "mind cures" that emphasized the power of thought and nature over and against the medical establishment.

Scholars suggest that modern Buddhists and Asian reformers embraced the idea of secular spirituality as a strategy of cultural and institutional survival by conforming to popular modern Western ideals.[10] The imperial context of modernism, with its unequal East-West power relations, certainly should not be glossed over. But the ease with which Buddhists took to this kind of secularism also suggests that the rejection of organized religion in favor of a this-worldly religiosity was already quite familiar to them, at least as a discourse. Buddhism has always been a monastic tradition, which is built on a distinction between the "worldly" (*Pāli: lokiya*) realm of lay people and the "otherworldly" (*lokuttara*) one of clerics. The institutional centrality of the monastic order, with its accompanying value of world renunciation, is the context for the Mahāyāna argument that there is really no distinction between religious and worldly paths. In Chinese Buddhism, this sentiment was presaged and influenced by the Daoist philosopher Zhuangzi (369–286 BCE), who famously averred that the Dao (the Way) is in the piss and shit.[11] This move of elevating the profane is readily applicable to the worldly phenomenon of cinema, in order to see it as a viable mechanism for Buddhist liberation.

Cinema in the Mirror of Emptiness

The first factor in regarding all cinema as religious entails the view that our experience of films is phenomenologically no different from our experience of "real life" when it comes to eliciting immediate emotions and broader effects, including dispositions and worldviews. I have made this argument in an earlier article by considering the Buddhist notion of "emptiness" (Sanskrit: *śunyatā*; Chinese: *kong*), which is calibrated to open our eyes to the false and insubstantial nature of everything that we take to be real.[12] This tenet is central to the Mahāyāna critique of the monastic ideal of world renunciation, essentially setting the deconstructive ethos of emptiness on to the institutions of earlier Buddhism itself. But the teaching of emptiness also recognizes that human activity—including Buddhist ones—requires social organizations and conceptual categories, such as the opposition between the good and the bad, the beautiful and the ugly, and the religious and the secular. The essential challenge is to remember that all these distinctions are expedient but insubstantial conventions, and to use them while remaining detached from these structures of our own making.

In popular East Asian parlance, the idea of emptiness is expressed by saying that "life is nothing but a dream." Dzongsar Jamyang Khyentse, the current incarnate lama of the Tibetan Khyentse lineage, is also an acclaimed filmmaker who effectively updated this adage in his short essay, "Life as Cinema."[13] It is significant that both analogies are tied to actual fictive art—to Khyentse's filmmaking and to the genre of dream tales in East Asia. I explore this in more detail below. But whether life is compared to a dream or to cinema, the idea of emptiness is not meant to gloss over the practical differences between life and fictive art. It is important to distinguish between an actual tree that can be climbed and a picture of one that cannot. But at the level of philosophical analysis, it becomes difficult to designate art as "less real" than life if life itself is thought to be an illusion.

To really make sense of this, it is important to understand that Buddhist thought is concerned with phenomenology, or with how human beings see and experience the world, rather than with an objective world separable from human thought and activity. Early Buddhist discourses reject ontological materialism that says matter is the ultimate reality, on the one hand, as well as religious assertions of an ultimate divine reality, on the other.[14] The Buddhist stance is simultaneously skeptical and phenomenological: It affirms that human beings experience what we call "matter" and "the divine"—and that they are very significant and consequential experiences, indeed. But it also understands such experiences to result from human capacities rather than external realities. Since all experience takes place within the human sensory manifold—which very importantly includes the mind in Buddhism—that is the only thing we can be certain of. The imperative then is to pay careful attention to these human capacities and cultivate them in salutary rather than harmful ways.

A contrasting philosophical system can help to clarify what is going on here. Plato defines art in his *Republic* (Book X, 596d) as mimesis—that is, as a mere imitation and secondary representation of life that is qualitatively separate from and ontologically less real than what it depicts. For Plato, the difference between life and art is like the difference between actual objects and their images reflected in a mirror. The comparison emphasizes that there is a practical distinction between an actual object and an image of one, whether in a mirror, painting, or a movie. One can eat an actual sandwich but not an image of one. Plato's concern is less with this kind of difference, however, than with a higher truth that he calls the "Forms." Ironically, the Form of a sandwich is just as inedible as images of it because Forms are purely abstract and ideational, in line with Plato's privileging of thought over the physical realm. The functional difference between art and life is of lesser importance to Plato than attaining metaphysical knowledge of the Forms. In this enterprise, art is a distraction at best, and more frequently a hindrance, particularly in its tendency to water "womanish" emotions that interfere with the workings of reason. It is this putatively harmful effect of art that leads Plato to pay attention to it.

In the Buddhist context, however, Plato's Forms are in the same category as matter and God. All three can be equalized by virtue of being human experiences, whether they are sensory, emotional, or rational. The important question is what kind of thoughts and dispositions these experiences are used to cultivate. In that case, the functional difference between an artistic depiction of something and an actual instance of that thing is less important than the actions and consequences each of them prompts. We cannot eat an image of a sandwich, to be sure, but the image can compel hunger and craving, and the subsequent actions of satisfying it. The intensity and salience of an artistic representation might be even more provocative than our encounters with daily objects, in fact. This worried Plato, and he countered with an appeal to reason as a way to tame the sensory and emotional persuasiveness of art. He does this for political reasons, but with the premise that Truth is a logical and mental reality apart from physical and affective events.

Mahāyāna thought eschews all appeals to such ultimate ontological essences—unless we consent to the claim that the denial of all essences (the emptiness principle) is itself a kind of ontology.[15] Whatever we call it, the important result of emptiness is that religious transformation is not dependent on accessing something other than the ingredients of everyday life. But it *does* require the deliberate and intensified manufacture of aesthetic experiences, which can be used to actively reform habitual thought and behavior that lead to suffering. This is a way of understanding the purpose of religious institutions such as monasticism—as providing a favorable environment or strategy for such work rather than access to an otherworldly reality. The same can be said for the variety of contemplative practices that have evolved in Buddhist schools.

From that point, it is not a stretch to include the experience of cinema as a religious practice, if it includes exercising awareness of how movies have the power to affect us. To be sure, not all films affect us equally—individual taste matters—and not all movies have religious or morally uplifting content. But in fact, the capacity of moving pictures to arouse hatred or sexual desire, as well as nobler feelings, is what should provoke reflection on the nature of human experience as a whole. We can do this by examining cinema in relation to Buddhist ritual practice, which in turn suggests how cinema can be seen and experienced in ritually intentional ways.

Cinema and Ritual Practice

Although the goal of Buddhist meditation is sometimes described in mystical terms, such as the attainment of "the infinity of space" or the realm "beyond consciousness and no-consciousness," such spatial imagery is intimately tied to mental phenomenology and the goal of overcoming the obstructions posed by our own thought systems.[16] At the highest levels of practice, one might travel beyond normal constructions of space, time, and thought. But in other contemplation traditions, such as Pure Land meditation, the focus is on visualizing very concrete entities such as the historical Buddha to overcome the fact that he is no longer present in the world. One is also instructed to cultivate visions of a pristine and beautiful world known as "pure lands" as a way of escaping the imperfect ones present to our normal consciousness.[17] This tradition of mental cinema is but one indicator of how readily established Buddhist ritual disciplines translate into an appreciation of the power and potential of films. As I noted earlier, the adage that life is nothing but a dream was tied to actual literary production, primarily of narrative fiction and poetry. This went beyond the well-worn trope that life is nothing but a dream, and produced a literary theory that sees artistic creations as simulacra of emptiness that can also awaken the reader to the truth of emptiness. I have examined how exemplary fictive and poetic works throughout East Asia express this notion of itself, and in that manner, function both philosophically and religiously.[18]

In considering the art of cinema, one can focus on the widespread Buddhist practice of image veneration as the most appropriate analogue for cinema. Image veneration bridges the separation between monastic and lay populations, and it is backed by a theory about the power and impact of visual experience, regardless of the material nature of the image. This theory is put into practice by three facts: first, Buddha images are treated as equivalent to the original historical Buddha; second, there is an unlimited variety of forms that the Buddha can take; and third, image veneration is recommended for its affective and religious impact on the viewer. I will elaborate on these points in turn.

The Status of Buddha Images

Buddhists have unambiguously and repeatedly affirmed that the historical Buddha Śākyamuni passed into eternal nirvana upon his death and is no longer present in the world. And yet when one looks at the language of donative inscriptions and land grants to Buddhist monasteries throughout India from the fifth to twelfth centuries, it "leaves no room to doubt that the Buddha himself was thought to reside in the specifically named monastery."[19] That is to say, images of the Buddha "residing" in a monastery were treated like the living Buddha in the official and legal donation records. The monastic codes of the *Mūlasarvāstivāda Vinaya*[20] confirm this with passages "that explicitly treat the Buddha [image] as a juristic personality and describe the appropriate procedures for dealing with *buddhasantaka*, 'that which belongs to the Buddha.'"[21] The legal and monastic practices are not a betrayal of the position that the Buddha is gone. Rather, it testifies to the fact that there are compelling proxies for the original Buddha, the logic and possibility of which are sanctioned by the doctrinal teaching that all things—including Śākyamuni himself—are inherently empty due to their impermanent and conditioned nature.

The ubiquity of this idea can be gleaned from the genre of Buddhist miracle tales popular throughout East Asia. These "tales of the strange" known as *zhiguai* in China, and *setsuwa* ("oral tales") in Japan, are legends in the sense that they claim to recount actual events.[22] A dominant motif of such tales concerns animate statues of the Buddha or bodhisattvas (particularly Guanyin) that walk, talk, emit light, and, most importantly, save beings in distress. These stories attest to the life and power that the populace attributed to images, and the popularity of recounting and retelling such tales suggest how easily the medium of film—which fulfills the idea of images that move and talk—can enliven their basic premise.

The treatment of images in the monastic and popular context replicates the status given to the physical relics of the Buddha, which are considered equivalent to the living Buddha. Relic veneration has been a central part of Buddhism since Śākyamuni passed away in the fifth century BCE. Relics are the physical remains of the Buddha after his cremation, which are housed in reliquary monuments known as *stūpas* and venerated with flowers, perfumes, and incense. One might argue that human remains have an organic physical connection to the original person, which puts the Buddha's relics in a different category from paintings and sculptural likenesses of him. But the Theravāda tradition puts images into the same category as relics because of their power to recall the Buddha and bring him back to life. Relics re-present the Buddha because it was a part of his original body; on the other hand, images "gain their authority by their capacity to re-present the Buddha visually."[23]

The common thread of "re-presenting" the Buddha is worth considering in some detail because it supersedes the criterion of physical identity. The latter puts a lot of stock in the primacy of the physical body, wherein relics share in its organic essence. This valuation, however, is not at all in line with Buddhist teachings about the insubstantial nature of the body, or with the Buddha's repeated admonitions against attachment to his body. The re-presentation of the Buddha, then, isn't a matter of connecting to something ontologically specific, such as the Buddha's physical body or to an otherworldly essence. Everything, including the Buddha, already shares the same essence by virtue of being empty. Experiencing the presence of the Buddha is entirely a matter of the devotee's spontaneous or cultivated response to various objects. Buddha relics and images are often associated together in temple complexes, creating spaces that "evoke and orchestrate devotional attitudes and behaviors."[24] There is an inner logic that allows Buddhists to venerate Buddha relics and Buddha images equally, which sees them both as no different from the original living Buddha himself. The implication for cinema is that its secularity as a medium and institution is irrelevant if it provides images of the Buddha that worshippers find moving. But more than this, the logic of Buddhist images extends this possibility to figural representations beyond the Buddha himself.

The Multiplication of the Buddha

The logic that links relics and images also allow for the possibility of encountering the Buddha in multiple and even infinite forms. The theoretical basis for this is articulated in the idea of "manifestation bodies" (*nirmāṇakāyas*) that is ubiquitous in Mahāyāna thought but also anticipated in early Buddhism. The *Sāmaññaphala Sutta* of the *Dīgha Nikāya* (in the Pāli Canon) states that beings in advanced stages of meditation have the power to draw another body out of their own, that is "complete with all its limbs and faculties," as well as the power of multiplication—"being one, he becomes many."[25] These "bodies made of mind" (*manomayakāya*) are thought to be a natural consequence of advanced mental discipline, and Mahāyāna texts develop this into the idea of deliberate incarnations projected by the Buddha in order to reach all beings in multiple and accessible ways. According to the *Daśabhūmika Sūtra* (contained in the *Avataṃsaka Sutra*), bodhisattvas (buddhas-to-be) attain the ability to create such bodies at the eighth stage of their tenfold path to buddhahood.

The most radical shift in Mahāyāna thinking, however, is the portrayal of the historical Buddha himself as one of these physical manifestations. This significant change in view is accompanied by the articulation of an umbrella category from which the historical Buddha and countless other buddhas are thought to emanate. This category is the ever-present and abstract "dharma body" (*dharmakāya*) that functions as the matrix of all manifestations. This reverses the early view of the Buddha as a mortal human being in favor of a broad cosmic conception of the buddha-nature that pervades all things. This is part and parcel of the Mahāyāna move of integrating samsara and nirvana: buddha-nature is always in the world as an abiding reality that is ever accessible, and it is not confined to the particular individual called Śākyamuni Buddha who lived in a specific time and who is now dead and gone.

Chapter 16 of the *Lotus Sutra* contains a famous narration of this, when the Buddha says, "My life-span is incalculable asaṃkhyeyakalpas ('innumerable eons'), ever enduring, never perishing."[26] The Buddha explains that he is eternal but makes a show of birth and dying as an expedient device to inspire the people of the world to hurry on to the Buddhist path of liberation. In one of the well-known stories told in the *Lotus*, the Buddha says it is like a doctor who has sons who are ill beyond reason and refuses to take the medicine their father has prepared. The doctor departs and sends word that he has died, in order to inspire his sons with remorse to finally take the medicine. The traditional understanding of the Buddha is hereby enveloped within a larger theory that makes Śākyamuni only one of countless buddhas, and which also explains why he created the fictional show of being a mortal being.

The *Lotus Sutra* also dedicates a chapter each to the bodhisattvas Gadgadasvara and Avalokiteśvara (Chinese: Guanyin) and their abilities to manifest themselves to sentient beings in diverse forms. Thirty-three different kinds of manifestations are attributed to Avalokiteśvara, which include non-Buddhist identities such as Hindu gods (Brahmā, Śakrā, Vaiśrvaṇā) and priests (Brahmins). The manifestations also include nonreligious figures such as householders and officials, as well as women and children. These are generic categories rather than specific individuals, which suggests that the bodhisattva can be encountered by interacting with ordinary individuals in daily life.

The *Śūraṅgama Sutra* explains why Avalokiteśvara takes on such particular forms. The bodhisattva accounts for one of his manifestations in the following way: "To beings who would like to be able to discuss celebrated writings and to live a pure life, I will appear as a layperson and will instruct them in the Dharma that will lead them to fulfillment of their wish." The account of yet another manifestation is the following: "To beings who would like to govern a country or to decide the affairs of a province or a district, I will appear as a minister of state, and I will instruct them in the Dharma that will lead them to fulfillment of their wish."[27] All of the manifestations follow the same logic—the form that Avalokiteśvara embodies depends on the needs of the individual receiving teachings. The unifying idea, however, is that the bodhisattva is a deliberate fictional projection who can bring people to liberation in the course of any number of activities.

The concept of manifested bodies quite likely evolved in tandem with the veneration of Buddha images. Robert Decaroli observes that in the extensive literature dedicated to the topic of the Buddha's bodies, "practical issues about art played a far greater role ... than is typically acknowledged."[28] We can, however, turn to an image that self-reflexively asserts the presence of the Buddha in images (and other objects). A silkscreen print from the tenth-century Chinese state of Wuyue (Hangzhou) depicts the Bodhisattva Guanyin with twenty-four manifestations, which are pictured around the periphery of the image.[29] The astonishing thing about these manifestations is how they take the idea of buddha bodies beyond human forms. In addition to real and mythical animals (dragon, lion, elephant, phoenix, turtle, and sparrow), the vast majority of them are inanimate objects. Some are natural—grass, lotus flower, the hand and foot of the Buddha, clouds, and the reflection of the moon in water. The rest are manufactured: a pavilion, a drum, a temple bell, a bridge, a hand bell, a stupa, a well-covering, a precious jewel, a wheel, and—significantly—a stone Buddha image.

At one level, the Wuyue print conveys the doctrinal teaching that buddha-nature is present in all things. East Asian Buddhism is well known for mapping the Buddha's body unto the natural landscape, with the idea that even rocks and trees possess buddha-nature and that mountains and rivers can teach the Dharma. Japanese Buddhism is particularly pointed about the buddha-nature in the landscape, although the idea goes back to Chinese Tiantai Buddhism. But the Japanese version of Tiantai (Tendai) asserts that the grass, trees, and land will all become buddhas,[30] making nature equivalent to sentient beings. The Japanese Sōtō Zen master Dōgen (1200–53) composed the *Mountain and Water Sutra* (*Sansuikyō*), which likens mountains and rivers to the body of the Buddha that can preach the Dharma.

The idea that fabricated objects are also incarnations of the Buddha, however, takes the manifestation theory to another level that asserts the need for art. This makes sense when one considers that images were the most available re-presentations of the Buddha, compared to the limited number of his physical relics. Images also have the advantage of presenting the human form of the Buddha, which elicits emotions more readily than abstract symbols and other non-figural objects. The evidence of traditions all around the globe testify to how automatically and strongly people respond to human likenesses. It is clear that Buddhists were also aware of this power and the expediency of using it for religious ends. This purpose is the basic driver of the Buddhist ritual process.

A Theory of Images

We can turn to a tale from the *Divyāvadāna* ("divine legends"), a Sanskrit collection of legends, to see how this ritual process is articulated as an explicit theory of images. The legend of the monk Upagupta is contained in the *Aśokāvadāna* ("legend of Aśoka"), the twenty-ninth of the thirty-eight stories comprising the *Divyāvadāna*. Aśoka (304–232 BCE) is the Mauryan dynasty king who united the Indian subcontinent and famously converted to Buddhism. Upagupta was a famous monk and teacher who lived in northern India (in Mathurā) and whom, according to the *Aśokāvadāna*, Aśoka engaged as a guide to all the important locations in the life of the Buddha. The *Aśokāvadāna* details the king's acts of Buddhist piety, such as his construction of 84,000 stūpas (Buddhist reliquary monuments) and his worship of the Bodhi tree under which the Buddha attained enlightenment. The legends illustrate a persistent theme of Buddhist tales both within and outside of the *Divyāvadāna*: the longing of followers to see the Buddha. In these acts, "Aśoka repeatedly creates a situation in which the Buddha, despite his parinirvāṇa, may in some sense be said to be present."[31]

Upagupta is also the subject of legends in various sources, and he is particularly credited with subduing and converting Māra, the "Evil One" and personification of sensory desires. The two encounter each other when Māra interferes with Upagupta's attempts to preach the Dharma to an assembly of monks by causing showers of pearls and gold to rain down, thereby distracting the crowd with greed. Divining that Māra is behind this ploy, Upagupta attaches a garland of corpses to Māra's body, which Māra finds impossible to remove. When Māra finally submits to Upagupta, the monk agrees to free Māra only after he (Māra) takes on the resplendent form of the Buddha for Upagupta to see. Upagupta explains this request, saying, "I have already seen the Dharma-body but I have not seen the physical body of the Lord of the Triple World, who resembles a mountain of gold."[32] Because Upagupta was born centuries after the Buddha, he cannot see the Teacher in the flesh. His longing can only be satisfied by turning to art.

Māra retreats into the forest to take on the form of the Buddha and then emerges, "like an actor wearing a bright costume":[33]

> Making manifest the Tathāgata's body,
> which abounds with the highest marks
> and brings tranquility to the eyes of men,
> he ornamented that forest,
> as though unveiling the fresh colors
> of a valuable painting.[34]

The comparison of Māra's transformation to acting and a painting is notable. It reinforces again the equivalence between Buddha manifestations and artistic images, the latter being the most accessible kind of manifestation available to Buddhists through the centuries. Upagupta is overwhelmed by the apparition, "and thinking that this image *was* the Buddha, he fell at Māra's feet with his whole body, like a tree cut off at the root."[35] When Māra protests that Upagupta has broken his promise not to revere him, which amounts to an act of idolatry, Upagupta offers up the following defense:

> Of course, I know that the Best of Speakers
> has gone altogether to extinction,
> like a fire swamped by water.
> Even so, when I see his figure,
> which is pleasing to the eye,
> I bow down before that Sage.
> But I do not revere you![36]

Upagupta elaborates further by referring to image worship:

Just as men bow down
to clay images of the gods,
knowing that what they worship
is the god and not the clay,
so I, seeing you here,
wearing the form of the Lord of the World,
bowed down to you,
conscious of the Sugata,
but not conscious of Māra.[37]

Upagupta offers a normative description of the proper human response to artistic projections of the Buddha. He emphasizes what's in his mind—what he is *conscious* of—upon seeing the likeness of the Buddha. Upagupta isn't concerned to know what the Buddha literally looked like—"He is, rather, craving a religious experience."[38] Images are necessary to trigger such experiences, but the art is strictly instrumental: "What it is made of—clay, wood, metal, or, in this case, Māra—is not the Buddha; but it itself comes to re-present the Buddha in a way that is obviously *religiously real*."[39]

But what does it mean for an experience to be religiously real? We can answer by referring to a traditional Buddhist meditative practice known as *buddhānusmṛti*, which means to "recollect the Buddha." Andy Rotman alludes to it when he says "[Upagupta] doesn't see the Buddha through Māra; rather, Māra's impersonation of the Buddha allows Upagupta *to bring the Buddha to mind*, and it is only then, with his mind fixed on an image of the Buddha, that he can really see him."[40] Buddhānusmṛti is primarily associated with Pure Land Buddhism, but it's mentioned in the Pāli *Nikāyas*, as well as Mahāyāna texts apart from the Pure Land tradition. The *Pratyutpanna-buddha-sammukhāvasthita-samādhi-sūtra* ("The samadhi of the one who stands face-to-face with the present buddhas") provides instruction in buddhānusmṛti practice, which consists of detailed visualization of the thirty-two iconic marks of the Buddha's body. The specificity and concreteness of the visualizations are hallmarks of Pure Land meditation. What's particularly interesting about the *Pratyutpanna*, however, is its repeated emphasis on the insubstantial nature of the vision, which reflects the influence of the emptiness doctrine. The recollection of the Buddha Amitābha, who is the primary focus of this text, is compared to dreaming, and the appearance of the Buddha is termed "nirmita," a magical creation, a term that is related to "nirmāna," or buddha manifestations.[41]

Underscoring the ultimately illusory nature of the visualized Buddha and Pure Land shifts the goal of meditation from the reality of what is seen to the process and effect of seeing itself. The point is that what is illusory is still powerful. The *Pratyutpanna* reveals that visions do not have to be of

Amitābha for this lesson to be conveyed. It tells the story of three men who hear about three famous prostitutes, and "just through hearing of their names, appearance, and beauty, they came to have lustful thoughts."[42] Fantasizing about the women, the men fall asleep and satisfy their sexual desires in a dream. Repeating a familiar trope of Buddhist dream literature, the dream experience proves to be quite educational and the men attain perfect awakening as a result. How does this happen? As Paul Harrison explains, the men see that their dreams were "apparitions so vivid and yet so empty of independent reality as to remain suitable objects of spiritual practice for them even after they have turned their minds to higher things."[43] The men meditate on the simultaneously vivid and empty nature of the dream, and this brings wisdom.

Buddhānusmṛti works in exactly the same way. The *Pratyutpanna* instructs that when a vision of the Buddha is obtained, one "should not entertain the apperception of an existing thing, but should entertain the apperception of empty space."[44] According to Harrison, the *Pratyutpanna* utilizes emptiness doctrine in order to correct Pure Land Buddhists who think that the encounter with Amitābha and rebirth in the Pure Land are literal experiences.[45] The sutra corrects this by teaching that those who obtain a vision of Amitābha did not go anywhere and nor did the Buddha come from somewhere. Instead, it is concentration meditation (*samādhi*) that brings things to life: "Whatever belongs to this Triple World is nothing but thought. Why is that? It is because however I imagine things, that is how they appear."[46]

Whether one visualizes an alluring woman or the Buddha Amitābha, it is the act of concentration that produces results. Being aware of this power of the imagination overrides the issue of what exactly is imagined, because this awareness turns even the sexual wet dream into an overtly religious lesson on emptiness. Similarly, what makes Upagupta's experience religiously real is this same balance between his ability to be moved by Māra's appearance as the Buddha, and his mindfulness of its illusory nature. This balance is an awareness of the fundamental nature of all things, as well as an ability to profit from this awareness. Recall that before Upagupta subdues Māra, the latter had been distracting monks with visions of pearls and gold. But notably, Upagupta does not forbid Māra from his conjuring tricks, per se. Māra is the king of sensory appearances, and Upagupta simply puts his talents to much more productive use. Herein lies the essential lesson, which consists of an awakening to the power of sensory and aesthetic experience.

A Theory of Cinema

This summary review of Buddhist image veneration and its theoretical underpinnings not only suggests how easily films extend this heritage, but, even more interestingly, how Buddhism can supply a new perspective on the significance of cinema. This perspective can only be gained, however, after a larger consideration of how to define what is "religious." In the Mahāyāna Buddhist logic of the Buddha's body, the Buddha is embodied in any and all material forms, and images of him are said to be animate in the same way that films bring bodies to life. Moreover, the Buddha's body is also thought to take on every character and personality that is relatable to the worshipper, meaning that the Dharma can be learned in the context of any worldly activity.

At this point, the distinction between religious and secular is disposable. If the Dharma can be encountered in relationships with kings, merchants, spouses, children, and so forth, then there is no point in distinguishing between religious and secular, or even between "Buddhist" and "non-Buddhist." What I am calling a Buddhist theory of cinema, however, is this tradition's appreciation of the primacy of the cinematic imagination in both engendering and cultivating personhood. This fact is recognized as a double-edged sword, in that the Buddhist diagnosis of the human condition is that we are mired in maladaptive fantasies. The solution is not to wake up to some higher and better reality, but rather to cultivate better imaginings with the help of aesthetic rituals.

A vignette from an actual movie may help to underscore the ritual power of cinema. Drew Goddard's *Bad Times at the El Royale* (2018) concerns four strangers who check into the eponymous hotel during the off season, and at the end it depicts a pretend priest who administers the rite of absolution to the dying hotel clerk named Miles. Jeff Bridges plays an aged bank robber just released from prison who disguises himself as a priest to retrieve stolen money hidden in the floorboards of one of the guest rooms. In the course of the movie, Miles attempts to engage "Father Flynn" to obtain absolution for his guilty conscience, having to do with the blackmailing operations run out of the El Royale and the men he shot during the Vietnam War. The movie comes to a climax with an explosion of violence triggered by the arrival of the cult leader Billy Lee and his brutal gang. Miles reluctantly employs his sharp-shooting skills to take out the intruders, but he's stabbed in the process. As Miles lays dying, "Father Flynn" is prompted by another guest to administer the rite of absolution, despite the fact that his true identity has been revealed.

Initially hesitant, Father Flynn says, "Confess, my son, confess." When Miles protests, "You're not a priest," Father Flynn replies decisively, "Of course I am. Miles Miller, my name is Father Daniel Flynn and I am here to absolve you of your sins." What follows is a transformation of pretense into ritual reality as the priest and penitent go through the scripted drama. Miles intones, "Bless me, Father, for I have sinned." Father Flynn recites, "Do you seek absolution for your sins? Do you give yourself to the mercy of the Lord? Will you give to him the time you have left? It's never too late.

You are forgiven. Miles Miller, in the name of the father, the son, and the holy spirit, you are forgiven."

Those who hold to Catholic canon law might be offended by this scene because only a *bone fide* priest is empowered to offer the rite of absolution, not a bank robber dressed up like one. But the scene also suggests a play in which performing the ritual empowers both participants to actually become who they imagine themselves (and each other) to be. This scene centers on recognizable religious identities and rituals, but that is immaterial to my thesis about the "religious" nature of cinema. Instead, the point is that engaging and entertaining the imagination produces results that are no different from what religious rituals strive to attain. As the scene shows, ritual truth is often more powerful than empirical reality.

The fact that it is a movie depicting the transformative effect of ritual experience offers a double-layered and self-implicating demonstration of this potency. If we ourselves feel the significance of what the absolution scene from *Bad Times at the El Royale* portrays, then we can see that the whole cinematic medium is a formal conveyance mechanism for countless pretend priests calling up real ritual moments. Being aware of this power of cinema, in turn, invites us to think long and hard about what experiences, dispositions, and worlds to cultivate with the help of this ubiquitous medium.

Notes

1 Herbert Fingerette, *Confucius: The Secular as Sacred* (New York: Harper and Row, 1972).
2 Anthony Yu, *State and Religion in China: Historical and Textual Perspectives* (Chicago: Open Court, 2005), 15.
3 Timothy Fitzgerald, *The Ideology of Religious Studies* (New York, Oxford: Oxford University Press, 2000); also see Robert Ford Campany, "On the Very Idea of Religions (In the Modern West and in Early Medieval China)," *History of Religions* 42, no. 4 (May 2003): 287–319.
4 Peter Van der Veer, *The Modern Spirit of Asia: The Spiritual and the Secular in China and India* (Princeton, NJ: Princeton University Press, 2014), 38.
5 Ibid., 37.
6 J. J. Clarke, *Oriental Enlightenment: The Encounter Between Asian and Western Thought* (London, New York: Routledge; 2003); Donald Palmer, *Qigong Fever: Body, Science, and Utopia in China* (New York: Columbia University Press, 2007); and David McMahan, *The Making of Buddhist Modernism* (Oxford, New York: Oxford University Press, 2008).
7 Van der Veer, *The Modern Spirit of Asia*, 45–61.
8 Ibid., 227.

9 Wakoh Shannon Hickey, *Mind Cure: How Meditation Became Medicine* (New York: Oxford University Press, 2019), 11.
10 Richard King, *Orientalism and Religion: Post-Colonial Theory, India and the Mystic East* (London, New York: Routledge, 1999); and Donald Lopez, *Buddhism and Science: A Guide for the Perplexed* (Chicago, IL: University of Chicago Press, 2008).
11 This line is from the eponymous text, *Zhuangzi*, section twenty-two. When asked by a student where the Dao exists, Zhuangzi first answers it is everywhere. When pressed for further details, Zhuangzi states progressively that it is in the ant, the grass, the tiles and shards, and finally in the piss and shit.
12 Francisca Cho, "Buddhism," in *The Routledge Companion to Religion and Film*, ed. John Lyman (New York: Routledge Press, 2008), 162–77.
13 Dzongsar Jamyang Khyentse (b. 1961) goes by the directorial name of Khyentse Norbu. He has directed and released four films to date: *The Cup* (1999), *Travellers and Magicians* (2003), *Vara: A Blessing* (2013), and *Hema Hema: Sing Me a Song While I Wait* (2017). "Life as Cinema" (2016) accompanied his release of *Travellers and Magicians*, see https://www.lionsroar.com/life-as-cinema.
14 There are numerous references to philosophical materialism in the Buddhist Pāli canon, such as the *Sāmaññaphala Sutta* (The Fruits of the Contemplative Life). The Indian school of matter-only reductionism is known as the Cārvāka, but Buddhists characterize it as the doctrine of "annihilationism" because it denies karma and rebirth. Buddhists have engaged in refutations of theism throughout its history, but one of the earliest is in the *Tevijja Sutta* (The Threefold Knowledge) also in the Pāli canon. In this text, the Buddha challenges the Vedic principle of divinity known as Brahmā, on the grounds that no Brahmin priest has ever seen it face-to-face to ascertain its existence and nature. Both of these suttas appear in the *Dīgha Nikāya*, or the "long discourses" of the Pāli canon.
15 This argument has not been lost on Mahāyāna Buddhists or their opponents. For example, the discourses of the Indian Buddhist philosopher Nāgārjuna (second century) documents his interlocuters who object that if Nāgārjuna is right in asserting that all is empty, then the assertion of emptiness is itself empty and therefore baseless. This is a negative form of the objection that emptiness is another way of asserting an essence—the essence of essencelessness. For my own purposes, this debate is purely semantic as I am primarily concerned with the *content* of emptiness doctrine and its effect of reversing distinctions between the worldly and transcendent, whether the latter is defined as divinity or rationality.
16 The "infinity of space" and "beyond consciousness and no-consciousness" are two of the "formless" realms named in early Buddhist cosmology, with each realm being explicitly equated with a stage of mental consciousness. The formless realms comprise the highest in this system, whereas there are multiple realms of hell comprising the lowest. See W. Randolph Kloetzli, *Buddhist Cosmology: Science and Technology in the Images of Motion and Light*

(Delhi: Motilal Banarsidass Publishers, 1983), esp. his account of the Buddhist single world cosmology known as the *Cakravāla*.

17 Pure Land Buddhism has a storied career throughout premodern Buddhist Asia and it is often described as the easy, populist path because it offers the masses automatic entry into the "pure land" of a Buddha (usually Amitābha) by reciting his name at the point of death. Although the recitation of the Buddha's name dominates Japanese Pure Land practice, precise visualizations of the Buddha and his pure land have been present from the beginning. See Charles Jones, *Chinese Pure Land Buddhism: Understanding a Tradition of Practice* (Honolulu, HI: University of Hawai'i, 2019) for a general account of Chinese Pure Land Buddhism.

18 Francisca Cho, *Embracing Illusion: Truth and Fiction in The Dream of the Nine Clouds* (Albany, NY: State University of New York Press, 1996); also see Francisca Cho, "Buddhist Literary Criticism in East Asian Literature," in *Buddhist Literature as Philosophy, Buddhist Philosophy as Literature*, ed. Rafal Stepien (Albany, NY: State University of New York Press, 2020).

19 Gregory Schopen, *Bones, Stones, and Buddhist Monks: Collected Papers on the Archeology, Epigraphy, and Texts of Monastic Buddhism in India* (Honolulu, HI: University of Hawaii Press, 1997), 267–8.

20 The Mūlasarvāstivāda is an Indian monastic order that appeared around the second century and declined by the seventh, although it survives today in Tibet. The monastic rules of the *Mūlasarvāstivāda Vinaya* are still observed by Buddhists in Tibet, Bhutan, Nepal, Ladakh, and Mongolia, whereas the Theravāda vinaya rules are followed by South and Southeast Asians (in Myanmar, Cambodia, Loas, Sri Lanka, Thailand), and the Dharmaguptaka vinaya is followed by East Asian Buddhists (in China, Korea, Japan, Taiwan, Vietnam).

21 Schopen, *Bones, Stones, and Buddhist Monks*, 272.

22 Chinese zhiguai tales were collected from the end of the Han dynasty (206 BCE–22 CE) into the Tang dynasty (618–907) and are considered the first examples of Chinese narrative fiction. Robert Campany has provided numerous translations and studies of zhiguai collections, including *A Garden of Marvels: Tales of Wonder from Early Medieval China* (Honolulu, HI: University of Hawaii Press, 2015). Japanese setsuwa were collected between the eighth and fourteenth centuries, one of the most famous collections being the *Konjaku Monogatarishū* ("tales from the past").

23 Kevin Trainor, *Relics, Ritual, and Representation in Buddhism: Rematerializing the Sri Lankan Theravāda Tradition* (Cambridge, New York: Cambridge University Press, 1997), 30.

24 Kevin Trainor, "Introduction: Beyond Superstition," in *Embodying the Dharma: Buddhist Relic Veneration in Asia*, ed. David Germano and Kevin Trainor (Albany, NY: State University of New York Press, 2004), 17.

25 See *The Long Discourses of the Buddha: A Translation of the Dīgha Nikāya*, trans. Maurice Walshe (Boston: Wisdom Publications, 1995), 105. The *Dīgha Nikāya* is one section of the Pāli Canon, which is the scriptural collection

of the Theravāda school. The Theravāda is one of the eighteen lineages that emerged from the original Buddhist monastic community. It is the only school whose textual canon survives in its entirety, making it the only extant school of Buddhism.

26 See *Scripture of the Lotus Blossom of the Fine Dharma*, trans. [from the Chinese of Kumārajīva] Leon Hurvitz (New York: Columbia University Press), 239.

27 See *The Śūraṅgama Sūtra-With Excerpts from the Commentary by the Venerable Master Hsüan Hua*, trans. Buddhist Text Translation Society (Ukiah, CA: Dharma Realm Buddhist Association, 2017), 238.

28 Robert DeCaroli, *Image Problems: The Origin and Development of the Buddha's Image in Early South Asia* (Seattle and London: University of Washington Press, 2015), 170.

29 This image was sponsored by the last Wuyue emperor Qian Shu (929–88), who was a devout Buddhist. None of the original 20,000 copies survive, but it is reproduced in the Taishō Tripitaka, in volume 6 of the *Zuzōbu* (Diagrams and Paintings) section. For a reproduction of this image, see Yu Chun Fang, *Kuan-Yin: The Chinese Transformation of Avalokiteśvara* (New York: Columbia University Press, 2001), 230.

30 Jacqueline I. Stone, "Realizing This World as the Buddha Land," in *Readings of the Lotus Sūtra*, ed. Stephen F. Teiser and Jacqueline I. Stone, Columbia Readings of Buddhist Literature (New York: Columbia University Press, 2009), 215.

31 John Strong, *The Legend of King Aśoka: A Study and Translation of the Aśokāvadāna* (Princeton, NJ: Princeton University Press, 1983), 101.

32 Ibid., 192.
33 Ibid., 193.
34 Ibid.
35 Ibid., 195.
36 Ibid.
37 Ibid., 196.
38 Ibid., 107.
39 Ibid., 108 (emphasis added).
40 Andy Rotman, *Thus Have I Seen: Visualizing Faith in Early Indian Buddhism* (Oxford: Oxford University Press, 2009), 172.

41 See *The Samādhi of Direct Encounter with the Buddhas of the Present: An Annotated English Translation of the Tibetan Version of the Pratyutpanna-Buddha-Sammukhāvasthita-Samādhi-Sūtra with Appendices Relating to the History of the Text*, trans. Paul Harrison (Tokyo: The International Institute for Buddhist Studies, 1990), 32.

42 Ibid., 34.
43 Ibid., 35 n.6.
44 Ibid., 39.

45 Paul Harrison, "*Buddhānusmṛti* in the *Pratyutpanna-buddha-sammukhāva sthita-samādhi-sūtra*," Journal of Indian Philosophy 6, no. 1 (September 1978): 52.
46 *The Samādhi of Direct Encounter with the Buddhas of the Present*, 42.

PART II

Situating Secularism

Culture, Politics, and Cinema

4

Ousmane Sembène's *Moolaadé*

Sacred Space as Refuge and Political Agency

Nikolas Kompridis

Resettling *Moolaadé*

The films of Ousmane Sembène were foundational for the unjustly delayed emergence of African cinema, and are an integral part of an international canon of decolonizing critique produced by Africans and the African diaspora. *Moolaadé* (2004), Sembène's final film before his death in 2007, crowned a remarkable sequence of feature films that began in 1966 with *Black Girl* (*La Noire de . . .*).[1] Perhaps the most successful realization of his activist conception of cinema, *Moolaadé* is a deceptively complex film that slyly disguises its ambitious agenda. The studied artifice with which Sembène depicts quotidian village life endows it with a countenance that is at once uncanny and soporific. At times, it is hard to know what to make of the film; in one moment what it is about seems altogether obvious, and in the next, altogether opaque. A plot that is as misleadingly simple as its naturalistic veneer only adds to the difficulty of finding one's bearings. If one does not watch attentively, making oneself look again (and again) at some of its (many) puzzling or peculiar details, one will fail to see just how much the film's far-reaching "argument" reposes on its most understated and elusive elements.

There are some very fine readings of *Moolaadé*, responding primarily to its uncompromising treatment of the practice of female genital cutting—a practice that, literally and figuratively, cuts across some of the most fiercely contested and entangled issues on the continent.[2] Most prominent among them, the array of contested practices that suppress and deny the agency of women. However, the understandable preponderance of responses to the issue of female "purification" has come at the cost of an unjustifiable neglect of the very phenomenon to which the film owes its name and around which everything in it turns—*sacred space*. This neglect could be attributed to a certain secular aversion to serious engagement with the sacred, especially because of the idiosyncratic causal role it plays in a West African village that might too easily be mistaken for the nondescript, stereotypically "backward" African village commonly portrayed in Western films. Its neglect could also be attributed to a reflexive reluctance to muddy a prima facie human rights issue with serious discussion of an ancient practice that carries associations with "primitive magic," possibly exposing one to accusations of "othering" or "exoticizing" African culture. Whatever the reason, such reluctance is altogether misplaced; above all, because it fails to do justice to Sembène's film.

Moolaadé is a word from the Dioula/Bambara language family, widely spoken across West Africa. It can be translated appositely either as sanctuary or as asylum. But translating it as sanctuary or asylum does not sufficiently convey in English the inviolability of *moolaadé* nor its distinctive standing as a sacred space. In part, its distinctive standing is owed to a precolonial, animistic tradition of belief interwoven with the founding history of the people whose contemporary descendants inhabit the secluded Burkino Fasso village in which the film is set. No matter whether they are threatened or empowered by the invocation of *moolaadé*, all the characters in the film are as unhesitating in their acknowledgment of its inviolability as they are wary of its disruptive power. This is because *moolaadé* is not inert and inanimate: it possesses an uncontainable, vexatious agency of its own.

From the moment it is invoked to secure provisional refuge for a group of terrified pre-adolescent girls unwilling to undergo the ritual of "purification," *moolaadé* triggers a cascading series of dissident and unruly actions, enabling one very courageous woman's public contestation of the practice of female genital cutting. Overturning the spatial and normative order of the village, *moolaadé* goes far beyond the protection and refuge it was called upon to provide. It actively permeates and unsettles the spaces around it, paralyzing the customary exercise of authority in the village. The destabilizing effects radiating outward from *moolaadé* can be set in motion only because, for a brief, evanescent moment, it simultaneously transcends and undermines all secular power and authority. This is why its presence in the film is not reducible either to a narrative device for kick-starting a story of heroic resistance to female "purification" or to a troublesome remnant of a pre-Islamic African religion in conflict with Islam. Indeed, *moolaadé* does not fit comfortably on either side of the sacred/profane or secularism/religion binaries. Rather, it exposes their conceptual limits by incarnating the variability and permeability of the spatial boundaries that putatively wall off the sacred from the profane. As *moolaadé* unsettles the boundaries between sacred and profane spaces, it also *resettles* spaces previously "occupied" through colonial dispossession and forced conversion, reclaiming them in the name of a politically transformative aspiration, precisely specified by Frantz Fanon: to bring about once and for all "not only the demise of colonialism, but also the demise of the colonized," by which Fanon meant the demise of the conditions that reproduce "the colonized" even after the "demise" of colonialism.

Remarkably, this venerable African practice offering temporary sanctuary to those in dire need extends beyond the boundaries of the film to which it lends its name. *Moolaadé* performatively enacts a vision of cinema that I am certain Sembène would have found extremely congenial: cinema as *a fugitive space of refuge and freedom*—a sanctuary for thought and imagination in which the task of envisioning how things might otherwise be is inseparable from exposing how things should no longer be. *Moolaadé*, the film, inhabits its own fugitive space of refuge and freedom to present a syncretic vision of politics in which long-standing traditions and practices confront one another, staging a process of reflection on the question of which should be critically exposed and abandoned, and which reflectively renewed and passed on. If *moolaadé* can generate political possibilities awakened by the traces of the sacred latent in precolonial African religious traditions, it is because these traditions have not simply "died off." On the contrary, as Sembène assures his principal audience, despite persistent denigration, "Our ancient religions have not disappeared; they are present and have taken different shapes."[3]

To do justice to the ambitions of *Moolaadé* will require a scrupulous analysis of the "shapes" in which the sacred appears—above all, distinguishing the "shapes" which generate violence from those which resist it. Read closely from this perspective, *Moolaadé* performs a *decolonizing* critique of violence, particularly of violence against women. Sembène's complex representation of *moolaadé* as a space of political refuge *and* as a political agency, refigures the relation between sacred space and politics.[4] How it does so is both fascinatingly inventive and extraordinarily sophisticated.

Spacing the Sacred

Moolaadé begins lyrically with a shot of the verdant outskirts of the village of Djerisso, into which a traveling merchant rides his bicycle, hauling a trailer full of wares under the midday sun. With a name as laden as his trailer, Mercenaire is enthusiastically escorted into the village by an exuberant group of young boys, loudly cheering his arrival. Soaring over their voices is a single female voice, intoning the haunting melody with which the film begins and ends. Although clearly not Mercenaire's first visit to the village, it will be his last. Toward the conclusion of the film, as *Moolaadé* approaches its denouement, he is escorted right back to the outskirts of the village, this time by a group of angry, vengeful men, not under bright sunlight but in the torchlit dark of night, where he will be executed for interfering with the public flogging of a disobedient wife. Although we are not shown Mercenaire's execution, it takes place at about the same distance from the village as the distance from which we saw him enter it.

In fact, throughout the course of the film, we are never given anything to see *beyond* the outskirts of the village. And just as consistently, we never see the village from a perspective outside its borders. Sembène's camera systematically circumscribes the spatial boundaries of the village, delineating a space that looks and feels enclosed. Individuals exit and enter the village, but the camera never follows them anywhere beyond its outskirts, as though the relevant "beyond" of the village were more ontological than geographical. The general impression that is conveyed, repeatedly, systematically, is that this village exists in a state of spatial enclosure: its default ontological condition. Rendered with a more Heideggerian inflection, we might call its ontological condition, *enclosedness*. This is not to be understood as an absolute, unchanging state, but as an entrenched tendency, a habitual spatial orientation—an enclosing that keeps the "outside," outside.

While nothing can be seen beyond the spatial boundaries of the village, something can be heard. Leaking into the daily life of the village are the sounds of the radio, of voices and music coming from afar, which discompose the condition of enclosedness, and, at the same time, expose its persistent presence. The everyday significance of the radio to village life is certainly magnified by the villagers' constant preoccupation with the acquisition of good batteries. The standing need to replace dead batteries with new ones is one reason why the return of the traveling merchant was always welcomed. For the women, in particular, the radio is not only a source of pleasure and edification but also an essential tool of resistance to the condition of enclosedness. Unlike the gender-coded language of the village drums, intelligible only to the men of the village, the voices transmitted by the radio across disparate and heterogenous spaces cannot be controlled. Alarmed by the belated recognition of their value as tools of resistance, and desperate to arrest the disintegrating authority of patriarchal power, the men of the village will confiscate the women's radios and burn them in a pyre. For a brief, peripatetic moment, the voices from outside will be silenced, and the village likened to a "soundless" graveyard—the very apotheosis of enclosedness.

Into this village, there is but one pathway, which the ill-fated Mercenaire follows to the village square. Having set up his wares under the generous shade of a banyan tree, he drinks thirstily from a water urn and surveys the village. On cue, the camera pans across the square at eye level, and as it moves rightward the first thing that comes into view is the prominent village mosque, constructed of mudbrick in the quintessentially spiky, cone-shaped style of West Africa. Adjacent to the mosque is a far more modest structure, but just as central to the cultural and religious identity of the people of the village. For the time being, however, Sembène withholds its (revelatory) appearance. As the camera continues panning rightward, we see and faintly hear young boys beneath another tree reciting verses from the Qur'an under the guidance of their teacher. Jarringly, Sembène cuts abruptly to an aerial view of a mudbrick compound, the domicile of the polygamous family of Ciré Bathily, whose second wife, Collé, is the film's chief (human) protagonist. In the center of the compound, there is a courtyard in the middle of which stand three cone-shaped storage towers. From this aerial view, we can see that the shape of the courtyard resembles the shape of the village square in the same way that the cone-shaped storage towers, each of which is capped by a spiky spire, resemble the cone-shaped, spiky spires of the mosque. In case we are not paying attention or have failed to notice the resemblance, Sembène, for no other possible reason, shows us a young boy climbing up and into one of the storage towers. We are meant to notice this resemblance, not to draw our attention to the continuity of a culturally defining architectural style, but to make us aware that these two spaces are (or will be) connected to one another in some fateful way.

From that same aerial view of the Bathily family compound, we are given another glimpse of the lush green environs of the village, part of a meticulously executed strategy to visually establish (1) that the borders of the village and the borders of the film are coextensive with one another and (2) that to enter this village and this film is to enter a space that is heterogeneous to what lies outside it. And this heterogeneity with respect to what lies outside it is reproduced and complicated by *moolaadé*, which permeates and reorders the normative and political space of the village. Sembène's assiduous spatializing strategy intensifies the condition of enclosedness all the more emphatically to expose, and, ultimately, to shatter it.

Shifting back to eye level, the camera shows the women in the compound engaged in their daily routines—caring for infants and children, tending to domestic animals, preparing food, sweeping the grounds, replenishing the urns with fresh well water. In barely more than two minutes, these laconic opening sequences allusively implicate the connections and differences between the two principal spaces of the film, setting in motion a propulsive spatial dialectic. Before too long, their respective positions in the spatial hierarchy of the village will be reversed, and the spatial boundaries between them, blurred. Corresponding to each of these principal spaces, two other spaces will appear, both of which lay claim to the sacred, each inimical to the other. First and foremost, the space of *moolaadé*, which will "occupy" the Bathily compound, demarcating a space of its own that is at the same time physically indistinguishable from the space it has occupied. As a consequence, to say that it "appears" is to speak, metaphorically. But that's not quite right, either. Describing the presence of *moolaadé* in the space of the Bathily home presses against the limits of both literal and metaphorical language.

The counterpart and antithesis of *moolaadé* is the bucolic grove within which the "purification" ritual takes place. Curiously, it is a "sacred space" whose exact location remains ambiguous throughout the film, as though it were somehow placeless. When it first appears in the film, one simply presumes that the space of "purification" must lie somewhere at the edge of the village. However, the consistently nebulous position it occupies in the spatial configuration of the film eventually creates the impression that the ambiguity of its location is somehow essential to the kind of space it is—its placelessness is not only indispensable to, but also constitutive of, its standing *as* a sacred space. Quite notably, and altogether deliberately, we are never shown anyone crossing its sacred threshold—neither the women who conduct the ritual nor the girls undergoing it.[5] The space where young girls are taken to be cut is itself cut off from the world of the village. Inaccessible and invisible to uninvited eyes, it comes across as a space that actively obscures and, indeed, mystifies, not only *where* but also *how* its "sacred" space is demarcated from the profane spaces that surround it.

By contrast, Sembène makes a point of showing us various individuals entering and leaving the Bathily compound *after* the invocation of *moolaadé* and its precise demarcation by a publicly visible threshold. A great deal of what is at stake in *Moolaadé* turns on the conflict between these mutually antagonistic and mutually incompatible visions of sacred space—one of which exists as a permanent space of "purification," the other, as a fugitive space of refuge, offering temporary sanctuary *from* "purification." Throughout the film *moolaadé* consistently appears to us as a fully transparent public space, embedded almost imperceptibly in the ordinary and everyday space within which it has settled; and yet, it projects a mysterious otherness of its own. By contrast, the unplaceable space of "purification" remains spatially sequestered and opaque, hidden from exposure to the ordinary and the everyday; the "otherness" it projects seems to depend entirely on mystification. One must assume that the space of "purification" cannot survive contact with other spaces; that it must, by necessity, remain placeless and impermeable. To be contaminated by other spaces—be they sacred or profane—would mean its annihilation.

When the camera finally pauses its movement inside the Bathily compound, it focuses upon a woman sweeping the grounds. This woman is Collé, whose daily domestic routine is suddenly interrupted by the desperate cries of four young girls running into the compound. Their ceremonial dress marks the girls as runaways, fleeing "purification." Supplicating themselves before her, they plead for protection and refuge: "We don't want to be cut!" As her grown-up daughter, Amsatou, quickly points out to the perplexed Collé, their pleas cannot be refused. They are appealing to an unwritten moral law, like the ancient law of the sea, requiring all to give aid to the helpless and vulnerable. But unlike the law of the sea, the "law" of *moolaadé* cannot be ignored with impunity. Troubled and uncertain about how she should proceed, Collé confers with the other wives, the eldest, Hadjatou, and youngest, Alima, both of whom immediately draw Collé's attention not to her inescapable moral obligation to the young girls but to its more immediate political implications. The women, especially the conflict averse Alima, want Collé to understand that as soon as she invokes *moolaadé*, it becomes an unavoidably political matter. Not least for Collé, who will be accused of inspiring the children's insubordinate behavior in order to vitiate the sanctity of "purification"—and, by implication, of challenging the extremely misogynistic relations of power that rule the village. As if stirred by the threat of some precipitous change, the village drums can already be heard in the background, beating out their message in an ominous rhythm: the normative order of the village has been disturbed.

Passed over completely in the discussion between the women is the question of whether Collé has the authority to invoke *moolaadé*. But for the standing she enjoys through marriage to one of the wealthy families in the village, she is in every other respect an ordinary woman, lacking any special secular or religious status. This tells us that *moolaadé* can be invoked by anyone, anywhere—*it is radically democratic*. In this instance, *moolaadé* is not only invoked by an ordinary woman; it is invoked in the very space where women do their daily care work—in the gendered space of care. By taking into her protective care these desperate internal refugees, Collé releases the practice of care from its domesticated confinement in the sphere of "women's work," transforming into an active political force of its own.[6] The "ordinary" care work observed in the first few minutes of the film acquires a public political significance that will be as unwelcome as it is unexpected, for Collé's invocation of *moolaadé* unleashes an unrestrainable nonhuman agency capable of turning the existing normative order upside down.

And yet, as extraordinary as the power of *moolaadé* is shown to be, it is fastidiously represented in the most ordinary, utterly mundane ways. To publicly mark the threshold separating *moolaadé* from the profane space around it, Collé draws a braided tricolored rope across the doorless entrance of the Bathily compound—at a height barely a foot off the ground. There are no witnesses, and no ritual-like gesture to denote that something out of the ordinary is taking place. It all looks so unremarkable, so disarmingly unremarkable, that it can make one insensible to how remarkable it actually is. One gets the feeling that Sembène is testing us, testing us to see whether we are really looking, looking attentively, discerningly. And as he is testing us, he is also delicately prompting us to notice how the ordinary and the extraordinary—and by implication, the sacred and profane—are as *distinct* and *intertwined* as the multicolored strands of an otherwise plain and altogether unobtrusive piece of rope. Receding from our everyday taken for granted ways of seeing, whatever lies unobtrusively before us may remain just as unseen and inscrutable so long as our sight is not released from their grip (Figure 4.1).

In spite of its quiet, unobtrusive ordinariness, or because of it, this mischievously humble piece of rope effortlessly absorbs the power of *moolaadé*, precisely marking and at the same time casually muddling its sacred boundary. For as we soon see, this boundary is irregular and porous, puzzlingly so. To ensure that her young charges honor the sacred boundary conditions of *moolaadé*, Collé warns them in an austere and grave tone of voice that they must never cross over the rope without her permission: "Whoever breaks that law will be killed by *moolaadé*." However, everyone else is quite free to cross over the rope whenever they need to—unless they are members of the *Salindana*, the solemn faced, pontifically attired women authorized to conduct the *salinde*, the Bambara word for the "purification" ritual. Whenever the other villagers must cross the spatial threshold of *moolaadé*, be they members of the Bathily family or village officials, they

FIGURE 4.1 *Rope, still from* Moolaadé *(dir. Ousmane Sembène, 2004)*.

do so evincing varying degrees of wariness and concern. Trying their best to look casual, they are betrayed in one way or another by their barely suppressed fear. Indeed, much of the comic relief in this deadly serious film comes from watching the hesitancy and awkwardness with which various villagers first confront the humble rope, as befits an encounter with something that could not be more ordinary, but in which lies dormant a dreaded, impish power that must not be awakened. Comic contrast is provided by interspersed episodes of young goats, a dog, and a toddler blithely interacting with the rope as they would with any other plaything. Sembène's camera lingers, unhurried, on each of these comic episodes, as though it were merely documenting the blissfully mundane charms of quotidian life.[7] Evidently, nonhuman animals and very young children are not subject to *moolaadé*'s reputedly punitive disposition—the ordinary piece of rope is just an ordinary piece of rope. And just as evidently, without even a hint of paradox, the sacred can itself appear altogether ordinary without losing any of its extraordinary power.

(De)sacralizing Colonial Conquest and Dispossession

What do we make, then, of the porous boundary between *moolaadé* and the profane spaces that surround it? Sembène's handling of that boundary seems to contradict Mircea Eliade's classic work on the subject, *The Sacred and the Profane*.[8] Contrary to Eliade's stringent criteria, the boundary demarcating the sacred space of *moolaadé* is neither strict nor fixed. Nor is there any ontological differentiation of levels of being, differentiating higher from lower; only *moolaadé*'s virtually inconspicuous "occupation" of the domestic space of care, which remains in place, essentially unchanged in its mode of being. Care activities go on just as before; however, the work of care—caring for one's own and taking others into one's care—has acquired an urgency and significance it did not manifest before, turning the question of care into "a question of life and death." The palpable truth of Collé's words identifies the *political* transformation of the domestic space of care, its daily domestication interrupted by the invocation of *moolaadé*. However, this takes place without the dramatic "hierophanic" interruption that, according to Eliade, ontologically separates sacred from profane space.[9] All we see is a generic piece of rope drawn without fuss across the entrance to Collé's home. It does not uniformly and unambiguously mark the threshold of the "holy"; indeed, the "holy," the *hieros* in the strict sense, does not appear. What does "appear" is a sacred space that can be permeated by the profane and yet retains its distinctness, emanating an inviolable, but not invariable, otherness.

Despite Sembène's resolutely deflationary representation of sacred space, his depiction of *moolaadé* nonetheless meets the most crucial of Eliade's criterial distinctions: it "introduces and is characterized by spatial variation and heterogeneity whereas profane space remains homogeneous and undifferentiated."[10] Just as messianic and revolutionary time interrupt homogeneous, empty time,[11] sacred space interrupts homogeneous, undifferentiated space. Its heterogeneity is constitutive of its power, not only to demarcate itself from profane space, but all the more importantly, to reorder space and to alter the relation between existing spaces. This is how a newly invoked sacred space becomes "the fixed point, the central axis for all future orientation."[12] Of course, Eliade is thinking of sacred space as permanently fixed in place by physically unambiguous and unchanging boundaries (e.g., temples, churches, and stone monuments); but a reordering and reorientation of space can also follow from a spontaneous, temporally discontinuous designation of sacred space.

Taking a more robustly historical and comparative approach, freed from the conceptual constraints of Eliade's rigid sacred/profane binary, subsequent scholarship presents a picture of sacred space that in just about every respect corresponds to the picture presented in *Moolaadé*.[13] A singular coincidence? Or simply a perspicuous attunement to the constitution (and diversity) of sacred space in situ? Given Sembène's geographic, cultural, and historical location, he would have found the emerging scholarly view of the sacred as politically constituted to be stating the obvious, not a serendipitous confirmation of the workings of sacred space in his film (or, indeed, in Africa).[14] The political is not anterior to the sacred; it is essential to its constitution. Rather than fixed in a particular space by some "hierophanic" event, sacred space can be mobile, set free to appear, if only temporarily, wherever it is invited or invoked.

Critics of Eliade have claimed, not altogether correctly, that power as an essential element of the sacred is entirely missing from his analysis. In a text contemporaneous with Eliade's, the philosopher of religion, Gerardus van der Leeuw, aptly described sacred space as "a centre of power" positioned in a place where "its effects become perceptible."[15] To become such a locus of power, the sacred has to settle in a space already occupied by others: the "settlement" of the sacred "is *always* a conquest."[16] But Eliade also recognized that the consecration of sacred space *always* involved "conquering and inhabiting a territory already inhabited by other human beings."[17] Indeed, the consecration of land "already inhabited by other human beings" became the performative foundation of colonial dispossession: consecration *as* dispossession.

> A territory can be made ours only by creating it anew, that is, by consecrating it. This religious behavior in respect to unknown lands continued, even in the West, down to the dawn of modern times. The

Spanish and Portuguese conquistadores, discovering and conquering territories, took possession of them in the name of Jesus Christ. The raising of the Cross was equivalent to consecrating the country, hence in some sort to a "new birth." For through Christ "old things are passed away; behold, all things are become new" (Corinthians, 5, 17). The newly discovered country was "renewed," "recreated" by the cross.[18]

The alarming moral blindness exemplified in this passage could justifiably monopolize all of one's critical attention. Not only does Eliade fail to question the use of consecration to sanctify colonial conquest and dispossession, but he also unwittingly (but not wrongly) identifies "religious behavior in respect to unknown lands" with acts of genocide. Eliade runs violence and the sacred so closely together that he more or less undercuts the claims of his critics that he failed to recognize power as an internal element of the sacred. On the contrary, he recognized it all too well. What he failed to do was to grasp the moral and political implications of that recognition. The ultimate value of this particular passage may lie less in the link Eliade makes between consecration and the violent dispossession of land than in the link he makes between consecration and a "new birth"—the creation or recreation of a territory, a space, a country. But is a genuine "new birth" even possible in a space "settled" by conquest and dispossession? For if consecrating an already occupied space is equivalent to "creating it anew," how can it be created "anew" without the freely given consent and equal participation of the "other human beings" who *already* inhabit this land? Otherwise, the "new birth" would be absorbed into yet another round of violent (re)occupation and dispossession—a still birth, not a new birth.

So how *does* one non-violently consecrate, which is to say, *recreate*, a land that was occupied by colonial conquest and dispossession? Can we even imagine what that would look like? If not, the failure of our moral imagination might be very costly. Bereft of any compelling alternative, we would not only be compelled to accept that violence and the sacred are inextricably linked; we would be rendered incapable of refuting the conclusion of René Girard's powerful and influential analysis of the sacred: "Violence is the heart and secret soul of the sacred."[19] As it happens, this is just how one of the village elders will describe the spirit of *moolaadé*. But it is by no means Sembène's own view—at least, not in *Moolaadé*. For if the anticipated telos of political and cultural struggle is not only "the demise of colonialism, but also the demise of the colonized," how can such a struggle be successfully realized without ending the cycle of violent (re)occupation and dispossession? Fanon's answer in *The Wretched of the Earth* seemed to be unequivocal: "colonialism is not a machine capable of reason, a body endowed with reason. It is naked violence and only gives in when confronted with greater violence."[20] Sartre, in his preface to *The Wretched of the Earth*, goes further still, ascribing to political violence a cleansing homeopathic power of mythic proportions: "Violence, like Achilles's spear, can heal the violence it has inflicted."²¹ By the time Sembène made *Moolaadé*, he was far less sanguine about the cleansing, "purifying" power of revolutionary political violence.

These perplexing questions converge on the more general problem most closely associated with the political thought of Hannah Arendt; namely, the problem of beginning or founding—the founding of a new political order, a new "world," a *novo ordus saeclorum*. Eliade already has such a connection in mind when he claimed that "settling in a territory is equivalent to founding a world."²² Unlike Eliade, Arendt thought deeply (if not always perspicuously) about what it means to *found* a world—politically. As *Moolaadé* intimates, such a founding may require a spatial as well as a temporal break—a break with the cycle of violent occupation and dispossession sufficiently decisive to enable the creation or recreation of a territory, a space, a nation. Of course, the concern with a new political beginning is always accompanied by the ubiquitous signs that an era is coming to an end. In the final sequence of *Moolaadé*, the chief's son informs his domineering, authoritarian father, that "the era of petty tyrants is over, forever." The end of the practice of genital cutting is intertwined with the end of an era. Together they are meant to herald the nascent end of patriarchal relations of power and domination along with the end of the post-independence politics of authoritarianism and corruption. In light of the bitter history of post-independence Africa, Sembène would have certainly agreed with Arendt that "freedom would not be the automatic result of liberation, that the end of the old is not necessarily the beginning of the new."²³

Whether he did so explicitly or intuitively, I believe Sembène was grappling with these questions in *Moolaadé* from inception to completion. The film does not fully speak to us unless we notice just how much these very questions structure the film, how much they shape each and every scene in the film, directly and indirectly. Of course, Sembène's answers to these questions are not final, nor can they be, but they are extremely suggestive, and, at the same time, layered with caution. The contrast he draws between two traditions of the sacred is certainly compelling, not least because he does not present his preferred tradition cleansed of its potential for violence—if only as a standing threat. Appearances to the contrary, Sembène does not end *Moolaadé* on a note of unambiguous triumph. There is a victory at the end, but it is partial, at once joyfully celebrated and soberly qualified. From the time *moolaadé* is invoked to the time it is revoked, a man is murdered for challenging the patriarchal norms of the village; two children commit suicide rather than submit to "purification"; and another child, tricked into leaving the protective sanctuary of *moolaadé* by her own mother, dies from "purification."

Sembène is most certainly not the Frank Capra of African cinema—but neither is he its Gandhi, nor, for that matter, its Fanon. Not quite.

He is looking for some way to negotiate the difficult political space between Gandhi at his most pacifist and Fanon at his most militant, each of whom represent philosophically and politically divergent pathways to decolonization. If the goal of decolonization is the mutual demise of colonialism and of the colonized, which pathway is the right one? We may infer Sembène's answer to that question by treating the single pathway into the village of Djerisso as a symbol of the misleading and dangerous thought that there is but *one* right pathway to decolonization. He would have surely agreed with Stuart Hall that there can be no "Bible of decolonization" for a people unquestioningly to follow.[24] Whichever pathway is identified as *the* single, correct pathway will create its own path-specific version of enclosedness—be it back-to-our-roots "negritude," Western-style modernization, or violent insurrection in the name of a sectarian religious or ethnonationalist identity.

Veering toward Gandhi, Sembène's film eschews Fanon's prescriptive violence, but retains his diagnosis of the perduring effects of violence on the colonized. When it comes to the choice between Gandhi and Fanon, Sembène does end up picking a side by virtue of *where* he chooses to settle *moolaadé* in the film. That it is settled in the gendered space of care, making the significance of care for the other subversively and explicitly political, is extremely telling, to say the least. The "occupation" of the Bathily home amplifies and enlarges the practice of care for the other, and, by implication, care for the world (in Arendt's expansive sense). Unlike the use of consecration by the conquistadores, *moolaadé* is not made an instrument of violent occupation or of violent insurrection. It is *called* into an already occupied space to provide refuge and sanctuary, and it settles there quietly, undramatically, without conquest and dispossession. Called forth by an ordinary woman, herself called upon by a group of desperate, helpless children, *moolaadé* is as inherently resistant to instrumentalization as it is constitutionally disposed to align itself with the work of care.

Once settled into the Bathily home, *moolaadé* redefines that space, "creating it anew," giving the work of care a new meaning for those whose work it is. The women of the Bathily home, in whose hands *moolaadé* is placed, soon realize that *moolaadé* requires its own kind of care, requiring them to become custodians of its law, ensuring it is consistently observed and respected. In caring for *moolaadé*, however, they also discover the political meaning of care, extending it well beyond the domestic space into which it has been segregated and by which it has been depoliticized. Their care work becomes politically salient as it becomes an expression of their political agency. Conversely, Collé's invocation of *moolaadé* binds her to an irrevocable commitment to remain true to its spirit, its *ethos*, one might say—a commitment neither to exploit nor to desecrate its space, and to protect the children in her care at any cost. She is supported to uphold this commitment by the women in the Bathily home, and, increasingly, by the other women in the village, turning that commitment into the basis of a newly binding solidarity among the women of the village.

Spacing Refuge and Resistance

Once *moolaadé* inhabits the domestic space of the Bathily home, it becomes the "central axis" around which all other spaces in the village now turn. As the locus of power in the village has shifted, the central actors entangled in the ensuing crisis of authority and legitimacy must confront the sudden reorientation of spatial relationships and the correlative alteration of power relationships. Apprised of the whereabouts of the missing girls, the *Salindana* are the first implicitly to acknowledge this change, grudgingly, resentfully. Seeking an audience with Collé, they arrive indignant and angry at the doorway to the Bathily compound, but maintain a cautious distance from the sacred threshold, wary of provoking the punitive spirit of *moolaadé*. They wish to reassert their authority, but they first have to contend with Collé, now the designated steward of this disruptive new center of power.

As Collé comes out to greet the *Salindana* at the entrance to her home, Hadjatou, the senior wife, arms her with a machete—conspicuously, an instrument for cutting, and a symbol of the putatively avenging power of *moolaadé*. Wielding a staff around which is coiled a silver two-headed snake, the leader of the *Salindana* rebukes Collé for thwarting the purification of the young girls and then reminds her just who it was that purified her and many other mothers in the village. To which Collé replies, "Truth be told you cut me and stitched me up twice. *Twice*. And you also buried my [first] two children. These [young girls] requested protection, and they'll get it." Tracing the line of the rope with her machete and then pointing it directly at the *Salindana*, Collé warns, "Anyone who crosses this rope will be punished by *moolaadé*." The *Salindana* retreat but not before their leader issues a warning of her own: "Collé, you are too subversive. I will have to neutralize your powers." Undaunted, waving her machete high in the air, Collé, leads a joyful celebratory dance of the women and children. The unexpected entrance of her visibly irate brother-in-law, returning from the fields to a village dramatically different from the one he left in the morning, brings the celebration to an abrupt end. Collé will not show such deference to any man when at the end of the film she again leads the women of the village in a much larger and much more emphatic celebratory dance.

Caught up in this tension-filled confrontation, we may not have noticed that the *Salindana*'s striking red coral robes with brown and yellow trim are composed of the very same colors as the braided rope marking the threshold of *moolaadé*. Doubtless, Sembène wanted to use the subtle interplay of matching colors to show both the proximity and distance between these discordant ideas of the sacred: an ordinary piece of rope humbly representing one idea of the sacred, pontifical robes worn with an imperious air, representing another. The distance between them is magnified yet further by the thin streak of silver on the *Salindana*'s robes, symbolizing their status and power. It is a contrast which Sembène develops systematically throughout the film, for it is not just a matter of discordant ideas of the sacred confronting one another; the meaning of the sacred as such is at stake. All of this is foreshadowed rather enigmatically in a prior scene, an offhand conversation between Collé and the child refugees. She learns that they ran to *her* for help because of Collé's refusal to let the *Salindana* cut Amsatou, thereby incurring the disapprobation of the villagers and the stigmatization of Amsatou as a *bilakoro*—an "impure" woman, unsuitable for marriage. At which point, without further comment or explanation, Collé tells them: "You should know that purification [*salinde*] is one thing; and *moolaadé* is a different thing."

In that moment, so very early in the film, it is not immediately evident how to parse the meaning of Collé's words. It is a puzzling distinction, without a clearly discernible purpose. Given the casual context in which it is inconspicuously stated, it would be all too easy to miss or dismiss its significance. Certainly, it comes across as a very odd thing to say, especially to these four still very shaken young girls, prompting the thought that perhaps it is not actually intended for their ears. To make sense of it, we must recognize that Collé's remark belongs to an altogether different conversation, addressed to an altogether different interlocutor. Not the conversation that Collé is having with these young girls, who are in no position to decipher its oracular expression; but rather, the meta-conversation Sembène is having with his principal addressees—his fellow Africans. The distinction Collé draws can now serve as a useful interpretive frame for making sense of the film as a whole; namely, as staging a confrontation between two inherited African traditions, and the competing ideas of the sacred internal to them. It then becomes transparently clear that Sembène is deploying this distinction to ground an argument whose goal is to initiate a process of collective self-reflection. One can imagine him putting it this way: "I know you can all see that *moolaadé* and purification represent different and separate traditions. Of course, they are both *our* traditions. But one of them is no longer worthy of our allegiance. Hear me out, and I will show you, why." Alongside this argument over which African traditions should be renewed and which abandoned, Sembène is staging another; a more oblique and more demanding argument over the very meaning of the sacred, for the traditions in question also claim a sacred status, appealing to altogether incompatible ideas of the sacred and its normative status in human life. The last thing we should suppose Sembène to be arguing is that the sacred has *no* place in human life, whether in Africa or anywhere else. The question of the sacred and its place in human life gives the film its name, and it is posed and reposed again and again in different ways in almost every scene.

In two scenes that immediately follow Collé's conversation with the girls—the confrontation with the *Salindana* at her home, and, subsequently, the scene in which we see the *Salindana* in theirs—Sembène develops his case through a succession of explicit contrasts. Licking their wounds after their unsuccessful attempt to retake the runaways from Collé, the *Salindana* return to their own "sacred space." Diligently consistent, Sembène's camera does not let us see where or how they enter it; they are already moving in that space when the scene begins. What we do see is a joyless space, bereft of life. The young girls awaiting "purification" appear thoroughly enervated, their bodies limp, devoid of the liveliness of youth, as though condemned to an inexplicable and indefinite detention. As the *Salindana* make their way through their idyllic grove, they seem just as enervated as the young girls. Their solemn faces have turned sullen, their mood overtaken by a foreboding loss of power and status—the aura of *their* "sacred" has been pierced, cut open, one might say, and left visibly exposed. They can no longer shield themselves from the thought, the fear, that their sacred space of "purification" cannot survive contact with other spaces—cannot survive, that is, *as* a sacred space. As the film unfolds, we witness the gradual disenchantment of this idea of the sacred, exposed not only by a materialist critique of the sacred, which Sembène clearly intends, but also by a series of confrontations with an altogether different idea of the sacred.

Simmering with anger and unnerved by the sudden reversals of the spatialized power relationships in the village, the *Salindana* take their places on their shrine-like dais, in the center of which is an ostentatious throne for their leader. The throne is positioned next to a ceremonial fire-blackened tree, on which various tokens of ritual practice hang, accented by smoke rising from burning incense, below. What we are presented here is the more familiar image of the sacred as the symbolically inflated antithesis of the ordinary and everyday. It is an image of the sacred that represents itself as a "center of power" but the power it represents differs starkly from the "power" of *moolaadé*. Most saliently, its power is *spaced* vertically, hierarchically, which is to say, undemocratically. Its power is not accessible to anyone; it is concentrated in the hands of a few upon whom the requisite status for wielding it has been conferred. For the *Salindana*, close association with this idea of the sacred and its familiar trappings gives them power—the power to cut into the bodies of young girls and young women. And it is this "sacred" power that is most directly threatened by Collé's emergence as the steward of *moolaadé*. As one of the *Salindana* indignantly complains, "She thinks her power is greater than ours. She wants us to give up our knives." In response, their leader declares, "Collé is challenging us. I will destroy her powers." But the *Salindana* completely misunderstand the threat Collé poses. The "powers" they face are not those of someone seeking to wield power as an instrument of domination and control of others. Collé is empowered by her moral commitment to *moolaadé* and the children she has sworn to protect. It should be increasingly obvious, then, that what is really at issue here is not a profane power struggle between Collé and the *Salindana*, but rather, a struggle over the very meaning of the sacred, over the source of *its* power and authority, a struggle over *whom* and *what* it should empower.

Implicitly conceding that the confrontation with *moolaadé* is draining their idea of the sacred of its symbolic power, the *Salindana* appeal to the chief and village elders at a public hearing in the village square. Collé is accused of disrespecting the sanctity of one of their revered traditions by invoking *moolaadé*. That this tradition is in conflict with *moolaadé*, another of their revered traditions, is conveniently ignored. Upon hearing that *moolaadé* has been invoked, one of the elders rises pompously from his chair and with considerable affectation points his silver embroidered staff at the structure which Sembène held from view during the camera's first sweep across the village square. Revealed finally from a dramatically acute angle directly behind the elder's outstretched staff, we finally see the bizarre grave of the first king. Over the centuries, his corpse was entombed within a red, mudbrick anthill and formed into a cone-shaped, spiky structure, no more than two meters tall. Recomposed from the detritus of organic life, the king's corpse became ideal material for the ingenious architectural activity of ants. The construction of the anthill obviously resembles the much larger, grandly built mosque directly next to it, for which it was surely the model. Its diminutive proportions notwithstanding, the anthill, much like its spiritual cousin and ally, the humble rope, possesses an outsize power to alter the political order of the village. As the elder points his staff at the anthill, he recites the story of how it came into existence in rhythmic, stentorian cadences (audible to the ear but not captured by the literal English subtitles):

> *Moolaadé!* You are in this anthill that embodies our first king. His people rebelled and he was transformed into this anthill. He had offended *moolaadé*. His rebellious subjects killed him, and after he was buried here. His swollen body transformed into this anthill. Years later our ancestors converted to Islam. To Allah they erected this mosque next to the tomb of the first king. None can transgress *moolaadé*. Its spirit is formidable. To calm its spirit, one needs to shed blood. (Figure 4.2)

The elder's story of the uncanny transformation of the king's "swollen body" into an anthill acknowledges the inviolability of *moolaadé*—not even a king can desecrate its space. By dishonoring a "law" higher than human law, the king forfeited his life. Even so, the king's sin was not entirely expiated; his corpse was subjected to an endless posthumous punishment. As the ontological and biological boundaries between human and nonhuman life broke down, blurring the categorial difference between the organic and the moral, the king's corpse decomposed into a living tombstone on

FIGURE 4.2 *Anthill*, still from Moolaadé *(dir. Ousmane Sembène, 2004)*.

which a moral lesson is inscribed. Now one could also say that the king's corpse was subjected to an equally endless posthumous atonement. In its posthumous life as an animate public monument, the king's abject corpse serves as a macabre memorialization of what befalls those who forget—or fail to acknowledge—our moral obligation to the other, an obligation which supersedes whatever secular law or sovereign power stipulates.

In traditional West African societies, when the king overreached it was the job of the *griot* to tell him, "You are over the line." A significant figure of West African social life, the *griot* performed multiple social roles—storyteller, historian, singer/musician, counselor, repository of cultural memory, and the most delicate and perilous of all these roles—the role with which Sembène himself most identified—internal social critic. Unlike the "new breed of griot," portrayed unequivocally and caustically in *Moolaadé*, "The griot was an honest eyewitness and messenger; the only one able to speak the truth and to humiliate the leader."[25] If the griot appeals to an immanent critical standard when the king has crossed "over the line," the invocation of *moolaadé* appeals to a transcendental critical standard when all immanent appeals go unheard or are denied—when, in other words, secular law does not *hold the line* against arbitrary power, oppression, and misrule. Spaces of refuge answered the need for spaces that can hold the line, which they could hold only because they were regarded as *supra legem*—above secular law and beyond the reach of sovereign power. Just what they *spaced* is captured in the literal meaning of the Greek word, *asylia*, from which asylum is derived, meaning a space in which one is *not (a) subject to seizure (sylia)*.[26] Much like asylum spaces in pre-classical Greece, *moolaadé* answers the call for an inviolable, heterogeneous space—literally, a space of otherness—where one is not subject to seizure. That call arises whenever and wherever untethered power is at liberty to cross the last remaining line protecting human beings from inhuman treatment. When no fixed space of refuge is available that space must be called forth spontaneously with equal inviolability.

The first of three crucial scenes set in the village square, manifesting the expanding spatial reach of *moolaadé's* power, the *Salindana's* appeal for help is very carefully constructed to work at multiple levels. In conformity with the patriarchal power relationships that structure the social life of the village, the *Salindana* seat themselves on the ground, while the chief and the village elders, all men, seat themselves on chairs opposite the women: to speak to the men, the women must look up from the ground. During their discussion, moderated by a fluently obsequious griot, the camera alternates between close-ups of individual speakers and medium wide shots of the women taken from behind and above the shoulders of the men. These medium wide shots of the women give us a clear view of the anthill at the back the frame, exerting its uncanny presence, as though it were bearing witness and preparing to render judgment. As though performing the role of a mute Greek chorus, this seemingly inscrutable anthill speaks without making a sound and is heard only by those willing to listen.

Despite the foreboding presence of the anthill memorializing the sin of their founding king, the elders *choose* not to listen. Tragically, this is a consequence of their alienated, intellectualized understanding of *moolaadé*, which allows them to deflect its morally binding expectations, turning them into non-moral obstacles to be overcome by instrumental reasoning. When the elder declares, "*Moolaadé!* You are in this anthill," he acknowledges its presence but not its moral claims. When he declares, "To calm its spirit, one needs to shed blood," he represents *moolaadé* as though it were an offended cult deity demanding a sacrificial offering. He therefore represents the relationship between *moolaadé* and violence in a way that overstates and at the same time misrepresents it. When the "people" rose against their king, it was because he violated the moral sanctity of *moolaadé's* space of refuge, not because the very invocation of *moolaadé* requires, ipso facto, the shedding of blood. Even the elder's professed acknowledgment of *moolaadé's* living presence in the anthill sounds superfluous and belated, for *moolaadé* has been in the anthill all along, ignored, yes, but always present, awaiting the need for which it must be called. But by this point in the story, *moolaadé* is not *only* in the anthill; nor *only* in the public space in which official political decisions are made and announced—the village square. It has *forcelessly* occupied the entire village, becoming a *centerless center of power*, paralyzing and at the same time suspending the inherited and naturalized political authority of the chief, the elders, and the *Salindana*.

As prefigured in the opening scenes, the interaction between the two principal spaces in the film—the Bathily family compound and the village square—together constitute a spatial dialectic propelling the action of the film to its resolution. Now that the spirit of *moolaadé* has fully occupied these two spaces, they operate as the two poles of an elongated magnetic field—the rope marking one pole, the anthill the other. As a consequence of *moolaadé*'s spatial elongation across the entire village, there is no longer a single axis of orientation or a single center of power. Unlike asylum spaces in pre-classical Greece and in early Christianity, *moolaadé* is not fixed to a dedicated space of refuge with which it is identified, be it a temple or church. Nor does it depend on the authority of a specific religious or spiritual institution (e.g., Delphi, the early Church) whose sacred spaces are administered by institutionally appointed officials (priests, priestesses, church officials). Therefore, to speak of *moolaadé* as a centerless center of power more precisely identifies its spontaneous mobility, its dynamism, and its agentic qualities. Speaking of it in these terms also more fully captures its radically democratic character.

Because *moolaadé* can be invoked by anyone, anywhere, anytime, it can become the vehicle through which a community, a people, expresses its democratic will—as was the case when "people rebelled" against the founding king, and as will be the case when Collé's public contestation of female "purification" turns into a collective act of political resistance led by the women of the village. While it is certainly possible for Sembène to tell such a story without *moolaadé*, it would not only be a different story; it would be bereft of all that is essential to this one. It would be missing the film's "argument" for the irreplaceable value of *moolaadé*-like spaces in a (more or less) secularized world not only to provide a space of refuge when it is everywhere else denied but also to enable a kind of democratic politics not otherwise possible. When the "people" rebelled against the founding king for violating *moolaadé*'s sacred space, they were certainly expressing their democratic resistance to untethered arbitrary power. But they were also expressing their allegiance to the *supra legem* status of *moolaadé*, to the inviolability of the *ideal* it represents, an ideal which they implicitly recognized as both a condition of their political agency and of the possibility of justice.

Although the chief and elders know they are powerless to change the sacred status of *moolaadé*, they believe they can get around it. To reassert their threatened patriarchal authority, they concoct a hubristic scheme, which, fittingly, draws on an especially hoary ancestral tradition—the "unlimited powers" of a husband over his wife. Because Collé invoked *moolaadé*, only she can revoke it. If she refuses to "utter the redemptive word," her husband's "unlimited powers" can compel her to do so by any means necessary, including violent force. Compelling her to "utter the redemptive word" is by itself, not enough, however; its performative utterance must be pronounced publicly in the village square. The scheme, unanimously endorsed, brings the hearing to an end, and we are shown the *Salindana* leaving the village square in single file, passing right by the anthill. Once again, the shot is taken from behind the seated elders, the *Salindana* and the anthill at the back of the frame. Walking as though they have already suffered defeat, their steps punctuate the slow time of a dirge. But much more than any grave doubts they may have about the scheme to restore their power and authority, what stands out is the alarming disquiet by which they are gripped as they pass by the symbolically charged plenipotentiary of *moolaadé*—as if each step bears the weight of an inescapable fate.

The scene ends with a medium close-up of the anthill; its visage, a riddle inscribed on a mask. A riddle, certainly, but not inscrutable. Sembène's deft use of dramatic irony here needn't be especially subtle. Since the elders and the *Salindana* see and hear very selectively, they can no more discern the spirit of *moolaadé* in the anthill than they can heed the voices of their ancestors. For the anthill is not only an animate public monument, reminding everyone of the founding king's fatal moral blunder; it also doubles as a "radio" through which the voices of the ancestors are transmitted, imploring their descendants not to repeat the same tragic mistake—in this instance, to no avail. The condition of enclosedness can make one as unreceptive to (dissident) voices speaking from inside one's own traditions as to voices challenging them from afar (Figure 4.3).

The very brief scene that follows, coda-like, trades the anthill's metaphorical mask for real masks, which, no less metaphorically, raise the confrontation between the competing ideas of the sacred to another level. The significance of the scene turns on the absolutely terrified response of the runaway children to the sudden appearance of the *Salindana* at the entrance to the Bathily home. When the children look up from the ground where they are sitting, it is not enrobed women with stern, resentful faces that they see; what they see—as benign daylight is precipitously usurped by malignant night—is an *apparition*: demonic spirits wearing intimidating ceremonial

FIGURE 4.3 *Mosque, anthill, radios, still from* Moolaadé *(dir. Ousmane Sembène, 2004).*

masks, moving toward them with threatening demeanor, as though they are about to reach across the threshold and *seize* them. Their cry of help is quickly answered by Collé, who confronts the hostile stares of the *Salindana* in a resolute martial stance, machete in hand, flanked by Hadjatou and Alima. This time the confrontation between them is wordless and terse, resulting in another retreat by the *Salindana*.

On this occasion, their confrontation is not about an empowered Collé facing down the *Salindana* once again; it is about the *face* of the sacred that appears in the fear-induced hallucination of young girls. The faces of the *Salindana* are turned into masks of terror, which, in turn, *unmask* this manifestation of the sacred, exposing the face of a menacing, malevolent power. As Collé remarks to Hadjatou after the *Salindana* retreat, "They are like vultures that smell blood"—the blood of children. Recall what the pompous, hypocritical elder said about *moolaadé*—to calm its spirit, "one needs to shed blood." And yet with this very brief scene, Sembène turns the question back on the elders and the *Salindana*: Just *who* needs to shed blood, here? And who believes it is a sacred right?

Does an idea of the sacred that produces terror in the hearts of our children, that inflicts violence on them, that violates them body and soul, deserve our reverence or allegiance?

Sembène presses the question of the sacred yet further, not only to expose the violence inherent in a particular idea of the sacred, but also to pose the question of whether *moolaadé*—or any "sacred space"—can find a place, can even be *spaced*, in a secular, presumably, desacralized age. If so, *how* should it be spaced, and *where*? I take *Moolaadé*, the film and the practice, to represent Sembène's answer to these questions—an answer which might be as contentious and contestable as the conclusion of Girard's *Violence and the Sacred*.

Rebirth: Decolonizing Violence and the Sacred

Less contentious and contestable, perhaps, is Fanon's claim that colonialism speaks in "a language of pure violence,"[27] creating a ubiquitous "atmosphere of violence" that sets the conditions under which the colonized respond to the world—cognitively, emotionally, physiologically.[28] Regarded from this Fanonian perspective, it is by no means surprising that an increasingly palpable "atmosphere of violence" permeates the misleadingly pastoral setting of *Moolaadé*. It is an "atmosphere" not only conducive to perpetuating colonial violence; it is also conducive to perpetuating the violence that inheres in precolonial traditions and practices. After all, they speak the same language. Sembène's film reframes the violence of female "purification" as an inseparable part of colonialism's bequest, thereby obliging us to see it in a new way—as a form of violent subjection continuous with the violence of colonial subjection. That continuity is not to be grasped as a linear causal sequence; it is to be grasped genealogically as a meaning-altering, historical experience. No practice, let alone female genital cutting, can preserve a pristinely independent precolonial meaning. The violence inherent in precolonial practices that were once shielded from challenge is as exposed as any of the practices and policies of colonialism. Indeed, on my reading of *Moolaadé*, Sembène turns genital cutting into a metaphor for colonial violence and subjugation.[29]

Reverberating in the trauma of "purification" is the larger trauma of colonization. Sembène's film perspicuously illuminates how "purification" sustains colonialism's "atmospheric violence"—sustains it by inscribing its idea of the sacred directly on the bodies of young girls, simultaneously obscuring and mystifying the violence latent within it. The quotidian iteration of this "atmosphere" is conveyed in a particularly visceral way in a parallel sequence, composed of three brief scenes, one of which we have seen before. The first is of a terrified young girl undergoing "purification," screaming, unbearably, in fear and in pain, tears flooding her face. The second is of the threatening ceremonial masks hallucinated by the young girls, revealing once more the violent face of its idea of the sacred. The third and longest is of Ciré Bathily engaging in rough, manifestly punitive, sexual intercourse with Collé, insensible to her obvious pain and the trauma of her own woundedness. Sembène's editing makes it hard for the viewer to regard Bathily's sexual act as an isolated example of merely symbolic violence—and not only because Collé must wash out from the bedsheets the blood she shed during intercourse. Sembène places all three parts of the sequence at the same semantic level, creating the appropriate context in which to grasp how everyday acts of violence "hide" below the surface of ethical perception *in virtue* of their mundane, commonplace reality. Although we do not yet know that Ciré Bathily will whip his wife viciously in the village square, the violence with which she is assaulted there differs only in intensity from the many everyday violations of women that constitute a diurnal transglobal regime of violence.

The second crucial scene in the village square involves an intensification and amplification of the spatial dialectic between the domestic space of the Bathily home and the public space of the village square. This dialectical interplay is set off at the end of the previous scene in the Bathily home, when Ciré finally succumbs to the relentless pressure of his belligerently misogynistic older brother to put Collé in her place: the stability of the patriarchal order must be restored. While a member of the *Salindana* escorts Collé out of *moolaadé*'s protective space to face the elders in the village square, her husband, whip in hand, follows closely behind. To the shocked disappointment of the elders and the *Salindana*, the patriarchal order is not restored; the spatial relationships are not turned right side up. Collé, as expected, refuses to submit to her husband's demand to publicly revoke *moolaadé*. Incited by his own anger and by the exhortations of the men and the *Salindana*—"Tame her! Break her!"—he begins to whip Collé with furious energy. But he is taken aback by the power of Collé's unyielding resistance. Tears appear on his face. He knows that he is doing something unforgivably wrong to a woman whom he loves. But he does not stop; he persists through his tears, striking her even harder, demanding again and again that she "Say it! Say it!" But Collé does *not* say it; she does not utter the "redemptive word." She does not utter any word. Collé will endure her husband's blows, silently; but her silent resistance, like the anthill's silent judgment, speaks in its own way. The elders, listening only for what they expected to hear, are stupefied by the disastrous outcome of their hubristic plan. "She did not say the word!" "After all this beating . . . not a word." "Unprecedented!" "What a failure!" Since they do not understand themselves as addressees of *moolaadé*, and therefore as *answerable* to its claims, they are insensible to the distinctly moral language in which it speaks. Not coincidentally, those who do understand themselves as *moolaadé's* addressees, *talk back to power*. Collé's muted heroism not only exposes the cowardice and hypocrisy of the elders; it also exposes the limits of their inherited patriarchal power.

During this very disturbing scene, we see the whip strike Collé's body only a few times. The camera dwells on her face, her husband's face, and the faces of the villagers. The only access we have to Collé's pain is through the expression on her face and the faces of the village women, themselves visibly pained by her public humiliation and the violence inflicted on her body. Pained also because of their shame and guilt for allowing the *Salindana* and the elders to turn Collé into the "the sacrificial lamb" of the village. Sembène's camera picks out one other face in the crowd, the outsider, Mercenaire. Since his arrival, he has been a mostly silent witness to the events in the village square. But now, claiming he is no longer able to "bear the violence" being inflicted on Collé, Mercenaire pushes his way through the crowd, rips the whip out of Ciré's hand and knocks down Ciré's unhinged older brother. For this violation of traditional patriarchal norms, the elders demand that the villagers take hold of "this motherfucker" and "make him disappear!"—which they do, come the night, in an act of ritualized murder.

Sembène went out of his way to offer a many-sided portrait of Mercenaire, one which corresponds to his polysemic name. Aside from Collé, he is the most important character in the film. No one else in the film is given such an elaborate backstory. There is a reason the film begins as he is approaching the village. Where exactly is he coming from? From another village? No doubt.

But we could also say that he is coming from a possible African future, the harbinger of a secular African modernity. When the children cheer his arrival with cries of, "Mercenaire is here! Mercenaire is here!," they could just as well be crying out, "Modernity is here! Modernity is here!" Sembène figures this complicated and internally divided character as a synecdoche for the contradictory and destructive tendencies of a "modernizing" Africa in the grip of neocolonial forms of globalization. From his conversations with the chief's son, we learn that for many years he served as a UN peacekeeper, until he was wrongly imprisoned for challenging the corrupt salary practices of senior officers. Ironically, he was given the name "Mercenaire" by the media, whose reporting sided with the senior officers rather than with the low-ranking soldier. He comes across as someone who is clearly contemptuous of Africa's moral and political "backwardness," impatient to see it become fully modern and secular—like Europe. He also comes across as morally inconsistent, if not morally incoherent, and, as shamelessly opportunistic—mercenary, you might say. He happily recites the homilies of capitalist globalization when his extremely inflated prices are questioned; he fondles with joy new bank notes from France and chides a poor villager for scrunching old bank notes into a pouch: "You must not torture bank notes like that!" He can brazenly flirt with the village women, obnoxiously hitting on each one that comes to his stall, and, without hesitation, angrily accuse the men of the village of being "pedophiles" because they won't abandon the custom of betrothing prepubescent girls to grown men. For all of his pronounced moral contradictions, Mercenaire is nonetheless prepared to stand up for his rights and the rights of others. How he does so, however, only intensifies those contradictions.

Doubtless, Sembène intended Mercenaire's ambiguously successful effort to stop the flogging as a critical comment on the interventions of the international human rights regime in Africa. That is why we were given his background as a UN peacekeeper. But that is not all we are invited to think about here. The flogging scene in the village square is also meant to initiate critical reflection on the difference between Collé's quiet "everyday heroism" and the louder, attention-grabbing heroism, with which Mercenaire brings this scene to an end, and, inadvertently, his life. The contrast Sembène draws is deliberately gendered. Mercenaire's self-aggrandizing heroism is unequivocally masculinist and soloistic. It does not lack courage, but it does lack sensitivity to context, which comes as no surprise, given Mercenaire's demonstrated contempt for the cultural context. While Mercenaire's intervention does bring the flogging to an end, rather late, since Collé is on the verge of collapsing from the blows, it fails to generate social solidarity and collective resistance. It is an isolated act performed in a masculinist register, however well intentioned. By contrast, Collé's courage is expressed altogether differently. Her stand is not soloistic; it is normatively and performatively *relational*—she is standing *for* the children placed in her care and standing *with* the women in the village who do the work of care—all of whom are thereby moved to stand with her. The stance she takes is not about her anymore than it is about the pain she can heroically withstand; it is about keeping faith with the moral obligations of *moolaadé*, a faith which is emphatically expressed in the final scene of the film as an affirmation of natality and the future.

Over and over again, Sembène has shown us the women of the village engaged in diverse self-decentering practices of care—caring for things, for others, and for the earth. The men, by contrast, appear not to care for the *work* of caring. The chief and the elders lead lives of conspicuous leisure. The other men in the village keep busy working the fields, pursuing their commercial interests, controlling their wives and daughters, and demonstratively displaying their piety. This striking contrast draws our attention to the apparently gendered disconnect between those who respond to the moral claims of *moolaadé* and those who do not: only those who undertake the work of care comprehend the call of *moolaadé*; only they understand what they are called to do. We are thereby drawn to infer that the inability of the village elders to hear the *call* of *moolaadé* is due to their disconnect from the practices of care. For almost without exception, only women understand themselves as its moral addressees—as called by *moolaadé*, and as answerable to it. That this disconnect from practices of care is a consequence of patriarchal and toxic forms of masculinity is strongly suggested by none other than Ciré Bathily, who comes to the belated realization that it "takes more than a pair of balls to make a man." This rather ambiguous premise underdetermines whatever it is that does or should make a "man." However, the implication underlying the denunciation Sembène puts in Bathily's mouth, is unavoidable: so long as our idea of what *makes* a "man" excludes or trivializes caring for things, others, and the earth, it will be thoroughly vacuous and unavoidably (self)destructive in practice.

Even with all the multiple connections Sembène develops between *moolaadé* and care, the threat of violence evidently required to motivate compliance with *moolaadé's* moral demands remains necessarily in force. Thus, the more the non-violent "face" of *moolaadé* appears to be its true face, the more it seems to be a practice in contradiction with itself. One way to resolve the troubling tension between its violence-resisting aspect and its violence-threatening aspect, is to regard the latter as the expression of a "legalistic" understanding of *moolaadé* that requires the coercive force of law. To disobey or disrespect these demands is to invite punishment and retribution. Sembène does not underplay or soften this understanding of *moolaadé*; on the contrary, he takes every opportunity to exhibit how much this understanding of *moolaadé* remains attached to the threat of violence. But Sembène also actively subverts this understanding of *moolaadé*, sometimes to the point of reducing it to a folk superstition, even to empty bluster. (The scene of the elder revealing the presence of *moolaadé* in the anthill borders on comic caricature.) Observed closely, it is not the threat of punishment or retribution that moved Collé to keep faith with her moral commitments to *moolaadé*. She took herself to be responding to an unconditional moral "ought," not to a threat, making her conduct throughout the film consistent with this understanding of her moral situation. Collé bears the moral burden of *moolaadé* not as an alien imposition but as rightly hers to bear, whatever the circumstances by which it became hers to bear; and she leaves no doubt that she experiences the bearing of it as the direct expression of her moral and political agency.

Sembène's moral attitude toward the violence that inheres in precolonial traditions and practices is equally consistent and unwavering—and that includes his attitude toward *moolaadé*. I have the impression that the various threats issued in its name are meant less to convey *moolaadé*'s awesome punitive power than to expose and, ultimately, to expel the precolonial residues of violence that adhere to it. Without making it explicit, Sembène wants us to notice that both "purification" and *moolaadé* are practices that are either sustained by or associated with the shedding of blood. As morally exemplary as Collé may be, no one issues more threats in the name of *moolaadé* than she. Sembène resolves this unignorable contradiction by treating as *transitional* the legalistic, retributive interpretation of *moolaadé* Collé inherits—transitional to a transformed understanding of *moolaadé* that renounces the threat of punitive violence and relinquishes the *need* of it. She outgrows and overcomes this inherited understanding *as* she expresses a new, empowering understanding of her own moral and political agency. That this transformation was enabled by her invocation of *moolaadé* is not all that we are meant to notice. If I am reading Sembène's intentions correctly—and if not his intentions, his intuitions—we are *also* meant to notice how *moolaadé* itself undergoes a transformation. Call it a decolonizing transformation made possible through its "occupation" of the space of care. The forceless occupation of the Bathily home is reciprocated by an equally forceless occupation of *moolaadé* by the women of the Bathily home: they not only act as the custodians of *moolaadé*, they also actively alter its identity, working with and against the violent, coercive form of its law. Its space of refuge is literally occupied and redefined by the work of care, through which *moolaadé* undergoes its own "new birth," shedding the threat of retributive violence, and its "need" of blood.

In his final film, Sembène is not reaching into the African past *only* to retrieve a revered but mostly forgotten tradition nor *only* to initiate a resurgence of precolonial African traditions. His reinterpretation of *moolaadé* creatively renews *and* profoundly transforms its identity and practice. I am here supposing that Sembène understood that *moolaadé* could not be retrieved in some pure precolonial form, untainted by the legacies of colonialism. Decolonization means many things, not least, a commitment to acknowledge and overcome the legacies of colonial violence and oppression; but to be internally consistent with itself, it must *also* mean a scrupulously critical analysis of the violence that also inheres or adheres to precolonial cultural traditions and social practices, no matter their provenance nor the reverence in which they are held. Bringing about the "demise of colonialism and the demise of the colonized" once and for all is inseparable from bringing about the demise of colonial *and* precolonial violence in its many forms, especially violence against women in the name of "sacred" practices or traditions. Sembène's reinterpretation of *moolaadé* subtly and compellingly induces the thought that decolonization not only requires an end to the violent legacies of colonialism but also requires an end to the "the atmosphere of violence" that *outlives* colonialism.

With the nocturnal execution of Mercenaire at the outskirts of the village, the film comes to an end in order to begin again—or rather, to instance its idea of beginning anew. Unable to outrun a murderous gang of egregiously pious men whose painted faces ritualize and sanctify the murder they commit, we see Mercenaire for the last time at the very spot where he first appeared. The spatial symmetry of Mercenaire's appearance and disappearance functions as a striking temporal disjuncture in the narrative: a story with an inescapable fate comes to an end as another story with an indeterminate future begins. Apropos, the open-ended final sequence of *Moolaadé* begins the very next morning. Against a pale blue sky, we are shown vultures circling around the remains of Mercenaire's corpse. A gruesome allusion to the murder the night before, to be sure, and yet, there seems to be something different about this morning. Given the location, precisely at the most prominently featured border of the village, it somehow portends a rupture in the condition of enclosedness and a momentous shift in the "atmosphere."

The expectant mood is maintained when the camera enters the Bathily home, where Collé's fellow wives are dressing her wounds. She hears for the first time of Mercenaire's murder and of Diatou's death by "purification," and is moved to call off *moolaadé*. Its job done, *moolaadé* is ended as it was begun, without fuss or ceremony. But when Alima goes out to untie the rope on Collé's behalf, she unties only one end of the rope. She then reties that end vertically up one side of the walled entrance as if to indicate that this space is not "entirely desacralized," that it remains under the sign of the sacred. Although *moolaadé* is publicly ended, it still occupies the Bathily home, reaching irrepressibly outward to encompass both the private and public spaces of the village. This humble rope, tied physically to the wall of the Bathily home and spiritually to the anthill in the village square, is now one more public reminder of *moolaadé's* abiding presence—a reminder that its unruly and sheltering space of refuge can always be spaced again, whenever and wherever it is called by someone in need.

A gathering in the Bathily courtyard later that morning reunites the surviving internal refugees with their mothers. The young lives lost are painfully remembered and mourned. Salba, Diatou's mother, utterly broken by unbearable loss and guilt, is inconsolable. *Astonishingly, no one is reproached; no one is blamed.* Instead, we witness an extraordinary act of generosity that culminates in an equally extraordinary act of consecration— *consecration as rebirth.* The spatial dialectic of the film still in play, the former act takes place in the domestic space of the Bathily home, the latter in the public space of the village square. It all begins when one of the mothers *gifts* her own newborn daughter to the inconsolable Salba, "Here . . . have her for life." The camera then cuts abruptly to a shot of men exiting the mosque after prayer service. Among them, perpetrators of Mercenaire's murder. As they exit the mosque, the chief and the elders enter the village square to take their appointed seats. One of the murderers sets aflame the radios piled directly in front of the mosque (Sembène, obviously referencing the book burning rituals of Nazi Germany). At this very moment, Salba enters the village square, leading a procession of women from the Bathily home. Holding her "reborn" daughter high over her head, and looking directly at the chief and the elders, she declares in a steadfast voice, "This one will not be cut!" Hadjatou and Collé on either side of her, just as steadfastly declare, "No girl will ever be cut!" With this passionate performative utterance, the women (re)consecrate the space of the village, reclaiming it, not in the name of a nation or religion but in the name of *natality*. Call this act "miraculous" in Arendt's sense, for *this* consecration of a space "already occupied by others" arises neither from vengeance nor from conquest: it performs a *nonviolent* new beginning.[30] If Arendt is right, the "actualisation of the human condition of natality"[31] is the actualization of freedom *as* beginning. But I would add that any creation of a new worldly space of freedom *also* aspires to the condition of sacred space, however transient and "improbable" its spacing. Now that would entail thinking of the sacred, counterintuitively, as essential to the creation of new spaces of freedom and new relations of freedom. I will return to this thought, but for the moment, I want to suggest that this is just how we should understand Sembène's (unclarified) claim that *Moolaadé* is "not about genital cutting," but "about freedom."[32]

As the final crucial scene in the village square unfolds, the chief and village elders discover that the new day does not mark a return to business as usual. More women enter the square, only to discover that their precious radios are ablaze. By this further act of violence, cutting women off from the world beyond the village, they are reminded of the events of the previous day, prompting one of them bluntly to remark, "Some give birth, others kill." That this particular day is marked for birth and rebirth is given further substance by the scathing response of the women to the entrance of the *Salindana*: "Here come the child killers." Their "sacred" power now completely disenchanted, and their authority publicly mocked, the *Salindana* are forced to relinquish their knives. When their leader drops her "sacred" staff on the ground, one of the women promptly steps on it as if she were stepping on a cockroach. The knives are collected and displayed before the disbelieving elders, whom Collé now confronts not as someone subject to their patriarchal authority but as a political agent asserting her own change-making power. A close-up shot of the anthill precedes her address to the elders, smoke from the burning radios seeping through it. "You have already burned our radios, but if you lay a hand on me, I, Collé Ardo, will set the village on fire and drown it in blood."

On this occasion, for the very first time, Collé threatens violence not in the name of *moolaadé* but in propria persona. She is of course speaking in the masculinist language of the elders to emphatically declare that she will no longer participate in her own subjection, nor resist, mutely. But does her defiant declaration require the threat of retributive violence? Given the previous scene in the Bathily home signaling if not promising a potential change in the "atmosphere of violence," Collé's threat is strikingly dissonant. If the possibility of a future different from the past depends on the kind of non-violent new beginning instanced there, is it not also the case that the "atmosphere of violence" that has outlived colonialism will require many successive and concurrent new beginnings before it can bring about its "demise"? While Sembène's *Moolaadé* has not veered completely to the side of Gandhi, its weight leans very heavily in that direction. And yet it retains Fanon's deep understanding of the tenacious "atmosphere of violence" bequeathed by the colonial system.

For now, there are only small victories to celebrate. After refuting the elders flawed, self-serving understanding of Islam, by referring them to the Grand Imam's proclamation on the radio that genital cutting is absolutely not required by Islam, Collé leads the women of the village in a triumphal dance around the burning pyre of radios, chanting "Wassa! Wassa!" ("Freedom! Freedom!"). As the women celebrate, the camera follows into the air the plumes of noxious black smoke rising from the pyre, arriving at a close-up of an ostrich egg that sits atop the highest spire of the mosque. The arrival seems to indicate a kind of finality, as though the camera's movement has arrived at its goal. But that feeling of finality is quickly dissipated by a further movement of the camera as it settles inexplicably on a close-up of a television antenna. These are the two final images of the film. The ostrich egg, whose significance was foreshadowed in an earlier scene, is a common sight atop mosques across the African Sahel (most famously, the Djenne in Mali). Following centuries-long practice that precedes Islam, Sembène positions the ostrich egg "as a visual signifier of sacred space"[33]—positions it not only over the reconsecrated village square but also over his own film, signifying it as a space of refuge and freedom for reflectively reimagining the world other than it is (Figure 4.4).

The image of the pedestrian antenna appears out of nowhere. It is not prepared by anything that preceded it. There are no television antennas

FIGURE 4.4 *Ostrich egg, still from* Moolaadé *(dir. Ousmane Sembène, 2004).*

FIGURE 4.5 *Antenna, still from* Moolaadé *(dir. Ousmane Sembène, 2004).*

sitting atop any house in the village, making the appearance of this phantom antenna at the very end of the film even more peculiar—uncanny, one might say. Because it appears unexpectedly, without any legible connection to the semantically rich, aesthetically pleasing ostrich egg, the close-up of the antenna enigmatically complicates the ending of the film, placing a question mark over it. We would be mistaken to think that Sembène chose to end his politically sophisticated fable simplistically with something meant to signify the "liberating" effects of modern technology. Once again, Sembène is asking us to look more discerningly, asking us to see something more in yet another very ordinary object on which his camera lingers. Discerning the symbolic significance of the antenna is literally a matter of seeing it for what it is and what it does: it is an apparatus of *receptivity*; it *receives*. We would therefore not be mistaken to think of this ordinary antenna as a parable condensed into a single image: When we are unable to receive the "frequencies" of others, and, indeed, the very otherness of the world, we are unable to disclose our world anew—we remain enclosed (Figure 4.5).

Heterotopias of the Sacred and the Ideal

Sembène's film is a gift of sorts, too, illuminating how sacred spaces can create passageways between our current normative order and a better one. Even though it is not yet founded, the better one is not beyond our reach; for it does not lie entirely in a future "to come," it has already been spaced—here. In a prescient 1967 publication, Michel Foucault claimed that, contrary to our secular assumptions, "contemporary space is perhaps not yet entirely desacralized."[34] This was particularly true of *heterotopias*—heterogeneous spaces that functioned as "actually realized utopias," occupying a space that was "outside all places," even though they could be located in an actual place.[35] Uncannily, Foucault's description of the effects of heterotopias on adjacent and surrounding spaces applies without qualification to *moolaadé*: heterotopias *are* "connected to all the other [spaces], but in such a way that they suspend, neutralize, or reverse the set of relations that are designated, reflected, or represented by them."[36]

The constant feature of Foucault's historical and contemporary examples of heterotopic spaces is the residue of the sacred they preserve, and on which, by implication, their heterogeneity depends. Given Foucault's definition of heterotopia, heterotopic spaces are virtually synonymous with sacred spaces. One could safely assume that Foucault would have recognized *moolaadé* as an exemplary and remarkable instance of a heterotopia. However, other than to claim that heterotopias are "animated by a silent or hidden sacralization"[37] Foucault, regrettably, does not offer an account of the sacred that could explain its persistence across centuries of ongoing desacralization. In spite of its uncanny congruence with Sembène's recreation of *moolaadé*, Foucault's intriguing characterization of heterotopias is unable to elucidate how heterotopic space, sacred space, can be *animate*—a catalyst of normative change that is at the same time a medium for collective democratic action. These questions were simply not on Foucault's mind, which at that time was preoccupied with epistemological questions in relation to the history of regimes of knowledge. More importantly, the kind of heterotopic spaces which Foucault singled out—notably, the institutional spaces on which some of his most influential research focused—for example, prisons, hospitals, museums, libraries—are generally fixed and inert spaces, self-enclosed spaces that do not possess the boundary-blurring dynamism and transgressive agency of *moolaadé*.

The questions that Foucault failed to address in his promising essay on space were the very questions that concerned Emile Durkheim in his final work, *The Elementary Forms of Religious Life*.[38] The sacred was precisely what Durkheim wanted to understand and explain, not as an account of religion and secularization, but as an account of the constitution of new bonds of sociality and new social institutions through "extraordinary, collective expressive action."[39] It is precisely this moment of founding a new normative order that Durkheim called the sacred. The sacred is not something that originates in the distant past, becoming an incongruous residue of some withering and soiled tradition; nor is it something which mature societies eventually outgrow through processes of rational "enlightenment." The sacred in this very different sense must be recreated anew in response to new historical conditions and challenges. Thus, whatever we call the sacred "is inherently impermanent and so must be added to the object again and again, just as it was originally."[40] Which leads to a suprirsng conclusion: *the sacred cannot be desacralized in principle.* If the possibility of new forms of freedom, new forms of sociality, and new social structures depends upon the successful rearticulation and re-embodiment of the sacred, then there can be no final and permanent desacralization of the sacred, for that would mean human history has come to an end.

However, the sacred in this Durkheimian sense cannot be added to anything at all without adding its equiprimordial counterpart—the *ideal*. Together they constitute the distinctively human additions to the real:

> [W]hat defines the sacred is that the sacred is added to the real. And since the ideal is defined in the *same* way, we cannot explain the one without explaining the other. . . . A society can neither create itself nor recreate itself without at the same time creating some kind of ideal by the same stroke. This creation . . . is the act by which society makes itself, and remakes itself, periodically.[41]

Beginning from very different starting points, Durkheim and Sembène converge on an altogether distinctive conception of the sacred. As I have argued in my reading of Sembène's film, the heterotopic space of *moolaadé* is not only animated by an idea of the sacred with the power to "suspend, neutralize, or reverse" relations between existing social spaces; it is also animated by a *supra legem* ideal of justice through which new spaces of refuge and freedom can be instituted. Today, when the "refugee camp" represents the catastrophic inversion of sacred space—the epitome of a desacralized, which is to say, of a depoliticized and self-enclosing space—Sembène's *Moolaadé* rescues an image of sacred space as an "actually realized" utopia. For without an image of an "actually realized" utopia, we cannot think anew "the act by which society . . . remakes itself."

Notes

1 The colonial powers prohibited sub-Saharan Africans from making films of their own. Sembène's very first film *Borom Sarret*, a twenty-minute short made in 1963, three years after Senegal's independence from France, was the first film ever made by a Black African in Africa. *Mandabi*, made in 1968, was the first feature-length fiction film made in an African language (Wolof).

2   I found the following papers particularly helpful: Jude Akudinobi, "Durable Dreams: Dissent, Critique, and Creativity in Faat Kiné and Moolaadé," *Meridians: Feminism, Race, Transnationalism* 6, no. 2 (2006): 177–94; Samba Gadjigo, "Ousmane Sembene's *Moolaadé*: People's Rights vs. Human Rights," *Framework: The Journal of Cinema and Media* 61, no. 2 (Fall 2020): 70–88; Karen Lindon, "Ousmane Sembene's Hall of Men: (En)Gendering Everyday Heroism," *Research in African Literatures* 41, no. 4 (Winter 2010): 109–24.

3   Sada Niang and Samba Gadjigo, "Interview with Ousmane Sembene," *Research in African Literatures* 26, no. 3 (Fall 1995): 2.

4   The idea of cinema as "a space of refuge and freedom" complements Sembene's somewhat didactic view of African cinema as a kind of night school, a cinematic pedagogy of the oppressed.

5   But for one peculiar exception presented in an almost surreal, overexposed flashback sequence. Even in this case, we do not see the threshold, only a dense grouping of thickly leaved trees.

6   Sembène's position on the role of women as irreplaceable catalysts of social change in Africa is especially prominent in his final two films, *Faat Kiné* and *Moolaadé*.

7   Sembène's affection for the cinema of Chaplin and Keaton is palpable in these scenes.

8   Mircea Eliade, *The Sacred and the Profane* (New York: Harper and Row, 1961).

9   Ibid., 11–12.

10 Ibid., 20.

11 Walter Benjamin, "On the Concept of History," in *Walter Benjamin. Selected Writings. Volume 4, 1938–1940*, ed. Howard Eiland and Michael W. Jennings, trans. Edmund Jephcott and others (Cambridge, MA: Harvard University Press, 2003), 395.

12 Eliade, *The Sacred and the Profane*, 21.

13 See the instructive overview of the literature by Alyson L. Greiner, "Sacred Space and Globalization," in *The Changing World Religion Map*, ed. Stanley. D. Brunn (Dordrecht: Springer, 2015), 363–79.

14 "[T]he sacred is nothing more nor less than a notional supplement to the ongoing cultural work of sacralizing space, time, persons, and social relations." David Chidester and Edward Linenthal, "American Sacred Space," in *American Sacred Space*, ed. D. Chidester and E. D. Linenthal (Bloomington: Indiana University Press, 1995), 6.

15 Gerardus van Der Leeuw, *Religion in Essence and Manifestation*, trans. Ninian Smart and John Evan Turner (Princeton, NJ: Princeton University Press, 2014), 397/399.

16 Ibid., 399.

17 Eliade, *The Sacred and the Profane*, 32.

18 Ibid., 33.

19 René Girard, *Violence and the Sacred*, trans. Patrick Gregory (Baltimore: Johns Hopkins University Press, 1977), 31.
20 Fanon, *The Wretched of the Earth*, trans. R. Philcox (New York: Grove Press, 2004), 23.
21 Jean-Paul Sartre, "Preface," in Fanon, *The Wretched of the Earth*, lxii.
22 Eliade, *The Sacred and the Profane*, 47.
23 Hannah Arendt, *The Life of the Mind. Willing* (New York: Harcourt Brace Jovanovich, 1978), 204.
24 From an interview with Stuart Hall, quoted by Homi Bhaba in his "Forward" to *The Wretched of the Earth*, xvi.
25 Interview with Sembène in Samba Gadjigo and Jason Silverman, *Sembène! The Inspiring Story of the Father of African Cinema*, a documentary about Sembène's life and work.
26 Simon Behrmann, *Space, Subject, Resistance* (London: Routledge, 2018), 8.
27 Fanon, *The Wretched of the Earth*, 4.
28 Ibid., 31.
29 Obviously, Sembène did not believe that colonialism ended with African independence; it too changed its "shape," retaining in neocolonial form its exploitative grip on the continent.
30 Hannah Arendt, *The Human Condition* (Chicago, IL: University of Chicago Press, 1958), 246–7; "What Is Freedom?" in *Between Past and Future* (New York: Penguin, 1993), 169.
31 Arendt, "What Is Freedom?," 178.
32 "*Moolaadé* is not a film about genital cutting. It is a film about freedom." Interview with Sembène in *Sembène! The Inspiring Story of the Father of African Cinema*.
33 Nile Green, "Ostrich Eggs and Peacock Feathers: Sacred Objects as Cultural Exchange between Christianity and Islam," *Al-Masaq* 18, no. 1 (March 2006): 53.
34 Michel Foucault, "Different Spaces," in *Michel Foucault. Aesthetics, Method, and Epistemology*, trans. James D. Faubion (New York: The New Press, 1998), 177.
35 Ibid., 178.
36 Ibid.
37 Ibid., 177, translation ammended ("*toutes sont animées encore par une sourde sacralisation*").
38 Emile Durkheim, *The Elementary Forms of Religious Life*, trans. Karen E. Fields (New York: Free Press, 1995).
39 Hans Joas, *The Creativity of Action*, trans. Jeremy Gaines and Paul Keast (Cambridge: Polity Press, 1996): 63–4.
40 Karen E. Fields, translator's introduction, Durkheim, *The Elementary Forms of Religious Life*, xliv.
41 Durkheim, *The Elementary Forms of Religious Life*, 424–5.

5

Cinema as a Secularizing Medium in the Middle East

Walid El Khachab

Talal Asad establishes a distinction between two notions of secularism: an ontological secularism and a political one. Ontological secularism is founded on the category of the secular, where the human subject is central. This notion entails that religion or transcendental divine power does not define the world or society, and its corollary is that the human in the world is governed by secular law. Hence, Asad's discussion of human rights in his history of secularism and his attempt at "Redeeming the 'Human' through Human Rights."[1] Therefore, one could argue that political secularism is about the separation of religion from power, that is, about state neutrality in matters of religion, in a manner that leaves the human free to embrace ontological secularism or not. Asad's critique of hegemonic discourses of secularism shows the said neutrality to be founded in theory but materialized in complex ways in specific real-life contexts. Based on this heuristic distinction, I will underscore, first, how cinema is ontologically a performance of the secular. Second, I will argue that the inherent secular agency of cinema is challenged by its simultaneous capacity to reintroduce the sacred, thus producing a world defined by a claim to religion, the sacred, or divine transcendence as primary organizing forces of the world and of society. Therefore, I claim that secularism cannot be efficiently produced by cinema unless it figures/represents/performs political secularism. This is at least true in the case of Middle Eastern cinemas' historical experience. In the following chapter, I will explore how the practice of cinema, particularly in the Middle East, is a practice of secularism, but that it overcomes the reintroduction of religion only by practicing some form of political secularism.

In *The Movement Image*, Deleuze suggests that cinema introduces a new understanding of form in its interface with time. Cinema, he argues, represents a critique of transcendence. For the ancient Greeks, the latter is materialized as a form, that of a statue, for instance, fixed in time, as is a film still. Transcendence, therefore, holds a privileged suspended time. Cinema, on the other hand, introduces a regular movement, that of the shutter and the flickering where the space of the film frames is evenly and regularly projected in a time continuum. This undermining of the uniqueness of transcendence and its fixed time represents an aspect of cinema's modernity.[2] One may argue that this is what makes modernity—and cinema—secularizing forces. Film—because of movement being its essence—undermines the stillness of transcendence—except in the rare instances of a still shot.

In this chapter, the focus will be on the Arabic-speaking Middle East for the sake of brevity. But I would argue that its claims can be safely generalized to the Turkish, Persian, and Hebrew segments of Middle Eastern cinematic productions. In the scholarship about the Middle East, it is often assumed that, because Islam is a major reference in the region, the cultural landscape was inhospitable to cinema at the end of the nineteenth century. It is also assumed that Islam prohibits the figurative representation of humans, as in the most conservative aniconic Semitic traditions. In *Taboo Memories and Diasporic Voices* Ella Shohat appears to be a strong proponent of the thesis about the prevalence of aniconism in the Semitic Middle East, which she applies to both Muslim and Jewish traditions.[3] In the chapter entitled "Sacred Word, Profane Image: Theologies of Adaptation," she suggests that cinema secularized literature and the entire epistemological apparatus in the Middle East. According to her analysis, the seventh art promoted the image, associated with the profane, thus undermining the centrality of the word and the logos, which are the foundations of a particular regime of the sacred dominating any cultural production in the region and marginalizing images, including those on film.[4]

These assumptions about aniconism and Islam require some nuance, as does Ella Shohat's thesis. There is a diversity of views on aniconism within Muslim traditions, as evidenced by the tens of thousands of paintings portraying the prophet of Islam in predominantly Muslim societies, during the entire existence of the religion. However, the essence of Shohat's thesis is pertinent, not because visuality secularizes the transcendental order of scripturality in the Middle East, but because cinema powerfully introduces movement into the visual dimension of cultural production. As per Deleuze's argument, it is the mechanic, even, movement of film that shatters the immobility of transcendence' fixed and hierarchical time. As I have argued elsewhere, this deterritorializing agency of cinema, decentering transcendence in the practice of the new media, was soon recuperated by a reterritorializing movement, which produced transcendence within the immanent workings of the seventh art. In a way, cinema is appropriated as a machine that produces the sacred.⁵ The obvious example of the production of transcendence within immanence as a byproduct of the agency of film technology is the genre of biblical films, particularly those producing the figure of Jesus Christ. In the Middle East, the reterritorialization of transcendence within cinema also materialized in the so-called religious films (*film dini*), reconstituting the history of the prophet of Islam, and producing the Quran as the transcendental source of world harmony brought by the prophet. By the same token, the Quran is elevated to the status of an icon of state power. But the epistemic nature of film—the immanence of cinema, to reverse Guattari's defense of a cinema of immanence⁶—makes the seventh art inherently part of a secular practice, because even when it produces transcendence, it does so with the means of, and within the sphere of, immanence. For example, as I argue in my analysis of the Arab classic *The Advent of Islam*, it makes the Quran appear as a discourse in the political history of Islam, not as a materialization of the Word constitutive of the universe.⁷

In the Middle East, these epistemological foundations of cinema's agency associate the institution of the seventh art and the medium of film with a modernist and secularist worldview. The ambivalence of cinema as evacuating transcendence but also as having the potential to reintroduce/produce it through technological means is particularly suited to account for the ambiguity of modernity in the Middle East and the prevalent brands of secularism in that geo-cultural region. It is safe to claim that an ontological secularism is rarely theorized in the Middle East, except in rare, extreme examples, such as in the famous polemical treaty by Ismael Adham: *Why I am an Atheist?*⁸ It is also rarely produced on film. Secularism is predominantly negotiated here as a political one, and cinema is a major arena of that negotiation, as well as a prominent actor. Suffice it to remember that a staple of secularists' demonstrations in Egypt, during the brief rule of the Muslim Brotherhood was the brandishing of major female movie stars posters.⁹ Major secular discourses in the Middle East are often criticized for not being radical enough in their propositions to distance religion, or the transcendence of the divine, from the public sphere. A symptom of this lack of radicality is the tendency to translate the concept of "secularism" using the Arabic word *madaneya*, which stands for civility, in the sense of "civicness," to avoid shocking Muslim conservatives.¹⁰ In all the discursive practices of and about modernity, secularism, and cinema in the Middle East, there is always a copresence of the religious and the civil, of transcendence and immanence. As a matter of fact, since cinema's early days, it has been historically the space for negotiating modernity in the Middle East.¹¹ Sporadically, a minor discourse about "Islamic cinema" emerges and purports to represent a worldview and an aesthetics that conform to Islamic orthodoxies, particularly in the Arabic and Persian Middle Eastern cultural-scapes. But this discourse represents only a fringe movement within the area of cinematic production in the Middle East. Most films in the region—including in the Islamic Republic of Iran—are in effect predominantly engaged in a secularizing process, at least because of the privileged epistemological position of movement inherent to the film medium.

Cinematic Enchantment/ Re-enchantment vs. Disenchantment

Secularism is often defined according to the Weberian notion of disenchantment. In the Middle Ages, the world was enchanted by a belief that transcendence was the organizing force of existence, while a disenchanted modern world was believed to be governed by rationality. Talal Asad and Saba Mahmood have extensively analyzed prevalent discourses of secularism and shown their grounding in Christian traditions. Interestingly, Asad analyzes the Protestant roots of secularism, for example in Weber's writings, while Mahmood presents a critique of Charles Taylor's views on the origins of secularism in what he calls "Latin Christendom."[12] It is therefore difficult to accept Weber's theory of rationality as an accurate description of the exclusion of religion from the workings of modern society, even though, as Asad points out, Weber's strategy can be understood as an effort to translate "an aspect of Protestant Behavior (morality) into the god of capitalist society (accumulation)."[13] However, Weber's concept of disenchantment is valid inasmuch as it refers to the exclusion of religion as the arch-reference of meaning and value, and as the organizing instance of society, not to the pure and simple exclusion of religion from the public sphere. On the other hand, enchantment as a "secularized" concept may account for the presence of discourses and practices of religious origin in secular modern society. Enchantment or re-enchantment here would not be about spirits animating the world, but about "the spirit" of religious discourses, epistemic models and vocabulary still detectable in the secular worldly sphere. Once again, this understanding of the place/trace of religion in the secular realm may explain the strong presence, not of religiosity, but of religious-based vocabulary, discursive patterns, and preestablished discourses in Middle Eastern societies and cinemas.

Using Weberian terminology in that sense, one may distinguish two types of cinema in the Middle East, originating in two different secularizing discourses. First, there is a *cinema of disenchantment*, advocating for a rationalist vision of the world, without necessarily completely removing religion from the public sphere, but always placing it hierarchically under the authority of a moderate rationalism. I claim that this take on the ambivalent relationship between religion and the public sphere is inferred from Asad's discussion of Muslim intellectual traditions as leading to a distinct formation of the secular.[14] In light of non-Western secular traditions, one may expand the reach of Asad's conclusion: "The secular as disenchantment is not to be seen simply as part of the move towards religious separation from political authority but as a vision of rational and therefore justified hierarchy."[15] In the Middle East, a cinema of disenchantment can possibly be atheist or theist, but would still reserve a place for religion, not as to be removed from the public sphere and confined to the private, but to be placed hierarchically under some form of rationalism, be it that of a modern society. In the Middle East, I would argue, there are only a handful of examples of a pure cinema of disenchantment.

A second type of cinema can be called a *cinema of multiple enchantments*, framed by a view of spiritualities and organized religions in the world as multiple, ambiguous, coextensive, and syncretic. It is a cinema that performs secularism as is understood in the mainstream of its advocates: not a cinema that evacuates religion, and not a cinema that contents itself with introducing religion as falling under the hierarchical supervision of a form of rationalism, that of the secular state for example, but as a cinema that acknowledges the multiplicity of faiths and religious references in the mosaic of faith communities characteristic of the region. A cinema both producing and being produced by multiple enchantments is one that does not evacuate the divine or the religious social references, but that acknowledges their multiplicity, in reference to at least two or all three of the major Abrahamic traditions, the most prevalent religious traditions in the region. It does not preoccupy itself with displacing or removing the centrality of transcendence, nor with confining it to an assigned social or private role. Rather, it challenges the hegemony of one and unique religious reference, that of the majority, by performing difference and acknowledging the diversity of these references within society.

Early in the history of Arab cinema, particularly with the rise of Arab nationalist sentiments, the reproduction of some glorious moments in the history of Islam became increasingly part of the cinematic discourse of Arabism (and of the promotion of Islam). One of the early examples is *The Advent of Islam* (*Zuhur al Islam*, dir. Ibrahim Ezzeddin, 1950). With the softening of the State's grip on cinematic production and censorship, The Coptic Church was allowed to produce and distribute low-budget religious Coptic fictions at the end of the 1990s. Whether the religious ideology is Muslim or Christian, these films are part of a process of enchantment or re-enchantment: they restore the protective narratives of institutional religion, particularly in the face of a modernization/Westernization process that threatens the traditional centrality of religious discourses in Middle Eastern societies.

Beyond the obvious examples of films promoting some institutional stories of respective organized religions, some early Arab films resisted the anxiety caused by the specter of disenchantment by reintroducing God on the screen. *Interview with the Devil* (dir. Kamel Telmissany, 1955) is an example of a cinema that is anti-atheist, which promotes religiosity as an ultimate degree of morality and makes it a point to reintroduce religion in the public discourse as a fundamental social and spiritual value. While doing so, films such as *Interview* are still secularizing religion because they reserve a place for it in society, but they do not place it as the ultimate arbiter of ethics and behavior within society. The film is a modern Egyptian take on the myth of Faust. The socially conscious generous doctor living in a popular neighborhood is poor. The Devil dressed as a modern mysterious scientist becomes friends with him and undertakes a Faustian pact with him. The doctor becomes rich but morally hollow. Having lost God's blessings, which he had enjoyed when he was poor, he can't save his own son who becomes critically ill and is on the brink of dying.

During that trial, the doctor expresses remorse and invokes God's name. Similar to the use of religious vocabulary in traditional vampire movies, once the repentant doctor mentions the name of God, the Devil is irritated and distressed. He completely disappears at the end of the scene—and of the film—in a dissolve editing trick, after the doctor recites a talismanic verse from Quran. *Interview* is one of the most daring Arab films of its time presenting a critique of religion. But the final coup de théâtre in the movie is that the re-establishment of the Good is done through religious vocabulary.

What I call the cinema of disenchantment is somehow comparable in its marginality to the "Islamic cinema," or to its softer version dubbed "Clean cinema," the latter being a popular term in the Arab-speaking world at the turn of the twentieth century, describing movies with minimal or no sexual references. The cinema of disenchantment is a fringe movement in the Middle East, because of censorship and of widespread respect for the symbolic standing of religiosity (not of faith per se). One can count a handful of films during the entire history of the Arab-speaking Middle East where cinema produces a radical critique of faith. A rare example is the Egyptian/Moroccan film *Where Do You Hide the Sun?* (1980, dir. Abdallah Misbahi), which depicts a hippie-style community of atheists, who end up discovering faith in the last fifteen minutes of the film.

Arab cinemas and, broadly speaking, Middle Eastern ones rarely would display an extreme secularist view calling for the complete removal of religion or the sacred from the screen or the public sphere. It would never advocate for anti-religious views. Historically, cinema was the medium and the virtual space for the negotiation and promotion of modernity, including secular values. But because it was a space of negotiation rather than one of propaganda, it has always focused on mitigating the fears from and the social effects of modernity. It never served as a mouthpiece—or an eyepiece, for that matter—for an entirely anti-religious ideology. Its function has been the negotiation and mitigation of modernity, not the performance of a cultural revolution. The two films previously discussed account for two types of cinema: one that is keen on reintroducing transcendence in the public sphere, and one that attempts to advocate for a form of disenchantment. The latter one is always tempered on screen by a return of the religious or of the sacred, at least to conjure censorship. Only the following examples perform secularism more consistently, through what I have called multiple enchantments.

Secularism and a Cinema of Multiple Enchantments

Most Middle Eastern films would fall into the category called here "cinema of multiple enchantments." It is a cinema where religious and cultural diversities are acknowledged, or where the lifestyle dominated by Islamic references is ambiguous, because of its entanglement with modern Western secular practices and ideals.

In the first decades of cinema, the entire Middle East was engaged with a progressive version of secularism, at least in its outlook, especially when it comes to the common grounds built between the three major Abrahamic faiths of the region: Judaism, Christianity, and Islam. The second quarter of the twentieth century was aptly called by historians, such as Selma Botman, "The Liberal Age," and it perfectly coincided with the birth of the Egyptian film industry.[16] The emergence of modern ideas of nationality and of constitutional monarchy, then of the theoretical ideal of liberal democracy, made the presence and coexistence of signs associated with the three Abrahamic faiths a staple mark of the cinematic Middle East. Up until the 1970s, the Egyptian film industry was the sole major hegemonic power on the film market in the entire Middle East and was aptly dubbed Hollywood on the Nile. It is striking that the theme of sympathy between members of the three Abrahamic faiths was somehow literally explored in the first half of the twentieth century in Egyptian films, roughly during that liberal age. The products of that era of secular nationalism and liberalism were comedies like *Fatima, Marika and Rachel* (1949, dir. Helmy Rafla) and *Hassan, Marcus and Cohen* (1954, dir. Fouad El Gazaerli). In both films, the protagonists' names suggest their community affiliation and perform a sort of multifaith unity, since in both cases, it sets the stage for a Muslim, a Christian, and a Jewish character altogether.

In the serious register, melodrama was the field of negotiation between secular modernity and religious-based ethical formulations. Melodrama was appeasing those who considered secularism as a Western immoral cultural invasion, either by actively criticizing "excesses" of modernity, or by promoting "civilized" secular and modern ideas. Historically, cinema in the Middle East was dominated by melodrama, which tends to reintroduce a sort of secularized transcendence in the sociohistorical sphere, replacing the implacable rationality of modernity, as a kind of social *fatum*. Hence, enchantment remained well and alive in the region, but in a secularized and ambiguous form. In that sense, Elsaesser's argument about melodrama being a secular genre is valid inasmuch as melodrama replaces the gods by social forces or passions or coincidences, which occupy the position held by transcendence in Greek tragedy.[17] Melodrama remains a site of resistance to disenchantment at least because, as Peter Brooks argues, it maintains the principle of the victim purifying the world through sacrifice. Interestingly, Brooks refers here to the villain as the modern equivalent of the sacrificial victim.[18] The melodramatic ethos maintains a space for the supernatural to sometimes regulate the natural world, and to accidents/coincidences to sometimes disrupt the implacable rationalist social order. This ethos is thus performing a re-enchantment of the world.

In the early years of cinema, the medium was an embodiment of technological modernity and a vehicle of modern ideas, including secularism, both in the West and the Middle East. Nevertheless, by the end of the twentieth century, cinema in the Middle East had become an indigenized medium, and a battlefield between secular ideals and the ideals of the far right using Muslim themes. Anti-secularism was, and still is, a priority for this far right.

Toward the end of the twentieth century, the debates about cinema's morality and the excesses of secularism strikingly resembled those raging in the early decades of the century, but with a shift in the balance of power between secularists and anti-secularists. After the Islamic Revolution of 1979, Iran created a sort of "Islamic Cinema." Ironically, because of the medium's nature, that cinema is an active agent of secularism in the Islamic Republic. The term "Islamic Cinema" is—in reality—as old as cinema in the Middle East. It has shifted from a discourse of high morality in the 1940s, to an active propaganda tool for the conservative moral agenda of the Muslim far right in the 1990s. A Christian equivalent has emerged for church-going audiences in Egypt, in the late twentieth century, which is a little-known phenomenon.

However, the nature of the medium, its primal engagement with matter, image, and movement, as well as its connections with the universal history of cinema, makes Middle Eastern films active agents of secularism, either through a discourse on worldliness or through a compromise between conservative morality and the entertainment market, resulting in what is fondly called "Clean Cinema."

In the following sections, the focus will be on the golden age of Egyptian Arab cinema, which spans the 1940s and the 1950s, but was still alive until the 1960s. As of the 1970s, the rise of Muslim fundamentalism and Islamist far-right extremism made the discussion of secularism almost impossible. The debate over secularism became partisan and antagonistic until today. Special attention to comedy allows for the discussion of subtle approaches to a serious topic in a non-partisan manner, where taboos can be transgressed without excessively shocking the audiences, since comedy is taken lightly. To further my earlier comment on melodrama's modernist agency, it may be that comedy, and particularly vaudeville, are more actively promoting modernity and secularism in Middle Eastern cinemas, precisely because no one takes them seriously at face value. I have argued here that the prevalent brand of Middle Eastern secularism, particularly in cinema, is political secularism, especially the trend which cherishes the acknowledgment of multiple cultural/religious references in the public space, or at least some sort of representation that accounts for the demographic diversity, in terms of faith communities. I have argued elsewhere that Arab comedy has promoted what I call the "Vaudeville ideology."[19] This agency of Arab comedy provided the entertainment and optimistic pendant of state propaganda about the democratization of access to the middle class in the 1950s and 1960s, thanks to major hiring programs in government positions and in the public sector. A byproduct of the massive importation of adapted vaudevilles in Egypt, for example, was the widespread cultural productions emanating from state-sponsored instances, such as the radio comedy shows, the national Television Theatre and the public sector film production, which promoted a light moral approach to romantic involvement with multiple partners, and its celebration as part of the access to the pleasures afforded to the newly educated middle class. This challenge to the conservative traditional discourses about the sanctity of marriage is only part of the questioning and undermining of traditional moral and religious discourses performed in comedy.

Fatima, Marika and Rachel

The ideal of secularism is understood here as a performance acknowledging the multiplicity of symbolic and cultural productions originating in a multiplicity of communities of faith, cohabitating in the public sphere. It is then a multicultural principle which guarantees a space in the public sphere, as well as a public discourse and popular cultural production for each faith/cultural community. Arabic films that include main characters from the three main Abrahamic communities in the Arabic-speaking world and in the entire Middle East (Muslim, Christian, Jewish) would come up as perfect examples of the secular agency of cinema. One is inevitably reminded of *Hassan, Marcus and Cohen* (dir. Fuad Al Jazaerly, 1954) and of *Fatima, Marika and Rachel* (dir. Helmy Rafla, 1949).

Thanks to the charisma and popularity of the movie's male star, Mohamed Fawzi, *Fatima, Marika and Rachel* is still today a widely watched and appreciated film, constantly shown on the classic movie channels in the

Arab World, such as Rotana Classic. Since the birth of the first major Arabic-speaking state television broadcast in Egypt, in 1960, the film is part of the repertoire of state-sponsored entertainment. *Fatima, Marika and Rachel* is actually more about a man, than about three women, whose names indicate their respective faith communities: a Muslim Arab, a Christian Greek-Egyptian, and a Jewish-Egyptian. The main protagonist is Youssef, the wealthy Muslim playboy who "collects" women. To ply them to his desire, he parades his wealth and promises engagement, sometimes offering actual engagement rings. The film is centered around this Muslim womanizer who is "inclusive" enough to court Muslim, Christian, and Jewish women.

The limits of "tolerance" appear strikingly tight when one examines the "place" assigned to each community in the kind of public discourse produced and reinforced by the film, which obviously displays a masculinist view of cultural diversity. It is the Muslim wealthy male who is the arbiter of cultural diversity. He is the lead character whose agency and choices determine the identity of the lucky girl who will end up marrying him. The lucky bride is expectedly the Muslim "entirely" Egyptian young woman, Fatima. The two other love interests, not only belong to minorities (Christian and Jewish) but also they are less "indigenous" than Fatima: Marika is Greek-Egyptian and belongs to the Greek Orthodox Church, and Rachel's Jewish identity makes her associated with recent—or old—histories of migrations around the Mediterranean sea. The gender dimension that focuses on male desire and pleasure is intertwined with a nationalist and faith community supremacism.

The gender power dynamics in the film are not just governed by male supremacy, which is, in itself, disturbing and indicative of the limits of good secular intentions. Its overarching morale is that minority communities have a place only inasmuch as they are feminized and subjected to the Muslim male desire. The heavy stereotyping of the female characters belonging to minority communities is quite troubling, once one sees through the lightness of the romantic musical comedy genre. Marika, the Greek Egyptian, speaks Arabic with a heavy accent which furthers the process of her "othering." Loula Sidky, the actress who plays Marika, has almost exclusively played the female villain for most of her career. Even more disturbing is the antisemitic stereotyping of Rachel and of her parents. The father is only interested in Youssef's wealth, about the minute details of which he inquires in a strident nasal voice. Rachel herself is played by Nelly Mazloum—who was Greek Egyptian—and is an unabashed gold digger. She is reputed to be Jewish, but there are competing stories about her belonging to the community.

The very first images of the film encapsulate the gender dynamics as introduced earlier. The camera shows a wedding, featuring a bride dressed in white, seated on a fauteuil as in traditional Arab weddings. Next to her, is an empty fauteuil signaling her groom has not yet arrived. A bridesmaid asks the bride about the name of her future husband. It is a recognizable Muslim name: Youssef Abdel Aziz, literally: "Joseph servant of The Noble

(God)." Most Arabic names ending with "Abdel" followed by traditional Muslim names of God are exclusively Muslim (with some exceptions where the name is reserved for Christians, for example, Abdel Massih, literally "Servant of Christ" or "of the Messiah"). The girls laugh and tease the bride about her wonderful groom.

The camera cuts to another wedding-like party. But instead of the Muslim cleric, it is a Coptic priest who is sitting next to the father of the bride. Later, it will be clarified that this is actually an engagement party, not a wedding. In real life, however, an Egyptian Christian engagement party—or a wedding celebration, for that matter—never includes a priest who blesses a bride's and groom's union at home. The priest's presence is merely a signal to the Muslim majority among viewers to confirm that the scene is one about officially uniting a man and a woman. It also strengthens the symmetry between the Muslim and the Christian ceremonies. As a matter of fact, the similar sets in which both the Muslim cleric and the Coptic priest appear seated intend to enforce the rhetoric of the parallel: the size and sequence of the frames in both scenes, the two decors are quite similar, the position of the major actors in both scenes, as well as the dialogue present strong symmetry. Here, a friend asks the bride about her groom's name. She replies: Youssef Morcos, literally: "Joseph Marcus," a clear sign that the groom is Christian. In both scenes, the groom never shows up. Editing and the order of successive scenes will explain that the Youssef who wakes up in his luxurious home in the third scene is the Youssef in question. This symmetry between the Muslim and the Christian ceremonies is probably implemented here as a comedic device, but it also establishes a cultural symmetry signifying that in basic universal matters of life, love, and sex, there are similarities and instances of "equity" between the two faith communities.

After two marriage/engagement scenes, in which he is absent, in the third scene, Youssef is in his bed, waking up wearing his tuxedo, clearly in a state of hangover. He explains to his best friend and confidant, Hummus, that the previous night, he skipped a wedding and an engagement party with two ladies altogether. This very sad story is introduced by him as a laughing matter. A jeweler comes in to deliver an order. He has brought to Youssef twenty-nine rings each engraved with one letter of the Arabic alphabet. Youssef explains that he keeps the rings at hand to put the one with the appropriate initial around the finger of the courted woman, so that they become engaged and can go out together, go to the movies, and party, and he can—in his own words—"enjoy her beauty," while avoiding social stigma, since they would be fiancés.

Still in its introduction, the film expectedly produces a romance between Youssef and a Jewish young woman, to both reinforce the comedic symmetry and repetition of narrative patterns dear to the genre, and to insist on the equivalence between the three major Abrahamic faiths: women from all backgrounds fall for the young handsome man. At timestamp 5:20, the film cuts into yet another wedding ceremony. Rachel dances ballet as part of the entertainment. Youssef meets her and immediately falls for her. He introduces himself as Youssef Hizqeel, literally Joseph Ezekiel.

Their interaction starts with a quarrel as in Marivaudage tradition. Rachel was dancing in front of the bride and groom. Youssef, a friend of the groom, enters the scene and performs a song where he leads a chorus of bachelors mockingly lamenting the groom. The music is dynamic and fast, but the lyrics are those of funerals lamenting the death of a dear one, pastiched by replacing references to death by ones to marriage. Rachel is outraged and quarrels with Youssef, mostly in French, arguing that she is *"une grande artiste,"* offended by Youssef's dashing and loud entry into the scene, which overshadowed *"mon succès."* But when a guest mentions that Youssef is a very wealthy man, Rachel immediately changes her attitude and apologizes.

Quickly the relationship evolves, and Youssef pays a visit to Rachel and her family to ask her hand for marriage. The screenplay provides an idea of how Youssef proceeds when seducing his female victims. Rachel's parents offer to serve him coffee and tea, but then mention that coffee affects the nerves and tea the intestines. Youssef declines to have any drink. They ask him about his wealth, and he replies that his father owns a 300-acre property in addition to 20,000 Egyptian pounds—an impressive amount in the 1950s—in his bank account. Rachel's mother asks him when his father will die. He replies maybe in a year, and she expresses shock because twelve months is a long time (before her son-in-law-to-be inherits his father's wealth).

These stereotypes of the miser Jewish family, grotesquely keen on marrying their daughter to an extremely rich man, are disturbing. Also problematic is the insistence on the daughter speaking French and dancing ballet, because these are elitist Westernized practices which alienate the majority and contribute to the othering of Jews, who appear as "not Egyptian" enough. Youssef adopts a nasal strident voice comparable to that of Rachel's father when he proposes, which is both ridiculous and tasteless. Nevertheless, the intentions of the filmmakers are not on trial in this chapter. I am confident that Helmy Rafla, the director of *Fatma, Marika, and Rachel*, is not in any way, shape or form harboring antisemitic views. His wife and children are Jews. Loula Sidky, the actress who plays the Greek Egyptian woman, is half Italian herself. Gracia Qaseen, who plays Rachel's mother, is actually Jewish. The antisemitic stereotypes seem to be a concession to the populist taste of the majority community in Egypt to secure cheap laughs.

Cinematic "Oecumenism"

Fatima, Marika and Rachel's "morale" may be best summarized in the film's title song. The star singer, Mohamed Fawzi, is filmed in a medium to wide shot in his living room, which is crowded with expensive furniture. The scene starts with him seated at his piano—another sign of major wealth—playing a few notes, like any Hollywood depiction of a rich kid who does not need to work to earn a living. He then hops on a coffee table and tap dances. Here the dance is completely void of its historical meaning and its roots in African American culture. It is just a sign of slick coolness showing that the young man is up to date with his immersion in American pop culture. He sings: "Fatima, Marika and Rachel—in my heart form a cocktail." The lyrics clearly are intended to emphasize the "oecumenic" nature of Youssef's relationship to women. They simply highlight his playboy status. "All my life, I have loved beauties—I am attracted both to white-skinned girls and to brunettes." His womanizing is merely motivated by his taste for variety.

The visual language of the film establishes a void: the non-Muslim women's desire is experienced as a want, a lack of manhood that the absent gorgeous Muslim male is hoped to fill. But the absence of that Alpha Muslim male from the first two scenes, while he is nevertheless at the center of the conversation, underscores this void. As in the Freudian model of female sexual desire, the non-Muslim women in the film experience their own bodies as lacking a penis and view the penis—here the Muslim male's— as an object of desire, something they "miss." The first two scenes display women in a position of desire expressed through their clothing signs (the bridal white dresses) and the spatial signs (the vacant fauteuil of the groom). The penis here would be the Muslim male. Indeed, Youssef acts like one.

It is also striking that the male in the film needs to possess language, in addition to the large bank accounts he also possesses and the women's bodies he constantly strives to possess. Buying as many rings as Arabic letters is a powerful production of cultural hegemony, particularly that the two non-Muslim women speak a minor version of the majority language. Buying the metonymy of marriage, the ring, "stamped" with language, is establishing the male's cultural and sexual grip on the virtual feminized non-Muslim bodies of the potential, prospective brides. Constantly buying rings, each bearing a single letter of the alphabet, Youssef is establishing the capital's grip on language, and the whole order of the Symbolic. It is the "merger" of capital as wealth and the symbolic capital as language that allows for both the physical and metaphoric possession of the female body.

Hassan, Marcus and Cohen

Hassan, Marcus and Cohen (dir. Fuad Al Jazaerly, 1954) is adapted from a namesake stage production from 1941. The play is the model after which *Fatima, Marika and Rachel* was made: in both cases, a trio belonging to the three Abrahamic faiths is at the center of a vaudeville plot. Even though it is also a comedy, Al Jazaerly's film has not had the same longevity as Rafla's, which is an all-time classic constantly shown on TV. However, *Hassan,*

Marcus and Cohen's story and its theatrical version have older and deeper roots in Arab pop culture than *Fatima, Marika and Rachel*, even though the former movie was released five years after the latter. Based on the stage hit from 1941 by the same title, written by Naguib Rihani and Badi Khairy, famed pioneers of Arabic vaudeville, *Hassan, Marcus and Cohen* was adapted to the screen in the aftermath of the Egyptian coup of 1952 which removed the king, and brought in the republic. The film's credits refer to the play as "The immortal theatrical masterpiece," even though the stage production was only thirteen years old when the film was released.

Hassan the Muslim, Marcus the Christian, and Cohen the Jew are the co-owners of a drugstore. They trick their clerk, Abbas, into signing a binding contract which obligates him to pay them a substantial indemnity should he leaves his job: 20,000 Egyptian pounds, a fortune by the 1940s' standards. They knew before him that he had inherited an extraordinarily large sum of money and were counting on him acquiescing to the dispositions of that contract and resigning, once he discovers the matter of his inheritance. However, Abbas decides to stay as clerk-assistant, thus ruining the wicked plot of his greedy employers, and keeping them from succeeding in various nefarious endeavors.

Indeed, Hassan, Marcus, and Cohen's greed is not just fed by personal con jobs; it takes the form of full-fledged corruption. Early in the film, Cohen, played by Stephan Rosti, speaks over the phone with an intermediary who agrees to facilitate a deal between the three partners and the cabinet minister in charge of importation concessions. In exchange for 3,000 Egyptian pounds, the intermediary would arrange for a belly dancer to have the minister sign the concession for importing phosphate in favor of Hassan, Marcus, and Cohen.

The fact that the crooked business owners somehow massively represent society, because they come from its three main Egyptian faith communities, makes the film a political statement against corruption and comprador capitalism, which appear to disregard community boundaries. It is for this reason that the film is carefully set in 1950. In his first face-to-face meeting with the three corrupt businessmen in their drugstore, the intermediary between them and those who will reach to the minister in charge of concessions, states that his 600 pounds commission is fair, because these are 1950 prices. The screenplay manages to emphasize to the audience that the film screened in 1954—the year of the proclamation of the Republic— is showing and condemning the kind of corruption that the 1952 coup-turned-revolution came to fight. The film's credits, using the rhetoric of "the masterpiece," is partly a contribution to the nationalist post-independence effort to manufacture a national modern heritage, and partly an ideological attempt to hide the new regime's mistrust of private capital developed during the monarchy, under the guise of a discourse that predates the 1952 coup, which ultimately brought in the republic.

The play on which the film is based appears therefore—even more so than the film—as a progressive, socially aware statement condemning a class of opportunists who thrived between the two world wars and after the second one. In a subtle way, both the play and the film are reminding the audiences that corruption and the rise of comprador capitalism are not the privilege of non-Muslims, as the far-right propaganda of the 1930s and 1940s insisted, but that it is a class issue to which all three major communities of faith contribute.

The film *Hassan, Marcus and Cohen* still does not evacuate religion as such. It uses religious vocabulary as an expression of ethics. The condemnation of the three partners' corruption is sometimes expressed in religious terms. Right before Hassan, Marcus, and Cohen are introduced on screen, after seven minutes, thirty seconds from the beginning, their clerk Abbas looks to the sky, raises his hands in a traditional gesture of prayers and implores God to save him from them. Abbas leaves his small room in a popular neighborhood in Old Cairo, heading to work. He goes through a dark tunnel connecting the medieval city to modern Cairo. When he emerges from the tunnel, and is thus symbolically reborn in the modern city, the sun casts even more light on him. He starts his day as a professional with a prayer like millions of Middle Eastern individuals do. It is emphasized by the accompanying soundtrack of nay music, traditionally used to signal intense spiritual moments. His prayer translates as the following: "O Lord, spare me those seven evils: Poverty, Sickness, Ignorance, Om Tintin (his landlady), Hassan, Marcus and Cohen."

Interestingly, Abbas repeats the discourses of millions of progressives in the nineteenth and early twentieth centuries regarding misery, disease and ignorance, the most challenging three ailments hindering Human's access to modernity and to a decent life. While these three plights are usually mentioned as the result of despotic policies adopted by backward regimes, here they are associated with corrupt parasite non-productive capitalism. Not only do they plot to obtain a concession by sexually bribing a public servant, but they do so in order to exploit natural resources (phosphate), not to manufacture a product or to initiate an agricultural production.

Somehow the "national unity" here between the three communities is conceived of in terms of the witty petit bourgeois who represents the "authentic" national, who also belongs to the Muslim majority, in the face of comprador corrupt capitalism, regardless of the faith of the capitalists. The company founded by the three corrupt partners to extract phosphate was named HaMaC or HMC, which stands for the first letter of the names of the three crooked partners. In a way, they are fused in one body, in one corporation, the Latin root of the word being literally corpus, body. Here, though, the body is not that of the nation, rather it is the body of corruption produced by parasite capitalism. Irony is at work here, not just because of the corporeal metaphor, but because "Hamak" in Arabic is colloquial for "Hamaq," which means "idiocy."

The three partners may form one corpus, but they are individually distinct, and one major sign of their diversity is the politics of their headgear. Western scholarship is always fascinated by women's headgear in Arab societies and in Arabic movies, which fascination is often grounded in an orientalist preoccupation by othered women. Women's headgear in this film are not particularly significant. They mostly wear Western-style hairdos. However, it is the semiotics of the men's headgear that is particularly complex in terms of its cultural significance. Hassan wears a fez, sign of Ottoman modernization, but still wears the traditional men's robe, Jilbab; Marcus wears a similar fez, but wears a Western-style modern suit and tie; Cohen wears a traditional black hat and a traditional men's robe, which is shorter than the Muslim one, but he wears on top of it a Western-style jacket.

This is the repertoire of hybrid modernities in a nutshell on screen: different combinations of signs of modernity with a Muslim reference (Ottoman) or a Western one (European), together with signs of tradition (Muslim and Jewish men's robes). The secularization of the public space is not just operated by including representatives of major faith communities, but by promoting different styles of compromise between Western modernity and diverse traditional anchorages. Secularization appears to be a matter of class as well. Abbas wears a Western-style suit and tie together with a fez, much like Marcus. However, when he becomes a rich man, thanks to his inheritance, and engages in a high society Western lifestyle, in his meals and clothing, he ditches the fez. In a way, he becomes fully westernized (fully secular and modern) by removing the symbolic headgear associated with a modernized Muslim identity.

This brief discussion of the politics of headgear requires a much longer study space to avoid stereotyping the characters. However, the play and the film do use stereotypes as a comedic technique, but sometimes do so in an abusive manner. Much like *Fatima, Marika and Rachel*, *Hassan, Marcus and Cohen* indulges in stereotypical antisemitic tropes. In a long scene—utterly superfluous—Cohen invites Abbas to have a drink in a popular coffeeshop, a few meters away from his own apartment. He uses a few rhetorical tricks to avoid ordering tea for Abbas, much like Rachel's father avoided serving coffee or tea to Youssef in *Fatima, Marika and Rachel*. Cohen's daughter calls him from the entrance of their building to complain about her younger brother who has swallowed a dime. Cohen is quick to instruct her to do whatever it takes to make the boy through-up the dime or go to the bathroom to evacuate the dime with his own excrements. It is troublesome that such rhetoric was at work in a play staged in 1941 at the decisive historical moment of the Second World War and the ramping up of the Holocaust horrors. It appears, only in hindsight, that the play, then the film, was unconsciously participating in the cultural erasure of the memory of Egyptian Jews being part of the national fabric, while purporting to perform cultural diversity. The play coauthor, Badi Khairy, has detailed in his memoires that the effort to include characters from the three faith communities was a deliberate attempt to enforce cultural diversity within the social fabric. The effort succeeded despite protestations from Jewish, Christian, and Muslim official institutions.

In all fairness, the film cast performs this purported diversity. Besides the director Fuad Al Jazaerly, who belongs to the Muslim majority, it includes the star Stephan Rosti, the Italian/Austro-Hungarian Egyptian Catholic, rumored to be Jewish, the future Egyptian Jewish star, Nagwa Salem, Victoria Hobeiqa, who is Syro-Lebanese Christian, and the Copt Iskandar Minassa. The dialogues were co-written by Naguib Rihani who was an Egyptian Chaldanian Christian.

Limitations of Cinematic Secularism

While cinema in the Middle East has promoted secularism by performing modernity and actively advocating for a modern lifestyle that was imported from Europe, thus importing secular practices, discourses, and values, it has never been a full-fledged agent of secularism. Rather, it has been the space of negotiation between forces tending to preserve tradition, and forces fascinated or subjugated by modernity. Hence, characters like Youssef and Abbas briefly analyzed earlier, enjoy modern life, flirt with a variety of women, and drink alcohol (which is a highly symbolic marker of westernization in predominantly Muslim societies as produced in Middle Eastern films), They implement their own personal moral code, which can be summarized as scrupulous in its respect of private or public property: they are in no way "thieves." But that code is extremely liberal in the department of romantic and sexual life and is in stark contrast with traditionally based religious morality. However, both Youssef and Abbas end up longing for a religiously sanctioned marriage and the films introduce that marriage as their reward for becoming good citizens.

Cinema in the Arab Middle East as a case study showcases this ambiguous role played by the seventh art: it has not engaged in disenchantment, radically replacing religion by rationality, but has promoted multiple enchantments, where multiple religious signs, characters, references, discourses, stereotypes associated with the major faith communities were introduced on screen. Hence, the ultimate authority of religion in matrimonial matters is never contested in the two films discussed earlier. But their secular agency is deployed in the construction of a web of desires where male and female representatives of the three major Abrahamic faith communities are represented. Youssef is exploring his desire for three women from three different faith communities. Abbas witnesses three men from three different communities pursue their desire for money. Cinema was not an entirely neutral space as much as it was a multicultural, multifaith one. However, that agency suffered from a serious shortcoming, precisely because of its adoption of stereotypes, let alone, sometimes, overt racism. In any case, the production of a multifaith scape translated power dynamics within society at large, thus always establishing a moral, social, and narrative hierarchy between the diverse communities. The Muslim male character is always the smart, funny, attractive lead, always gets the Muslim girl who is the female lead, and always is or becomes the richest among members of the three Abrahamic communities.

Notes

1. Talal Asad, *Formations of the Secular: Christianity, Islam, Modernity* (Stanford, CA: Stanford University Press, 2003), 127–33.
2. Gille Deleuze, *The Movement-Image* (Minneapolis: University of Minnesota Press, 1986), 8–11.
3. Ella Shohat, *Taboo Memories and Diasporic Voices* (Durham, NC: Duke University Press, 2006).
4. Ibid., 70–104.
5. Walid El Khachab, "*Le mélodrame en Égypte. Déterritorialisation, Intermédialité*," PhD diss. (Montreal: University of Montreal, 2003), 301–6.
6. Félix Guattari, "Un cinéma de l'immanence," in *La révolution moléculaire*, ed. Félix Guattari (Paris: Éditions Recherches, 1977).
7. El Khachab, *Le mélodrame en Égypte*, 294–7.
8. Ismael Adham, *Lemaza Ana Molh'ed? (Why I am an Atheist?)*. Alexandria: Ta'awon Press. 1937.
9. See Mariz Tadros, *Resistance, Revolt and Gender Justice in Egypt* (Syracuse: Syracuse University Press, 2016).
10. See Amr Katbeh, "The Civil State (Dawla Madaniya) A New Political Term?" *IFAIR*, February 24, 2014, https://ifair.eu/2014/02/24/the-civil-state-dawla-madaniya-a-new-political-term/.
11. Walid El Khachab. "Cinema and Modernity in The Middle East: Postcolonial Newness and Realism," in *The Modernist World*, ed. Allana Lindgren and Stephen Ross (New York: Routledge, 2015).
12. Talal Asad, *Secular Translations: Nation-State, Modern Self and Calculative Reason* (New York: Columbia University Press, 2019); Saba Mahmood, "Can Secularism be Other-Wise? A Critique of Charles Taylor's A Secular Age," in *Varieties of Secularism in a Secular Age*, ed. Michael Warner et al. (Cambridge, MA: Harvard University Press, 2010), 282–99.
13. Asad, *Secular Translations*, 22–3.
14. Assad, *Formations of the Secular*, 205–15.
15. Asad, *Secular Translations*, 22–3.

16 Selma Botman, "The Liberal Age, 1923–1952," in *The Cambridge History of Egypt*, ed. M. W. Daly (Cambridge: Cambridge University Press, 1998), 285–308.
17 Thomas Elsaesser, "Tales of Sound and Fury: Observations on Family Melodrama," in *Imitations of Life: A Reader on Film & Television Melodrama*, ed. Marcia Landy (Detroit: Wayne State University, 1991), 68–89.
18 Peter Brooks, *The Melodramatic Imagination* (New Haven, CT: Yale University Press, 1976).
19 Walid El Khachab, *Fuad El Mohandes and The Unconscious of Egyptian Cinema* (Cairo: Maraya Publishing House, 2022).

6

The Impossible Possible

Secularism and Hindi Popular Cinema

Sheila J. Nayar

Setting the Secularist Stage

If ever there was an evergreen secular Hindi film, *Amar Akbar Anthony* is it. While this classic *masala* (spice-mix) movie[1] may have acquired super-hit status in 1977, it has nostalgically grown since to blockbuster proportions. The plotline? Three male protagonists—a Hindu (Amar), a Muslim (Akbar), and a Christian (Anthony)—turn out to be blood brothers who were separated in their youth. By the end of the film, the three brothers reunite and marry without issue in their respective religions, notwithstanding an emotional reunion with their Hindu parents. Indeed, when Amar, Akbar, and Anthony are together, "the impossible becomes possible," as that mixed religious trio sings in the film's last scene.

Today, the phrase "Amar Akbar Anthony" implies "harmony among all religions," says journalist Sidharth Bhatia,[2] perhaps wistfully indicating a happier, more avowedly secular time than the nation today—which in early 2021 was downgraded to the rank of "partly free" democracy due to governmental scotching of social dissent. Indeed, in the last twenty years, according to political critics, India's *competing* nationalisms—between a "plural, secular and composite India (in contrast to Islamic Pakistan)" and an India encouraging and promoting Hindu nationalism (paradoxically echoing Islamic Pakistan)[3]—have come to serious loggerheads.[4] But as we shall see, India's political landscape in these last two decades does not always correlate with what audiences endorse by way of their having granted only a small contingent of films super-hit, blockbuster, and all-time blockbuster (ATB) status.[5] In fact, when it comes to secularism today—no less than in *AAA*'s day—the impossible becoming possible remains the prevailing Bollywood mantra. Even more, India's secularism, whether politically or cinematically speaking, does not exist *without* religion.

Given the seeming paradoxes of India's unique brand of secularism, let me provide some context before going on to address the recent audience-approved trends regarding its negotiation in Hindi popular cinema. If references to India's "deep diversity"[6] are frequent, they are also well warranted—and not merely religiously, given that religion is always transected by geography, history, linguistics, ethnicity, politics, and socioeconomics, and in the case of India, this has sometimes been ongoing for thousands of years. (What other mainstream cinema industry has opening title credits that often appear in three different scripts: Devanagari, Urdu, and English?) According to the 2011 Census of India, 98.75 percent of Indians identify themselves with a specific religion community—a percentage that rises to 99.41 percent if one includes the category of "other religions," including tribal ones ("Religion").[7] Mahatma Gandhi famously stated that religion is written into the fabric of India's cultural landscape—something with which the Constitution's writers agreed. Indeed, when Indians speak of their republic as having been founded on principles of secular modernity, what they really mean, advises Rinku Lamba, is that its founders staunchly opposed proclaiming an *established* religion.[8] Instead, the promotion was of "goodwill toward all faiths."[9]

Moreover, in being topographically sandwiched between a new neighbor that was decidedly Islamic (East and West Pakistan, now Pakistan and Bangladesh), India was unavoidably tied *to* religion, even as it positioned itself as a state proclaiming religious amity. Or, in slightly cruder terms, India would be a non-Hindu state—as distinct from the decidedly Muslim state of Pakistan, which likewise gained its independence from colonial rule in 1947. This was in spite of Hindus comprising 84 percent of India's population at the time—with the 30+ million Muslims electing to remain in India comprising just below 10 percent (now 15 percent). Constituent assembly members like B. R. Ambedkar also anticipated difficulties in transforming Hinduism if India were to declare itself a Hindu nation, predicting that the beneficiaries of its hierarchical order would never endorse deeply progressive change, such as regarding untouchability.[10] Religion in India possessed a public dimension and was not simply a private matter. In fact, the unevenness of that religiously diverse fabric mandated allowances for state intervention.[11]

As for the threads of that fabric, they are everywhere apparent in the public sphere: identifiable in styles of architecture and even in the names given to neighborhoods; in roadside Hindu altars, Sufi tombs, and Jain bird hospitals; in clothing like Sikh turbans or Parsi ceremonial caps, or appurtenances like steel bangles, crucifixes, and *Om* tattoos. They are there in the commercially printed religious calendars one might find on a bureaucrat's office wall or in the form of a private shrine next to a restaurant's cash register. They underpin India's myths and imagery, its music, and philosophies—which may have originated with one sect only to get picked up by others, including those modern secular sects known as advertising and popular entertainment. As art historian Kajri Jain expresses with judicious felicity, spirituality in India unfolds "through material engagements that blur—without erasing—distinctions between spirit and matter; religion, commerce, the state, and the public sphere; interiorized, individual, private faith and collective ritual performance."[12] One might even say that attempting to excise religion from India's public landscape would be signaling faith as no longer constituting a *way of life*—whether for good or for bad, whether as utopic celebration or interfaith chafing. Indeed, the cinema industry is often taken up with the conflicts, crises, and myriad entanglements that emerge when this coexistence is put (or felt to be put, or targeted as being put) in jeopardy.

True, for much of its history—especially from the 1970s to 1990s—Hindi popular cinema was deemed trite, juvenile, ahistorical, melodramatic, kitschy, and sentimental; too much of a spicy salmagundi, especially given its obligatory inclusion of songs that made genuine strides toward realism impossible. Still today, such qualifiers can roll off the pens of many an intellectual, with reviews deeming this or that movie escapist or uncritical—or, more colorfully, "retrograde, bloated, and formulaic" with "toxic levels of cheesiness" and "more red meat than grey matter" (these were some of the descriptions applied to the blockbuster *Tiger Zinda Hai* [Tiger Is Alive, 2017]). This is even the case as the films have become technically slicker and less narratively piecemeal, enough so that they are now sometimes reviewed by the likes of the *New York Times* or rogerebert.com.[13]

Still, Bollywood remains a profit-oriented industry; and as a commercial enterprise interested in the widest, most broad-based market possible, that means, too, that it yearns to appeal to the most *secular* market, in the Indian (religiously pluralistic) sense of that term.[14] (Many writers tried, in fact, in the nascent post-independence film industry to bring "a political left-wing and overtly secular outlook" to their movies[15]—which is to say, by jettisoning religion altogether—but they found their attempts unsuccessful at the box office.[16]) Prominent lyricist and Bollywood screenwriter Javed Akhtar publicly declared in 2006, "[I]f you want everybody to see your film, if you want to communicate with everybody, you will have to be secular. The producer cannot afford to be selective about his audience. He is desperate; he wants everybody."[17] After all, there are crores riding on these films. But as already noted, religion is too deep a determinant—a way of life, recall—that demands its also being a vital constituent of practically every film.

Notwithstanding that these films intend to "communicate with everybody," only a handful of the hundreds of films produced yearly become actual hits. The majority are received lukewarmly or are designated "flops" or, worse yet, "super-flops." Obviously, there is something more complex at hand, in terms of hitting the right chords apropos secularism. In restricting my analysis to films that have been unmitigated super-hits, blockbusters, and ATBs, my aim is to disclose what, when it comes to secularism, spectators are willing ideologically to submit or consent to, not to mention what they insist upon and also—sometimes, rather adamantly— reject. This feels especially pertinent given that the last two decades also align with the creeping rise of right-wing nationalism, including the massive success of the Hindu nationalist party, the Bharatiya Janata Party (BJP), to which the current prime minister, Narendra Modi, belongs. This party ideologically promotes Hindutva, or "Hindu-ness," as a cultural national identity, sometimes propagandistically tampering with how the mythology and history of Hinduism, and so of India more broadly, gets told. As such, we might glean something about the sentiments of the human on the ground regarding religious accommodativeness—that is, whether the more recent spate of successful films exposes shifts toward a more majoritarian and less tolerant attitude toward nationhood, or if those films have, instead, retained their "inclusive quality."[18]

The All-India Team-Players Approach

Projecting India's secular map in a unifying way has hardly dwindled since *Amar Akbar Anthony*. When it comes to co-religious assemblages reflecting a coalescent impulse, many top twenty-first-century films continue that trend. In the colonially set *Lagaan* (Taxation, 2001), a puckish Hindu villager manages to persuade villagers from his region to form a cricket team that will take on their insidious British oppressors. It is a team narratively intended to reflect India's pluralistic makeup, consisting as it does of caste Hindus, a Muslim, a Sikh, and even—in what is projected as the most initially repellant expectation of inclusivity—a Dalit sweeper. This initially inept all-Indian team must struggle with and overcome (or, at the least, temporarily suppress) their internal prejudices in order to take on the all-India oppressor.

More cosmopolitan is the ensemble cast of *Rang de Basanti* (The Colors of Spring, 2016), which comprises Delhiite college pals, including a charming, if nationalistically cynical, bad-boy Sikh; a modern Muslim; the rich son of a corrupt Hindu capitalist; a nonspiritual nationalist who is a pilot in the Indian Army; his Hindu girlfriend; and even a Hindutva nationalist, who will join them as actors for the production of a historic film that an Englishwoman has come to the capital city to make. Together, they will not only learn about their nation's fight for independence but also visit the Golden Temple in Amritsar, and not merely as tourists, but as participants in Sikh prayer. They will bicker, argue politics, condemn government rot, critique orthodoxy, and ultimately learn to act together in the name of social justice, which, in this film's instance, means fighting state corruption foremost. They will also dance or be accompanied to music embracing hymns, Hindu lamentations, Punjabi *bhangra*, and modern Hindi rock. Indeed, music is said to be one of the deepest, most creative, and most brilliant wellsprings of pluralism in Hindi popular cinema, given the industry's evocative and oft-sophisticated emotional use of Hindustani *ghazals*, Sufi *qawwalis*, and a wide variety of other religiously originated styles and genres. Alas, the inflamed activist impulses of *Rang de Basanti*'s Indian ensemble of friends—which echo those of the freedom fighters whom they are playing in the Briton's movie—lead to their deaths. Or is that fortunate, we might ask, in the sense that their deaths also quash any open-ended rebellion or revolt against the status quo, such that the movie's spectators can leave the theater cathartically intact?

In *Chak De! India* (Let's Go! India, 2007), catharsis comes in an entirely different manner. Here, a Muslim field-hockey player of old, Kabir Khan, seeks redemption from a humiliating past psychological wound: accusation that, as a player for Team India, he intentionally lost a match to Pakistan.[19] Now, he coaches the women's team, which is composed of all religious and regional stripes. Between negotiating the young women's exposed prejudices and internecine frictions—religious, ethnic, linguistic, urban-rural, and class-based—as well as some of their more personal battles, such as with male chauvinism, ultimately Khan leads them to victory on the international stage. In this film's case, it is the internal divisiveness eradicated for the sake of global supremacy that is fictionally fundamental, as is the through-line of a Muslim needing to prove himself loyal to the Indian nation. Indeed, such a demographically diverse set of characters learning to work jointly in order to combat a bigger adversary is not unlike the sort one sees in *Avengers: Endgame*—a film that, by the way, earned ATB status in India.

This coexistence model is the case even in films that critique some of the distasteful excesses, mindless rituals, or fractiously ugly rifts in religiosity. In *OMG: Oh My God!* (2012), an atheist Hindu (yes, Hinduism can sometimes be just that fluid) sues God in the courts when lightning demolishes his shop. With the aid of an urbane avatar of Krishna and a poor Muslim lawyer, not only does the shopkeeper pull the veil off commercialized religion, as distinct from true faith, but finds the latter himself at the end. In one of Bollywood's hugest ATBs to date, *PK* (2014), a space-alien struggles to comprehend India's bafflingly complex and contradictory multireligious landscape, including holy hucksters of sundry religious stripes, especially a rotund Hindu guru, who spends most of his time sowing seeds of communal discord and shoring up his profitable media-saturated racket based in superstition. Ultimately, the alien-protagonist's ambition is, unlike that guru's, to propagate pan-religious values of love, honor, and compassion for humanity (he even succeeds at reuniting his Hindu journalist-helper with her Pakistani lover). At one point, to make his case, he brings out several men whose outfits and appurtenances immediately convey their communal identities, only to reveal after that the Muslim is actually a Hindu; the Sikh, a Muslim, and so forth (By the way, both *OMG!* and *PK* were publicly criticized by orthodox Hindu contingents for desecrating Hinduism while downplaying Muslim hypocrisies.)

Indians Abroad

When religion in successful popular Hindi films is sidelined or pushed into narrative retreat, that opportunity often comes by way of displacement, with the story transpiring in New York City or Chicago, in Australia or Canada. There—and, to some degree, there alone—are characters afforded varying degrees of liberation from the familial-cultural pressures that can come with religious identity in India. True, characters will still recognizably belong to a faith, by virtue of an identifiably Hindu or Muslim surname, or the way they pray, or the name they use for God (Bhagwan, Allah, Waheguru) or other verbal markers (Long Live Hanuman, Inshallah, Sat Sri Akaal[20]). But in being away from the homeland, even if only as a Bombay staging of "abroad," characters are able to evade or, at the least, appear more independent from the domestic sway of extended families and communal networks. Indian-Hindu Jaggu and Pakistani-Muslim Sarfaraz's romance in *PK*, for instance, is implicitly predicated on their having been together at school in Europe. And if, in *Tiger Zinda Hai*, India's greatest spy is married to a Pakistani with whom he shares a child, that is aided by his never setting foot in India, in spite of his working for its intelligence agency. These Indians are also typically depicted as wealthy and educated and, so, aligned with foreign cosmopolitanism—with an imagined Western kind of secularism, we might even say.

At the turn of the millennium appeared the "NRI film," a romance subgenre devoted to narratives about non-resident Indians—and intended to attract that newest consumer of Bollywood films, the Indian diaspora. Either that or they served as a useful and even safely distant stage on which to negotiate tensions between modernity and "Indian values." Social dramas like *Kal Ho Naa Ho* (Tomorrow May Never Come, 2003) might never even set foot on Indian soil (or encounter an American "foreigner"). In the last decade, however, the concept of Indians abroad has taken a different turn as India, what with India, rather than merely its NRI population, having "gone global,"[21] giving rise to a more confident India, internationally speaking—something visible in the recent flurry of sports and thriller-spy films. One of the biggest box-office grossers of all time, the biographical film *Dangal* (Wrestling

Competition, 2016), is even bereft of the standard song-and-dance numbers of virtually all other ATBs. The film is based on the family saga of amateur wrestler Mahavir Singh Phogat, who raised his daughters, Geeta and Babita, to become international wrestling champions. Here, the main ideological canvas is that of gender discrimination, as well as of fatherly and filial duty. Indeed, we might aver that because this family follows the majoritarian faith, their celluloid practice of it can afford to remain peripheral. Phogat—unlike the Muslim Indian wrestler at the center of *Sultan* (2016) or the Muslim hockey coach in *Chak De! India*—is *not* under narrative obligation to prove his allegiances to the nation.[22] But like those films, *Dangal*, too, prides itself in demonstrating Indian competitiveness on the global stage, such that audiences get to extol that *larger* family, the nation.

In *Dhoom 3* (Blast 3, 2013), "abroad" signifies a fantasy space that is more construct than actual location. Sahir Iqbal Khan and Samar Iqbal Khan are, by virtue of their monikers, Muslim twins. They also happen to be seeking familial revenge on Anglo-American bankers, with Jai Dixit, the Hindu law officer, coming from India in the company of his Muslim colleague-cum-sidekick to assist the Chicago police in apprehending the Khans. So, are these names now merely marginal tokens of identity, relics of an absconded past, or are we being asked to read their identities allegorically? Is it conceivable that *Dhoom 3*'s flattening of religious identity would not have received the same level of audience approval had the film been set in India, where insulation from contingencies like community and socioeconomic inequities is more trying? We might even postulate that a movie like *Dhoom 3* is *escaping* India, in an attempt, paradoxically, to get out from under that nation's particular breed of secularism. In other words, such movies arguably permit a temporary displacement from the religious diversity—as enmeshed in power relations—at home.[23]

Tiger Zinda Hai attempts an even more radical shift in negotiating secularism abroad: via a legitimately international approach to human rights. From their (fictional) location in Syria, India's counter-terrorism intelligence forces, who are working with Tiger, agree to *join forces with Pakistan* in order to combat the greater global Jihadi threat. As the movie plays up, the Pakistanis are far more *like* the Indians than they are the Arab Muslim aggressors. "We can make it better when we come together," as Tiger declares.[24] Utopic, perhaps; but his words are crucially motivated by a secularist exhibitionism that is also decidedly Indian. For, not only do those words morally hinge on collaboration between the Indians and their (ideally secularist) Pakistani equivalents. They doubly mitigate the typical Western secularism's cult of the individual, given the additional (and explicitly played up) pluralistic makeup of Tiger's fellow agents, including a Sikh, a Muslim, and Hindus of various doctrinal stripes. (As for why I call this exhibitionism "decidedly Indian": Pakistan banned the film for its "demeaning" depiction of the state's law enforcement institutions and symbols [IANS, "Pakistan"], notwithstanding that the actor playing Tiger, Salman Khan, has a major following in that nation.)

"Good" Muslims and "Bad" Muslims

As we have already seen, when it comes to Muslim characters, often a narrative frisson comes in their being asked to prove their allegiance to India—first—and then, only secondarily, to their religion. In *Tiger Zinda Hai*, for instance, a young Muslim soldier, when religiously harassed, proves his patriotic mettle by displaying to his colleagues that what he is carrying in his backpack is not the Quran, but the Indian flag. In the action-thriller *War* (2019), a Muslim intelligence agent whose father was a traitor is brusquely questioned regarding his own loyalties. "I'm my mother's son, too," he reminds his senior officer (and future co-protagonist of the film). She is also a mother who prays for *all* of his colleagues, we are explicitly shown, thus certifying that she is, like he is, a "good" Muslim. Better yet, this son will unambiguously articulate his fidelity to India when espousing that one's country is supposed to come first, second, and last. Certainly, this dovetails with Wendy Brown's contention that, as a societal practice, tolerance is generally granted by the majoritarian group (the "tolerant"), which ultimately determines the extent to which the practices and behaviors of the minority group (the "tolerated") will be withstood.[25] In every lexicon, from plant physiology clear to medicine and engineering, tolerance, she says, "signifies the *limits* on what foreign, erroneous, objectionable, or dangerous element can be allowed to cohabit with the host without destroying the host."[26] In the Hindi film context, "the hegemonic group is typically constructed as universal and secular," argues Priya Kumar, "while minority groups are viewed as saturated by their religious and cultural identities."[27] But when one confines one's scope to the super-hits, blockbusters, and ATBs, what becomes swiftly apparent is that *all* orthodox extremes are reflected as minority positions potentially destructive of the host.

Consider the scene in *Tiger Zinda Hai* where the Indian and Pakistani agents collectively opt for privileging humanity over regional politics. In the process of deciding whether an Indo-Pak alliance is even feasible—the "impossible made possible," as that *AAA* trio once crooned—the agents imagine what a non-Partitioned India *could* have been: winning sports teams; really good music. One soldier even mentions an earlier ATB, the highest grossing film of 2001, *Gadar: Ek Prem Katha* (*Mutiny: A Love Story*), in which, during the time of Partition, a highborn Muslim girl falls in love with and marries the Sikh truck driver who saved her from attack by a Hindu mob. When the joint forces in *Tiger Zinda Hai* finally commit to their utopic compromise—they will jointly save the Indian and Pakistani nurses kidnapped by ISIS while working in Iraq—a member of the Indian contingent queries, "Does the PM know?" Apparently, this was intended as a tribute to Prime Minister Modi, who had negotiated the safe release of forty-six Indian nurses in much the same plight (though I'll confess that, upon screening the film, I interpreted this as a swift comical swipe at the right-wing nationalism promulgated by Modi's party because of the fictitious portrayal of Indian agents working with the Pakistanis). The film also takes some potshots at the United States for having promoted the rise of rebel factions in Afghanistan and the Middle East in the 1980s—factions that later regrouped into fundamentalist organizations like Al Qaeda. In fact, one of the undercurrents of the film seems to be "Shouldn't Indian *Muslims* be afraid?" This is not only the case because of global terrorism, so the film projects, but because the Middle East, with its oil economy that relies on exploited migrant workers from both India and Pakistan, becomes a means of uniting those of differing religious and national identities under the banner of *subcontinental* heritage.

Still, Muslims have of late been more recurrently maligned, perhaps nowhere more distressingly than in (the historically inaccurate and outright Islamophobic) *The Kashmir Files* (2022), with its conspiratorially fictitious recounting of the 1990 exodus of Pandit Kashmiris by Muslim insurgents. Alas, vilification is arguably there, too, in the recent spate of blockbuster "historical" epic dramas. In *Padmaavat* (2018), this comes via the historical Delhi Sultanate Allaudin Khilji, depicted here—and rather electrically, at that—as a vile, vicious, morally bankrupt, and ravenously meat-eating obsessive, a moral counterbalance to the film's stoic, principled Hindu Rajput leader. (This description alone likely accounts for why I put the word historical in quotation marks.) Far more glamorous fable and fantasy than any attempt at fact, this latest genre of films—including *Jodhaa Akbar* (2008) and *Tanhaji: The Unsung Warrior* (2020)—employs an aesthetic occasionally equated with India's longtime series of comic books, *Amar Chitra Katha*.[28] These films also sometimes deploy incongruously Arab tropes and stereotypes when depicting their Muslim villains. Consequently, and certainly understandably, some critics lament that the films are capitalizing on the Hindutva-oriented mood of the nation. The recent mythico-medieval *Tanhaji*, for instance, which topped the box office in 2020, was disparaged for its hyper-majoritarian nationalism and "saffronization" of events (the Mughals/Muslims as plunderers; the Marathas as godsends, etc.).[29] Then again, back in 2001, *Gadar: Ek Prem Katha* was critically rebuked for its similarly polarized canvas, which even led to protests and communal rioting. To complicate matters even further, only the year before *Tanhaji*, the mythico-medieval *Panipat* (2019) proved a super-flop.

Tanhaji garnered additional disapproval for anachronistically referencing the militaristic term "a surgical strike," thereby alluding to the retaliatory measures taken by the Indian Army against Muslim insurgents in Jammu and Kashmir in 2016. Of course, this is also a patent reference to a successful filmic precursor, the military action drama *Uri: The Surgical Strike* (2019). Such intertextual borrowings from earlier movies are a cultural constant in Bollywood. Consider, for instance, that, at one point in *Tiger Zinda Hai*, we get a musical paean to an earlier film of Salman Khan's, *Dabangg* (Fearless, 2010); and, in 2019's *Bharat* (India), an Indian ship crew are at near death at the hands of sub-Saharan African hijackers—that is, until Anthony Gonzales from *AAA* and the actor who played him, Amitabh Bachchan, become the topic of discussion, which subsequently leads to the hijackers' amiable departure. Even *AAA* makes reference to the goddess Santoshi Maa, who had only just gained popularity in India, thanks to the blockbuster *Jai Santoshi Maa* (Hail Santoshi Maa, 1975). Not only does this intertextually bind the films as a popular cultural form, it also constellates their secular potency in another complex way.

No, Hindus Aren't All (or Always) "Good"

If a film is to appeal to spectators across India's religious communities, identity reciprocation is key. So for every Muslim/Christian/Sikh ("brother," sidekick, sympathizer, profiteer) on the Hindu's side, a Hindu ("brother," sidekick, sympathizer, profiteer) can be found on the Muslim's/Christian's/Sikh's. Indeed, India's biggest blockbusters frequently attest to the presence and toxicity of demonstrably "bad" Hindus. For impetuously selfish reasons, the insidious Brahmin priest in *Padmaavat* aids the impetuously selfish Khilji. In *War*'s case, unabashed concession is made to how the world's neoliberal landscape has given rise to Hindu citizens dissolutely willing to sell out their nation for the sake of personal profit (here, to a ring of global Islamic terrorists). Reference in these movies to the secularly wide gambit of black-money corruption cannot be overstated. In *PK*, that corruption comes in the form of a Hindu guru-cum-media star who is basically fleecing his worshipful flock. Intriguingly, while conservative Hindu groups lambasted *PK* for not being critically tough enough on Islam but glibly mocking their religion, as earlier I mentioned, so too did Muslims complain that *Padmaavat* projected them in an entirely Islamophobic light. In the long run, either everybody is winning—or nobody is. Or, in another turn of phrase, in a land of diversity, there is always going to be a diversity of complaints regarding hurt sentiments.[30] Still, I would not want to make light of the fact that some Muslim stars have refused "out of fear" to speak up regarding the cinematic saffronizing of history recently promoted.[31]

Equally essential, however—and far less addressed in critical circles—is that the actual socioeconomic conditions of the majority of India's Muslims are *not* reflected in the sorts of villainously depicted figures in these movies, just as they are not in its Muslim protagonists either, whether the professional, educated, and fair-complexioned heroes in *War*, or the aristocratic, educated, and fair-complexioned heroines in a romance film like *Veer-Zaara* (Veer and Zaara, 2004). The conditions under which most of India's Muslim community lives are, in fact, "pitiable."[32] But an outsider spectator coming to these movies would hardly glean that Muslims are among the poorest sections of Indian society today (Vanaik). Even more, the majority of those who comprise this minority group in India descend from Hinduism's Dalit communities and "Other Backward Classes" (OBC), having converted from Hinduism in an attempt to escape its irredeemably crushing caste system, which sociologist Khalid Anis Ansari labels "a Brahminical disease."[33] There is a sad irony, thus, in the (potentially Hindu nationalist) projection in these recent films of Muslims as foreign invaders, since the majority of the extant Muslims in India (as well as its Christians) were trying historically to escape the injustices *of* Hinduism. Sadly, brandings of "Muslim Dalits" and "Christian Dalits" persist today—something rarely attested to on the Bollywood screen, much as one rarely sees representations of Dalit or even low-caste Hindu protagonists, and certainly not dark-skinned characters (unless as thugs).[34]

Could the cinematic depiction of Muslims as dominating over Hindus be, in some sense, a deflection from the true nature of the socioeconomic conditions of Muslims *in* India, and also of the more complex and sticky connections between Hinduism's caste biases and its minority populations? The painful intricacies, indeed the scourge, of caste are typically kept out of, or at least kept at bay in, Bombay cinema—and *attractively* so, we need speculate, since the movies discussed here have all been sanctioned by viewers based on domestic collections. Perhaps, then, there is a deep-seated sense that the aspirational hinges on an *escape* from the politics of caste and colorism or, at the least, demands an onscreen obliteration of such impingements—not unlike those Hollywood films conveniently set in comfortable and hermetically sealed upper-middle-class milieus.

But there are serious ramifications to Hindi cinema's figuration of the hero as someone typically fair-skinned, northern Indian, and high-caste or, if Muslim, *Ashraf*—which is to say, representative of the mere 15 percent of Muslims in India who trace their lineage back to western or central Asia or who are upper-caste converts (Ansari). And said hero *is* virtually always male, with the female conventionally ensconced in the role of "love interest" or "helper."[35] Accordingly, this recurrent (and, lately, highly muscularly steroidal) sort of hero becomes narratively aligned with the security and propping up of the Indian state. He becomes the lone signifier, the exclusive arbiter and face *of* secularism, with Bollywood thereby repeatedly injecting into its narratives a precariously colorist, patriarchal, regionalist, and casteist secularism—even when that hero is Muslim.

Such impingement even applies to a nobly intended film like *Lagaan*, in which Aamir Khan, in the role of the villager cricket-team captain, implores his bigoted (Hindu, Sikh, and Muslim) teammates to accept a crippled, Dahlit sweeper among their numbers. Why? Because the latter man's disability enables him to put a wicked spin on the ball. Of course, Khan doesn't exactly ask that sweeper if he wants to join. Even more, that sweeper, in being portrayed as physically infirm, also safeguards that he will not, in the end, disrupt the status quo by rebelling against his Indian oppressors. By being made to feel human *in* his lot, the film, in a kind of shrewdly Gandhi-esque move, preempts any upset of the film's secularly all-inclusive apple cart. Otherwise, Hinduism itself would require becoming the enemy, which would be far too disruptive given the predominant "Us-versus-Them" (Indians-versus-British colonizers) conflict that the film wants to maintain. The pluralized Indian secular network requires, in other words, that the multiple constituencies involved give up their claim to embodying *in themselves* the "living essence of the nation."[36] In the case of *Lagaan*, that means a necessary submission or subservience to the secularly fairer (and also physically fairer) leader of the group—a role amplified, and also consented to, by audiences because of Aamir Khan's star power. So, while *Lagaan* admirably includes a representative of a minority that is entirely tethered to India's majority religion, ultimately national identity must override all other societal allegiances, including religious, linguistic, and regional.[37] The paucity of Dalit representation in these films, as well as the general marginalization of lower-caste Hindus, is, in effect, the elephant in the secularist filmmaking room. There are, after all, as many Dalits as there are Muslims in India, with each group comprising 15 percent of the current population.

The Secularizing Text Beneath the Text

But there is one big and beautiful complication, at least, to all these films' projections of religious identity, one that no address of Hindi popular cinema would be complete without. The industry is notorious for running on "star power"—and male star power, at that. And for the last two decades, the biggest Bollywood stars, those who have appeared in so many of the ATBs addressed in this chapter, are themselves Muslim. While spectators in the West may rarely know or care about the religious persuasions of their movie stars, the same cannot be said of the subcontinent. This applies even to those films courting explicitly Hindu characters, like the Phogats whose nationalism is never in question in *Dangal*. After all, it is Aamir Khan starring as that villager-wrestler, much as he stars, too, in the aforementioned *Lagaan* (as a Hindu villager again) and also in *PK* (as its religiously baffled space-alien). Shah Rukh Khan, who appears as the Muslim field-hockey coach in *Chak De! India*, takes on a Hindu mantle in the ATB *Chennai Express* (2013), where the conflict pertains, in part, to regional cultural discrepancies; and in *Veer-Zaara*, as an Indian Hindu-Punjabi air-force pilot who falls in love with a bubbly Pakistani-Muslim-Punjabi. Salman Khan, meanwhile, plays an acolyte of the Hindu god Hanuman in *Bajrangi Bhaijaan* (Brother Bajrangi, 2015) who risks his life to get a mute Pakistani girl back to her parents and home country; but then slides, just as easily, into the role of the Muslim wrestler in *Sultan* who works his way into a startling comeback in order to represent his beloved nation.[38]

So, even when one of the Khans may be playing a Hindu protagonist, Muslim viewers—including Pakistani ones (Ghosh 13)—retain consciousness that beneath their played exterior of Hindu (or Sikh, or Christian) is someone who identifies as Muslim. And the same applies the other way around, with Hindus donning the roles of that nobly nation-loving Muslim agent in *War* and also that ignobly outsize sultan in *Padmaavat*. As for the actor Amrish Puri: he plays the strict, even rabid orthodox Muslim father in *Gadar: Ek Prem Katha*, a role which he performed in pretty much identical fashion in the earlier *Dilwale Dulhania Le Jayenge* (The Big-Hearted Will Take the Bride, 1995)—only that time as a Hindu. In fact, it's this capacity for easy re-costuming—of Muslims playing Sikhs, who themselves may be playing Christians, with those Christians effortlessly playing Hindus—that *PK* brings comically to the fore, as a warning of the deceptive ease with which externals can mask and even undercut true faith.[39] And so, a hero characterized as one religion may well elicit empathy and identification by spectators of other religions because of the "star text" operating beneath that portrayal; or, in Kumar's apt phrasing, spectators come to "listen to the other as if it were the self."[40]

Often remarked upon, too, is the secular nature of the film industry *behind* the camera. The industry writ large has historically proven itself to be "one of the most enduring secularist cultural sites of contemporary India with its diverse personnel coming from various religious and regional backgrounds."[41] Screenwriter Javed Siddiqi contends that this is because, in India, "cinema is primarily a business product" and, so, when it comes "to signing an actor or a technician, film makers don't look at their religion and [instead] strictly go by what suits their business interests."[42] No less of note is that many of the industry's actors are married to partners whose religion is not their own. Aamir Khan and Shah Rukh Khan have both been married to Hindus (something, again, virtually all Bollywood aficionados know). In this sense, these stars' own religiously pluralistic family lives may appear aspirational to viewers who could never imagine their own families allowing such interfaith marriages. In fact, sometimes the religious syncretism of their family dynamics even makes them fodder for troubling orthodox censures and screeds.

The *Sine Qua Non* of the "Good" Secular Film

If India remains a land where "prohibiting caste discrimination in public contexts would be insufficient to effect the kind of social change needed to give credence to claims that India in now a liberal-democratic state,"[43] perhaps that explains why so many blockbuster Hindi films suppress that discrimination or, even more familiarly, erase it altogether through representationally erasing the oppressed *from* the screen. And this, it bears repeating, is an erasure often sanctioned by film viewers, given their having collectively deemed these films meritorious, through that most precious means of judgment: their wallets. Perhaps this is because otherwise the entertainment would become too "real"; too depressing; too non-escapist; too marked with an open-ended despair of Us *versus Us*. While Indian politics today may be coming to reflect more of the latter, internally riven by a collapse of Hindu-Muslim unity, competing orthodoxies, and the rise of majoritarian impulses that suggest citizens no longer want to accommodate minorities, that is *not* overall what the resolutions to the last two decades of the cinema industry convey. In fact, what emerges foremost in limiting one's analysis to the super-hits, blockbusters, and ATBs is not what they narratively do when it comes to religious tolerance but what they virtually always *refrain from doing*.

Virtually no hero ever compels others to convert. Even, or maybe especially, in those films where interfaith romances do occur—*Gadar: Ek Prem Katha*, *Veer-Zaara*, *Tiger Zinda Hai*, *PK*—there is rarely the hint of one partner assuming that the other will change their religion, or of their being asked to convert, and certainly never of their being *forced* into conversion (though that may be initially demanded by extended family members, who may, just as likely, attempt to thwart the romance). Could this be because audiences recognize that religious genealogy matters—that it reflects the larger, cultural community to which every individual is inherently connected? Or is it because for most Indians this remains the *greatest* fantasy when it comes to religious pluralism—and, so, is read more as national allegory than as a personally negotiable feat? In the former case, Bollywood, like its spectators, may instinctively feel that one's identity is inherently woven from one's family religion (certainly as culture, if not as faith), rendering one's identity too much a part of one's being to simply or involuntarily let it go. In the latter case, the conversion motif remains suppressed because it would rip apart the "test" of the secular idea (and ideal) of India.

In that sense, the "good" secular film is one where one religious protagonist could just as well be replaced by that of another religion because, in the end, communal redemption is acquired through the same means: by defending India's honor. There is, of course, no lack of irony in Émile Durkheim's definition of religion, which emphasizes "beliefs and practices relative to sacred things" that unite a people "into one single moral community,"[44] applying just as well to these films' secularist appeals to the nation. The same could be said regarding evolutionary psychologist Robin Dunbar's argument with respect to religion: that it generally looks beyond the individual because it is more keenly sensitive to the survival of *the group*.[45]

But let me end by returning full circle to *Amar Akbar Anthony* and the lack of conversion at that film's end among its three brothers. As journalist Sidharth Bhatia declares, "[W]hat could be a stronger message of harmony?"[46] As I already posited, the pressures *off* screen to change one's faith (or, more likely, not to intermarry at all) may be substantial. We cannot ignore, after all, the extent to which intercaste and interfaith marriages remain a point of (sometimes horrifically violent and homicidal) contention. But in the films, if such anxieties are raised—and by any one of a number of religiously orthodox communities—it is in order that they may be allayed or pleasantly elided. What these movies more often promulgate, from *AAA* all the way to *Zinda*, is that one be a more principled person of one's respective faith. It is advice far more in line with housecleaning than revolutionary overthrow: if Hindu, be a *better* Hindu; if Muslim, a *better* Muslim; if Christian, a *better* Christian. Certainly, it's a message that dovetails with the existential principle Mahatma Gandhi promoted: that humans ought not to extricate themselves from their religion, but pursue truth from within it. And given how deeply the roots of these religious communities extend into the national soil, India can hardly begin from a blank slate. Instead, what Bollywood's spectators prefer, based on the imprimatur they have given select films, is that any "real" Hindu, any "real" Muslim—or Parsi, or Christian, or Buddhist, or Jain—is always one who, in the name of their religion, ethically puts *India first*[47] (or, at the least, sacrifices oneself trying). It is the cinematic projection of a land that perhaps never was—and yet must persist.

Notes

1 The term designates films that consist of a rather formulaic assortment of song, dance, fights, romance, melodrama, moral oratory, and comedic shtick.

2 [Qtd. in] IANS, "Hindi Cinema Has Greatly Contributed to a Secular Idea of India," *Business-Standard*, August 18, 2013, https://www.business-standard.com/article/news-ians/hindi-cinema-has-greatly-contributed-to-a-secular-idea-of-india-ians-books-113081800109_1.html (Retrieved June 29, 2020).

3 Edward Luce, *In Spite of the Gods: The Rise of Modern India* (Albany, NY: Anchor Books, 2008), 15.

4 Ibid., 151.

5 *See* Boxofficeindia.com, https://boxofficeindia.com/hit-down.php (Retrieved July 22, 2021).

6 Rajeev Bhargava, "Rehabilitating Secularism," in *Rethinking Secularism*, ed. Craig Calhoun, Mark Juergensmeyer, and Jonathan VanAntwerpen (Oxford: Oxford University Press, 2011), 95.

7 "Religion Census 2011," https://www.census2011.co.in/religion.php (Retrieved July 16, 2020).

8. Bruce J. Berman, Rajeev Bhargava, and André Liberté, "Introduction: Globalization Secular States, and Religious Diversity," in *Secular States and Religious Diversity*, ed. Bruce J. Berman, Rajeev Bhargava, and André Liberté (Vancouver, BC: University of British Columbia Press, 2013), 20–1.

9. Deepa Das Acevedo, "Secularism in the Indian Context," *Law & Social Inquiry* 38, no. 1 (2013): 160.

10. Rinku Lamba, "State Intervention in the Reform of a 'Religion of Rules': An Analysis of the Views of B.R. Ambedkar," in *Secular States and Religious Diversity*, ed. Bruce J. Berman, Rajeev Bhargava, and André Liberté (Vancouver, BC: University of British Columbia Press, 2013), 190.

11. Acevedo, "Secularism in the Indian Context," 160.

12. Kajri Jain, "Le mal des fleurs," *The Immanent Frame*, May 16, 2019, https://tif.ssrc.org/2019/05/16/le-mal-des-fleurs (Retrieved July 20, 2020).

13. The quotations come from: Abrams, who also, admittedly, called *Tiger Zinda Hai* "consistently sincere, energizing, and charming." See, Simone Abrams, "Tiger Zinda Hai," *Rogerebert*, January 1, 2018, https://www.rogerebert.com/reviews/tiger-zinda-hai-2017 (Retrieved July 22, 2020).

14. A new genre of indie-type films has indisputably arisen in the last two decades, produced for the educated cosmopolitan set that frequents the multiplex theaters ensconced in India's upscale malls. This is definitely ramifying the industry, since films are now being made with an eye exclusively on "the classes" (as distinct from "the masses").

15. These writers were Saadat Hasan Manto, Ali Sardar Jafri, Rajinder Singh Bedi, Sahir Ludhianvi, Kaifi Azmi, and Khwaja Ahmed Abbas.

16. Shyam Benegal, "Secularism and Popular Indian Cinema," in *The Crisis of Secularism in India*, ed. Anuradha Dingwaney Needham, Rajeswari, and Sunder Rajan (Durham, NC: Duke University Press, 2007), 230.

17. The same is true of Hinduism in today's hyper-mass-media environment: with the "god channels" on TV "aggressively inclusive, since their main aim is to maximize audience share." See Luce, *In Spite of the Gods*, 311–12.

18. Benegal, "Secularism and Popular Indian Cinema," 237. State censorship certainly has its part to play, given the Indian film board's proclivity toward eradicating anything judged too politically subversive, including scenes that might stoke communal unrest.

19. According to Kumar, it is only recently that Muslim protagonists in mainstream films are actually *played* by Muslims. See Priya Kumar, *Limiting Secularism: The Ethics of Coexistence in Indian Literature and Film* (Minneapolis: University of Minnesota Press, 2008), 180.

20. This last one, meaning the "Eternal Lord is Truth," is a Sikh greeting or blessing. In *Tiger Zinda Hai*, Tiger persuades his bomb specialist to save a nurse who has been strapped to explosives. Only after succeeding at the task is the soldier's religion identified—through Tiger's thanking him via the words "Sat Sri Akaal."

21 While economic liberalization began in the early 1990s, India's international presence has grown substantially since due to IT, partnerships with multinationals, digital communications, satellite TV, and greater disposable income on the part of the upper classes. At the same time, satellite TV and the like have resulted in greater exposure *in* India to the global landscape.

22 Director Ali Abbas Zafar articulated why Hindus would identify with the Muslim wrestler at the heart of *Sultan*: "It was the story of the struggle of an average Hindustani." [Qtd. in] Giridhar Jha, "Gully Boy, Sultan, Tiger Zinda Hai . . . How Bollywood Has Broken Free from Stereotyping Muslim Characters," *OutlookIndia.com*, February 17, 2020, https://www.outlookindia.com/magazine/story/ entertainment-news-gully-boy-sultan-tiger-zinda-ha i-how-bollywood-has-broken-free-from-stereotyping-muslim-characters/30 2756 (Retrieved June 29, 2020).

23 Bharghava, "Rehabilitating Secularism," 95.

24 Tiger himself appears something of a religious amalgam or religiously moving target. While his character's name is Hindu, he often wears a *keffiyeh*-patterned scarf.

25 Wendy Brown, "Introduction," in *Is Critique Secular? Blasphemy, Injury, and Free Speech* (Berkeley, CA: University of California Press, 2009).

26 [Qtd. in] Kumar, *Limiting Secularism*, xviii.

27 Ibid., xviii.

28 These are serialized stories of Hindu epics, myths, and saints, as well as of important religious, historical, and political figures in India.

29 The later films likely owe something, too, to the South Indian spectacular *Baahubali 2: The Conclusion* (2017), which now ranks as the biggest national box-office grosser *ever*. While that film is set in a mythological, pre-Islamic past, it unequivocally emphasizes that the kingdom at the heart of its story includes *non*-Hindu subjects.

30 Uday Bhatia, "How Bollywood Is Rewriting History," *Livemint*, December 1, 2019, (Retrieved July 4, 2020).

31 Javed Akhtar, "The Role of Cinema in Secular India," *JavedAkhtar.com*, February 17, 2017, http://javedakhtar.com/Article-4.html.

32 Christophe Jaffrelot, "The Fate of Secularism in India," *Carnegie Endowment for International Peace*, April 4, 2019, https://carnegieendowment.org/2019/04 /04/fate-of-secularism-in-india-pub-78689 (Retrieved July 18, 2020).

33 Khalid Anis Ansari, "India's Muslim Community Under a Churn: 85% Backward Pasmandas Up Against 15% Ashrafs," *The Print*, May 13, 2019, https://theprint.in/opinion/indias-muslim-community-under-a-churn-85 -backward-pasmandas-up-against-15-ashrafs/234599/ (Retrieved September 6, 2020).

34 One notable exception is the biting satire *Peepli Live* (2010), about a rustic farmer's planned suicide and the media's ensuing parasitic descent. (While not a major grosser, the film was deemed a super-hit on the basis of the ratio of its budget to domestic collections.) For films that do foreground Dalit

protagonists, see director Nagraj Manjule's Marathi-language films *Fandry* (Pig, 2013) and *Sairat* (Wild, 2016).

35 *Padmaavat* is arguably an exception here, what its climax of the titular queen committing self-immolation to escape the clutches of the unscrupulously infatuated Khilji. Of course, she did request and receive permission from her husband to do so before his entering and dying in battle.

36 William E. Connolly, *Why I Am Not a Secularist* (Minneapolis: University of Minnesota Press, 1999), 94. Connolly is here addressing not the Indian scenario but the recent rise in the West of pluralized networks as a modus vivendi.

37 Kumar, *Limiting Secularism*, 67.

38 Salman Khan is the product of a Hindu-Muslim marriage and prides himself as such.

39 Sheila J. Nayar, "Bollywood Religious Comedy: An Inaugural Humor-Neutics," *Journal of the American Academy of Religion*, 83, no. 3 (2015), https://academic.oup.com/jaar/article/83/3/808/727116 (Retrieved July 18, 2020).

40 Kumar, *Limiting Secularism*, 203.

41 Ibid., 179.

42 [qtd. in] Jha, "Gully Boy, Sultan, Tiger Zinda Hai . . . How Bollywood Has Broken Free From Stereotyping Muslim Characters." This does not mean that they cannot—they, in fact, do—show signs of elitism that are class- and education-based.

43 Acevedo, "Secularism in the Indian Context," 161.

44 Émile Durkheim, *The Elementary Forms of the Religious Life*, trans. Joseph Ward Swain (London: George Allen and Unwin, Ltd, 1964), 47.

45 Brandon Ambrosino, "How and Why Did Religion Evolve?" *BBC.com*. April 18, 2019, https://www.bbc.com/future/article/20190418-how-and-why-did-religion-evolve (Retrieved June 30, 2020). I have insufficient space here to address *alternative* reasons for why, beyond cathartic reconstitution, this modus vivendi might be favored. While intellectuals keenly foreground the historical wherefores of secularism—for example, the Enlightenment, the rise of the nation-state—rarely, if ever, do they acknowledge or dissect its absolutely fundamental link to *literacy*. The alphabetically literate milieu was paramount to secularism's rise, not to mention its very potential for existence. Secularism's origins lie not with its atomization from religion, I would argue, any more than they do with print culture, which permitted such atomization. In other words, when we negotiate that originally western European concept, what we are dealing with at heart is not secularism so much as *print*-secularism (cf. Benedict Anderson, on print-capitalism). Benedict Anderson, *Imagined Communities: Reflections on the Origin and Spread of Nationalism* (London: Verso, 2006).

46 [qtd. in] IANS, "Hindi Cinema Has Greatly Contributed to a Secular Idea of India."

47 I allude here quite intentionally to Prime Minister Modi's declaration of what his version of secularism meant: "Everyone has defined secularism in their own way. So, I always say that to me secularism means 'India first.' My India should stand foremost." (I need [to] note that in extrapolating on this notion of "My India," Modi turned to decidedly Hindu concepts.) See, Narendra Modi, "Narendra Modi Answers a Question on Meaning of Secularism," You Tube Video, 3:55, https://www.youtube.com/watch?v=PS--nIVAO4o/ (Retrieved July 18, 2020).

7

Observational Secular

Religion and Documentary Film in the United States

Kathryn Lofton

Documentary film addresses religion poorly, and there is little significant documentary film criticism that engages with religion.[1] Yet religion has been a significant subject for documentary film throughout its history. This conjoined declaration—that there are few quality documentaries about religion and no significant film criticism about religion, but religion is determining of documentary film—is the subject of this chapter. Documentary film historians do not acknowledge religion as a substantive subject, and documentary filmmakers have a vexed record of its capture.[2] In this silence and these stumbles, historians continue the modernist impulse defined by religion's denial, and filmmakers maintain its documentary persistence as a form of signified other. Looking at the kinds of visibility afforded religion in documentary offers a view into the secularizing work of nonfictional thinking of which documentary is but one emblematic genre.

This chapter explores the visibility of religion within documentary film through the analysis of three films from a particular epoch of documentary, observational or Direct Cinema, and the observational secular this movement advocated to achieve. This work is critical and constructive, seeking to evaluate preceding documentary attention and encourage better documentary artistic and critical acuity in the future. Trinh T. Minh-ha and Fatimah Tobing Rony have articulated well the political infrastructure of the documentary genre, underlining the racialized legacies of colonial exploration in documentary production in which the salvaging of "culture" served as an imperative inaugural force.[3] To this appraisal, I add the complicit religiosity of this documentary impulse to observe and educate. By "religiosity," I do not mean to identify a specific denomination or sect whose cosmologies influence a filmmaker's decisions, although this information can contribute to the interpretation of religion. Rather, the religiosity of documentary is in its inherent humanism—what Alexandra Juhasz and Alisa Lebow have called its "intent on changing the world."[4] Making documentaries and viewing documentaries have long been components of a broad pedagogical mission to raise awareness and encourage the tolerance of difference through the exposure of what is assumed to be, or is being rendered to be, unknown, mysterious, strange, and other.

In reference to the mid-twentieth-century US film archive of Direct Cinema, I argue that this humanism is indistinguishable from a performance of secular politics in which the documentarian is cast as the nonsectarian broker of subjects imagined to be less neutral than the filmmaker because the filmed subjects are sectarian—Catholic, Pentecostal, Lutheran. The making of documentary has frequently—but not exclusively—been a component to the broader aesthetics of control in which religion is something to be contained, rendering documentary itself an articulation of secular freedom. If one casts the documentarian as someone exploring subterranean spaces, traversing borders, and transgressing intimate boundaries, that figure emerges as the ultimate cosmopolite for whom religious life would be a contradictory piece of prejudicing baggage. If the critic or scholar understands the documentary director as necessarily secular, the resultant documentaries they make are secularizing, insofar as the documentary is often a viewing assignment imagined to be a pathway to assimilating into a plural society with compassion and intercultural understanding.

Assigning the word "secular" to documentary acknowledges its long-standing journalistic role in the public sphere while underlining the ideological, even homiletic, hope for such nonfictional persuasion. Like ethnographic writing and the postcolonial novel as described by Johannes Fabian and Benedict Anderson, documentaries produce a political ideology of hierarchical relations in and through the occupation of a cosmopolitan secular genre.[5] Naming the documentary as not just colonial in its anthropological origins but also secular in its educational purpose allows us to see more clearly its ideological valence. In the specific history of religion and its discursive operations in the United States, the secular is not an absence of religion but a series of contested and competing claims to religious authority. As many recent scholars of religion have demonstrated, the secular describes a context in which certain kinds of religions, certain ways of *being* religious, are preferred and protected, while others are stigmatized and prohibited by law and social expectation. More often than not, in the

United States, the forms of religion that jurisprudence and etiquette secure are those that submit to the norms of speech and act of white Christianity after the Reformation.[6]

For those outside of religious studies, it is sometimes hard to move from seeing the secular as a space of nonreligion or irreligion to seeing it as a tool for adjudicating competing ideas about religion. For most of the twentieth century, references to the secular usually meant allusions to the state's religious disestablishment. What post-9/11 studies of the secular have worked to expose is how this absence of official state religious authority does not diminish religious vibrancy among the people or claims to religious authority within and by the state. If anything—as, again, the robust sectarianism of the United States suggests—disestablishment increases the competitive social sphere for religion. Most scholars of religion now agree: the secular is not the absence of the sacred as much as it is a reterritorializing of what *is* sacred.[7] In this chapter, the word "secular" should be associated not with irreligion but rather with control over the absence or presence of religion.

Here I introduce a complicated category, the secular, into documentary studies, suggesting it is an imperative category to comprehend the ideology of its nonfictional pretense and aesthetic power. "If ever there is a set of filmic practices that contradict the spiritual side of life, it would be those associated with documentary," Juhasz and Lebow suggest. "But like all general claims made about the documentary, this omits important contributions to the practice of documentary that challenge its range and scope."[8] Documentary is not spiritual, these scholars note, but this doesn't mean that its nonfictional forms don't supply spiritual or religious power. Consider a recent survey of documentary directors by the British Film Institute's *Sight & Sound* magazine, which lists among its top ten documentaries the films *Man with a Movie Camera* (Dziga Vertov, 1929), *Shoah* (Claude Lanzmann, 1985), *Night and Fog* (Alain Resnais, 1956), and *The Thin Blue Line* (Errol Morris, 1988).[9] Watching these films, you will see nothing that the regular viewer might catalog as religion. Nobody prays; the camera does not linger on temple edifices; the subjects of the films say little about God. However, for admirers of these films, it seems strange not to use words like "sacred" or "sublime" as they describe these films' accomplishments. Two of these films address the Holocaust, all meditate in some way on the spiritual effects of trauma, and one offers a ramble in a mechanized urbanity in which ethical inquiries abound. Insofar as these movies ask where modern subjects sit in the universe, and under what material constraints and with what existential opportunities, the concept of religion seems useful to get at the existential bigness of what these films do, even as there is no minutiae of religious life on display.[10] These films are not depictions of spiritual life, but in their secular sight, they are not without spiritual meaning to their directors or viewers.

When documentary more overtly addresses religion, such sublimity transfigures to work either more sentimental or more hectoring than the classic works just cited. The vast majority of documentary films addressing religion do not offer accounts of religious lives that are generously disposed. Indeed, their entertainments exist on the grounds of cruelty toward the religious: cruelty as manifest in how the films show some aspect of religion brainwashing its followers, or how invariably self-contradictory religious belief is, or how proximate piety is to mental illness or sexual sublimation. Religion in documentary film is rarely a site of individual or social complexity or ingenuity. Rather, documentary films in the United States such as those often produced by National Geographic celebrate the splendor of religion, or documentary films try to explain the experience of conservative American Christianity, such as in *The Eyes of Tammy Faye* (Fenton Bailey and Randy Barbato, 2000), *Hell House* (George Ratliff, 2001), or *Jesus Camp* (Heidi Ewing and Rachel Grady, 2006). Whether one views debunking treatments of religion such as *Religulous* (Larry Charles, 2008) or investigative treatments of religion such as *Going Clear: Scientology and the Prison of Belief* (Alex Gibney, 2015) or *8: The Mormon Proposition* (Reed Cowan and Steven Greenstreet, 2010), the verdict on religion in documentary film is the same. Documentary film on religion condemns religion as an overbearing source of anti-intellectual sensory wonder or social control. According to Brian Winston, the "tradition of the victim" suffuses documentary filmmaking from the late-nineteenth-century capture of exotic subjects in salvage ethnography to the depiction of human beings as social problems in *The March of Time* (Time Inc., 1935–51) newsreels.[11] We could decide that religion is just another subject in that documentary tradition of victimhood.[12]

This would be a mistake. Like any nonfictional genre, the documentary form can be deployed to better and worse realizations of its educational imperative. As Anna Grimshaw and Amanda Ravetz have argued, the term "observational cinema" designated a media formation that included a wide variety of films whose production worked overtly to break from earlier anthropological approaches toward the recording of social and cultural practice.[13] Taking up the secular in observational documentary—and marking it as the observational secular—allows us to see what hermeneutic good can exist in documentary film considering religion. The emergence of observational documentary encouraged filmmakers and critics alike to consider reflexivity in the relationship between filmmaker and filmed. During the heyday of observational cinema, nonfiction was itself a highly contested cultural form, and observational documentary contributed to querying what mediated truth can exist. Three Direct Cinema films about religion—*A Time for Burning* (Bill Jersey and Barbara Connell, 1966), *Holy Ghost People* (Peter Adair, 1967), and *Salesman* (David Maysles, Albert Maysles, and Charlotte Zwerin, 1969)—offered religion not as a subject in opposition to the self-proclaimed secular of the filmmakers but as a form of interpersonal reckoning and intimacy. As will be conveyed in their own voices, Direct Cinema documentarians strive for a relational performance of neutrality. This is what I will call the observational secular, namely the effort by filmmakers to set themselves in the middle of relationships defined by religion and use their cameras and editing to depict what comprises those relational forces without deciding on a side to take.

As I researched these individual Direct Cinema filmmakers, I found in every directorial case an overwhelming verbosity about their formal, and expressly *irreligious*, ambitions as documentarians. Their repeated references to their neutrality toward their subjects were simultaneous with their disavowals of religion. The latter is, of course, a contradiction of the former: one cannot be neutral toward that which one ardently claims not to be. Denying religion is still a relationship to religion. Even more, in this instance, we find that in this space of fierce neutrality, the filmmakers are not quiet about what they prefer to be or do; they had rules. Whatever success or failure Direct Cinema was, it had many of the components of a new sect, including doctrine, commandments, charismatic leadership, and a significant following. As archival records consistently show, vérité documentarians intended to do something different with their human subjects than what had been done before. They did not want to idealize human subjects as congruent icons or potential heroes; they also did not debunk their subjects, seeking hypocrisy in their choices. Instead, they sought to find the humanity that emerges through everyday acts of relational interpretation and reconciliation. This often leaves the edges of the films, and the subjects, more ragged than romantic and the films more boring than dramatic.[14]

In his definition of documentary, philosopher and communication studies scholar Carl Plantinga says that a grounding principle for documentary is that the filmmakers must "take an attitude of belief toward relevant propositional content."[15] Returning to these filmmakers and these particular films exposes something else. For observational filmmakers of the 1960s, the effort was to capture resistance and presence. Talking about this ambition led to grandiloquent claims, such as by Albert Maysles:

> I think the most essential element in my work is my love for people and my understanding of people and the success that I have in understanding them through my work. You see it on the screen. It's a hard relationship I have with the people I am filming ... they pick up on my empathizing.... Anyone watching one of my films should have no difficulty getting very close to the people on the screen and I think become all the better person for having had that experience.[16]

I do not claim that the Direct Cinema films on which I focus achieve their stated relational objectives. Instead, I contend that one can see in these films an effort to depict the recording gaze as a relationship for the filmed to engage. Arguing that these films achieve an observational secular that reckons with the camera's objectification, this chapter concludes with recommendations for future work in the study of religion and documentary film.

Observational Secular, 1966–68

Documentarians have stigmatized or erased religious subjectivity in ways related to, but not perfectly isomorphic with, the pedagogical role of race in documentary film. Stephen Charbonneau argues that the history of documentary film is indistinguishable from the representation of racial otherness, since its genre origins date to nineteenth-century efforts to integrate filmmaking into anthropological excursions. It is also difficult to disentangle race from the documentary film's broader liberal tendency to train citizens, promote social pedagogy, and, to some extent, manage the excesses of modern life in the twentieth century.[17] The subject of religion in twentieth-century documentary film is similar in its position relative to race: documentary exists as a context for teaching the public about something presumed to be *other than that public*.

Writing about the Second World War newsreels, Sumiko Higashi describes how the "voice of God" narration in Paramount News continued in the rational investigative tradition of the interwar American urban reporter, "while its moral exhortation, rendering ideology more transparent, expressed a Manichaean view of the cosmos."[18] Postwar educational movies lightened a bit on its wartime rhetoric, but the moralizing narrative remained. Documentary film, especially in its relationship to educational film, has always had an inferred needful viewer who requires the humanistic education documentary provides. Historians have explained how American infrastructure for the use of educational films grew exponentially after the Second World War as a feature of Cold War efforts to program civic identity.[19] Documentary played a critical role in establishing the impression of American democratic society as tolerant, not only through its depictions of America as a civic ideal but also—through their distribution and screenings—making a common civic space for Americans to learn how to be American. Higashi suggests that as postwar America became increasingly less churchgoing and ostensibly secularized, the "moral polarity of a melodramatic world of absolutes . . . served the rhetorical purposes of discourse on the 'Other.'"[20] As fewer people attended actual churches, the gospel of the nation, depicted in educational films, emerged as a ritual commons.

Beginning in the late 1950s, Direct Cinema sought to resist the moralizing sentimentality of postwar documentary realism, especially manifest in the use of somnambulant narrators, sit-down interviews, and static compositions. The filmmakers associated with these movements, known as Direct Cinema in the United States and Canada, cinéma vérité in France, and, slightly later, Free Cinema or observational documentary in Britain, shared certain aesthetic conventions, including the rejection of carefully scripted cinema. Filmmakers associated with these schools seemed unconcerned if their images were grainy and wobbly or went out of focus. This rougher aesthetic became an aesthetic signifying the "real" of what they recorded.[21] The films also emphasized indirect address rather than individuals speaking directly to the camera, thereby minimizing the viewer's sense that the onscreen figures acted conscientiously, in light of the filmmakers' presence, and placing the viewer in between the on-camera speakers. Films further conveyed this sense of the noninvasive filmmaker through long takes, synchronous sound, and the eschewal of voice-over narration. "The virtue of the long take," said Albert Maysles, a leading artist in Direct Cinema, "is that it involves necessarily less artificiality. The artificiality of the author-editor is thrown out for the duration of the take. The viewer is put in the driver's seat: the continuity that he selects from gives him a feeling of really knowing exactly what's happening."[22] Resulting films tended toward spatiotemporal continuity rather than montage, invoking the feeling of a perpetual "present tense" to the recorded proceedings.[23]

In her brilliant reading of *Primary* (Robert Drew, 1960), Jeanne Hall suggests that *cinéma vérité* may be defined as a style that is specifically interested in examining the nature of persuasion.[24] For some critics, the self-importance of *vérité* directors, as well as subsequent debates about how "truthful" their realism was, undermines the power of this stylistic genre. Hall rejects these debates over the *veritas* (truth) of *cinéma vérité*, asking instead that we focus on how these films help us think about documentary as a form of textual criticism about persuasion. Breaking down the editorial work in *Primary*, Hall argues that as a comment on ideology and argument, the film exposes how the *vérité* documentarian isn't producing truth but illustrating how the documentary is produced to be read *as* truth.

Adding to Hall's significant insight about how *cinéma vérité* comments on the editing process, I suggest that *A Time for Burning*, *Holy Ghost People*, and *Salesman* each render their subjects participants in the formation of the secular attention given to them. When I point to the observational secular in these three films, I am trying to describe the relationship between the documentarians' attitudes toward their films' formal qualities and the aims and focus of their documentary looking. These films focus on the space *between*: between human beings, between filmmaker and subject, and between named ideals and lived practices. Reading *Primary*, Hall asks us to think about how *vérité* aesthetics—grainy, wobbly, occasionally out-of-focus images; indirect address; long takes; synchronous sound; and spatiotemporal continuity—reflect an attempt to represent the editorial process of assemblage. I suggest that these same aesthetics are likewise emblematic of the relational techniques they show, including the hesitations of racial and religious reconciliation, the queer possibilities for public intimacy, and the hardship of professional failure. The roughened forms of Direct Cinema express the ragged edges of interpersonal life, of political life, and of economic survival. That they do so in and through religion is not random but appropriate, since religion is a structure of relational life, between self and other, self and deity, self and institutional systems of rule and authority.

Advocates for Direct Cinema believed that their films allowed greater freedom of interpretation on the part of the viewer, because the filmmaker pulled back their role as arbiter, editor, or moralizer and let the scene they observed play out.[25] Its documentarian leaders stressed an empathetic, nonjudgmental, participatory mode of observation that attenuated the authoritative posture of traditional documentary narrative exposition and control.[26] Robert Drew, producer of *Primary*, conveyed this position: "The film maker's personality is in no way directly involved in directing the action."[27] Descriptions of Direct Cinema repeat this promise that it "conveys a sense of unmediated and unfettered access to the world" and that "this quality of observation-without-intervention became one of the key claims of its truth-value."[28] This sense of being "unmediated" was the editorial craft of the filmmaker, and it is in this work of rendering the space of the viewer as one of all-access intimacy that we find something better for religion's perception. The observational filmmaking movement was an explicit reformation of documentary to improve upon its didacticism and legacy of colonial anthropology.[29]

Influenced by postwar independence movements in Asia and Africa, observational filmmakers understood themselves as replying to the problem of colonial control by locating themselves differently toward the subjects, in a way that closed the interpretive gap. As Albert Maysles explained, "in this case, [the] filming technique, consists of it letting it happen . . . . Then, when it begins to turn off a little bit, without even saying anything, you can pull it back in. It's that subtle sort of thing."[30] Like many sectarian reformers before them, they quickly codified, and disagreed about, rules for the right and wrong ways to make documentaries.[31] "Paradoxically, the film-making movement which seemed to stand for iconoclasm and freedom became one of the most codified and puritanical."[32] Students of religion will be unsurprised that an effort to purify and democratize a particular field—here, documentary film—led to new forms of chauvinism and control. Filmmakers in this idiom thought that what they did was truer than preceding anthropological or educational films, because they did not judge what they witnessed but instead sought to observe the relationships people had with one another and how relationships and choices were never all bad or all good.[33] The conscientiousness of Direct Cinema did not produce perfect films, but it did offer forms of secular observance indicative of the capacities for documentary to find its footing in the subject religion. Let us turn to three instances of Direct Cinema's observational secular to watch it at work.

A Time for Burning

This 1966 film records the efforts of L. William Youngdahl, the ingenuous pastor of a white Lutheran Church in Omaha, Nebraska, to initiate an exchange between his church and neighboring all-Black churches. Segregationists within his church oppose the plan, and they force the pastor to resign. The plot of this film is this simple: an overly earnest white man asks his white flock to do something they are still too racist to do, and he loses his job for it. The climactic event of the film transpires offstage. In a proximate experiment at a nearby high school, a teacher encourages white high school students to visit a Black congregation and a group of Black high school students to visit a white Lutheran church. The white students visit the Black congregation without incident. After the Black high school students make their visit, members of the white Lutheran congregation threaten to quit the church if it becomes a regular occurrence. Church leaders see this as a dangerous portend if any further racial exchanges take place.

The two most prominent figures in the film are Youngdahl, the earnest white pastor, and Ernie Chambers, a brilliant, Black atheist community leader.[34] Aside from their regular onscreen appearances, the film primarily listens into conversations among churchmen and laity as they wrestle with the idea of integration in a moment of national civil rights conversation. The majority of the film focuses on white and Black Christians talking about the idea of exchange and the upset after the student visits to the churches. There are some interior shots of church services, but mainly we see churchmen talking in church offices or meeting in church basements or students talking in what appears to be some sort of club. There are many good one-liners. There are no hugs, no handshakes, and no happy resolutions between the disconnected parties; instead, the film depicts many awkward, failed efforts at relational connection in service of racial and religious reconciliation.

The film has denominational origins. Lutheran Film Associates, a media company established in 1952 as a joint venture between the Evangelical Lutheran Church in America and the Lutheran Church–Missouri Synod, was assigned to produce a film that would address the era's radical social and political shifts and offer guidance to church members wrestling with these changes. The company's executive secretary, Robert E. A. Lee, then commissioned Quest Productions and its producer, Bill Jersey, to make the film.[35] Throughout the history of Christianity, churches have found ways to educate their parishioners on social issues through these kinds of educational media, whether through tract societies, broadcasting networks, or the embrace of film, television, and documentary film as a genre useful for missionary conveyance. Educated at the evangelical Christian colleges Houghton College in New York and Wheaton College in Illinois, Jersey made the film with a strong cultural understanding of white American Christianity, despite considering himself to be a humanist, not a Christian, by this time.[36]

By his own testimony, Jersey saw more reason in Chambers's political resistance than in Youngdahl's hopeful piety, mainly because Chambers's arguments proved true: "If you listen and try to do something," Chambers says to Youngdahl, "you'll get kicked out of your church. That's the way your people are." At the beginning of the film, and before the students visited the congregations, Chambers explains to him, "You did not gain control of the world like you have it now by dealing fairly with men, keeping your word. You're treaty breakers; you're liars; you're thieves; you rape entire continents and races of people then you wonder why these very people don't have any confidence or trust in you. Your religion means nothing." Chambers tells Youngdahl that his Jesus is "contaminated" and that he is wary of engaging him, however well-meaning the pastor may intend to be. "I have a terrible feeling against preachers since I think you're responsible for the problem in the first place," Chambers says. "And for you this may be an excursion across the line." When he leans into his enunciation of excursion, into the second syllable, the meaning is clear: he will not be anyone's experience. He refuses to be an ethnographic subject like Nanook in *Nanook of the North* (Robert J. Flaherty, 1922), and he won't let the Black people of Omaha be Youngdahl's anthropological encounter. Chambers is not going to help a white man get what he needs to feel better about anti-Black systems of injustice with which he is complicit.

The film is memorable because it unblinkingly exposes how arguments for civility produce racist systems. Not a single figure goes on record in the film articulating racist sentiment as such. Yet the majority of white speakers repeatedly insist that it is not the right time to engage with Black people through the church. They are anxious about property values; they are anxious about diminishing numbers in the pews. They wonder why Youngdahl has chosen this social issue rather than another. "Why pick this one?" a white leader asks. "Why be so revolutionary?" Although a few voices in the white church resist such calls ("If we don't start now as a church, the world is going to pass us by," says one), the overwhelming majority articulate a fear of the mimetic effects of any appearance of integration. This description might suggest that the film focuses on white voices, when the primary cinematic reversal it makes—reversal relative to the history of colonial ethnography that preceded it—is to make Black voices the organizing authorities of the film. Although Youngdahl's face is the first one seen on camera, the first voice heard is a Black male student speaking about the universality of prejudice, then a Black woman resisting his assertion. Through the film, argument never achieves resolution. There is less action than reaction to occurrences off-screen and the anticipation of potential occurrences. The editing of the film fades in and out of discussions, suggesting that part of the problem in social change isn't silence as much as it is indecisive positioning. The film concludes with images of white and Black churchgoers worshipping separately, reflecting a sociological fact of American Christianity that has few exceptions.

As a depiction of religion, *A Time for Burning* is unique in its effort to expose simultaneously liberal and conservative views within a religious tradition and in its depictions of critique of a religious tradition as internal to the occupation of a religious world. The film practices an observational secular in the way it nestles into religion as a relational practice of interpretation. Although Jersey is clearly a fan of Chambers—a fact the filmmaker reiterated in interviews over the next five decades—he offers a disciplined account of everyone's viewpoint in the documentary, and he avoids turning Black spirituality into a romantic good or white spirituality into a racist tool of power. Everyone, Christian and not, communicates their beliefs: to other Christians, to other community members, and to the camera. Jersey focuses not on landscapes or physical environment, honing instead on dialogue and close-up shots of faces as they speak. This is a depiction of a very real history of racial and religious reconciliation in its hesitant movements, intense discussions, and ultimate failures. Youngdahl preaches from the pulpit, "I think the Christian community has a great opportunity today to help change the climate." Some in the crowd nod. When he asks if there is any hope for reconciliation, Chambers says no. This doesn't stop Youngdahl from continuing to work, and it doesn't stop many Christians, white and Black, from continuing to debate. In the discussion among Black students, a woman says, "the people make up the church and not the other way around," and one of the reasons *A Time for Burning* is such a successful depiction of religion is that it holds true to this vision. There is no hegemonic power or blind devotion. There are simply people, debating and deciding what to resist and what to maintain.

Holy Ghost People

The premise of the 1967 documentary *Holy Ghost People* could hardly be anything other than exploitative: a filmmaker with self-professed atheist views goes to the mountains of West Virginia and watches a Pentecostal service that includes snake handling. Because serpent handling occurs primarily in the Appalachian South, popular coverage of snake handling constructs its handlers "as exotic, bizarre, and grotesque denizens of a southern nether world, as a trivial sideshow spectacle beyond the ken of humanity."[37] Historian of religions Robert Orsi echoes this sentiment, arguing that people are simultaneously attracted to and repulsed by individuals who, in the case of serpent handling, "'do forbidden things with their bodies' and, in doing so, claim intimate access to transcendent power."[38] *Holy Ghost People* fulfills these worries, partaking, in nonfiction form, of the realistic traditions of Southern Gothic fiction.[39] Is this all it does? A closer look at the film, as well as the filmmaker's own legacy, suggests that the film is not only offering depictions of the other or the bizarre but also capturing relational intimacy.

The film does traffic in many primitive tropes. The opening voice-over in the film establishes these religious people as hidden in the backwoods ("thousands are scattered among the hills") and in possession of beliefs that lead them to speak in tongues, drink strychnine, and handle snakes as a sign of the presence of the Holy Spirit. The camera's view as we hear this explanation is that from a driver's side of a car, careening through mountain communities that seem abandoned. After the introduction, we see two unnamed men and two unnamed women in a series of monologues, describing how they first got the Holy Ghost. They speak in detailed, loping ways, unhurried and easy in the story. Viewers familiar with the Pentecostal tradition can see these are testimonies that have likely been said before, spoken in church services as testimonies of their ties to the faith.

After the monologues, there is a jump in style, from individual speeches to an exterior nighttime shot. We see cars pull up, headlights bright and almost blinding to the viewer; the adults and children from the cars enter a nondescript building. The preacher begins, "I believe it's time we should start the service. And we want everybody here that's got the Holy Ghost to get in the service, put something in the service. And if you haven't got the Holy Ghost, come and seek the Lord and get it, 'cause you need it." Aside from the main preacher, we do not hear the people during the service. We do not hear their chatter, gossip, or prayers. They are bodies and murmurs, tambourines shaking, and hands in the air. The subjects are white, but the filmmaker casts their lives in shadows and darkness.

Reviewers at the time loved the film. In *Film Quarterly*, Ernest Callenbach wrote, "the film follows the very informal procedures in a cool, descriptive, ethnographic way. There is no condescension and no phoney [sic] explanation in the film; it simply presents these remarkable people to us."[40] Folklorist William Clements said, "*Holy Ghost People* ... avoids sensational treatment of snake-handling by placing the ritual in its worship context."[41] And Margaret Mead extolled, "The audience, whether a sophisticated audience of specialists or a mixed group of students, becomes completely entranced, as opposed to 'in trance,' and emerges from viewing the film ready for new levels of discussion of the realities of religious experience."[42] The summary reaction was that *Holy Ghost People* achieved the goal of observational film, letting events unfold and thereby giving viewers access to a whole world of experience.[43] Contemporary scholars might see the film as a reductionist rendering of the religious subject rather than a quality interpretation of religious lives. In addition, robust studies of the secular thoroughly contest

Mead's distinction between a secular audience that can be entranced but not deceived, available to be enthralled but still able to wake up and discern "realities."[44] Whatever positive words the contemporaneous reviews offer, they still distinguish between the film's subjects and the audience, the former who were understood to be religious and the latter who were not. Such presumptions—that the people in the film couldn't be in its eventual audience and that the audience, though enthralled, wouldn't ultimately be this kind of religious—define the problems produced by the observational secular.

There is no doubt that the film fails to adequately put the snake handlers' beliefs and practices into any sort of general cultural context and thereby refuses opportunities to think about the relationship—economic, political, psychological, gendered—between what the on-camera practitioners do and what they think. Filmmaker Peter Adair's public comments about his personal history, combined with a rereading of the film, invite understanding the specific observational perspective of *Holy Ghost People*. Adair did reproduce certain tropes of the colonial gaze; he also used his cinematographic gaze to focus on particular physical elements of how his physical subjects spoke to one another in and through the ritual idiom they practiced.

Born in Los Angeles County, but raised in Navajo country, Adair was the son of the visual anthropologist John Adair, whose most famous work, the Navajo Filmmaking Project, involved teaching a group of Navajo people to make subjective films about themselves and their culture; he intended these films to both supplement the work of outside anthropologists and to explore broad questions about cross-cultural communication.[45] John Adair was a stock anthropological figure, "loving" Native American art and understanding that love as a meaningful mutuality and perceiving Navajo ingenuity with silversmithing as an emblem through which to expose the depth and substance of Indigenous cultures of the Southwest.[46] Peter Adair would later credit the experience of growing up on a reservation with shaping the way he approached his own films. "Being in the minority, and sometimes the only white kid around, started me looking at everything from the eyes of an outsider. So in a sense, all my films, even if they are about my peers, are cultural studies."[47]

Such a genealogy could implicate the long anthropological legacy in Peter Adair's documentary approach. Many of those archivists and anthropologists associated with the broad practice of salvage ethnography worked to record cultures they understood as "vanishing," and they narratively structured this reclamation around paradigmatic figures—craftsmen, shamans, hunters—who became a metonym for an evaporating Indigenous nobility. Yet Adair's film career did not evince an obsession with individual mythic subjects or the otherness of their power. Rather, his work increasingly focused on an effort to see *his* tribe, the LGBTQ community, as a broad social reality of diverse individual experience. In the two decades following *Holy Ghost People*, Adair became a legendary recorder of gay experience, perhaps most famously with his landmark collaborative project, *Word Is Out* (Mariposa Film Group, 1977), a documentary by and about queer men and women.[48] For the major part of his career, he spoke passionately about the work of bringing gay voices to light and to making their lives seem familiar, complicated, and human rather than exotic or dangerous.[49] He would not return to overtly religious subjects in his filmography, leaving *Holy Ghost People* as a topical exception to his work. How might we connect the filmmaker of *Holy Ghost People* with the filmmaker of *The AIDS Show* (with Rob Epstein, 1986) and *Absolutely Positive* (1991)? The obvious connection is the work of using a number of individual cases to comment on aggregate and marginalized social experience.

Yet a return to *Holy Ghost People* after reviewing Adair's longer filmography invites a more intimate connection, focusing on the physical intensity he records in the film. The last scene shows the preacher after a snake bit his hand. As the preacher sops up the blood with a kerchief, he is heard saying some words of prayerful calm. The film concludes with a shot of his swollen hand. Hands are everywhere in the long worship scene that comprises the majority of the film. Hands in the air, hands on cheeks, hands covering mouths, hands holding babies. Hands grabbing other hands. The unfocused ritual allows for multiple parallel physical realities. There are bored toddlers, quietly singing grandmothers, teen women speaking in tongues, and middle-aged men praying over someone. There is a coed duo singing a gospel tune. Physical intimacy predominates the scene. The camera tracks in and out of song and testimony, in and out of the bodies dancing, falling onto other bodies, as some sing. The film conveys a room in which no one is exactly synchronous as individuals access the spirit in a variety of ways but unite in delicate, quickly shifting moments through touch: touching one another, touching the snakes, touching his back or her neck, hugging quickly and moving forward languidly, rhythmically. Nobody once visibly shirks off a touch. Nobody slaps a hand away. You see women touching men but also men holding onto other men, accepting that touching is component to the spirit's presence.

The sexualization of religious behavior by nonreligious and differently religious observers has a long and problematic interpretive history, including the sensationalizing of Catholic religious women by anti-Catholic Protestants, the description of African religious rites by colonial European settlers, and lurid accounts of polygamy in multiple traditions. But something about what Adair creates is not sexual, exactly. It is about the freedom to touch. In her work on Appalachia, Deborah Vansau McCauley writes:

> Because tactility, touching, is so important to worship services, and has such a long tradition in the mountains, mountain people have their own norms and unspoken guidelines for where individuals can touch and

how, so that this loving tradition in worship that is supposed to signify a little bit of heaven in the here and now—what social relationships are supposed to be like—is not corrupted by inappropriate behavior ... By literally giving their hands to each other in worship, and by hugging and embracing with deep emotion, and often kissing, mountain people are giving their hearts, an act of profound faith boldly embodying their "hope of heaven."[50]

McCauley describes exactly what *Holy Ghost People* records. With Adair's subsequent documentary interests in view, it becomes possible to read this film as documenting a queer parenthesis in heteropatriarchy, a ritual space where humans can feel each other out without coming out. Critics can rightly see the recorded result as exoticizing, as Adair depicts the world as remote, sequestered, and strange to the everyday lives of the presumptively irreligious audiences for the film. But the film invites us also to see how religious worship affords opportunities for physical expression not as available in irreligious life and how ritual structures a space where certain norms sit down others stand forward. Adair's observational secular sets him in the in-between spaces where the communion, control, and freedom of religion reside. It would have been nice to hear the worshippers think about what is unspoken, to name what that space meant to them in their physical life and erotic life. It is also possible that Adair worried what risk it would be to those he filmed if he forced them to voice what was freer in silence. In his cinematographic focus, he left a record of unnamed intimacy for subsequent audiences to debate.

Salesman

One of the most actively promoted and widely distributed films of the observational documentary era in the United States, *Salesman*, directed by Albert and David Maysles, received mixed appraisal from early critics in 1969. Tough reviewers decided that the filmmakers disliked their subjects; kinder ones saw it as a document of the present capitalist situation without parallel.[51] The filmmakers felt they did something special and spoke frequently in the subsequent decades about the passion with which they committed to telling a humane story. "A couple of critics have been talking about some kind of condescension on our part, in selecting it," Albert Maysles observed. "I don't know what they're talking about. Because I think what we're doing is just the opposite of that."[52] The film focused on a quartet of door-to-door Catholic Bible salesmen: Paul "Badger" Brennan; Charles "Gipper" McDevitt; James "Rabbit" Baker; and Raymond "Bull" Martos. McDevitt is the undisputed king of the salesmen, so successful at selling that he coaches his colleagues, but Brennan is the indisputable star of *Salesman*. The main narrative of the film is the realization of Brennan's depth of character and his professional failure. It concludes with him in despair about his work and future. The main characters of *Salesman* seem gloomy even when—perhaps especially—under bright Florida skies.

The capitalist relations that structured the film's subject made plain everyone's consent in the picture. Mid-American Bible Company, the salesmen's employer, cooperated with the film. The four salesmen volunteered to be onscreen, arguing that their sales improved when the cameras were present. Although they did not have approval of the final cut, they spoke in praise of what they saw. Even the door-to-door sales exhibited in the film were consensual, with salesmen only visiting houses of individuals who had filled out a card at church expressing interest in the Bible and the salesmen (and cameramen) only let inside with the resident's consent. As Albert Maysles observed, "You knock on the door, and if you can't be trusted right away, then you can't get in the house."[53]

Critics thought that the film staged the "ironies of capitalism" either very well or very poorly. As one writer observed, *Salesman* showed how "materialism had saturated even the religious sector—and how stealthily it had done so, as neither seller nor buyer was fully aware of the problematic nature of the relationship . . . of religion and business."[54] Such viewers saw in the film a group of peddlers hustling wares that should be sacred, not profaned by marketing. This reaction misses what the salesmen understood about their work and what the Maysles brothers show them doing onscreen. The salesmen do not see selling the Bible as a hypocritical practice. "Some of you at one time or another may or may not have had a higher income," the vice president of the company preached to them, "but you have never held a higher position of esteem in the minds of the world or in your own self-satisfaction." The problem in the film isn't that selling contradicts Christian values; it is that being successful at selling makes a person feel good and being unsuccessful makes a person feel badly. *Salesman* shows and has its characters articulate the relentlessness of work-discipline. The film tracks the daily work of getting up, going to work, trying again, succeeding or failing, returning home, relaxing briefly, and then returning anew to the work again. Religion is not only coincidentally the salesmen's product but also the thrum of their ritualized return to work after yesterday's failure.

The personal investment in the subject emerges from the filmmakers.[55] "The whole process of making the film is exactly the process of our own personal discovery of the subject," David Maysles observed.[56]

> Interviewer: By this same token, when you make a film about Bible-salesmen, does this mean that you'd like to sell Bibles?
> Albert Maysles: Yes, in a sense, I think that the reason we choose a subject for a film has to do with the fact that we begin to find a lot of ourselves in the subject.[57]

The Maysles brothers were the children of Russian-Jewish immigrants, raised in the ethnically diverse, but historically Irish-Catholic, Dorchester area of Boston. In their early adulthood, both brothers initially transferred curiosity about ethnic difference to the study of psychology; they majored in the subject at Syracuse University, and Albert taught psychology at Boston University in the mid-1950s. They both sold products door-to-door—David sold Avon; Albert sold encyclopedias. When an interviewer asks if they were Irish Catholic, David said, "No, Jewish. But I always wanted—I think I wanted to be one. I'm finding that out. . . . I wanted to be one when I was a kid. . . . Instead of a love-hate thing . . . there were sports heroes in our school and, I guess, I wanted to be a sports hero. I like to play ice hockey and I—the team was all Irish-Catholic."[58] Filming *Salesman*, the Maysles brothers nestled near those who had tormented them and those whom they had hoped to be. The observational secular again finds the filmmaker depicting relations of intimacy in order to convey human difference humanely.

The Maysles brothers wanted to solve the problem of their own otherness by studying people familiar to them. The brothers repeatedly spoke of how Paul Brennan reminded them of their father, insofar as he was an unsuccessful salesman and often played around with an Irish brogue.[59] For the filmmakers, the focus on Bible salesmen was not a condescending look but a familial stare: these were people they knew, grew up with, and felt they understood. This sense of commiseration comes through in what the Maysles brothers chose to include onscreen. Frontstage and backstage are on full display. We see the salesmen joke, self-remonstrate, push one another, and articulate irritation. They complain about the people to whom they sell even as they also offer compassion to those who seemed hard up. The viewer isn't seeing sales as much as discussions of the sales in hotel rooms, conference halls, and walking from place to place. Everyone onscreen can be serious and funny, normal and weird, competent and failed. When Catholic Brennan repeatedly hums and sings the chorus from "If I Were a Rich Man," from the Jewish musical *Fiddler on the Roof* (Jerry Bock, Sheldon Harnick, and Joseph Stein, 1964), the camera doesn't force the viewer to see this moment as ironic. The observational secular of the Maysles brothers meant that they set themselves in a relational imminence without judgment or partiality. The camera watches as Brennan works through his day, hums to energize, even as failure hounds him. *Salesman* shows the human effort to make a single day a success. It suggests that success is, in part, how individuals explain to themselves why they are failing and whether they can continue to develop such alibis without falling into despair. *Salesman* is a metonym for documentary itself, insofar as the film observes how individuals try to get people to do what they want them to do without divulging the truth of who they are.

Conclusion

In an interview, Albert Maysles recalled a scene deleted from the final cut of *Salesman*, in which two salesmen were refused entry to a house with a supposedly promising lead. One of the two Bible salesmen muttered as he walked away, "No matter what you do, after Wednesday the leads are no fucking good." Maysles sees in this moment everything he valued. "Geez, I mean, all of life is right there," he said. "The whole concept of this is so beautiful. What a man can do in his own territory. That's everybody's life. What can a man do with what's given him?"[60] Here, Maysles points to a throwaway moment when a salesman walks disappointed from a home. It is *throwaway* in multiple senses: it is a moment on which filmmakers did not previously focus; it is a moment cut from the picture; it is a moment when the subjects feel thrown away. In this self-description of a salesman's frustration—with his company, with his job, with the limits of his daily effort—the filmmaker finds a thesis for his perception of all of life.

Critics haven't decided whether those who engaged in observational cinema succeeded in their ambitions.[61] Claims of observational neutrality by Direct Cinema filmmakers camouflaged their shaping influence and left them open to subsequent accusations by critics and viewers that they had failed to fulfill their ideals.[62] Even as Direct Cinema filmmakers resisted any suggestions that they staged scenes, they admitted that they still played a role in what the audience saw. "I think there's always something in the rushes that's better than what's in the final film," Albert Maysles observed to an interviewer.[63] Maysles suggests that the best parts of documentary are the pieces left behind in the final cut. As Hall's work on *Primary* suggests, understanding Direct Cinema requires recognition that its editing style is a strong component to its conscientious argument. As David Maysles noted, "We are very, very objective in the shooting. I call them less objective in the editing."[64] In this chapter, I did not focus on the editorial process for documentary filmmaking. Rather, I asked whether another form of categorical enclosure, religion, is a way to talk about how editorial choices in documentary default more often to certain hermeneutic emphases over others. Insofar as documentary has not represented religion as well as its other topics, talking about what it means to do it well exposes the unstated ideological seams of documentary's secularism.

To watch the best documentaries is to see films that have beautiful, even breathtaking shots; that have a sense of unveiling through their seeing; and that have a lingering look on things not often seen. Even more—perhaps most of all—the best documentaries don't let us get away with thinking that what they document is something wholly other from the audience for the documentary. The best documentaries don't let us think we, the viewers, aren't in this too. Instead, they show us that we might not have been heroes during the Holocaust. That we might have been a part of the system that wrongly convicted Randall Dale Adams, the man sentenced to death for a murder he did not commit, in Morris's *The Thin Blue Line*. That we see our city as ours to own, just as *Man with the Movie Camera* shows Soviet citizens in Kiev, Kharkov, Moscow, and Odessa at work and at play and interacting with the machinery of modern life. These great films show us not only something the director is looking at but also something that we participate to create. Most depictions of religion in documentary film cannot achieve this quality of documentary engagement because the filmmaker cannot get over the occupational hazard of their secularism. Focusing on three films from Direct Cinema, we find filmmakers who are, indeed, self-identified secular subjects. Yet they worked to see inside the space of religion rather than decide its oppressions at the outset. The observational secular in these films is the perspective that leads filmmakers to give space for their subjects to join the conversation: to correct, to reply, to explain how they exist in "the ordinary, uncontrolled, course of things."[65] These replies can be in fierce monologues spoken to others on camera; they may be in gestures of intimacy in worship spaces; they may also be in letting people feel frustrated in the slow fact of life's layers of disappointments.

A great documentary on a religious subject would require a gaze that could account for its complicity with the world it saw. Not as an exhibit to be in awe of, or an idea to debunk, or a problem estranged from us to understand, but as a thing we, too, need; we, too, make; we, too, believe. Trinh T. Minh-Ha has said, "the 'documentary' often forgets how it comes about and how aesthetics and politics remain inseparable in its constitution."[66] Religion is at the origin of the aesthetic choices for documentary and the colonial politics that gave rise to its first makers. From the beginning, documentary was a missionary tool of secular life. Knowing how this influences what we want from documentary film will also change how we judge its success.

Acknowledgments: This chapter began as a response to a prompt offered in 2017 by the Center for the Study of Religion at the Ohio State University for a public discussion with Judith Weisenfeld on "Religion, Media and Narrative." I give thanks to her for many years of personal commiseration, intellectual provocation, and field leadership, as well as to Sarah Johnston, Hugh Urban, and Isaac Weiner for their incisive questions. I am grateful to Faye Thompson at the Margaret Herrick Library, May Hong Haduong at the Academy of Motion Picture Arts and Sciences Film Archive, Laura Russo at the Howard Gotlieb Archival Research Center at Boston University, and the staff at the James C. Hormel LGBTQIA Center of the San Francisco Public Library. The three anonymous reviewers recruited by *JCMS* were among the best reviewers I have engaged; I thank them for their generosity and detail. I am also deeply grateful to Marko Geslani, Jacqueline Goldsby, Lucia

Hulsether, Tina Post, Caleb Smith, and David Walker for their readings of earlier drafts. This chapter is halfway to what Kati Curts saw was possible; I dedicate it to her and the conversation we share.

Notes

1. Here I concur with Alexandra Juhasz and Alisa Lebow when they observe, "Religion has almost never been a topic in any visible evidence conference (with exceptions, of course), and to date no book addresses it head on with regard to documentary." Alexandra Juhasz and Alisa Lebow, introduction to "Religion," in *Companion to Contemporary Documentary Film* (West Sussex: Wiley-Blackwell, 2015), 337. The three subsequent chapters included in the Blackwell companion address documentaries about religion outside of the United States. Within the fields of film studies and documentary studies, no scholarship on religion and US documentary exists. The one exception to this is Judith Weisenfeld, "Race, Religion, and Documentary Film," in *The Oxford Handbook of Religion and Race in American History*, ed. Paul Harvey and Kathryn Gin Lum (New York: Oxford University Press, 2018). Weisenfeld's path-clearing work demonstrates how early documentary film reflected and produced ideas about the relationship between religion and race and how representations of religion and race helped to support the authority of the documentary as a form understood to be axiomatically truthful and educational.

2. The latter claim is a normative one, the former a bibliographic description: the silence on religion in documentary film in film and media studies is striking because religion is a frequent topic of documentary films. Outside of Weisenfeld's work, however, there has been little work on religion as a topic in documentary film and none on religion as a topic in US documentary film.

3. Fatimah Tobing Rony, *The Third Eye: Race, Cinema, and Ethnographic Spectacle* (Durham, NC: Duke University Press, 1996); and Trinh T. Minh-ha, *Woman, Native, Other: Writing Postcoloniality and Feminism* (Bloomington: Indiana University Press, 1989).

4. Juhasz and Lebow, introduction to "Religion," 340.

5. Johannes Fabian, *Time and the Other: How Anthropology Makes Its Object* (New York: Columbia University Press, 1983), chaps. 1 and 3; and Benedict Anderson, *Imagined Communities: Reflections on the Origin and Spread of Nationalism*, rev. ed. (London: Verso, 1991), chap. 2.

6. Saba Mahmood, *Religious Difference in a Secular Age: A Minority Report* (Princeton, NJ: Princeton University Press, 2016); and Tisa Wenger, *Religious Freedom: The Contested History of an American Ideal* (Chapel Hill: University of North Carolina Press, 2017).

7. For key works in the study of the secular, see Gil Anidjar, "Secularism," *Critical Inquiry* 33, no. 1 (Autumn 2006): 52–77; Tracy Fessenden, *Culture and Redemption: Religion, the Secular, and American Literature* (Princeton, NJ: Princeton University Press, 2006); Kathryn Lofton, *Consuming Religion*

(Chicago, IL: University of Chicago Press, 2017); and John Lardas Modern, *Secularism in Antebellum America* (Chicago, IL: University of Chicago Press, 2011).

8   Juhasz and Lebow, introduction to "Religion," 338.
9   "Filmmakers' Greatest Documentaries of All Time," BFI.org, April 25, 2019, https://www2.bfi.org.uk/sight-sound-magazine/filmmakers-greatest-docs.
10 Juhasz and Lebow observe that the films of Werner Herzog particularly invite discussions of "ecstasy, sublimity, truth" as components to the "documentary pursuit." Juhasz and Lebow, introduction to "Religion," 338. In his work on religion and film, S. Brent Plate considers *Man with a Movie Camera* for its spatial elements and their formal relationship to ritual. S. Brent Plate, *Religion and Film: Cinema and the Re-creation of the World*, 2nd ed. (New York: Columbia University Press, 2017), chap. 2.
11 Brian Winston, "The Tradition of the Victim in Griersonian Documentary," in *Image Ethics: The Moral Rights of Subjects in Photographs, Film, and Television*, ed. Larry Gross, John Stuart Katz, and Jay Ruby (New York: Oxford University Press, 1988), 34–57.
12 A reviewer identified documentary films that they suggest depict religion better than this indictment suggests. These include *Satya: A Prayer for the Enemy* (Ellen Bruno, 1992), *Chasing Buddha* (Amiel Courtin-Wilson, 2000), *Trembling Before G-d* (Sandi Simcha DuBowski, 2001), *The Smith Family* (Tasha Oldham, 2002), and *Love Free or Die* (Macky Alston, 2012). I think this reviewer watches these films and sees the dignity and moral courage of their lead figures: Kim, the betrayed matriarch of the Smith family; the queer figures struggling to reconcile their sexuality with their Judaism; or Mark, Gene Robinson's devoted partner in his battle with the Episcopal Church. I watch these films and see how these characters battle religions or states oppressing their freedom; oppression is the inescapable thematic companion to religion's depiction. The main characters become surrogates for the filmmaker, a heroic seer of secular truth amid confounded unreason.
13 Anna Grimshaw and Amanda Ravetz, *Observational Cinema: Anthropology, Film, and the Exploration of Social Life* (Bloomington: Indiana University Press, 2009).
14 "Unfortunately, it continues true that the only way to suggest tedium is tedium, and *Salesman* is almost unsittably tedious," argued Charles Champlin in "'Fifth Street' and 'Salesman' to Open Run," *Los Angeles Times*, June 10, 1969. For a film review that again conveys this sense of an unexciting result to good documentary ethics, see Ernest Callenbach, review of *Salesman*, *Film Quarterly* 23, no. 1 (Autumn 1969): 54–5.
15 Carl Plantinga, "What a Documentary Is, After All," *Journal of Aesthetics and Art Criticism* 63, no. 2 (Spring 2005): 114.
16 Quotation from Academy Visual History with Albert Maysles, recorded in Harlem, New York, with interviewer Sienna McLean LoGreco (October 4, 2013). This is the edited, public version of the visual history interview with Albert Maysles, which Maysles has viewed and approved for public access. Available at the Academy of Motion Picture Arts and Sciences Film Archive.

17 Stephen Charbonneau, *Projecting Race: Postwar America, Civil Rights, and Documentary Film* (New York: Columbia University Press, 2016), 19.

18 Sumiko Higashi, "Melodrama, Realism, and Race: World War II Newsreels and Propaganda Film," *Cinema Journal* 37, no. 3 (Spring 1998): 39.

19 Lisa M. Rabin, "A Social History of U.S. Educational Documentary: The Travels of Three Shorts, 1945–1958," *Film History* 29, no. 3 (Fall 2017): 2. Despite resisting the narrativizing impulse of postwar educational film, many films from the Direct Cinema movement contributed to the same Cold War political project, advocating for the linked power of capitalism and democracy to improve individual lives at home and abroad. Many of the techniques of cinéma vérité—a "technique that constitutes a kind of domestic spying," as Jonathan Kahana writes—were the direct result of the military use of such equipment in World War II. Jonathan Kahana, *Intelligence Work: The Politics of American Documentary* (New York: Columbia University Press, 2008), 13.

20 Higashi, "Melodrama, Realism, and Race," 41.

21 Michael Renov, *The Subject of Documentary* (Minneapolis: University of Minnesota Press, 2004), 174–6.

22 "Interview: Albert Maysles and David Maysles; Friday, the 31st of March, 1967," David Maysles Papers (hereafter cited as DMP), box 2, folder 10, Howard Gotlieb Archival Research Center, Boston University, 13.

23 Bill Nichols, *Representing Reality: Issues and Concepts in Documentary* (Bloomington: Indiana University Press, 1991), 38–44. Several technical innovations in filmmaking, including handheld cameras, the portable sound recorder, tuning fork control, and sound camera synchronization, contributed to this development of the movement.

24 Jeanne Hall, "Realism as a Style in Cinema Verite: A Critical Analysis of *Primary*," *Cinema Journal* 30, no. 4 (Summer 1991): 24–50.

25 Plantinga, "What a Documentary Is," 109.

26 Nichols, *Representing Reality*, 42.

27 Brian Winston, "The Documentary Film as Scientific Inscription," in *Theorizing Documentary*, ed. Michael Renov (New York: Routledge, 1993), 43.

28 Nichols, *Representing Reality*, 43; and Michael Chanan, *The Politics of Documentary* (London: British Film Institute, 2007), 177.

29 Often to the purpose of serving social problems. See Stephen Mamber, "Cinéma Vérité and Social Concerns," *Film Comment* (Nov/Dec 1973): 9, 6. A historical illustration of this is the fact that *Salesman* made its debut at Manhattan's 68th Street Playhouse on April 18, 1969, with a gala premiere for the benefit of the Cesar Chavez grape workers union, United Farm Workers. For its viewers and its filmmakers, an alliance between progressive causes and Direct Cinema was axiomatic. Yet it's worth underlining that documentary historians would not catalog the films examined in this article as social documentary, that is, films (often connected to public media) that documented injustices and worked to advance minority rights at home and third world liberation struggles abroad. While many of the filmmakers who produced social documentaries drew on Direct Cinema techniques, their films had

different aims. Each of the filmmakers profiled here understood themselves as artists first and activists or journalists second, whereas social documentarians prioritized the activist journalism of their efforts.

30 "J" interviews Albert Maysles, "Manuscripts: Interviews of DM + AM, complete 2-part transcript," DMP, box 2, folder 7, 18. DMP does not identify "J."

31 The Maysles brothers engaged in an extended discussion about their rules for documentary film in "Interview: Albert Maysles and David Maysles; Friday, the 31st of March, 1967," DMP, box 2, folder 10, 7–12.

32 Kevin Macdonald and Mark Cousins, *Imagining Reality: The Faber Book of Documentary* (London: Faber and Faber, 1996), 250.

33 Michael Fox, "Albert Maysles: The Discerning Eye," program for the 27th Annual Mill Valley Film Festival (2004), 54. Located in the Albert Maysles file at the Margaret Herrick Library.

34 Chambers would go on to become one of the most prominent local politicians in Nebraska and one of the most radical legislators in public office in the United States. See Tekla Agbala Ali Johnson, *Free Radical: Ernest Chambers, Black Power, and the Politics of Race* (Lubbock: Texas Tech University Press, 2012).

35 Bill Jersey, director's commentary, *A Time for Burning* (Lutheran Film Associates, 2005), DVD.

36 Bill Jersey, e-mail correspondence with the author, March 7, 2019.

37 Jim Birkhead, "Reading 'Snake Handling': Critical Reflections," in *Anthropology of Religion: A Handbook*, ed. Stephen D.Glazier (Westport, CT: Greenwood Publishing Group, 1997), 20.

38 Robert A. Orsi, *Between Heaven and Earth: The Religious Worlds People Make and the Scholars Who Study Them* (Princeton, NJ: Princeton University Press, 2005), 182; see also Jenna Gray-Hildenbrand, "The Appalachian 'Other': Academic Approaches to the Study of Serpent-Handling Sects," *Religion Compass* 10, no. 3 (2016): 48.

39 Peggy Dunn Bailey, "Coming Home to Scrabble Creek: Saving Grace, Serpent Handling, and the Realistic Southern Gothic," *Appalachian Journal* 38, no. 4 (Summer 2011): 424.

40 Ernest Callenbach, review of *Holy Ghost People*, *Film Quarterly* 22, no. 1 (Autumn 1968): 4.

41 William M. Clements, "Review Essay: Snake-Handlers on Film," *Journal of American Folklore* 90, no. 358 (October–December 1977): 503–4.

42 Margaret Mead, review of *Holy Ghost People*, *American Anthropologist* 70, no. 3 (1968): 655.

43 Elizabeth Mermin, "Burden of Representation: 1996 Margaret Mead Film and Video Festival," *Nka: Journal of Contemporary African Art*, no. 6–7 (Summer/Fall 1997): 51.

44 Emily Ogden, *Credulity: A Cultural History of US Mesmerism* (Chicago: University of Chicago Press, 2018); and David Walker, "The Humbug in

American Religion: Ritual Theories of Nineteenth-Century Spiritualism," *Religion and American Culture: A Journal of Interpretation* 23, no. 1 (2013): 30–74.

45 Sol Worth and John Adair, *Through Navajo Eyes: An Exploration in Film Communication and Anthropology*, 2nd ed. (Bloomington: Indiana University Press, 1972).

46 Clifford Barnett, Richard Chalfen, James C. Faris, Susan Brown McGreevy, and Willow Roberts Powers, "John Adair, 1913–1997: Work across the Anthropological Spectrum," *Journal of Anthropological Research* 55, no. 3 (Autumn 1999): 429–45.

47 David W. Dunlap, obituary of Peter Adair, *New York Times*, June 30, 1996, 30.

48 Thomas Waugh, *The Fruit Machine: Twenty Years of Writings on Queer Cinema* (Durham, NC: Duke University Press, 2000), 25; and Greg Youmans, *Word Is Out: A Queer Film Classic* (Vancouver: Arsenal Pulp Press, 2011), 37–8.

49 Interview with Linda Actel, August 1977, found in "Interview with Filmmakers—1977," Peter Adair Papers, box 44, folder 14, James C. Hormel LGBTQIA Center, San Francisco Public Library.

50 Deborah Vansau McCauley, *Appalachian Mountain Religion: A History* (Urbana: University of Illinois Press, 1995), 387.

51 "*Salesman* is a very shallow, remarkably superficial, predisposed and suspect of a quartet of door-to-door salesman." John Mahoney, review of "Salesman," *Hollywood Reporter*, June 12, 1969.

52 "J" interviews Albert Maysles, "Manuscripts: Interviews of DM + AM, complete 2-part transcript," DMP, box 2, folder 7, 5.

53 "J" interviews Albert Maysles, "Manuscripts: Interviews of DM + AM, complete 2-part transcript," DMP, box 2, folder 7, 4.

54 Jonathan B. Vogels, "*Salesman* and the Limits of Language," in *The Direct Cinema of David and Albert Maysles* (Carbondale: Southern Illinois University Press, 2010).

55 Wheeler Winston Dixon, "An Interview with Albert Maysles," *Quarterly Review of Film and Video* 20, no. 3 (2003): 177–92.

56 "Interview: Albert Maysles and David Maysles; Friday, the 31st of March, 1967," DMP, box 2, folder 10, 9.

57 "Interview: Albert Maysles and David Maysles; Friday, the 31st of March, 1967," DMP, box 2, folder 10, 8.

58 "J" interviews David Maysles, "Manuscripts: Interviews of DM + AM, complete 2-part transcript," DMP, box 2, folder 8, 4.

59 "Z" interviews David Maysles, "Manuscripts: Interviews of DM + AM, complete 2-part transcript," DMP, box 2, folder 10, 6–7; and "J" interviews David Maysles, "Manuscripts: Interviews of DM + AM, complete 2-part transcript," DMP, box 2, folder 8, 39.

60 "J" interviews Albert Maysles, "Manuscripts: Interviews of DM + AM, complete 2-part transcript," DMP, box 2, folder 7, 33.

61 The recent reclamation of observational technique suggests its endurance as a reformer impulse. See Erika Balsam, "The Reality-Based Community," *E-Flux Journal*, no. 83 (June 2017).

62 Bill Nichols, *Introduction to Documentary* (Bloomington: Indiana University Press, 2001), 100.

63 "J" interviews Albert Maysles, "Manuscripts: Interviews of DM + AM, complete 2-part transcript," DMP, box 2, folder 7, 28.

64 "Z" interviews David Maysles, "Manuscripts: Interviews of DM + AM, complete 2-part transcript," DMP, box 2, folder 10, 19.

65 Jonathan Z. Smith, "The Bare Facts of Ritual," *History of Religions* 20, no. 1/2 (1980): 125.

66 Trinh T. Minh-Ha, "Documentary Is/Not a Name," *October* 52 (Spring 1990): 89.

PART III

The Dis/Enchantment of the World in Moving Images

8

The Wonder of Film

Science, Magic, and the Endurance of Enchantment

Catherine Wheatley

Against a verdant landscape, a pair of jeeps carrying several men and a woman comes to a pause. The passengers chat idly among themselves, unsure as to why they have stopped. Slowly, one of their number, a tanned white man in a straw hat and red neckerchief, stands and removes his mirrored sunglasses to peer at something. He nudges a fellow passenger, a blonde-haired woman, who turns her head, and—apparently noticing what it is that he sees—removes her glasses too and rises. There is a cut to the pair framed in close-up: eyes wide, gazes intent, and mouths agape. We look at them for several seconds, our feeling of anticipation growing as we wait to see what has caught their attention. On the film's soundtrack, the music—hitherto gentle, melodic—builds slowly in volume and depth. Finally, the camera cuts again to reveal what they are looking at. It is, of course, a living dinosaur.

The scientists' host moves into shot. "Welcome," he smiles, gesturing in the opposite direction, "to Jurassic Park." The camera moves in once more on the man's face as he turns in the opposite direction and we wait, again, to see what he sees. Another cut, and there it is: a whole herd of dinosaurs, drinking at a lake. The score swells into that famous refrain we know so well. We cut back to the two scientists' rapt expressions.

The man whispers: "How d'you do this?"

Steven Spielberg's 1993 *Jurassic Park* has been much discussed within film studies in terms of spectacle and special effects. Only Michele Pierson, however, gestures toward the importance of an experience of *wonder* to the scene described earlier: an experience in which both the characters on screen and the audience in the theatre or at home participate. For the diegetic and non-diegetic viewer alike, the dinosaurs' appearance—their appearance *there*, before us—leads us to land upon the same question as Sam Neill's Dr. Alan Grant: How did he (Hammond, Spielberg) do this?

The aims of this chapter are twofold. First, I want to outline the hidden history of wonder within film theory. It is my contention that from what Tom Gunning has called the "cinema of attractions" through science fiction to contemporary theories of the long take and slow cinema, the significance of wonder has often been masked by film theory's preoccupation with questions of belief and credence. It is part of my task here to invert that dynamic, arguing that whether or not we believe in what we see on screen is of little importance relative to the image's capacity to generate curiosity about it: where it came from, what it means. Confronted with the dinosaur, we (Dr. Grant, the audience) wonder not whether it is real, but how it got there and what it will do. Second, as I position "wonder" as definitive of film watching, I will demonstrate that it leads us toward the question of humankind's capacities for creativity and compassion through what I shall term, after Paolo Costa, a mode of "secular enchantment." By tracing the relationship of wonder to film-viewing, I shall demonstrate that even at its most ragged, naïve, and chaotic, cinema offers us reassurance about our species' knowledge of and mastery over the world, but at the same time it asks us, through wonder, to acknowledge the responsibilities that come with such mastery.

What Is Wonder?

What is wonder? In a first instance, it is something we feel. But wonder can also be an object or phenomenon that causes great admiration or surprise, as in the seven wonders of the world. And wonder is not only a noun but also a verb. To wonder *at* something is to be impressed by it. To wonder *about* something is to ask oneself questions about something.

Looking at the etymological roots of the term, it seems that there are at least two lineages of the concept: a Greek one stemming from the word *thaumazein*, emphasizing surprise and amazement and cognate with the word *theaomai* (I look); and a Latin one stemming from *mirari* and *miraculum*, relating it to incomprehensibility on the one hand and magic on the other.[1] In the old Scandinavian *wundar* means a prodigy or a marvel. To feel wonder at something originally meant to see it as a sign of something important. The German word *Wunder* translates as miracle or marvel, but it is also cognate with *Wunde* (wound) suggesting suddenness and even violence: a sense of something having been punctured. Vlad Glaveanu connects it to being *wonderstruck*.[2] In his definition of the term, he suggests that there is a fundamental connection between wonder and the possible—arguing:

> Wonder and wondering define a particular type of experience whereby the person becomes (more or less suddenly) aware of an expanded field of possibility for thought and/or action and engages (more or less actively) in exploring this field. This experience is generally accompanied by uplifting emotions (without all of them being necessary positive).[3]

Here we also see Glaveanu gesture to the experience of wonder as something pleasurable, "uplifting." The philosopher Martha Nussbaum agrees, describing it as "outwards-moving, exuberant." "In wonder," she writes, "I want to leap and run."[4]

Other theorists, philosophers, and historians lend further nuance. In Plato's dialogue between Socrates and Theaetetus, wonder is aligned with ignorance. It is the young Theaetetus's admission that he knows little and is much prone to wondering about how the world works that leads to Socrates's celebrated assertion that "philosophy begins in wonder." For Aristotle, too, wonder was essential to the process of philosophical inquiry because it arose from ignorance about the causes of natural phenomena and therefore led people to search for those causes. In their study of wonder's place in society and culture from 1150 to 1750, Lorraine Daston and Katherine Park are led to describe two forms of wondering audience: the educated philosophers and scientists whose wonder at natural phenomena led to knowledge, and the naïve dupes whose wonder was bound up with credence in marvels, curiosities, and phantasmagoria.[5] They make a modern-day comparison with cultivated admirers of the wonders of science and nature (volcanic eruptions, huge geodes, meteor showers), on the one hand, and the not-so-cultivated wonderers agog at tabloid reports of monstrous births and Unidentified Flying Objects on the other.[6]

Both Daston and Park and Genevieve Lloyd also link wonder to novelty, and hence to childishness and the childlike.[7] For children, rather than adults, so much of the world is new, that they are naturally prone to wonder.[8] Philip Fisher prefers the term "rare experiences" to new experiences, and argues, after Wittgenstein, that we are able to wonder at everyday objects if only we are able to notice them.[9] That is, we find the everyday wondrous when we look at it differently—we might say when we see it as if anew. The metaphor of sight is crucial to Fisher and to the argument I wish to make below, for following Fisher I believe that wonder is a relation to the visible world: "the outcome of the fact that we see the world."[10] From here, it is no great leap to claim that visual arts—and film in particular—hold a privileged relationship to wonder. In Fisher's words, moreover, wonder lies at "a border between sensation and thought, aesthetics and science."[11]

What better way to describe the cinema?

Wonder and Film Theory 1: Attraction, Astonishment

Early film theorists were quick to make the association between wonder and film. For example, Fulgence Marion's 1870 book, *The Wonders of Optics*, links magic and science in its examination and elucidation of the workings of the then new visual technologies deployed in service of crowd-pleasing optical illusions. In section "Natural Magic," Marion refers to early pre-cinematic devices such as the magic lantern, the camera obscura, and the spectroscope as modern "wonders." Through these wonders, he writes, "we are led astray by others whose knowledge of the laws of optics is greater than our own, enabling them to construct instruments capable of amusing us or imposing on us, according to our ignorance of the natural law."[12] Here Marion echoes Daston and Park's distinction between educated audiences for whom these devices might be amusing and "ordinary observers," who are "prone to belief in wonders."[13] His book was intended to serve a double purpose: debunking the illusions generated by the new technology for the naïve spectator, and explaining precisely how they are achieved for those who have marveled at their showmanship but shown sufficient self-possession not to fall prone to their "deceptions."[14]

Marion thus re-inscribes—or perhaps pre-inscribes—the foundational myth of cinema's first audience's belief in the cinematic illusion: the spectators terrified at the sight of the Lumiere's *Arrival of a Train at the Station*; screaming, hiding beneath their seats, running from the auditorium, overwhelmed by credulity and opposed, no doubt, to both the educated men behind the curtain who know very well that the train isn't there, and the more sophisticated spectators who are amazed but not overawed by this vision and the new technology behind it. Skeptical about the extent to which such a panic in fact took place, the film historian Tom Gunning has—across a body of work dedicated to what he calls "the cinema of attractions"—worked to debunk this myth. In an article titled "An Aesthetic of Astonishment: Early Film and the (In) Credulous Spectator," Gunning reframes the reaction of the crowd at the Grand Café's Salon Indien not in terms of "childlike credulity," but an ongoing fascination with magic, marvels, and wonder.[15] Gunning describes these early spectators as "astonished," "amazed," and "shocked" by these "marvellous" and "astounding" sights. This astonishment is inspired not by a train they believed to be moving before their eyes, but by a magical metamorphosis from stillness to movement: the novelty—after a decade of seeing still images—of seeing one *that moved*. This transition "startled" audiences, bringing about a "sense of shock," which came "less from a naïve belief that they are threatened by an actual locomotive than from an unbelievable visual transformation occurring before their eyes, parallel to the greatest wonders of the magic theatre."[16]

The thrills generated by the early cinema were sensational and immediate. This was a cinema of instants, rather than developing situations. As a result, the wonder generated by early cinema is similar to what Descartes refers to as *étonnement*. *Étonnement* (translated as astonishment) is for Descartes an excess of wonder which leaves us stunned, immobilized, and unable to process anything beyond the immediate sensation of surprise and amazement. Astonishment can "never be anything other than bad,"[17] since it paralyzes our intellect.[18] On the other hand, wonder proper—what Descartes calls *l'admiration*—is the act of noticing with pleasure something new and unprecedented. In this way wonder, for Descartes "the first of the passions," may act as a stimulus to learn more: a prompt to curiosity. The instant of *wondering at* gives way to the more durational process of *wondering about*. For that reason, those who are prone to wonder are, according to Descartes, rarely ignorant or naïve—an argument that seems to echo Gunning's claim that the spectators of early cinema are more knowing than they are often given credit for.[19]

While Gunning uses the terms "shock," "astonishment," and "wonder interchangeably," then, the experience of early cinema that he describes cleaves more closely to Cartesian *admiration*.[20] He argues that astonishment does not stop with the instant of beholding. Rather, the direct, confrontational address of early cinema makes the spectator highly aware of the film image's constructedness, and as such "engages the viewer's curiosity."[21] He makes a direct link to the secular by drawing upon St. Augustine's fifth-century definition of curiosity as a "lust of the eyes" that entails a fascination with seeing and insatiable desire for knowledge, ultimately leading away from God and toward the twin "perversions" of magic and science.[22] Gunning also argues that it is precisely due to a decline of belief in the power of magic, spirituality, and the marvelous—and by extension, the miraculous and the divine—that the spectators in the Grand Café were not fooled by the rushing train.[23] At the same time as such belief was waning, expanding urbanization, the growth of consumer society, and the escalating horizons of colonial exploitation both decentered a Christian God, piqued the curiosity, and expanded (Western) humanity's sense of its dominion over the earth. As Gunning points out, it can hardly be a coincidence that the slogan of one early film company was "an invention which puts the world within your grasp."[24]

Wonder and Film Theory 2: Science Fiction, Curiosity

Given that Gunning himself has drawn a direct link between the cinema of attractions and what he refers to as the "Spielberg-Lucas-Coppola cinema of effects,"[25] it is perhaps no surprise that wonder re-emerges as a term for thinking about film spectatorship in Michele Pierson's 2002 book *Special Effects: Still in Search of Wonder*. If the movies are magic, much of their appeal lies with their use of effects: a series of technological innovations used in service of illusionism. While Phillip Maciak has written eloquently about the (post)secular significance of special effects in resurrection films in early cinema,[26] it seems that wonder has a special relationship to science fiction. The opening section of Vivian Sobchack's ground-breaking book, *Screening Space: The American Science Fiction Film*, for example, is titled "Images of Wonder,"[27] while Sean Redmond calls the introductory section of *Liquid Metal: The Science Fiction Reader*, "The Wonder of Science Fiction." How appropriate, then, that the company that created Jurassic Park's wondrous dinosaurs is called Industrial Light and Magic: a moniker that invokes technology, the visual, and enchantment—as well, of course, as commerce.

It is important not to underplay wonder's vexed relationship to capital. Science fiction's audiences are a particularly specialized, knowledgeable audience, both in terms of narrative tropes and industrial practice. As a genre, it exacerbates or extrapolates an attachment to cinema fostered through cultures of appreciation and connoisseurship.[28] This appeal to expertise is significant here since it reiterates Gunning's argument that audiences of cinematic spectacle are far from naïve, but are rather driven by a desire for novelty, in the form of technical, stylistic, and/or aesthetic innovations. If wonder is attached to the new or the rare, it is not—nor arguably can it be—a neutral term. Daston and Park's study of wonder charts among other things its attachment to questions of class, education, consumerism, and capital. Pierson notes that the science fiction genre is driven by an endless pursuit of novelty, making appeal to Adorno, who wrote on more than one occasion that Hollywood has always traded on its feats of technological ingenuity and visual display to entertain audiences, and adding that effects cinema seems to exercise a peculiar "astonishment" at its cinematic "tricks." In the collective gasp of the wondrous audience, Pierson writes, Adorno heard the tremor that "lives off the excess power which technology as a whole, along with the capital that stands behind it, exercises over every individual thing."[29] A similar sentiment is expressed by *Jurassic Park*'s venal lawyer Donald Gennaro (Martin Ferrero): the camera zooming in on his rapt face as he gazes at the dinosaurs and murmurs: "We're going to make a fortune with this place." Certainly, the experience of wonder can easily be co-opted for capitalist ends: and in this case, perhaps wonder is indeed the quintessential Hollywood experience.

And yet the matter of curiosity remains. Warren Buckland explains that the wondrous vision of Spielberg's dinosaurs opens onto the question of "possible worlds"—imaginary worlds "that could possibly emerge from a state of affairs in the actual world."[30] He gestures toward a number of documentaries and books produced in the wake of *Jurassic Park*'s release, which loosely fall into two categories.[31] On the one hand, we have the film-related investigations devoted to the making of *Jurassic Park*, which posed variants on the question: How did he do that? On the other, the paleo-geological studies devoted to unpacking the science that informed *Jurassic Park*: the central question was, in effect, Could *we* do that? Buckland explains:

> When presented with a possible world on screen, spectators do not make a high ontological commitment to the reality of the objects on screen, but neither do they simply reject them as imaginary. The digital image can, by means of special effects, make the possible believable.[32]

In this sense, believable does not refer to belief in the image as real, but to belief in the possibility of a world in which the image might be real. How does the possible become believable? Through speculation—or put otherwise, through wonder. As wondrous visions, Spielberg's dinosaurs prompt us to wonder about where they come from: they thus lead us to speculate on the technical artistry of Industrial Light and Magic's personnel. But they also prompt us to ask whether dinosaurs might ever inhabit our world, by making visible the possibility of their existence. Spielberg's films not only present, that is, "what is technologically possible in genetic engineering in another world," but also "what is possible in digital special effects technology in the actual world."[33] Through wonder, we admire humankind's creative abilities (in bringing the computer-generated imagery [CGI] dinosaurs to screen) and celebrate its creative potential (in having the technological resources and scientific know-how to potentially bring these dinosaurs to life). In both cases, ontological questions precede epistemological and even metaphysical ones.

Wonder and Film Theory 3: Realism, Contemplation

We can see, now, how, in looking toward wonder, questions of belief can be reframed as questions of curiosity. Just so, Gunning's essay has been referred to as an essay on cinema's (un) belief-function, but it is, really, an essay on how an initial moment of wonder at something gives way to a more extensive period of wondering about its origins and mechanics. For this reason, the perceived split between *actualités* and trick films—realism and spectacle—matters little to the spectator's capacity for wonder. We wonder not only at rushing trains and CGI dinosaurs but also at the sight of workers leaving factories and feathers floating on the afternoon breeze. This is because, as Genevieve Lloyd and Philip Fischer have variously argued, we are able yet to wonder at everyday objects.[34] Fisher, following Wittgenstein, claims that the ordinary is transformed into the wondrous when we are prompted to notice it.[35] He gives the example of a shoe: we might notice our shoes if they start to pinch us, or if they have paint spilled on them, for example. But it is not only change or defectiveness within or to the object that calls objects to our attention. We might also notice our shoes if we are surprised by them: by a new placement, or angle. A change in perspective. Suddenly, our shoes become unexpected, extraordinary. As Fisher states, when we are struck by wonder, either "in time what happens was not expected" or "in space it was not ordinary."[36] Wonder is then, like cinema, both a spatial and a temporal experience.

In his 2017 book, *The Long Take: Art Cinema and The Art of the Wondrous*, Lutz Koepnick indicates the importance of time and space to cinematic wonder when he claims that long takes—"extended shot durations and prolonged experiences of moving image environments"—allow filmmakers "to reconstruct spaces for the possibility of wonder."[37] For Koepnick, wonder is a response that allows for the possibility of newness without shock, fear, or defensiveness,[38] registering instead as "quiet and pensive, judicious and discriminating."[39] He describes it as a form of "quiet awe," rather than "edgy astonishment" in response to "attention-grabbing spectacle," implicitly setting up an opposition once more between *étonnement* and *admiration*.[40] Wonder is therefore a very different experience for Koepnick than it is for Gunning (wonder an antonym, rather than the synonym, of astonishment). He is uninterested in films that display their own technological virtuosity—he dismisses, for example, the long take that opens Robert Altman's *The Player* as "showing off"—and in wonder as a spur to thinking about the medium and its makers.[41] Indeed, Koepnick states explicitly that his interest "is in long takes that result not in spectators shouting 'Wow, how the heck did they do that!' but in viewers who find themselves investigating possible relations among the different temporalities on screen, the temporal orders of the projection situation, and the rhythms of their own physical and mental worlds."[42]

It is tempting to read Koepnick's work in a Bazinian tradition, given its emphasis on the long take, the everyday, and spectatorial autonomy. And yet there is a key distinction to be made between Koepnick's theory of the wondrous spectator and André Bazin's theory of cinematic realism and its connection to hierophany, or the manifestation of the divine in the ordinary. This distinction lies with the fact that Bazin is working within a Protestant, post-Enlightenment tradition, one that associates both spectacle and the paranormal with "superstition, Asiatic idol worship, and the Oriental Despotism of hoodwinking priests, especially Roman Catholics."[43]

Indeed in his essay "Cinema and Theology," Bazin explicitly contrasts Catholic spectacle with Protestant asceticism, in which the presence of God isn't signified "by anything extraordinary, either on the physical or the psychological level."[44] This tracks with Barbara Maria Stafford's argument that after the Reformation, wonders came to be denounced as "the dazzling effects of diabolic technologies": smoke and mirrors charlatanism that exploited the gullibility and sentiment of the masses.[45] In the Protestant era, the term assumed a dual meaning, which led in both senses away from God. On the one hand, it was associated with magic and trickery: the Catholic "wonders" that contrast with the Protestant miracle. Or else it assumed a scientific sense, marked by a disenchanted rationality and an obsession with demystification, a conviction that all that is new, rare, inexplicable, or vague demands to be made precise. In both cases wonder departs from religion—hence, perhaps, Bazin's avoidance of the term. Sure enough, wonder is not a commonly used term in Bazin's writing (the sole usage that I could find comes in reference to Méliès's 1905 *A Trip to the Moon*, perhaps the quintessential spectacular film—Bazin, 1946). Instead, he prefers the "miraculous" and the "miracle," terms with a distinctly religious cast. For Bazin, cinema, and neo-realist cinema in particular, returns us to an age of enchantment by restoring God's presence: "the movie camera, by the simple act of photographing the world, testifies to the miracle of God's creation."[46]

The Long Take also sees cinema—or at least a certain type of cinema—as offering response to the disenchantment of modern life. Koepnick argues that through their use of long takes, films such as Béla Tarr's *The Turin Horse* (2011) "exhaust our endurance beyond redemption, and yet they thus precisely activate something forgotten amid the pulsating images of contemporary screen culture: a desire for a world in which we can again afford the pleasure and passion of wonder."[47] Offering us a new experience of wonder, the contemporary long take is thus able "to rekindle our hope for a different order of contemporary experience, one able to release us from the secret standstill of our frantic present and its fast-track pursuit of the next big thing."[48] To some extent, then, whether we perceive film as miraculous or wondrous is a question of perspective: both Bazin and Koepnick implicitly agree that slow cinema offers new ways of seeing the world and arouses the spectator's curiosity. In doing so, it leads the spectator to probe beyond the frame of representation, the time and space of display, to what lies beyond the film itself: to its makers, to the world it (re)presents. But where for Bazin, the process of contemplation leads ultimately to God, for Koepnick there are no fixed answers, only an open-ended reflection. He does not explicitly connect wonder to secularism in his book, but the process of wondering that he experiences might be well described as what Paolo Costa, among others, calls "secular enchantment": "a stance toward things that is intentional without being appropriative . . . a suspended gesture that makes room for an experience of sheer presence."[49]

Secular Enchantment. Or, Why Does Wonder Matter?

According to Costa, secular enchantment is "a form of enchantment especially suited for a modern 'secular' age; which does not necessarily mean an unbelieving or unspiritual time, but one in which, nonetheless, the general tone set by a fractured, restless, horizontal, skeptical, urbane and ironic climate."[50] It has commonly been argued that this is a fitting description of our current time, most prominently by Max Weber, who writes in his essay "Science as a Vocation" that: "The fate of our times is characterised by rationalisation and intellectualization and above all by the disenchantment of the world." In the modern age, "one need no longer have recourse to magical means in order to master or implore the spirits, as did the savage, for whom such mysterious powers existed. Technical means and capabilities perform the service."[51] Put otherwise, disenchantment is not simply a matter of the death of God, but a "dismissal of the very notion of mystery from our encounter with the world."[52]

Jane Bennett paraphrases the disenchantment narrative as follows:

> There was once a time when Nature was purposive, God was active in human affairs, human and other creatures were defined by a pre-existing web of relations, social life was characterised by face-to-face relations, and political order took the form of organic community. Then, this premodern world gave way to forces of scientific and instrumental rationality, secularism, individualism, and the bureaucratic state—all of which, combined, disenchant the world.[53]

In this version of the story, inspired in no small part by Weber, the mysteries of magic and divinity fall victim to the pursuit of knowledge, in the form of science, and humanity is left adrift: denied the consolations of religion or indeed the certainties of belief.[54] But Bennett, along with such thinkers as George Levine, Paolo Costa, and Charles Taylor, argues that secularization and disenchantment are not intrinsically linked and that in the modern world, mysteries continue to abound. Taylor, for example, writes that one of the very things that is held to have disenchanted the world—the theory of evolution—is itself "a cause for wonder at the greatness and complexity of the universe, of the love of the world it inspires within us."[55] For Taylor, enchantment is a sensibility, an openness to letting the world shape our lives, both psychic and physical.[56]

Materialism can thus generate its own form of wonder. For the religious person, the mystery of the universe leads us upward and outward, to God. For the materialist, it leads us onward, downward, into the detail: hence the proliferation of "devices of wonder" such as microscopes, telescopes, and all other instruments of modern technology that allow us to see the world on different scales (2001). It is this same sense of secular enchantment that underpins what Richard Holmes calls "Romantic science":[57] the scientific counterpoint to Romantic poetry or painting, artforms that try to forge a connection with a meaningless through world through the artist's subjectivity. Romantic science and Romantic art are linked, Holmes argues, by the experience of wonder that underpins both. Holmes, writing in particular of the period of the second scientific revolution (loosely 1768–1831 "although we have not yet quite outgrown it"), describes the following features: a single solitary scientific genius (Newton, Darwin), the Eureka moment of singular, almost mystical vision and the notion of a mysterious nature as yet explicable, waiting to be discovered (with the help of newly invented scientific instruments).[58]

It seems to me that film—whose prehistory, as detailed by Fulgence Marion, coincides with the Romantic era[59]—lies at the intersection of Romantic science and Romantic art. A technological form designed to capture the living world, it has been used in the service of both learning and discovery (as in anthropological films, informational documentaries, medical and exploratory films) entertainment and poetry. Across its many forms, it carries the potential to engender an experience of wonder, as it allows its audiences to see the world on screen, the same world that we inhabit, from new perspectives and in new lights.

Conclusion

In an article entitled "A Secular Wonder," Paolo Costa argues that wonder allows us to appreciate the world *as it is*, without hope for a better or more perfect one. It is, he argues "an exceptionally intense way of being affectively aware" of the things that we see that results in a powerful experience of presence: of both the object and of ourselves.[60] Costa refers to this experience as a "dilated present," in which physical activity is precluded but mental activity is not. Wonder, he writes, is "an objectless gratitude that turns outwards.... An expansive response to the world's allure that encourages respect, gentleness, humility, unpossessiveness."[61] In this reading, wonder takes on rather conservative undertones: it encourages us to be grateful for what we have, rather than to seek change.

On the other hand, the phenomenologist and cultural theorist Sarah Ahmed claims that wonder allows us to experience a phenomenon "as if" for the first time,[62] it can encourage the scales to fall from our eyes. Through wonder, we are disabused of our assumptions, habits, and taken-for-grantedness.[63] As a result, Ahmed writes, wonder allows us to reframe the world, seeing the ways in which it has been socially constructed. She suggests that wonder allows us to see the surfaces of the world as human-made and that as such "wonder opens up rather than suspends historicity."[64] Historicity, that is, is what is concealed by our acceptance of it as the "ordinary": something that is already familiar, or recognizable. When we are prompted to see it as something strange, its contingency is revealed. Thus, wonder opens once more onto the possible: the possibility of sociopolitical change, of a better world, a world whose present and future is determined by its human inhabitants.

In briefly tracing the hidden history of wonder's significance to film and its theorization, I hope to have shown that, whether spectacular or realist, factual or fictional, film is able to emphasize and condense the experience of wonder as a visual relationship between the wonderer and the world, a relationship that opens up a space of thought and action and which relates to questions of ontology and ethics. Wonderstruck, we are prompted to ask: What is this thing that appears before me? Where did it come from? What might its appearance before me mean for how I see and understand the world more broadly? Over time "How did he do this?" becomes "What should I do?" The shift from the other to the self analogizes the shift from a world which finds its meaning in the transcendent to one that is defined in relation to human action. Cinematic wonder thus demands an ethical response through its spur to appreciation and admiration, and its call to think about our responsibilities to that the wondrous world on screen. As the great Romantic poet Samuel Coleridge put it, "In wonder all philosophy began, in wonder it ends.... But the first wonder is the offspring of ignorance, the last is the parent of adoration."[65]

Notes

1. In Greek mythology, Thaumas was the God of wonder, and his daughter's first child (with Electra, daughter of Ocean) was Iris, the Rainbow. It is surely no coincidence that nowadays the term "iris" denotes part of the eye, as well as referring to a particular type of shot masked in a circular form and typically has been employed to gradually begin or end a scene. The use of irises calls attention to an object or character and/or creates the impression of looking through a small area like a keyhole—in short, it calls attention to the act of seeing and focusing, both essential aspects of wonder, as we shall see.
2. Vlad Petre Glaveanu, "Creativity and Wonder," *Journal of Creative Behaviour* 53, no. 2 (2017): 182.
3. Ibid., 172.
4. Martha Nussbaum, *Upheavals of Thought: The Intelligence of Emotions* (Cambridge: Cambridge University Press, 2001), 54.
5. Lorraine Daston and Katherine Park, *Wonders and the Order of Nature, 1150–1750* (New York: Zone Books, 1998).

6 Ibid., 365.
7 Genevieve Lloyd, *Reclaiming Wonder: After the Sublime* (Edinburgh: Edinburgh University Press, 2019), 1.
8 Hence, perhaps, the significant place of children and innocents in the fantasy and science-fiction genre, including *Jurassic Park*. As Caspar Salmon puts in a scathing review of the 2020 film *Dolittle*, the film includes "a pair of under-directed, gorgeous, doe-eyed kids in main roles, reduced to vapid reaction shots to convey the wonder we should be feeling at all times." See Caspar Salmon, "The Worst Thing About Robert Downey Jr's Incomprehensibly Welsh Dolittle? It Can't Even Commit to Being Bad," *Prospect Magazine*, February 10, 2020, https://www.prospectmagazine.co.uk/arts-and-books/robert-downey-jr-doolittle-review-caspar-salmon.
9 Philip Fisher, *Wonder, the Rainbow, and the Aesthetics of Rare Experiences* (Cambridge, MA: Harvard University Press, 1998), 19–20.
10 Ibid., 17.
11 Ibid.
12 Fulgence Marion, *The Wonders of Optics*, trans. Charles W. Quin (New York: Charles Scribner and Co, 1870), 173.
13 Ibid., 178.
14 Ibid.
15 Tom Gunning, "An Aesthetic of Astonishment: Early Film and the (In)credulous Spectator," in *Film and Theory*, ed. Robert Stam and Toby Miller (New York: Blackwell, 2000).
16 Ibid., 118–19.
17 René Descartes, *The Philosophical Writings of Descartes*, vol., trans. John Cottingham, Robert Stoothoff, and Dugald Murdoch (Cambridge: Cambridge University Press,1985), 354. Descartes writes: "When the first encounter with some object surprises us, and we judge it to be new, or very different from what we knew in the past or what we supposed it was going to be, this makes us wonder and be astonished at it. And since this can happen before we know in the least whether this object is suitable to us or not, it seems to me that Wonder is the first of all passions. It has no opposite, because if the object presented has nothing in it that surprises us, we are not in the least moved by it and regard it without passion." See *The Passions of the Soul*, trans. Stephen H. Voss (Indianapolis: Hackett, 1989), 52.
18 We might note a correspondence of sorts here with Apparatus Theory and its variants, with their emphasis on the spectator as "chained, captured, or captivated"; Jean-Louis Baudry, "Ideological Effects of the Basic Cinematic Apparatus," in *Narrative, Apparatus, Ideology: A Film Theory Reader*, ed. Philip Rosen (New York: Columbia University Press), 294.
19 For more on Descartes and wonder, see Daston and Park, *Wonders and the Order of Nature*, and Lloyd, *Reclaiming Wonder*.
20 In a 2020 interview with Annie van den Oever, Gunning acknowledges the nuances in the different terms, while arguing for their continued

interchangeableness: "Wonder, astonishment, the sublime, and even shock are all terms I think could be related to the concept of *ostrannenie*. I think though they all have slightly different connotations. Philip Fischer in his book *Wonder, The Rainbow and the Aesthetics of Rare Experiences* argues for the term 'wonder' as opposed to such concepts as the sublime or shock or the experience of what he calls estrangement as the equivalent of *ostrannenie*. He sees 'wonder' as more gentle and less 'melodramatic' than these terms. I would resist this Spielbergian understanding of wonder and would rather relate *ostrannenie* to the full gamut of a sudden perceptual discovery from simple surprise through aggressive shock. Therefore, astonishment remains my favored term, but I certainly think wonder fits in here, if we avoid seeing it as an aesthetic of reassurance." See Annie van den Oever and Tom Gunning, "Viktor Shklovsky's *Ostrannenie* and the 'Hermeneutics of Wonder,'" *Early Popular Visual Culture* 18, no. 1 (April 2020): 23–4. doi:10.1080/17460654.2020.1751915.

21 Gunning, "An Aesthetic of Astonishment," 121.
22 Ibid., 124.
23 Ibid., 117.
24 Ibid., 125.
25 Tom Gunning, "The Cinema of Attractions: Early Film, Its Spectator and the Avant-Garde," in *Early Cinema: Space, Frame, Narrative*, ed. Thomas Elsaesser and Adam Barker (London: British Film Institute, 1990), 56–62.
26 Philip Maciak, *The Disappearing Christ: Secularism in the Silent Era* (New York: Columbia University Press, 2019), Ch. 3.
27 Vivian Sobchack, *Screening Space: The American Science Fiction Film* (New York: Rutgers University Press, 1997).
28 Michele Pierson, *Special Effects: Still in Search of Wonder* (New York: Columbia University Press, 2002), 123.
29 Ibid., 8.
30 Warren Buckland, "Between Science Fact and Science Fiction: Spielberg's Digital Dinosaurs," in *Liquid Metal: The Science Fiction Film Reader*, ed. Sean Redmond (London: Wallflower, 2004), 24.
31 For a list of some of these, see Buckland's "Between Science Fact and Science Fiction."
32 Buckland, "Between Science Fact and Science Fiction," 32.
33 Ibid., 33.
34 Lloyd, *Reclaiming Wonder*; Fisher, *Wonder, the Rainbow, and the Aesthetics of Rare Experiences*.
35 Fisher, *Wonder, the Rainbow, and the Aesthetics of Rare Experiences*, 19.
36 Ibid., 20.
37 Lutz Koepnick, *The Long Take: Art Cinema and the Wondrous* (Minneapolis: University of Minnesota Press, 2017), 1.
38 Ibid., 2.

39 Ibid., 8.
40 Ibid., 8–9.
41 Ibid., 9.
42 Ibid., 10.
43 Barbara Maria Stafford and Frances Terpak, *Devices of Wonder* (Los Angeles: Getty Research Trust, 2001), 48.
44 André Bazin, "Cinema and Theology: The Case of Heaven Over the Marshes," trans. Bert Cardullo, *Journal of Religion & Film* 6, no. 2 (2002): 9, Article 15, https://digitalcommons.unomaha.edu/jrf/vol6/iss2/15. "The history of religious themes on the screen sufficiently reveals the temptations one must resist in order to meet simultaneously the requirements of cinematic art and of truly religious experience. Everything that is exterior, ornamental, liturgical, sacramental, hagiographic, and miraculous in the everyday observance, doctrine, and practice of Catholicism does indeed show specific affinities with the cinema considered as a formidable iconography. But these affinities, which have made for the success of countless films, are also the source of the religious insignificance of most of them. Almost everything that is good in this domain was created not by the exploitation of these patent affinities, but rather by working against them: by the psychological and moral deepening of the religious factor as well as by the renunciation of the physical representation of the supernatural and of grace. As for 'mysteries,' the cinema has been able to evoke only those of Paris and New York. We're still waiting for it to deal with those of the Middle Ages. To make a long story short, it seems that, although the austereness of the Protestant sensibility is not indispensable to the making of a good Catholic film, it can nevertheless be a real advantage" (Bazin, "Cinema and Theology," 1–2).
45 Stafford, *Devices of Wonder* 48.
46 Peter Matthews, "Divining the Real: The Leaps of Faith in André Bazin's Film Criticism," in *Sight and Sound*, August 1999, https://www2.bfi.org.uk/news-opinion/sight-sound-magazine/features/andre-bazin-divining-real-film-criticism-overview (accessed March 3, 2023).
47 Koepnick, *The Long Take*, 12.
48 Ibid., 18–19.
49 Paolo Costa, "A Secular Wonder," in *The Joy of Secularism: 11 Essays for How We Live Now*, ed. George Levine (Princeton, NJ: Princeton University Press, 2011), 142.
50 Ibid.,151.
51 Max Weber, "Science as a Vocation," in *From Max Weber: Essays in Sociology*, ed. H. H. Gerth and C. Wright Mills (New York and Oxford: Oxford University Press, 1946), 189.
52 Jeffrey L. Kosky, *Arts of Wonder: Enchanting Secularity* (Chicago, IL: University of Chicago Press, 2013), xii.
53 Jane Bennett, *The Enchantment of Modern of Life: Attachments, Crossings, and Ethics* (Princeton, NJ: Princeton University Press, 2001), 7.

54 The philosopher Stanley Cavell, for example, argues in *The Claim of Reason* that post-Enlightenment we have lost our natural relation to the world, that is, been plunged into the condition of skepticism; Stanley Cavell, *The Claim of Reason: Wittgenstein, Skepticism, Morality, and Tragedy* (New York: Oxford University Press, 1979).

55 Charles Taylor, "Disenchantment—Re-enchantment," in *The Joy of Secularism: 11 Essays for How We Live Now*, ed. George Levine (Princeton, NJ: Princeton University Press, 2011), 66.

56 Charles Taylor, "Buffered and Porous Selves," *The Immanent Frame*, September 2008. http://tif.ssrc.org/2008/09/02/buffered-and-porous-selves/.

57 Richard Holmes, *The Age of Wonder: How the Romantic Generation Discovered the Beauty and Terror of Science* (New York: Vintage, 2010), xv.

58 Here, we may find another for the close relationship between wonder and Science Fiction, which has to do with science fiction's emphasis on rational explanations for wondrous experiences, as opposed to say, Fantasy, in which we find no rational explanation—we might compare, for example, *Jurassic Park*'s cloned dinosaurs with *Jumanji*'s mystical, vaguely Voodoo, herd of rhinos.

59 The magic lantern became a popular entertainment in the period 1770–1831; the thaumatrope was invented in 1830. For more see Fulgence Marion's *The Wonders of Optics*.

60 Costa, "A Secular Wonder," 147.

61 Ibid.

62 Sara Ahmed, *The Cultural Politics of Emotion*, 2nd edn (New York: Routledge [2004] 2015), 179.

63 For more on seeing "as if" and "phenomenology," see Bonnie Mann, "Feminist Phenomenology and the Politics of Wonder," *Avant: Trends in Interdisciplinary Studies* 9, no. 2 (2018): 43–61. Mann, incidentally, connects her experience of wonder to her apostasy from the Christian Church (54–5).

64 Ahmed, *The Cultural Politics of Emotion*, 179–8.

65 Quoted in Holmes, *Age of Wonder*, xx.

9

Vegetal Life, Plant-Soul

Early British Film Flowers

Sarah Cooper

When F. Percy Smith's *The Birth of a Flower* was screened at the Electric Palace in Lewisham, London, in the final week of March 1911, it was greeted with an unprecedented response. Fritz W. Wolters, the manager of the theater, reported that the film had received more applause than any other since he had been in charge. The audience at the Electric Palace demanded an encore, the management obliged, and Wolters wrote to the film's producer and distributor Charles Urban afterward to tell him about this rousing reception and to thank him for allowing the theater to keep the film for the rest of that week.[1] Wolters enclosed a letter from T. W. Sanders, a leading horticulturalist who attended the screening, who wrote approvingly to him in the hope that more such "highly intellectual and educative" films would be shown in the future.[2] Urban, the astute businessman and marketer, included in his subsequent catalogue listings emphatic reference to "THE FILM THAT WAS ENCORED!" He also published the correspondence of Wolters and Sanders, adding a summative statement: "Exhibitors should see to it that the growing interest of their audiences in educational subjects is satisfied. The URBAN SCIENCE SERIES supplies just what is wanted—amusement and instruction combined."[3] Popular appeal through a combination of entertainment and education made this brief film exemplary of what Urban was aiming to achieve in his Science Series. In the same catalogue publicity, there is mention not only of the "immense scientific value" of the film but also of its "great beauty" (Figures 9.1–9.3).[4]

FIGURE 9.1 *Narcissus, still from* The Birth of a Flower *(dir. F. Percy Smith, 1910).*

FIGURE 9.2 *Garden anemone, still from* The Birth of a Flower *(dir. F. Percy Smith, 1910).*

The Birth of a Flower is thereby promoted as bridging science and aesthetics, amusement and instruction. What concerns me centrally here, though, is that the catalogue entry is further supplemented by a quotation from an article that praises the film for its capacity to open on to religion from within the secular context of cinema.

While this early response that I shall go on to discuss introduces a relation between religion and the secular in the screening of this film, other respondents

FIGURE 9.3 *Roses, still from* The Birth of a Flower *(dir. F. Percy Smith, 1910)*.

variously divinize or anthropomorphize plant life when reviewing this and other works by Smith. My opening aim in this chapter is to explore these tendencies toward the divinization and anthropomorphization of the vegetal within the initial reception of Smith's work. Early reviews of his films invoke discussion of the soul in a spiritual and nonspiritual sense, as well as attributing human or animal sentience to the plants that are filmed, which posits them in terms of something they are not. Viewed thus historically in religious and secular terms, Smith's filmed plants are not however constrained by these framings, and re-viewing them alongside current work in critical plant studies is helpful in this regard. Recent plant scholarship has retained reference to the vexed category of the soul in order to designate vegetal specificity that floats free of the sacred and secular anchor points of the past, with the objective of seeing the plant as a plant rather than in divine or human terms, but without losing sight of connections to other forms of life. It is with this attention to vegetal particularity and relationality in mind that I revisit the religious and secular discussion of Smith's filming of plant life, especially his flowers, to consider what it means to talk of plant-soul in the context of these films today.

From Divinized Nature to the Human Soul of Flowers

The article in which Smith's *The Birth of a Flower* is praised for opening on to religion is titled "The Cinematograph and Theology."[5] It begins with a question being discussed by the UK Council of the Metropolitan Hospitals Fund of whether Hospital Sunday Funds should accept the contributions of cinematograph shows. The issue of whether or not the funds would be acceptable hinges on the fact that the cinematograph is positioned as secular: "One can understand, of course, the disfavour with which the competition of these shows are regarded by good people who think that churches and chapels are the only lawful resorts on a Sunday. But the facts remain that very many people who cannot be induced to attend public worship find their way to enterprises of a more secular kind." Cinema is positioned as secular because it is an alternative venue for the otherwise church-going population on a Sunday. The secular institution of cinema as described here is clearly no place of worship but one of its saving graces is deemed to be the revelatory capacity of what is screened there. The article singles out the forthcoming release of the film that will "reveal to the audience the growth of a flower," continuing to describe how the whole "cycle of plant life" can be witnessed in minutes, and concluding the outline of the film with the sentence that Urban cites in his catalogue publicity for *The Birth of a Flower*: "It is impossible that the most thoughtless and miscellaneous audience should look on enacted miracles like this without having the sense of wonder stirred, and wonder, by consent, is the first step to religion." There is a distinction here between cinema/the secular and nature/religion, even as the "enacted miracles" referred to owe something to both. This chimes with film historian Colin Williamson's sense of how time-lapse footage of plants has been framed throughout cinema history as a technique of scientific discovery and a device of wonder, with wonder being ascribed to the technique as well as to the subject of the plant growing.[6] As philosopher Bruno Latour notes, there is no divinity whose force has been less contested than "Nature".[7] It is the relation between film and this force that is at issue here.[8] Nature is divinized in the eyes of the author of "The Cinematograph and Theology," with film being intricately bound up with its miracles, and a respondent to another of Smith's flower films of the period imbues it similarly with the power of the divine.

Indeed, the divine is in the eyes of the beholder once again when a reviewer writes of another work by Smith, *From Bud to Blossom* (1910), in terms that resemble those used in "The Cinematograph and Theology": "a child who should see these wonderful things must not only have his soul awakened to beauty but to the knowledge that science brings us close to the divine."[9] It is science that paves the way to the divine in this quotation, and reference to the soul of the child who is watching this film conjures a term that in this context supports the religious weight of the reviewer's admiration. These connections to religion and the divine notwithstanding, the majority of initial reviewers did not, however, see these films through an overtly religious lens, even though reference to the soul reappears elsewhere. Intriguingly, in the broader reception of these and other plant films of the time, it is not the soul of the audience that is referred to directly; rather, it is that of plants, stripped of its religious sense and standing for a life, rather than spiritual, principle. A review of the first demonstration in New York of the newly patented color system of animated photography begins with the declaration: "If you do not believe flowers have souls you would have been convinced tonight at the meeting of the New York Electrical society."[10] The flowers written about in the ensuing paragraph are described as "smiling," "nodding their heads," and opening their "eyes." The soul of flowers is not divinized and positioned in religious terms but nor is it exactly vegetal. This curiously uprooted life principle that is unearthed through the early reception of these and other of Smith's natural history films finds its place first of all in a literal deracination effected in *The Birth of a Flower*.

Smith made many botanical films in later years for the "Secrets of Nature" and "Secrets of Life" series and he worked frequently with filmmaker Mary Field along with other collaborators, who did the editing and handled other key aspects of the production, including voice-over commentary after the transition to sound film.[11] In contrast to many of these later "Secrets," which show their subjects planted in soil either indoors or outdoors, *The Birth of a Flower* charts the opening up of many of the flowers in vases. The flowers are placed in conditions that optimize their recording on film.[12] But those that appear in vases recall flowers positioned for a still life painting of a bygone era, colorful blooms against a black background, poised between life and death. The cut flower in particular carries over from the Victorian period the fascination with exquisite beauty heightened by the proximity of death. The true antonym of death, birth not life, is thus bound to its opposite, and through the use of speed magnification, the film charts the journey toward the extinguishing of life while still tracing the flowers' movements in the process. In the case of cut flowers, light and water continue to sustain them enough so that they can open before they fade. Inspired by Jacques Derrida's scattered meditations on flowers, philosopher and critical plant scholar Michael Marder refers to the cut flower as existing on the edge of culture, saying that as soon as it is picked from its root, it is no longer distinguishable from its artificial counterpart.[13] The resemblance of the cut flower to the artificial flower, coupled with the slowness of its movement under ordinary circumstances, can therefore suggest lifelessness.[14] Time-lapse footage of plants animates the animate, enlivening that which is already alive, but there is a strong sense too when a subject seems initially so static that it is bringing the dead back to life, or introducing the inanimate to life. The use of time-lapse in *The Birth of a Flower* speeds up movement almost to the point of the flowers' total collapse but then restarts that growth again and again, with the same kind of flowers and then with different flowers, creating a syncopated movement and iterative time within the sped-up life cycle. I have written elsewhere of what I term the performative constitution of techno-flowers in Smith's film with reference to this conjunction of technology and real flowers, along with the queer potential of the endless flowering of the flower.[15] The recursive logic of flowers opening up repeatedly not only enhances the dissolution of boundaries between nature and artifice; it also ensures that such successive resurrections appear as a wonder of science and technology rather than religion.

While the religious claiming of flora in some of the initial reviews of *The Birth of a Flower* attests to the abiding belief in these and other natural phenomena as subjects of creation, the filming of flowers emerges from a scientific lineage that begins with the experiments of evolutionary biology and that can therefore be said to have a more secular organizing principle from the outset. From the botanical studies of Charles and Francis Darwin onwards, scientists had relied on enhanced observational technologies to perceive and understand the life of plants, drawing first upon photography and later on film. Early experiments with time-lapse cinematography date back to the 1880s and the representational resources of cinema served botanical research.[16] The soul of the flowers spoken about at the New York Electrical society that breaks free of religious attachment is rooted otherwise in the ontology of film that speeds up the movements of the flowers blooming to make them visible to human perception. Pointing to the interweaving of movement and vegetal life from cinema's inception, film scholar Graig Uhlin notes—referring to André Bazin's "The Ontology of the Photographic Image"—that if the photograph is a flower, the cinematic image is the act of flowering.[17] The birth of a flower is synonymous with the birth of cinema, yet the intricate association of film and the soul is also to be found elsewhere in film history. Classical film theory is replete with discussion of the soul of cinema quite apart from that of the flower, the qualities of which it borrows mainly from the human or animal and not the plant soul.[18] In keeping with this theoretical context, but bringing these areas of interest in the soul together, the filmed flowers spoken about in the journalist's report on the screening at the New York Electrical society reveal their soul through movements described in terms of individualized human actions and attributes: smiling, nodding heads, and opening eyes. Corresponding with the fact that the seat of the soul has been more readily located in the human, other responses to the films of Smith bring out vital qualities that have been attributed historically to the human, or animal, soul.

Anthropomorphic Secular Sentience and the Electric Flower

Thus far, we have seen how responses to Smith's filming of flowers links them to religion by bringing in reference to the divine and to the viewer's soul, but we have also seen how pointing to the soul of these flowers in other writing more frequently breaks the sacred tie, understanding the soul as a life principle that is there in nature and that technologies are charged with revealing but which is cast in human terms. Broadening this latter secular, nonspiritual resonance, it is a reference to sentience that provides the continuing, though tacit, connection to the more explicit mentions of the soul as a life force. The legacy of eighteenth-century scientific theories of vegetal sentience is palpable here, but so too is a longer history of hierarchical discussion of characteristics of the soul. For both Aristotle and Linnaeus, sentience distinguishes the animal and human soul from the vegetal, and in the early writings on Smith's work in the film and popular press, cinema is said repeatedly to lend plants this characteristic. Speaking about speed magnification in *The Birth of a Flower*, the reviewer in *Picture Theatre News*, March 8, 1911, declares: "By this process plants are transformed, as it were, into sentient beings." *The Evening Standard* article "Botany by Bioscope" of March 11, 1911, makes exactly the same reference to the flowers as sentient beings to praise this as a remarkable film. In the 1920s, it is a nasturtium featured in *The Life of a Plant* that catches the attention of reviewers in similar terms. S. R. Littlewood, writing in *The Sphere*, January 16, 1926, and who gives *The Life of a Plant* a far better review than any of the other films playing in London's West End, notes of the nasturtium: "This flower is alive—a delicately perceptive, sentient, purposeful thing." Aliveness, equated with perception, sentience, and purposiveness, is more than the life principle associated with the Aristotelian nutritive soul of plants, and is brought to light through cinema.[19] G. A. Atkinson too, writing in *The Sunday Express*, September 18, 1927, notes that *The Life of a Plant* "concerns the death agonies of an uprooted nasturtium, and you find it difficult to believe, as you view the picture, that the life of a plant is not as sentient as your own." The film critic for the *Daily Mail*, January 11, 1926, also waxes lyrical about the death agony of the nasturtium when it cannot strike a root.[20] Through attribution of sentience to plants, cinema is understood in the eyes of these critics to give access to belief in a life "as sentient as your own." This view of plant life made possible through cinema that confers upon it the sentience of the animal and the human soul is different from a more recent focus on vegetal soul on the part of philosophers and naturalists that aims to valorize the plant in and on its own terms. I shall return to this contemporary attention to vegetal specificity since it attempts to move beyond both the divinization and anthropomorphization of nature with implications for both the religious and secular claiming of plant life. For the time being, there are further aspects of recognizing qualities of an animal or human soul in Smith's vegetal work that warrant consideration. Whether seeing the divine in nature or whether flowers are understood to have lives as sentient as one's own through these films, the praise of plant life in terms of something it is not risks denaturing it, and even descriptions that foreground Smith's naturalistic depictions cover over the fact that viewers are being distanced from, rather than taken closer to, their floral subject.

At the time of its first release, *The Birth of a Flower* received widespread rave reviews. Focusing on the initial UK reception context alone, the laudatory vocabulary enumerated how *natural* or *real* the flowers were, how *vividly* they appeared, and how cinema *imparted life*.[21] Such recognition of life, the actual, and the natural was encouraged by Urban through the promotion of Kinemacolor.[22] On the front of programs advertising the films screened at the Scala Theatre in London (Urban had leased the Scala in order to be able to screen entire programs in Kinemacolor from 1911 to 1913), reference is made variously to "Reflecting Nature in Her Actual Colors," "The World's Events in Their Natural Colors," "Reflecting Nature in Actual Colors and Movements," and inside the latter program, Kinemacolor is said to stand for "the thing-as-it-is in Nature."[23] This replica of nature can also be understood as a replacement for it, however. I have sought elsewhere to distinguish what I term the performatively constituted techno-flower of Smith's filming from talk of a mediated or electric flower.[24] It is nonetheless possible here to see the birth of the "electric flower" in the very specific sense that film scholar Akira Mizuta Lippit intends when describing the appearance of the "electric animal" and charting the vanishing of actual animals from the world from the nineteenth to the twentieth century.[25] That Smith's nature films flourish during a period of widespread urbanization is no coincidence.

In Lewisham, in particular, the location of the encored screening of *The Birth of a Flower*, the transformation of farmland into housing estates accomplished by Archibald Cameron Corbett between 1896 and 1913 involved the building of thousands of houses across hundreds of acres of land.[26] The flowers of the film, which the horticulturalist T. W. Sanders described in his letter to Wolters as "so typically good and well known," would have been so from public and private cultivated spaces—parks, gardens, and inside homes—all a sign of the urban encroachment and reshaping of the terrain of the vegetal, as well as a reminder of the dissolution of a boundary between the natural and the cultural already apparent in the farmland that was replaced by houses. Smith's filmmaking, whose written reception crosses boundaries between religion and the secular, as well as art and science, education and entertainment, exemplifies the rattling of dichotomies that political theorist William Connolly writes of in the advent of the Anthropocene.[27] The beauty, educational, and entertainment value of Smith's filming of flowers, praised as natural, real, and vivid, and described additionally with the attribute of the sentience of the animal and human soul, cannot disguise the fact that these are images of flowers that do not stand for themselves in reality but for humans in those early anthropomorphic responses—for life "as sentient as your own." They are doubly distanced from themselves from the outset, whether described subsequently in religious or secular terms.

Ostensibly different from celebrating the wonder of nature as divinity, the move to express the soul of the plant in human terms grounds and anthropomorphizes, bringing with it its own issues that we have already begun to explore. As naturalist Jacques Tassin observes, there is a long-standing tradition of seeing continuity rather than barriers between living creatures. He cites Pierre Louis Moreau de Maupertuis, G. W. F. Hegel, Jean-Henri Fabre, Maurice Maeterlinck, and Raoul Francé, as just some of the precursors to contemporary scholars devoted to exploring resemblances between humans and plants, and studying sensibility, intelligence, and behavior, referring invariably to the animal model.[28] In the case of Smith's later botanical films, analogy is built into them in order to serve educative purposes, permitting the description of something difficult to grasp in terms that are more familiar. Time-lapse cinematography serves the purposes of showing spectators what had hitherto never been seen in the growth of both flowering and nonflowering plants. This rendering visible of the invisible is part of what instigated that initial opening onto the wonder of religion and the divine in the eyes of some early viewers, even as the hitherto unseen miracles were worked by secular technology in a secular setting. In Smith's later films the entwinement of the cinematic and the vegetal does not stand alone as it did with *The Birth of a Flower* and is related verbally—via more detailed title cards, or voice-over with the advent of sound after 1927—to human life once again.

In *Floral Cooperative Societies* (1927), for example, title cards provide information about globe-thistles, daisies, and dandelions. With these latter flowers the female part of the flower is said to divide and thereby becomes "marriageable," the prelude to reproduction being inaugurated through reference to the ceremony in the human world. Furthermore, *Scarlet Runner and Co* (1930) begins with the flower of a broad bean followed by that of the scarlet runner, which is then visited by a bee, before Smith's mechanical model of the flower and his handmade mechanical insect Bertie the bee are brought in to demonstrate how pollen appears and is carried. The transfer of pollen to the bee is conveyed humorously not just through Bertie's presence but also through the commentary, which explains that he sometimes gets an eyeful as in a custard pie comedy. Later, the runner bean is described as the Samson of the bean world, capable of pushing up through the earth and knocking out concrete. And still further on the leaves of the bean open out in the sunshine but then are said "like all young things" to get tired in the evening and hang down to rest. Finally, through Smith's more minuscule cinematography, the magnified cells of moss which produce tiny flower-like growths when fully developed in *Gathering Moss* (1933) (Figure 9.4), are said to wake up slowly in the daytime, work feverishly by noon, but rest by evening, although "sudden jerks suggest nightmares and uneasy sleep."

Across all of these examples, description functions analogically, explaining plant life in terms of the human rather than the divine, and continuing that

FIGURE 9.4 *Still from* Gathering Moss *(dir. F. Percy Smith, 1933)*.

thread of secular sentience that links back to the nonspiritual life force of the human or animal soul. Anthropomorphism was originally the attribution of human features to the gods, but from the 1800s, it shifted to apply to other entities and names a broader phenomenon that occurs across secular thinking too.[29] In an era of human exceptionalism, anthropomorphizing has been subject to serious questioning due to associations with human dominance over all other life forms on earth. But anthropomorphic description, such as that which is used in the commentaries of Smith's aforementioned sound films or in those initial responses to *The Birth of a Flower*, need not be thought of as irredeemably problematic and can be understood in fact to gesture toward the very connections between other forms of life that it apparently suppresses by seeing human attributes everywhere. As political theorist Jane Bennett notes: "Maybe it is worth running the risks associated with anthropomorphizing (superstition, the divinization of nature, romanticism) because it, oddly enough, works against anthropocentrism: a chord is struck between person and thing, and I am no longer above or outside a nonhuman 'environment.'"[30] The world seen in our own image is followed swiftly by what she terms a "swarm of 'talented' and vibrant materialities (including the seeing self)."[31] For Bennett, anthropomorphism is not an end in itself, but is a point of access to seeing the distinctive material complexities of all actants in any ecosystem. Following on from this, the anthropomorphizing of the commentary in these films, along with the earlier reviewers' talk of the human/animal soul and the sentience of their flora, can pave the way toward more phytocentric possibilities of analysis envisaged in the recent research of Marder, among others. For Latour, it is not by adding the word soul to an agency that you will make it do anything more: actants are just actants.[32]

For Marder, in contrast, the soul is central to his philosophical project of reclaiming vegetal specificity from a history of marginalization. And for my purposes here, the focus on what Marder terms plant-soul permits me to revisit the initial viewers' divinization and anthropomorphization of Smith's plants and flowers in order to show how their resultant status as neither wholly sacred nor wholly secular returns us to the plants and flowers even in this altered filmic context, while still relating the vegetal to other forms of life.

Film and Plant-Soul

The initial reception of Smith's films paints a different picture of the vegetal from the centuries-long history that critical plant scholars Natania Meeker and Antónia Szabari excavate in cinema, fiction, and art in which science and the arts combine to posit plants as the model for all animate life.[33] As we have seen, the early reviewers of Smith's films who speak variously of the soul from religious or secular perspectives recuperate nature in divine or human/animal terms with both analogical moves (the latter of which is repeated in the commentary of his later films) serving to view plants in terms of something other than themselves and thereby working against their being a model for all animate life. Moreover, time-lapse can be understood as fundamental to such recuperation and Marder, in tune with Heidegger in this respect, is critical of this cinematic technique.[34] The plants may be active rather than passive in their filmic presence—they are actually growing and moving irrespective of speed magnification—but the technology of cinema, along with the spoken/written language used to describe them in film commentary and reviews, frame, claim, and objectify them repeatedly, with time-lapse speeding up their own time. Paradoxically, though, it is Marder's work on plant-soul that opens up the possibility for a reengagement with Smith's films that suggests a reconnection with the history that Meeker and Szabari outline, with the vegetal offering a model for other animate life.

To talk of the soul of plants today is immediately, as Marder concedes, to be met with suspicion by modern readers due to the term's heavy metaphysical and theological baggage.[35] Philosopher Jeffrey T. Nealon comments on this too, noting how the translation of the Aristotelian nutritive soul from Greek (psukhe) into Latin (anima) lends it Christian weight and an individualist sense of identity that are inapplicable to plants, and asserting that it is better understood as a vital principle or a kind of life.[36] Marder notes that plants are capable of three of the four kinds of movement that Aristotle speaks about in *De Anima* (altering their state, growing, and decaying) thereby preparing the theoretical space for an understanding of plant-soul that not only renders the specificity of the vegetal but also forms the basis of being as being-with.[37] As Marder argues in a later dialogue with feminist philosopher Luce Irigaray, ensoulment is expansive and energetic: "Rather than a vegetal soul setting itself to work in the body of a plant, the life of this plant is a conduit of nondestructive energy to which other vegetal, animal, or human beings can also be privy."[38] To speak of plant-soul in this way is therefore neither to posit a transcendent spiritual animating principle, nor an immutable nonspiritual essence or secular life force hidden inside plants, but nor is it to deny rapprochements between plants and other forms of life.[39] It is, however, to join with Marder, among other recent scholars, who have sought a phytocentric approach to life in which the vegetal is fundamental to a web of relations to other life forms with which it is energetically entwined.

By beginning with the locus of the soul beyond the human or rather at the end of the human or the beginning of something other than the human, all life can be seen to emerge from and return to a shared soil if not a common root: from soul to soil, "u" and "i" exchange places in order to think differently about what is shared, and this is where Marder's work is not so antithetical to that of Latour. In his Gifford Lectures, Latour recalls that human means soil, and to this we can add the rich layers of Donna J. Haraway's humus, humusities, and compost from *Staying with the Trouble*. She refers to a mad gardener chipping, shredding, and layering the rubbish of the Anthropocene and the exterminism of the Capitalocene to make a steaming compost pile for still possible pasts, presents, and futures, and these float free of religious and secular moorings: "This Chthulucene is neither sacred nor secular; this earthly worlding is thoroughly terran, muddled, and mortal—and at stake now."[40] If we take comparisons between flowers and plants with human or animal life as ensouled to suggest how much we are like them rather than they are like us—the difference is subtle but important and involves moving toward them rather than moving them toward us: considering how like a leaf we are, as Haraway puts it[41]—then vegetal life can be understood to subtend and connect with the lives of others, as Marder's sense of the ethics of plant-soul also suggests. This differs from the move to attribute a human or animal soul and their sentient qualities to plants that many of the early reviewers made when talking about Smith's filming of flowers and other plants. De-individuating *the* soul and viewing it as energy that is neither a transcendent nor an inner animating principle, plant-soul exists apart from both divine and human anchor points, and from both the sacred and the secular renderings of the soul in writings on these films in the past, while borrowing the impulse toward synergy underlying the anthropomorphism of Smith's films and the terminology of the initial reviews. Rather than seeing ourselves wherever we look, though, the ethics of vegetal soul suggests that we see plants instead without losing sight of our differences. For Marder, there is a living intelligence in plant-soul, and he recognizes that human and animal psyches derive from this figure, which is "sublimated (and, to a significant extent, dematerialized) in them."[42] Plant-thinking when articulated by Marder as a mode of thinking proper to plants is anti-metaphysical and it begins with the explosion of identity, a form of thinking "without the head," which lets the other pass through them without appropriating their alterity.[43] This is a life of tendrils, roots, and petals, of growth as well as decay, that reaches out and nourishes not only itself but others—leaves that breathe, plants that decompose, compost that fertilizes, life that pulses from the ground upward, outward, and downward, in darkness as in light.

In their writings on their filmmaking, Smith and Field also insist on thinking about plants and animals relationally, based on a sense of common ancestry.[44] The kinds of synergies that they speak about are precursors to the symbiosis that Haraway talks about, drawing upon the work of biologist Lynn Margulis.[45] This more recent research stresses connectedness between different species, rather than an expression of one life form in terms of another that denies difference, and it is exactly this plant-based synergy that the early nature films can also be understood to promote. The film *Nature's Double Lifers: Ferns and Fronds* (1932), for example, while partaking of the anthropomorphism of Smith's other films, encourages its viewers by means of voice-over to attend to the cell division witnessed through magnification (which it shows on screen as this is described), since this is the basis of formation of all organic life, whether animal or vegetal (Figure 9.5).

Through the very techniques that Marder understands to rob the plant of its own time, the common foundation of all forms of life is shown to stem specifically from the plant here, as film enables rather than hinders recognition of the qualities of vegetal soul. The films that bring the life cycle of flowering and other plants up to the speed of human perception thereby regulating their time also point to the generative and pervasive energy of

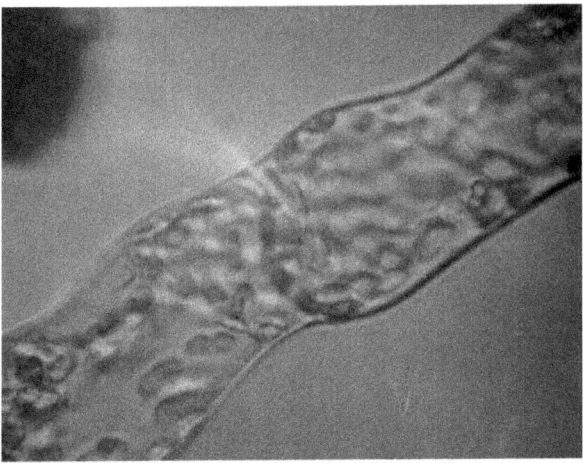

FIGURE 9.5 *Still from* Nature's Double Lifers *(dir. F. Percy Smith, 1932).*

plant-soul that exists apart from film and human regard. Plant time is not ours, as time-lapse makes clear, but even as these films manipulate time, they point simultaneously to plant-soul beyond human control and to being as being-with.

It is the dual possibility of vegetal specificity and relationality that my recourse to recent discussion of plant-soul in this filmic context is intended to recognize, resonating with the very connectivity on the basis of common ancestry that Field and Smith also point to in their own writings on their work. Viewed by their initial respondents in religious and secular terms, Smith's films imbue the plant with qualities that are neither wholly religious (they have been said to possess a secular soul or life principle, to be animated by science, to use naturalistic depiction, and to exhibit human/animal sentience) nor wholly secular (they have been understood to connect with a spiritual soul, to divinize nature, to convey wonder, and to make the invisible visible). Attributing to the plants of these films the sentient qualities of the human or animal soul is not the same as recognizing plant-soul, and the latter is no more religious than it is secular in its entwinement with other forms of life. How future viewers will relate to the flowers and the other plants filmed by Smith will vary, as both the religious and secular claiming of them in the past has shown.[46] But these filmed plants create a seemingly endless fascination with vegetal life as both bound up with but different from that of their spectators then as now and will continue to do so for many more years to come.

Notes

1. Letter from Electric Palace High Street Lewisham, March 29, 1911, Charles Urban Archive, URB 8/1, 1908–1911. Smith came to work for Urban after being sacked from his previous job at the British Board of Education in 1910. See Luke McKernan, *Charles Urban: Pioneering the Non-Fiction Film in Britain and America, 1897–1925* (Exeter: Exeter University Press, 2013), 59.

2. Letter from T. W. Sanders to Mr. F. W. Wolters, Charles Urban Archive, URB 8/1, 1908–1911.

3. *Catalogue of Film Subjects*, Kineto Limited, January 6, 1912.

4. Ibid., 7.

5. In the catalogue, the date of publication of this article is given as March 12, 1911 (ibid., 7), but the newspaper article that is also part of the Charles Urban Archive gives the date as March 13, 1911.

6. Colin Williamson, *Hidden in Plain Sight: An Archaeology of Magic and the Cinema* (New Brunswick, NJ: Rutgers University Press, 2015).

7. Bruno Latour, "The Anthropocene and the Destruction of the Image of the Globe," 2013 Gifford Lectures, University of Edinburgh, "Facing Gaia: A New

Enquiry into Natural Religion," https://www.giffordlectures.org/lectures/facing-gaia-new-enquiry-natural-religion (accessed February 25, 2020). These have since been reworked and published as *Facing Gaia: Eight Lectures on the New Climatic Regime* (London: Polity, 2017 [2015]).

8 For a broader discussion of the relationship between nature and technology in the filming of flowers beyond these religious and secular debates, see Sarah Cooper, "Techno-Flowers: Entwinements of Technology and Nature in *The Birth of a Flower* (F. Percy Smith, 1910) and *Little Joe* (Jessica Hausner, 2019)," *Screen* 63, no. 1 (Spring 2022): 1–21.

9 Cited in McKernan, *Charles Urban*, 63. A number of Smith's flower films circulated in Urban's programs throughout the world: *Floral Friends* (translated as *Nos amies les fleurs* and *Blumen Freunde* for programs in France and Germany, respectively) and *The Birth of Flowers* were longer programs that included a more extensive selection of flowers than *The Birth of a Flower*. See URB 3, volume 1 and URB 12, 1–6, Charles Urban Archive.

10 URB 3, volume 1, Charles Urban Archive, press cutting "Real Flowers Open and Bud on Moving Picture Screen." The date of 1910 is written in hand on the cutting.

11 For more on Smith's involvement with these nature film series, see Timothy Boon, *Films of Fact: A History of Science in Documentary Films and Television* (London: Wallflower, 2008). In addition to filming botanical subjects, Smith was famous for filming insects.

12 For a discussion of the technological equipment that facilitates this, see my "Techno-Flowers."

13 Michael Marder, *Plant-Thinking: A Philosophy of Vegetal Life* (New York: Columbia University Press, 2013), 123.

14 Smith and Field comment on the slowness of growth and resulting complexity of the production process with regard to the later "Secrets of Nature" series. See Mary Field and Percy Smith, *Secrets of Nature* (London: The Scientific Book Club, 1939), 236.

15 See my "Techno-Flowers."

16 See Oliver Gaycken, "The Secret Life of Plants: Visualizing Vegetative Movement, 1880–1903," *Early Popular Visual Culture* 10, no. 1 (February 2012): 51–69.

17 Graig Uhlin, "Plant-Thinking with Film: Reed, Branch, Flower," in *The Green Thread: Dialogues with the Vegetal World*, ed. Patrícia Vieira, Monica Gagliano, and John Ryan (Lanham: Lexington Books, 2016), 205.

18 See Sarah Cooper, *The Soul of Film Theory* (Basingstoke: Palgrave Macmillan, 2013) for discussion of the multifaceted conceptualizations and contestations of the relationship between cinema and soul in the history of western film theory.

19 Aristotle, *De Anima*, trans. Hugh Lawson-Tancred (London: Penguin, 1986), 162–4.

20 These press reviews can be found in the Charles Urban Archive, URB 8/1, 1908–1911 and URB 8/2, 1910–1935.

21 Such vocabulary features in horticulturalist T. W. Sanders's letter regarding the Lewisham Electric Palace screening (Charles Urban Archive, URB 8/1, 1908–1911), as well as in *Gloucester Journal* (March 25, 1911), *Portsmouth Evening News* (April 18, 1911), and in a report by the headmaster of the Belfast Municipal Technical Institute (April 14, 1911). The newspapers and report are consultable through the online British Newspaper Archive, https://www.britishnewspaperarchive.co.uk/ (accessed March 2019).

22 Although completed in April 1910, *The Birth of a Flower* was not released until March 1911. This delay was so that it could be distributed in Kinemacolor, a natural color cinematography developed by Urban. See McKernan, *Charles Urban*. The equipment for screening films in Kinemacolor was less widely available than standard projection equipment, so a tinted version of the film was screened in more places than the Kinemacolor version and it is the former that survives today.

23 Charles Urban Archive, URB 3.

24 See my "Techno-Flowers."

25 Akira Mizuta Lippit, *Electric Animal: Toward a Rhetoric of Wildlife* (Minneapolis: University of Minnesota Press, 2008 [2000]).

26 See https://boroughphotos.org/lewisham/torridon-road-hither-green-lewisham-3/ (accessed February 28, 2020). Archibald Cameron Corbett's vision was however for healthy living and his estates are characterized by low density housing with generous gardens, along with wide streets and plenty of green space. See https://thecorbettsociety.org.uk/ (accessed June 26, 2020).

27 William E. Connolly, *Facing the Planetary: Entangled Humanism and the Politics of Swarming* (Durham, NC: Duke University Press, 2017), 3.

28 See Chapter 1 in Jacques Tassin, *À quoi pensent les plantes?* (Paris: Odile Jacob, 2016).

29 S. E. Guthrie, "Anthropomorphism," in *Encyclopedia of Sciences and Religions*, ed. Anne L. C. Runehov and Lluis Oviedo (Dordrecht: Springer, 2013), https://doi.org/10.1007/978-1-4020-8265-8_1495 (accessed June 16, 2020).

30 Jane Bennett, *Vibrant Matter: A Political Ecology of Things* (Durham, NC: Duke University Press, 2010), 120.

31 Ibid., 98.

32 Latour, "Once Out of Nature: Natural Religion as a Pleonasm," Gifford Lectures (2013).

33 They contrast Smith's films with the early French vegetal avant-garde films they discuss in detail, noting that his work is frequently framed with narratives that highlight similarities to animals and people: see Natania Meeker and Antónia Szabari, *Radical Botany: Plants and Speculative Fiction* (California: Fordham University Press, 2020), 121 and 138.

34 Michael Marder, "The Place of Plants: Spatiality, Movement, Growth," *Performance Philosophy* 1, no. 1 (2015): 185–94. See also Marder, *Plant-*

Thinking, 103–4. I discuss the technology and implications of time-lapse further in "Techno-Flowers."

35 Marder, *Plant-Thinking*, 17.
36 Jeffrey T. Nealon, *Plant-Theory: Biopower and Vegetable Life* (Stanford: Stanford University Press, 2016), 34.
37 Marder, *Plant-Thinking*, 20 and 51.
38 Luce Irigaray and Michael Marder, *Through Vegetal Being: Two Philosophical Perspectives* (New York: Columbia University Press, 2016), 189.
39 Nealon is critical of Marder's *Plant-Thinking*, saying that he preserves a life-as-hidden-secret model with an anthropomorphic identity logic that he extends to plants (Nealon, *Plant Theory*, 12). The aspects that Nealon points to—Marder's reference to the inexhaustibility of vegetal soul and his attention to darkness and obscurity—can be read differently, however, not to signal hidden depths of a plant body or an interior to be mined but to be subject to Marder's vegetal deconstruction of depth/surface, interior/exterior.
40 Donna J. Haraway, *Staying with the Trouble: Making Kin in the Chthulucene* (Durham, NC: Duke University Press, 2016), 55.
41 Donna J. Haraway, *How Like a Leaf: An Interview with Thyrza Nichols Goodeve* (New York and London: Routledge, 2000 [1998]).
42 Marder, *Plant-Thinking*, 13.
43 Ibid., 42–3.
44 Mary Field, J. Valentine Durden, F. Percy Smith, *See How They Grow: Botany through Cinema* (London: Penguin, 1952), 12.
45 See Haraway, *Staying with the Trouble* and Lynn Margulis and Dorion Sagan, *What is Life?* (Berkeley, CA: University of California Press, 1995).
46 As I note in "Techno-Flowers," Smith's *The Birth of a Flower* has never been out of distribution, indicating its abiding popularity: see Bryony Dixon, "Smith, F. Percy," BFI screenonline, http://www.screenonline.org.uk/people/id/594315/index.html (accessed June 25, 2020). Most recently, it is featured on the BFI BluRay/DVD (released June 2020) of Jessica Hausner's *Little Joe* (2019), having also preceded theatrical screenings of her film at BFI Southbank and the ICA in London.

10

"There's a sort of evil out there"

Uncanny Secularity in Lynch's *Twin Peaks: The Return*

Robert Sinnerbrink

Critics have described David Lynch's *Twin Peaks: The Return* as the boldest, most experimental work ever screened on television. In this chapter, I consider Lynch's Third Series as an (unorthodox) contribution to contemporary secular/post-secular cinematic television, exploring the tension between secularist and post-secularist dimensions of post-war American culture. I examine, in particular, how *The Return* is characterized by its explicit intertwining of this worldly and otherworldly, or materialist and "spiritualist" perspectives, and how Lynch's experimental aesthetic articulates a tension between these contrary yet intertwined dimensions of American culture. In addition to Lynch's aesthetic fascination with mystery, film and television genres, and surrealist/absurdist drama, *The Return* is characterized by a rich cluster of metaphysical/mythological themes drawing on an eclectic range of sources (Vedic and Hindu mythology, Jungian archetypes, transcendental meditation, Greek mythology, esoteric and occult traditions, theosophy, etc.). We can view the entire *Twin Peaks* universe, I suggest, as a post-secular Manichean mythological allegory of societal corruption and a social-cultural as well as metaphysical struggle between good and evil in the postwar world.

At the same time, the Lynchian *Twin Peaks* universe remains strongly secularist in orientation, weaving spiritualist themes and concerns within a framework and aesthetic that remain committed to an intriguingly materialist metaphysical worldview. Examining Part 8, "Gotta Light?" in the Series, I consider how these religious and spiritualist threads are framed by a secular ideological perspective that manifests in the strange or uncanny secularity characterizing the *Twin Peaks* universe. Reflecting or doubling Kafka's fascination with the allegorical and theological dimensions of modern social institutions (here the police/FBI, government and the military, media communications technology, organized crime and the criminal underworld, conspiracy theories, and the like), *Twin Peaks* focuses on contrasting secular institutional and post-secularist "spiritualist" dimensions that structure both the experimental narrative and aesthetic qualities of the Series. In *Twin Peaks: The Return* these metaphysical and spiritualist aspects are articulated in a medium (television) shaped via a strongly secular cinematic aesthetic, one that, in Lynch's work, also owes much to surrealism, experimental film, and modernist art cinema. The ecumenical pluralism of these religious, mythological, and esoteric threads, I suggest, is not only reflective of an American secular cultural sensibility but also finds expression in the strikingly dualist nature of the Lynchian *Twin Peaks* universe, in both its cinematic-aesthetic and sociocultural dimensions. The latter combines secular ordinariness with metaphysical speculation, crime detection with conspiracy theories, socio-psychological and contextualist accounts of violence with moral and spiritualist conceptions of evil: all of which present us with an unstable and conflicted cultural-aesthetic sensibility that I am calling uncanny secularity.

Uncanny Secularity in *Twin Peaks: The Return*[1]

Many critics have commented on the manner in which David Lynch's *Twin Peaks (Season 3/The Return)* offers an aesthetically daring and ethically complex meditation on contemporary American culture and society.[2] The small-town focus of the earlier two seasons has been expanded beyond the North-West of the United States to incorporate the South-West, the Mid-West and the East Coast (New York), as well as other cities and countries around the globe (Argentina and Paris).[3] It also places a strong emphasis, as ever in Lynch's work, on electronic media, audio, and digital telecommunication technologies, which not only link different locations, times, and events but also serve as portals between the secular materialist world and a supernatural/metaphysical realm.[4] Even in the earlier two seasons, it was clear that the Twin Peaks universe,[5] as a number of critics have noted, comprised a dualistic or two-world metaphysics reminiscent of Gnostic traditions such as Manicheanism.[6] This dualistic metaphysics linked the secular world of Twin Peaks as an idealized version of small-town America, incorporating an ambiguous depiction of the 1950s, with the dualistic otherworldly metaphysical-spiritual realm of the (Demonic) Black Lodge and the (Angelic) White Lodge. The latter, although opposed, are defined by syncretic theological/spiritualist features derived from various traditions and are inhabited by quasi-mythological denizens (the Arm, the Experiment, the Fireman, Señorita Dido, Naido, Laura Palmer, and Agent Dale Cooper and his various avatars) who communicate with, and have access to, the mundane world of secular social reality.[7] We could call this dualistic metaphysics structuring the Twin Peaks universe a Manichean Gnosticism defined by the coexistence of a good, spiritual, world of light and an evil, material, world of darkness as metaphysical (rather than psychological or moral) domains that remain in perpetual struggle with each other in ways that affect our fallen, "secular," yet metaphysically ordered reality. There is also in *Twin Peaks* an emphasis on and valorizing of personal spiritual or metaphysically esoteric "secret" knowledge as a means of traversing these dualistic realms and overcoming the dualism between light and darkness, spirit and matter, good and evil, this-worldly and otherworldly existence. This dualistic metaphysical framework provides the foundational structure for the series' uncanny combination of soap opera drama, crime drama mystery, surrealist sensibility, theological-spiritual themes, speculative fiction, and metaphysical reflection. *Twin Peaks: The Return* expands and intertwines these dualistic elements and metaphysical themes, reflecting not only Lynch's and Frost's own trajectories as a collaborative artistic writing/directing team, but the emergence of cinematic television as a powerful medium in its own right (for which Lynch's original series was pivotal). It also reflects the intervening historical changes in American culture and society in the twenty-five years since the cliffhanger ending of Season 2 back in 1992, exploring these changes via the dualistic figures of the Doppelganger or Double, and the Return, while exercising a subtle resistance to nostalgia.[8]

Although clearly resistant to any simple plot summary, it is worth sketching the basic outlines of *Twin Peaks: The Return* in order to explore these intertwining secular and post-secular dimensions in more depth. As is well known, according to the end of Season 2, Agent Dale Cooper (Kyle MacLachlan) remained trapped in the otherworldly realm of the Black Lodge while his evil doppelganger, possessed by Killer BOB (Frank Silva), wreaked havoc back on Earth. This scenario provided the entry point for Season 3, which commences with a prophetic pronouncement by an uncanny supernatural Giant, familiar from the earlier series, who is later dubbed the Fireman (Carel Struycken).[9] In a striking black-and-white sequence, peering directly into the camera, he tells us (and Cooper) to "Listen to the Sounds" because "[i]t is happening again," to remember "430" and "Richard and Laura," and, pointedly, to mark that, "[i]t is in our House now." Precisely what is "happening again," what these sounds mean, what, exactly, is in our House now, and what this implies for Cooper (we assume), not to mention all the other characters we recall from Seasons 1 and 2, all remain to be seen. As becomes clearer later, The Fireman appears to be referring to the recrudescence of a dangerous form of evil, generated by a powerful force of negativity known originally as Jowday or Joudy (later nicknamed Judy) and now personified by BOB.[10] The latter has the dual character of being (as we learn later) a powerful spirit engendered by supernatural means, but also, in more mundane secular terms, a personification of the "evil that men do" (as Albert remarks in "Twin Peaks Series 1"). We therefore have two ways of understanding what the character BOB represents, namely, as supernatural demonic power and as a human manifestation of evil that feeds on pain and sorrow (Garmonbozia). This evil force is manifesting itself again on the Earth—across various locations in the United States—personified via the unleashing of BOB on the world, harbored by Cooper's evil doppelganger, Mr. C. (Kyle MacLachlan), who has been enjoying a crime spree during the intervening twenty-five years. For reasons yet unclear, Cooper himself still remains trapped in the Black Lodge, and can only return to Earth once his doppelganger is made to return to the Black Lodge as well. Cooper's task is thus to orchestrate the elimination of BOB/Mr. C. from the Earth, which will allow the case of Laura Palmer's death to be closed. This outcome would also open up the possibility of rewriting history and conjuring an alternative past/future/present in which Laura was never killed—a clear violation of fate and necessity with potentially disastrous consequences. More broadly, Cooper's return and Laura Palmer's transfiguration will also be, in effect, a redemption of the corrupted principle of goodness and light (personified by Laura) in its perpetual struggle with evil and darkness (personified by BOB). These two metaphysical principles or cosmic forces, intensifying their conflict, were unleashed on Earth in a powerful and toxic material form thanks to the world-disrupting 1945 Trinity nuclear explosion in New Mexico—an event that appears to have profoundly disturbed the cosmic order. These cosmic themes and metaphysical-spiritual dimensions of the series, however, are cinematically expressed in thoroughly secular and materialist terms: via electronic networks and cryptic underground relations linking the Law, the Federal Bureau of Investigation (FBI), the criminal underworld, telecommunication networks, geographical nodal points, as well as wormhole-like temporal portals to alternative dimensions of the Universe that remain causally connected with our secular materialist world. Together these intertwining secular and metaphysical elements make *Twin Peaks: The Return*, as many critics have noted, the most experimental and challenging work in television history.[11]

The popularly adopted subtitle of the series—*The Return*—suggests not only a return season of *Twin Peaks*, a return to Twin Peaks (town and world) with its beloved cast of characters, but also more philosophical, mythological, and metaphysical senses of return.[12] These include Freud's idea of trauma involving a "return of the repressed," Nietzsche's "eternal return of the same" as an ethical test, and the Vedic/Hindu idea of reincarnation as the restoration of karmic balance in the perennial cycle of birth/death and rebirth. As Franck Boulègue points out in his magisterial study, *The Return of Twin Peaks: Squaring the Circle* (2021), we can also regard *The Return* as a palimpsest-like rewriting of Homer's *Odyssey*, with Agent Dale Cooper playing the role of Odysseus who is fated to return to Ithaca/Twin Peaks and to his Penelope after the trials of the Trojan War. There are further literary references (T. S. Eliot, Dante, Kafka) and other textual/cinematic layers woven together, spanning speculative fiction (Lovecraft), movie genres like the Western, cinematic references (Kubrick, Hitchcock, Brakhage), esoteric literature and theosophy, the Book of Revelations, Vedic and Mesopotamian cosmologies, and religious poetry such as Valmiki's Hindu epic, *Ramayana*.[13] For my purposes, the most significant and suggestive reference point is the work of Franz Kafka, whose portrait appears twice in the series: "once in William Hastings' home, and once in Gordon Cole's office, facing his poster of a nuclear mushroom cloud"[14] What do we make of this uncanny conjunction of Kafka and the Cold War, *The Trial* and the Trinity Test? In what follows, I attempt to answer this question by articulating a conception of "uncanny secularity" that might help us understand these overlapping features of the Twin Peaks universe: its dualistic metaphysics and its disorienting, unsettling conjunction of the social and the supernatural, the secular and the post-secular.

Dialectic of the Secular and the Post-secular

Before turning to the Kafkaesque dimensions of *Twin Peaks: The Return*, which I shall explore via the concept of "uncanny secularity," I wish to offer some context for my discussion of the series by outlining what we might call the dialectic of the secular and non-secular and articulate its role in the constitution of modern democracies. According to a well-known philosophical-historical narrative, one of the defining features of social and cultural modernity is the rise of secularism, broadly defined as the separation of religion from civic culture and political government.[15] Secularism, however, also encompasses a range of related meanings and phenomena. These include the increasing authority of science (both natural and human) and technology as authoritative forms and instruments of knowledge applicable to society; and the development of independent spheres of knowledge and culture (science/morality/art) with their own norms, practices, and institutions. We can add the "privatization" of religion in becoming a matter of personal belief or conscience rather than a foundation for community or basis for politics; and the autonomy of art, as independent of religion, with artistic expression no longer bound to religious authority. Secularism arises with the rejection of religion as a foundation for the state, and the recasting of social institutions, moral norms, and political practices as separate from, although protective of, religious institutions and theological beliefs.

It treats religion as "private" matter of belief for individuals and groups, protected under law, but not mandated, or endorsed by, the political state.[16] Secular states are also characterized by the rise of a civic participatory culture and public sphere where principles of rationality, transparency, and equality govern the communication of opinion and ideas rather than the authority and conventions of hierarchical institutions or privileged forms of selectively controlled knowledge.[17] Contemporary liberal democracies, with their institutional structures of procedural representative politics, rule of law, formal autonomy of art and culture, free market systems regulated by government, and social institutions governed by bureaucratic rationality, offer representative models of the modern secular form of society.

This idealized model of secularism—vigorously developed by Habermas and Rawls—has faced critiques from both non-secular and post-secular perspectives. As Peter Berger declared in 1999, the founding premise of secularism—that modern states are defined by the separation of religion and politics, which itself reflects the decline of religious authority—has been historically "falsified"; far from witnessing the decline of religion we have witnessed its resurgence and its increasingly influential role in politics.[18] The model of secular liberal democratic societies held up as a paradigm of (Western) modernity has been challenged as reflecting a Eurocentric/colonialist bias against non-Western, non-Christian, and postcolonialist societies and ideological values.[19] Moreover, as philosophers from Charles Taylor and Giorgio Agamben to John Gray have argued, secular values, concepts, and norms (within political philosophy but also as a basis for democratic institutions and societal practices) are often "secularized" versions of religious norms, values, and beliefs.[20] Secular society, from this point of view, is still dependent upon and profoundly shaped by non-secular (religious/spiritual) forms of belief, values, practices, and institutions.

In the third phase of this critique, which we might call its "deconstructivist" variation, the anti-secular critical response to secularism shifts toward a model of ambiguous coexistence: a postsecular deconstructive interplay of secular and non-secular elements within an ambiguous "post-secular condition."[21] There are many variations of this model, some emphasizing "multiple modernities," some emphasizing anti-Eurocentric postcolonialist critiques, some emphasizing a "post-metaphysical" pluralist model of postsecular society with secular and religious forms of normativity coexisting within a broadly democratic form of society. Whatever model one adopts, all of these accounts acknowledge the persistence of religion as a community-binding, culturally pervasive, and politically influential force, which continues to contribute to addressing the "meaning-deficit" that sociologists have long identified as one of the hallmarks of secular modernity. At the same time, there is no doubt that secular sensibilities still prevail across the majority of social and cultural institutions and moral-political debates, not to mention the globalized economic and technological spheres, however much all of these domains may be contested by religious beliefs, spiritual-cultural practices, and faith-based politics. What is also evident is the increasing skepticism toward, or questioning of, traditional secular institutions, rationally grounded forms of knowledge, and procedural forms of politics. In other words, the dialectic between secular and post-secular attitudes, practices, and beliefs constitutes an ongoing dynamic that has come to play a defining role in how relations between morality, culture, society, and politics are articulated within our increasingly globalized world.

Indeed, we could even talk of the "paradox of secularism," which circles around the unresolved tension between secular humanist conceptions of freedom, morality, and progress and scientific conceptions of the naturalistic limits of human existence. As John Gray observes:

> Here we have the paradox of secularism. Secular societies believe they have left myth behind, when all they have done is substitute one set of myths for another. It is far from clear that this amounts to an improvement. Christian myth has harmful aspects, not least its ingrained anthropocentrism. Even so, in insisting that human nature is incorrigibly flawed it is far more realistic than the secular doctrines that followed it. In effect, liberal humanism has taken Christianity's unhappiest myth—the separation of humans from the rest of the natural world—and stripped it of the transcendental content that gave it meaning. In so doing, it has left secular cultures [. . .] stuck between a humanist view of mankind that actually comes from religion and a more genuinely scientific view in which it is just one animal species, no more capable of taking charge of its destiny than any other.[22]

Gray offers an updated version of Nietzsche's critique of modernity as founded on a secularized humanistic Christianity, which lacks the social-psychological (and mythic) resources that could create forms of post-secular morality and culture capable of addressing the enervating "meaning deficit" that confronts us socially and politically (hence the return of religion). This unresolved dialectic between secular and post-secular dimensions of modern societies means that we cannot define modernity in relation to one pole while ignoring the other. Although discourses of the secular describe modernity in purely secular terms, which exclude religion and spirituality from the domains of culture and politics proper, these nonetheless remain haunted by religious/spiritualist traditions. This suggests that the purely secularist account offered by many political theorists and philosophers is thus inadequate for describing contemporary experiences of modernity in relation to everyday social practices as well as culture and politics. It is within these ambiguous and crisis-riven horizons of meaning and value that artists, writers, and filmmakers have attempted to grapple with our social-cultural condition of "uncanny secularity" and its hybrid forms of postsecular sensibility. It is against this unstable background of attitudes and values concerning contemporary post-secular culture that I return to Lynch and Frost's attempt at such a mythology in *Twin Peaks: The Return*.

Kafka and Lynch

Moving away from the philosophical and sociological versions of this debate, we can find anticipations and explorations of these ideas on secularity/postsecularity in literature and cinema. It is given literary expression, for example, in Kafka's work, which combines secular institutional contexts with theological themes and absurdist motifs (in *The Castle* and *The Trial*, for example), both revealing not only the non-secular (religious/theological) core of secular institutions and contexts but also how this deactivated core of meaning still shapes their values and orientation. Kafka's novels famously explore the "irrationality" of postsecular social reality, the absurdity of its bureaucracy and impenetrability of institutions, the opaque and anonymous character of its political authority, from the perspective of an individual confronting an alienating form of social reality. They hint at an inscrutable metaphysical and/or theological background that renders quotidian social experience as uncanny and unsettling. As Agamben and other philosophers argue, the "theological core" of secular social institutions and political concepts still shapes and articulates fundamental concepts of secular modernity and politics. Secular liberal democracy, with its ideals of rational progress, social equality, individual liberty, and moral progress through technological advancement, remains deeply indebted to a Christian theological worldview, which continues to influence discourses of moral, social, and technological progress.[23] The idealized version of secular, technological, procedural democratic society must still reckon with the role of the religious, not only as supplemental source of personal and communal value and meaning but as a residual yet active core of prevailing secular values, attitudes, and practices. The related crises in meaning concerning the legitimacy of democracy, trust in social institutions and political processes, the questioning of morality, the universal validity of art, and increasing skepticism about science, are all linked with need for "thicker" foundations for shared norms and values than are currently available within a narrowly secular way of life. Hence, the need to acknowledge the dialectic between secular and post-secular perspectives; the necessity of acknowledging the "return" of religious and spiritualist perspectives within modern society, culture, and politics looms large again.

Kafka's work was a harbinger of these related strands of critical reflection and cultural skepticism, highlighting the "absurdity" of modern social institutions, secularized culture, personal morality, and bureaucratized politics. A persistent question in the study of Kafka's works is the extent to which we should take his novels as existential allegories of the present age, modernist-absurdist dramas with a psychoanalytical core, or theologically imbued mysteries that resist secular interpretation. As Anke Snoek observes (drawing on Susan Sontag's famous typology), Kafka interpretation falls into three broad schools. There is the political approach, reading *The Trial* and *The Castle* as allegories of the evils of modern bureaucracy and the threat of totalitarianism; the biographical-psychoanalytical approach, focusing on Kafka's fear of his father and the role of Oedipal guilt and psychic repression in his work; and the theological approach, reading his texts as theological-political fables set within a fallen, modern, secular world.[24] Agamben combines the first two approaches, with elements of the third, which together enables us to consider Kafka as both a political and psychological, secular and post-secular author. We could say the same, I suggest, about Frost and Lynch's *Twin Peaks: The Return*, which not only suggests a Kafkaesque influence but also explicitly acknowledges its indebtedness to Kafka's legacy. Despite these important parallels, the main difference between them, I suggest, is that, for Kafka and other "modernist" theorists, the religious/theological/spiritual core remained empty or neutered in modernity, whereas for contemporary post-secular theorists and artists like Lynch, this core remains (radio) active—a continuing source of ambiguous meanings and ambivalent effects.

Lynch scholars have noted numerous parallels and affinities between Kafka and Lynch.[25] Lynch intended to direct a version of Kafka's classic story, *The Metamorphosis*, and his admiration for Kafka remains an abiding inspiration and influence on his later work.[26] *Twin Peaks: The Return*, I suggest, can be viewed as a contemporary American version of postsecular work with close affinities to Kafka and other authors working in the genre of the uncanny, the fantastic, and speculative fiction. At the same time, it constructs its own original and complex mythology that interconnects contemporary social reality with occult sources and transcendent metaphysics.

Adam Daniel, for example, has examined the relationship between Kafka and Lynch, exploring the parallels, allusions, and overlaps between Kafka's novels and *Twin Peaks*, drawing attention to the shared themes, motifs, and parallels between the novels and the series.[27] According to Daniel, these include the alienation of the familiar and the role of gesture; the "defamiliarization" of the bourgeois home and its transformation into a gestural theater; and the shifting interplay between reality and unreality. There is the role of generality coupled with detail in place names, characters, and situations; the unmooring of reality and interpenetration of this-worldly and otherworldly concerns; the prominence given to "mystery and abstraction" that resist interpretation; and the mundane absurdity of life and its reverberation in art that is at once tragic and ironic.[28] Although Daniel also notes the importance of the crime story, police procedural, and detective fiction in *Twin Peaks: The Return*, he does not go on to focus on the broader parallel concerning the ways in which secular ideas and social institutions are linked with a religious/theological background and (increasingly defunct) horizon of meaning.

Lončar, in her study of Lynch, draws on Espen Hammer's concept of the "metaphysical crime narrative" to explore the manner in which *Twin Peaks: The Return* mirrors Kafka's novel, *The Trial*.[29] As she observes, other Lynch scholars have explored these parallels. Hagemen, for example, reflects on the relationship of "the uncanny dreamworld of *The Return*, as well as other *Twin Peaks* instalments, with Kafka's *The Metamorphosis* (*Die Verwandlung*, 1915)." For Hageman, it is "Lynch's and Kafka's common formal and thematic interest" in the "weird space between waking and dreaming worlds," as well as "metamorphoses of characters" that defines their shared artistic ground.[30] Like Hagemen, Daniel too underlines the theme of metamorphosis as key to the Lynchian universe of *Twin Peaks*, and he notes the importance of crime narrative for both Lynch and Kafka, without, however, citing *The Trial* as a key reference point. According to Lončar, this is intriguing, since Kafka's novel serves as a prime example of unconventional crime fiction, and would amply fit Hammer's concept of "metaphysical crime narrative," according to which "it is the crime and not the supposed culprit that is unknown."[31]

Like Kafka's works, *Twin Peaks: The Return* explores the contemporary sense of crisis concerning social institutions and personal morality. It goes on to link this with political upheavals, skepticism toward secular social institutions (the law, FBI, Government agencies, scientific inquiry, and political structures), and the combination of ambivalence and skepticism toward prevailing forms of secular morality (exploring the metaphysical question of evil in the modern world). Again like Kafka, we find the secular world linked with the metaphysical world, social institutions linked with their social underbelly (the criminal underworld) as well as with the broader "cosmic" metaphysical background to these social phenomena that also intrudes upon and shapes our modern world (the Black Lodge, the Fireman, Doppelgangers, Tulpas, etc.).[32] As remarked, this engagement with the secular world is framed by a Gnostic/Manichean dualism combining syncretic elements adapted from many religious and spiritualist traditions (Hinduism, theosophy, and so on). This metaphysical dualism bears on *Twin Peak*'s diagnosis of the nihilism of modern American society, locating the source of moral decay, evil/negativity, and pervasive disconnection or dehumanization in the simultaneous social/political and metaphysical/cosmic rupture introduced by the unleashing of the destructive power of the atomic bomb. We can add to this the "disenchantment" of nature, which retains an aspect of sublime mystery and metaphysical resonance in the Twin Peaks universe, and by the alienation, fragmentation, and anomie characteristic of the modern world reflecting deeper sources of violence and negativity. This mythological struggle between good and evil, endemic to humanity but made acute in modernity, pervades social institutions and modern communities, and would require metaphysical/messianic intervention in order for societal and cosmic balance to be restored, which is a fair summary of what transpires in *Twin Peaks: The Return*. There are Christological and other religious/theological resonances in the narrative framing of Cooper's mission to return to Earth from his exile in the Black Lodge. His task takes on similarly messianic overtones: to redeem the death of Laura Palmer and thereby restore the disturbed cosmic balance that would combat the extreme negativity of the "evil force" deriving from Jowday/Joudy/Judy but embodied or incarnated by BOB/Mr. C. and other malevolent forces/characters within the Twin Peaks universe. At the same time, *Twin Peaks: The Return* explicitly signals the simultaneously metaphysical-cosmic and social-technological dimensions of this force of negativity, presenting its own postsecular origin myth concerning the sources of our contemporary sense of disenchantment, moral corruption, social disintegration, and irrational violence.[33]

Season 3 Part 8: "Gotta Light?"

Described as one of the most extraordinary shows ever screened on television, Part 8 of *Twin Peaks: The Return* brings together the secular and post-secular elements of the series—or episodic long-form cinematic feature—in a surreal and challenging manner.[34] The work falls into three main sequences: (1) the shooting of "Bad" Cooper/Mr. C. by his criminal accomplice, Ray, and his subsequent "resurrection" with the help of simultaneously supernatural and earthy figures known as "The Woodsmen." (2) The detonating of the first atomic bomb in White Sands, New Mexico, in 1945, rendered in an extraordinary black-and-white experimental sequence accompanied by Penderecki's "Threnody for the Victims of Hiroshima." We also see the simultaneous birth of BOB, spewed forth by a disturbing humanoid-alien figure in an ectoplasmic steam. Finally, (3) the arrival of the Woodsmen in the New Mexico Desert eleven years later, in 1956, along with the hatching of a bizarre frog-moth creature in the desert. The Woodsmen cause havoc in the community, terrorizing locals, with one of the Woodsmen breaking into a local radio station and broadcasting an unnerving poem while the insect creature enters the mouth of a sleeping girl. Let me consider each sequence in turn and reflect upon how Lynch weaves together these dimensions in *Twin Peaks* as an expression of uncanny secularity.

(1) *The shooting of "Bad" Cooper/Mr. C. and his "resurrection" by The Woodsmen*

"Bad" Cooper or Mr. C. (Kyle McLachlan) and Ray Monroe (George Griffith) are driving on the highway at night after blackmailing their prison warden to ensure their escape from prison. Ray has memorized some vital information (numbers, coordinates) that Mr. C. needs but is reluctant to convey it without payment. Ray pulls over "for a leak"; Mr. C. takes his gun out of the glove compartment. After a tense exchange, in which Mr. C. demands the information he is seeking, he shoots Ray but the gun fails to fire. Ray laughs, shooting Mr. C. twice at close range. What to this point has been a dark " noir-like" crime story then takes on a disturbing supernatural character. Darkened spectral figures (The Woodsmen) emerge from the forest. They start tending to Mr. C., treating him for his wounds, performing a bizarre form of "psychic surgery" on his wounded chest— the figures superimposed on Cooper's injured body—while others perform a ritual dance around him, smearing him with blood. Ray is on the ground, yelling in disbelief, unable to make sense of what he is seeing. The soundtrack is muffled and slowed-down, intensifying the disturbing and disorienting spectacle. As Ray groans in horror, the Woodsmen remove a darkened Orb, with BOB's face visible within it, from Mr. C.'s bleeding chest. Ray runs back to the car, and speeds away. He calls an unknown "superior" (Philip Jeffries?) saying that he thinks he killed Cooper but is not sure, and that what he just witnessed (the wounded Cooper releasing the dark Orb containing BOB's spirit) may be "the key to it all." The Woodsmen continue dancing around Mr. C., striving to revive him from the dead. We see and hear electrical flashes, muffled groans, and snatches of strange musical and industrial sounds, followed by darkness. There is a cut to the Roadhouse Club, where experimental industrial electro-rock band Nine Inch Nails perform a menacing version of their song, "She's Gone," live on stage. Their performance and song resonates powerfully, in lyrics and mood, with the sequence we have just witnessed. At the conclusion of the performance, we cut back to the scene of the carnage, where Mr. C., bloodied but alive, wakes up suddenly in the darkened forest.

The contrast between the secular crime story and supernaturalist Woodsmen is striking in this sequence. The Woodsmen themselves combine a familiar depression era/mid-century worker/hobo/miner appearance with a spectral ghostly presentation, and their disturbing demeanor combines "earthy" bearded physicality with shamanic dance, unnatural physical strength, and supernatural powers of intervention in worldly events. There is even an uncanny historical dimension to their appearance, one of them closely resembling Abraham Lincoln, which suggests a dark and violent undercurrent to more optimistic accounts of American history and democracy.[35] The intersection of crime drama, horror, and supernatural "resurrection" offers a clear example of the intertwining of naturalist and supernaturalist, secular, and postsecularist dimensions of *Twin Peaks*.

(2) *Trinity Atomic Bomb Test and the Birth of BOB*

The second sequence is announced by a plain intertitle reading "July 16, 1945 / White Sands, New Mexico / 5:29 am (MWT)" against a stunning black-and-white image of the Trinity Atomic Bomb Test, accompanied by

Penderecki's "Threnody for the Victims of Hiroshima." It commences with a high-angle long shot, the camera zooming toward the toxic mushroom cloud from above, as the screen dissolves into disintegrative molecular images.[36] What follows is cacophonous stream of images: pulsating energy and light, molecular power, explosive fire, disintegrating matter, the primal origin of matter/energy revealed thanks to the cataclysmic explosion. This extraordinary sequence, as Monique Rooney remarks, locates "the 1945 atomic explosion and air-contamination as a creation myth for the toxicity that pervades the entire *Twin Peaks* narrative and attributing to the testing of the atomic bomb a centrifugal disturbance of planetary-level scale and impact."[37] Moreover, as Donato Totaro observes, critics who have written on Part 8 "have noted how the bomb is both a literal and figurative birthing of the ultimate evil, how the floating image of BOB sprouts from the bomb (and also its antithesis Laura Palmer)."[38] Other scholars, such as Joel Bocko, point to what I have called the Gnostic Manichean dimensions of this sequence; the image of the bomb, he remarks, "magnifies this dualistic opposition between man's inherent goodness and evil to cosmic proportions, staging it as a fundamental struggle between light and dark on a mythic scale."[39] Soller Seitz notes the cinematic predecessors of this sequence, observing that Part 8 alludes "to a rich tradition of post–World War II science-fiction cinema in which monsters birthed by atom bomb tests (and other scientific or military experiments that were essentially stand-ins for atom bomb tests) menaced teenagers and their adult guardians in Norman Rockwellian small towns and suburbs."[40] Indeed, Lynch gives surreal cinematic expression to what Seitz describes as the "hideous evil unearthed by the bomb" in what follows.

The Trinity Atomic Test sequence dissolves to another scene, an abandoned gas station or Convenience Store in the New Mexico desert area. We now see black-and-white fast-stop motion animation of the Woodsmen, appearing and disappearing at random, moving in abrupt staccato motion across the front of the Store. Mysterious gas or smoke emanates from the door, while lights flash erratically within the building. The Woodsmen mill around outside, with jarring, intermittent, scratchy, crackling electrical sounds creating a menacing background. The Convenience Store remains illuminated in lightning flashes, the Woodsmen now visible inside, which creates a disorienting effect of striking visual images accompanied by unearthly disturbing sounds, a nightmarish vision of mid-century desolation, primal electrical disturbance—a simultaneously technological and supernaturalistic disruption of ordinary life.

A strange unearthly humanoid figure now appears suspended in a darkened void (identified in the titles as "The Experiment"), projecting an ectoplasmic cloud from its mouth. A Dark Orb within the mass comes slowly into view with BOB's maniacal face clearly visible inside. We cut back to the atomic explosion, the camera penetrating to the heart of the elemental flux. Molecular images of golden globules, pulsing light/energy, a *2001: A Space Odyssey*-style sequence of space-time/matter distortions, appear in a mesmerizing sequence, both perceptually dazzling and metaphysically illuminating.[41]

This strange molecular vision of primal energy and vibrant matter then gives way to an oneiric, otherworldly image of a Purple Sea. The camera zooms across the waves toward an island looming in the distance. As the camera climbs up the sheer cliffs, we see a strange pale building perched atop a rocky crag, white and modernist in design (suggesting a de Chirico painting). The camera focuses on a single rectangular window opening in concrete wall, and then enters the building as the image fades to blackness. We hear now quite different music playing in the background on an antique phonograph, a mellow, circular, melancholy otherworldly melody (David Lynch's "Slow 30's Room"). An elegantly dressed woman, Señorita Dido, is seated on a sofa, listening to the phonograph in a surreal-retro room. The languid music is interrupted by a harsh warning sound or alarm ringing from a large Bell-shaped device placed in the center of the room, which appears to be an old-style electricity generator.[42] The tall figure of The Firemen appears and takes note of the warning sound, looking over to Señorita Dido. He checks the Bell, presses a button to turn off the alarm on the device, then leaves the room to enter what appears to be an empty theater with a movie screen.

The Firemen switches on a projector and watches the footage we have just seen of the atomic blast, looking shocked and concerned. The screen shows the images of the mushroom cloud, disintegrating matter, followed by shots of the Woodsmen outside the desert Convenience Store. He watches images on screen of The Experiment's ectoplasmic cloud with the Orb revealing the birth of BOB, then freezes the images to focus on BOB's face. The Fireman then begins to levitate, as Señorita Dido enters the theater, climbing to a point many meters off the ground, as a golden light begins to emanate from his head. Señorita Dido looks amazed, gazing at the golden light, which forms a scintillating cloud of particles above him, out of which a Golden Orb is released and descends toward her. Señorita Dido catches the Orb, kisses it tenderly, as we see the face of Laura Palmer within it. She releases the Orb into the air and it floats up into a tube-like instrument, which looks like a cross between a curved metal flute and a Fallopian tube. The Orb emerges from the tube and enters the movie screen, which shows a black-and-white image of the Earth, reminiscent of 1950s alien invasion science-fiction movies.[43] Once "injected" into the screen, like a fertilized egg on its way to womb, the Orb makes its way toward the United States.[44] This strange mythological sequence, featuring the reaction of two godlike figures to the atomic blast, the simultaneous birth of an evil force of negativity (BOB) and subsequent conception and birth of an incarnation of good

(Laura Palmer), provides a metaphysical/occult background myth to the secular narrative of *Twin Peaks*.

(3) *Arrival of the Woodsmen and Hatching of the Frog-Moth*

The third sequence commences with a black-and-white shot of the Mexican desert, accompanied by another intertitle: "1956 / August 5 / New Mexico Desert." On the desert sand at night, we see a resting egg that begins to hatch; out comes a creature (which Lynch calls a "frog-moth") that scuttles away across the rippled ground. The sequence cuts to the Convenience Store again and we see a charming teenage couple walking together, obviously attracted to each other. The Trinity Test and birth of BOB sequence we have just seen stands in stark contrast with this idyllic scene, followed by the uncanny arrival of the Woodsmen in the New Mexico desert. They appear as dark shadowy figures suddenly materializing in the desert, who roam and torment the local passers-by with their disturbing request ("Gotta Light?"), which they repeat menacingly in gruff, distorted voices.

One of The Woodsmen approaches a building in the dark, a radio studio in the desert. The Platters' poignant tune "My Prayer" starts suddenly, a diegetic song played by a DJ on a turntable in the studio. A man working on a truck, a woman working in an empty diner, and the young girl in her bedroom, are all listening to the Platters' song on the radio. The Woodsman approaches the radio station, repeating his menacing phrase, "Gotta Light?" before brutally killing the receptionist in her office.[45] He then attacks the DJ, clamping his skull with his hand. The record suddenly cuts out; the people we have seen listening to the music are disturbed. The Woodsman takes over the microphone, reciting the following poem in a dark voice: "This is the water / and this is the well / Drink full and descend / The horse is the white of the eyes / and dark within." As the Woodsman violently grasps the DJ's skull, we see both the woman working in the diner and the man in the garage collapse after hearing the poem. The frog-moth creature crawls slowly over the sand, approaching a building, which turns out to be the girl's house. The girl too is disturbed by poem recited on the radio but she, unlike the others, does not collapse. She lays down on her bed, facing us and listening, and then falls asleep. The frog-moth flies up to her window and enters her room. We see the girl in a mid-close-up, asleep on her bed, as the frog-moth approaches her face, enters her mouth and disappears down her throat. The Woodsman keeps reciting the poem as he slowly crushes the DJ's skull. His task complete, he leaves the building and walks slowly into the darkness. The intertwining of mass media technology, Gnostic dualism, evil haunting sites of historical and physical trauma, and possession in spiritual and physical terms, is expressed in violent and visceral ways in this sequence, which when taken together gives full expression to Lynch's uncanny secularity.

The "Lynchian Universe": Uncanny Secularity and Post-secular Myth

In each of these three sequences, mundane and metaphysical, secular and spiritualist, social-historical and supernaturalistic elements are juxtaposed and synthesized in disturbing and uncanny ways, drawing links between the present and the past (1940s/1950s America), violence and sublimity, elemental atomic energy and surreal oneiric imagery. In the third sequence, this amalgam of secular and post-secular elements is particularly striking: the Trinity Atomic Bomb test is linked with a nihilistic materialization of evil in the post-war American context. An American gothic "horror" style expresses a traumatic historical and cultural haunting figured via parasitic bodily infection, inscrutable violence, and demonic possession.[46] Mass media vectors (radio), music, and mesmerizing language (poetry) are used to hypnotize, beguile, and "possess" the population; these various media are used to boost the technological spread of the nihilistic moral and cultural malaise that was to become pervasive in the US postwar period. The latter is depicted, in *Twin Peaks: The Return* (but also other Lynch films) as a dualistic historical-cultural world defined by prosperity and optimism but also spiritual devastation and moral confusion following the unleashing of an unearthly power capable of destroying humanity: a power requiring a combined cultural-artistic and mythological-spiritualist response.

Twin Peaks: The Return offers the lineaments of post-secular eschatological myth that narrates the origins of a technological rupture in the cosmic order that ushers in an age of chaos, violence, and uncertainty. It depicts the technologically mediated emergence of redemptive figures locked in a Manichean struggle with forces of evil or metaphysical negativity unleashed by the violent human disruption of the cosmic order. As ever in Lynch's films, secular (psychological, materialist, sociological) accounts of evil are contrasted and combined with non-secular (metaphysical, transcendental, spiritualist/immaterialist) accounts.[47] The callous and egoistic evil of, for example, minor character Richard Horne [Eamon Farren] (whose cruelty and indifference toward others is exemplified in his shocking hit-and-run killing of a young boy while on a drug-fuelled rampage) is contrasted with the seemingly motiveless, relentless, impersonal malevolence of "Bad" Cooper/Mr. C., whose evil is a manifestation of a pure force of negativity. It is the inadequacy of the former to explain the persistence and pervasiveness of arbitrary malevolent violence that motivates the Lynchian turn to a "metaphysical" power of negativity: one that shapes and grounds, but also distorts and destroys, authentic subjectivity and social community. This tension between secular and post-secular senses of evil is both exacerbated and rearticulated in the contemporary world. Lynch and Frost present post-war America as a "test case" in their simultaneously surreal and psychological, occult and historical, post-secular mythology. The latter provides the mythological, metaphysical, and historical backstory behind Laura Palmer's murder, the appearance of BOB, and the unleashing of metaphysical evil as the threat of postwar Armageddon. The genre of the "metaphysical crime story" links these mythological and historical elements together, providing a grounding framework for the implicitly Kafkaesque dimensions of *Twin Peaks: The Return*. According to the latter, we cannot adequately grasp the nature of the contemporary world in purely secular materialist terms, a world in which the deeper metaphysical roots of evil as pure negativity become manifest in material, social, psychological, and secular forms and actions. In this respect, the uncanny secularity of *Twin Peaks: The Return* can be viewed as an allegory of our contemporary cultural and political senses of moral uncertainty and existential malaise.

All of this occurs in a medium that has been metamorphosed by Lynch and Frost, transfigured into what Boulègue calls "expanded television" (recalling Gene Youngblood's concept of "expanded cinema" but adapting it to the medium of serial television).[48] Lynch and Frost subject the secular/materialist medium of television to a post-secular/surrealist treatment, transforming the televisual/cinematic medium into a mode of "expanded consciousness" via the dialectic between secular and post-secular perspectives, the syncretic combination of mundane and supernatural domains. *Twin Peaks: The Return* thereby gives expression to a televisual post-secular mythology, an oneiric exploration of uncanny secularity as a way of probing the nihilism of our age.

Notes

1. Lynch's version of the title was simply *Twin Peaks* (2017) or *Twin Peaks (Season 3)* but Showtime altered this to the version now most commonly used, *Twin Peaks: The Return*.

2. Donato Totaro, "*Twin Peaks: The Return*, Part 8: The Western, Science Fiction, and the Big BOmB," *Offscreen* 2, no. 11–12 (December 2017), https://offscreen.com/view/twin-peaks-the-return-part-8-the-western-science-fiction-and-big-bomb; Walter Metz, "The Atomic Gambit of *Twin Peaks: The Return*," *Film Criticism* 41, no. 3 (Fall 2017), https://quod.lib.umich.edu/f/fc/13761232.0041.324?view=text;rgn=main.

3. On the depiction of the North-West and South-West as well as other US locations in the new series, see Rob E. King, "The Horse is the White of the Eye: Pioneering and the American Southwest in *Twin Peaks*," *NANO: New American Notes Online*, no. 15, *Twin Peaks: The Return* (February 2020), https://nanocrit.com/issues/issue15/The-Horse-is-the-White-of-the-Eye-Pioneering-and-the-American-Southwest-in-Twin-Peaks. Richard Martin, "David Lynch Sprawls," *NANO: New American Notes Online*, no. 15, *Twin*

Peaks: The Return (February 2020), https://nanocrit.com/issues/issue15/David
   -Lynch-Sprawls.

4 As Goddard and Burt point out, here the role of sound, audioscaping, and
   music, along with the notion of technological mediation of reality more
   generally, are crucial in creating the rich sense of world via mood and
   atmosphere relevant to the creation and transmission meaning within the
   Twin Peaks universe. Michael Goddard, "Telephones, Voice Recorders,
   Microphones, Phonographs: A Media Archaeology of Sonic Technologies in
   Twin Peaks," *Senses of Cinema* 79 (July 2016), http://www.sensesofcinema
   .com/2016/twin-peaks/sonic-technologies-in-twin-peaks/ and Andrew T. Burt,
   "Is it the Wind in the Tall Trees or Just the Distant Buzz of Electricity?: Sound
   and Electricity as Portent in Twin Peaks' Season 3," in *Critical Essays on Twin
   Peaks: The Return*, ed. Antonio Sanna (Cham: Springer/Palgrave Macmillan,
   2019), 253–68.

5 I use the term "Twin Peaks Universe" to encompass all three Twin Peaks
   series, the prequel film, *Twin Peaks: Fire Walk with Me* (1992), but also the
   related "paratexts," including Mark Frost's *The Secret History of Twin Peaks*
   (2016) and *Twin Peaks: The Final Dossier* (2017), and Jennifer Lynch's *Laura
   Palmer's Secret Diary* (1990).

6 See Zachary Sheldon: "Many critics have attached significance to the moral
   and religious aspects of Lynch's filmography in a way that ties a pervasive
   American identity and culture to Eastern religious influences. Jeff Johnson,
   for instance, argues that Lynch 'follows an intrinsically American moralistic
   obsession with the ideas of innate depravity, a Zoroastrian notion of goodness
   and evil, and the schizophrenic concept of innocence as both an ideal state
   and a treacherous, ultimately corrupting vice of the wickedly naïve' (3).
   Johnson ties this Zoroastrian conception of evil to the American national
   identity (3). Likewise, John Alexander has characterized Lynch's moral
   messaging as emerging from the tradition of the American Gothic, even as the
   nostalgic elements of Lynch's work—the deceptive 1950s-esque tranquillity
   of the town of Twin Peaks, for example—evoke a kind of Manichean belief
   system rolled into the postmodern sentimentality of contemporary American
   culture (8–13). Similarly, John Carroll sees Lynch's work as exemplifying
   'the most fundamental myths of American culture' as interpreted through
   'the Manichean strain of Christianity'" (291, 294). Sheldon, "The Artistic
   Evangelism of David Lynch: Transcendental Meditation, World Peace, and
   Laura Palmer," *NANO: New American Notes Online*, no. 15, *Twin Peaks:
   The Return* (February 2020), https://nanocrit.com/issues/issue15/The-Artistic
   -Evangelism-of-David-Lynch-Transcendental-Meditation-World-Peace-and
   -Laura-Palmer.

7 As Antonio Sanna (2020, p. 7) observes: "Particularly interesting is the show's
   depiction of the two opposite spiritual realms known as the 'Black Lodge' and
   the 'White Lodge,' where evil spirits and angels are respectively said to dwell.
   According to the fictional universe of *Twin Peaks* the evil spirits can inhabit
   the bodies of those weak humans who are unable to resist them and feed on
   their 'garmonbozia,' a term that is explicitly glossed as 'pain and sorrow.'

The entrances to the two domains are triggered respectively by fear and love. Many critics have investigated the depiction of such spiritual realms and have identified their origin in a series of texts that include the writings of the Theosophical Society and the Order of the Golden Dawn. The Black and the White Lodges are also mentioned in the volumes *Moonchild* (by Aleister Crowley, 1917), *The Devil's Guard* (by Talbot Mundy, 1926) and *Psychic Self-Defense* (by Dion Fortune, 1935)." Antonio Sanna, "Entering the World of Twin Peaks," in *Critical Essays on Twin Peaks: The Return: The Return*, ed. Antonio Sanna (Cham: Springer/Palgrave Macmillan, 2019), pp. 3–21.

8   Dominic Lash, "The Dangers of Getting What You Asked For: Double Time in *Twin Peaks: The Return*," *Open Screens* 3, no.1 (2020): 1–26. Tyler S. Rife and Ashley N. Wheeler, "'I'll see you Again in 25 Years': Doppelganging Nostalgia and Twin Peaks: The Return," *Critical Studies in Media Communication* 37, no. 5 (2020): 424–36.

9   In the Credits for Part 1, he is described as "???????" and only later named as "The Fireman."

10 According to Agent Tammy Preston's entry on "Judy": "Joudy, it turns out, is also the name of an ancient entity in Sumerian mythology (This dates back to at least 3000 B.C.). The name was used to describe a species of wandering demon—also generically known as an *utukku*—that had 'escaped from the underworld' and roamed freely throughout the earth, where they feasted on human flesh and, allegedly, ripped the souls from their victims, which provided even more meaningful nourishment. They particularly thrived while feeding—and I quote—'on human suffering.' These beings were said to appear in both male and female forms—'Joudy' indicated the female, and the male was known as 'Ba'al'—and, while they were considered beyond dangerous individually, if a male and a female ever *united* while on the earth, the ancient texts claimed, their resulting 'marriage' would create something far more perilous. As in: the end of the world as we know it." Mark Frost, *Twin Peaks: The Final Dossier* (London: Macmillan, 2017), 121–2.

11 Sean T. Collins, "Why 'Twin Peaks: The Return' Was the Most Groundbreaking TV Series Ever," *Rolling Stone*, September 4, 2017, https://www.rollingstone.com/tv/tv-news/why-twin-peaks-the-return-was-the-most-groundbreaking-tv-series-ever-115665/.

12 Matthew Ellis and Tyler Theus, "Is it Happening Again? *Twin Peaks* and 'The Return' of History," in *Critical Essays on Twin Peaks: The Return*, ed. Antonio Sanna (Cham: Springer, 2019), 23–36.

13 Franck Boulègue, *The Return of Twin Peaks: Squaring the Circle* (Bristol and Chicago: Intellect Books, 2021).

14 Karla Lončar, "Kafka, Lynch, and Frost: The Trial and Tribulations in *Twin Peaks: The Return*," *NANO: New American Notes Online*, no. 15, *Twin Peaks: The Return* (February 2020), https://nanocrit.com/issues/issue15/Kafka-Lynch-and-Frost-The-Trial-and-Tribulations-in-Twin-Peaks-The-Return.

15 See Jürgen Habermas, "Notes on Post-Secular Society," *New Perspectives Quarterly* 25, no. 4 (2008): 17–29. In March of 2007, Habermas delivered

his now famous lecture on "post-secularism" at the Nexus Institute of the University of Tilberg, Netherlands. Habermas pointed to three factors that characterize modern social orders as post-secular: 1) the broad perception that many global conflicts hinge on religious strife and the changes in public consciousness and weakening of confidence in the dominance of a secular outlook that such acknowledgment accedes; 2) the increased importance of religion in various public spheres; and 3) the growing presence in Europe and elsewhere of immigrant or "guest workers" and refugees with traditional cultural backgrounds.

16 Gordon Graham, "Religion, Secularization, and Modernity," *Philosophy* 67, no. 260 (April 1992): 183–97.

17 Jürgen Habermas, *The Philosophical Discourse of Modernity: Twelve Lectures*, trans. Frederick G. Lawrence (Cambridge MA: The MIT Press, 1985). John Rawls, *Political Liberalism* (New York: Columbia University Press, 1993).

18 P. L. Berger, "The Desecularization of the World: A Global Overview," in *The Desecularization of the World: Resurgent Religion and World Politics*, ed. Peter L. Berger (Washington, DC and Grand Rapids, MI: Ethics and Public Policy Center; W.B. Eerdmans Pub., 1999), 1–18. See also Peter L. Berger, "Secularism in Retreat," *The National Interest* 46 (December 1996): 3+, https://nationalinterest.org/article/secularism-in-retreat-336. Interestingly, in 1968 Berger predicted the decline of religion worldwide, with secularization becoming dominant and religious believers "likely to be found only in small sects, huddled together to resist a worldwide secular culture." Peter Berger, "A Bleak Outlook is Seen for Religion," *New York Times*, February 3, 1968.

19 Talal Asad et al., *Is Critique Secular? Blasphemy, Injury, and Free Speech*, 2nd ed. (New York: Fordham University Press, 2013). For overviews of the postsecular turn, see James Hodkinson and Silke Horstkotte, "Introducing the Postsecular: From Conceptual Beginnings to Cultural Theory," *Poetics Today* 41, no. 3 (September 2000): 317–26; and Peter Coviello and Jared Hickman, "Introduction: After the Postsecular," *American Literature* 86, no. 4 (December 2014): 645–54.

20 Giorgio Agamben, *State of Exception*, trans. Kevin Attell (Stanford: Stanford University Press 2005); Giorgio Agamben, *The Time that Remains: A Commentary on the Letter to the Romans* 149, trans. Patricia Daley (Stanford: Stanford University Press, 2005); Charles Taylor, *A Secular Age* (Harvard: Harvard University Press, 2007); Beata Polanowska-Sygulska and John Gray, "Moral Hysteria and the Myths of Secular Humanism: An Interview with John Gray," *Salmagundi*, no. 160/161 (Fall 2008–Winter 2009): 53–97.

21 Ananda Abeysekara, *The Politics of Postsecular Religion: Mourning Secular Futures* (New York: Columbia University Press, 2008); Bruce Robbins, "Is the Postcolonial also Postsecular?" *boundary* 2 40, no. 1 (February 2013): 245–62.

22 John Gray, *Heresies: Against Progress and Other Illusions* (London: Granta Books, 2004), 46–7.

23 Ibid.
24 Anke Snoek, *Agamben's Joyful Kafka: Finding Freedom Beyond Subordination* (London and New York: Bloomsbury, 2012).
25 Dennis Lim, *The Man from Another Place* (New York: Houghton Mifflin Harcourt, 2015); Justus Nieland, *David Lynch* (Urbana, IL: University of Illinois Press, 2012); Hossein Eidizadeh, "When You See Me Again It Won't Be Me: *The Metamorphosis*, Franz Kafka and David Lynch's Lifelong Obsession," *Senses of Cinema*, no. 88 (October 2018), https://www.sensesofcinema.com/2018/feature-articles/when-you-see-me-again-it-wont-be-me-the-metamorphosis-franz-kafka-and-david-lynchs-life-long-obsession/.
26 Cf. Lynch's response to Chris Rodley's question regarding his attitude to Kafka: "When he reviewed *Blue Velvet*, novelist J. G. Ballard said that the film was 'like *The Wizard of Oz* reshot with a script by Franz Kafka and decor by Francis Bacon.' Kafka certainly comes to mind in *Eraserhead*. Do you like his work? LYNCH: Yeah. The one artist that I feel could be my brother—and I almost don't like saying it, because the reaction is always, 'Yeah, you and everybody else'—is Franz Kafka. I really dig him a lot. Some of his things are the most thrilling combos of words I have ever read. If Kafka wrote a crime picture, I'd be there. I'd like to direct that for sure." Chris Rodley, *Lynch on Lynch: Interviews,* ed. rev. (London: Faber and Faber, 2005), 56.
27 Adam Daniel, "Kafka's Crime Film: *Twin Peaks: The Return* and the Brotherhood of Lynch and Kafka,'" in *Critical Essays on Twin Peaks: The Return*, ed. Antonio Sanna (Cham: Springer/Palgrave Macmillan, 2019), 221–35.
28 Ibid., 224–8.
29 Lončar, "Kafka, Lynch, and Frost."
30 Andy Hageman, "Twin Peaks Backstory Investigations: The Metamorphosis, Written by Franz Kafka (1915)." *25 Years Later*, January 14, 2019, https://25yearslatersite.com/2019/01/14/twin-peaks-backstory-investigations-the-metamorphosis-written-by-franz-kafka-1915/.
31 Lončar, "Kafka, Lynch, and Frost." See also Espen Hammer, "Introduction," in *Kafka's* The Trial*: Philosophical Perspectives*, ed. Espen Hammer (Oxford: Oxford University Press, 2018), 7.
32 "Tulpas" refer to conjured doubles of individuals who are created through concentrated thought along with "a seed and organic material from the template—such as hair—and [that] . . . retain memories from their [biological human] templates." See "Tulpa," Twin Peaks Wiki, https://twinpeaks.fandom.com/wiki/Tulpa. Agent Tammy Preston refers to Diane as a "Tulpa," which becomes evident when irascible Diane is revealed to be an uncanny Doppelganger who disappears with a scream. Twentieth-century Theosophists adapted the concept of the "Tulpa" or thought-form from the Vajrayana notion of the "emanation-body."
33 In this respect, Lynch and Frost's *Twin Peaks*, with its fusion of technology, science, metaphysics, and spiritualist ideas makes a contribution to a distinctive thread in the history of American secularity that weaves together

religious evangelicalism, spirituality, technology, cultural practices, and political traditions. John Lardas Modern argues that nineteenth-century Evangelical Americans understood themselves as secular by connecting the ideas of technology, electricity, circuitry, and energy to the notion of "spreading the Word" (evident in the birth of Evangelical publishing, with a Gideon Bible in every hotel room, for example). See J. L. Modern, *Secularism in Antebellum America* (Chicago, IL: University of Chicago Press, 2011). Lynch and Frost's vision is darker, more syncretic and speculative, but also emphasizes the role of electricity and communication technologies as media that connect secular and post-secular dimensions of modernity. My thanks to Mark Cauchi for pointing out this connection.

34 Lynch refers to each "episode" as "Part," confirming his contention that *Twin Peaks: The Return* is in fact an eighteen-hour cinematic work. See Sanna, "Entering the World of Twin Peaks' and Allister McTaggart, "'I am Dead Yet I Live": Revealing the Enigma of Art in *Twin Peaks: The Return*," *NANO: New American Notes Online*, no. 15, *Twin Peaks: The Return* (February 2020), https://nanocrit.com/issues/issue15/I-am-dead-yet-I-live-Revealing-the-Enigma-of-Art-in-Twin-Peaks-The-Return for illuminating discussions of the relationship between film and television in the case of *Twin Peaks: The Return*.

35 The Woodsman who enters the radio station is played by Lincoln lookalike actor, Robert Brodski. The young girl walking with the boy we see earlier finds a penny on the ground and rubs Lincoln's face on the coin, saying that it brings good luck, but unfortunately later ends up ingesting a frog-moth.

36 These images recall the disturbing void of nonexistence—"In-exist-ent!" as "The Arm" proclaims—into which Cooper falls before materializing in the strange black box experiment set up on the New York City warehouse apartment site that we see in Part 2.

37 Monique Rooney, "Air-Object: On Air Media and David Lynch's 'Gotta Light? (*Twin Peaks: The Return, 2017*)," *New Review of Film and Television Studies* 16, no. 2 (March 2018): 123–43, and 145.

38 Totaro, "Twin Peaks, The Return, Part 8," np.

39 Joel Bocko, "Secret Histories Return to Twin Peaks," *Offscreen* 21, no. 11–12 (December 2017), http://offscreen.com/view/secret-histories-return-to-twin-peaks.

40 Matt Zoller Seitz, "The Eight Episode of Twin Peaks: The Return is Horrifingly Beautiful," *Vulture*, June 26, 2017, http://www.vulture.com/2017/06/twin-peaks-the-return-part-8-atom-bomb-flashback.html.

41 Totaro notes the allusions here to the "Star Gate sequence" Kubrick's *2001: A Space Odyssey* (1968).

42 The Bell-shaped device has attracted much speculation from *Twin Peaks* fans, but it is most likely an old electricity generator, as suggested by the two insulated electrical cables protruding from the top of the device. Its shape may also be alluding to Alexander Graham Bell, inventor of the telephone, photophone, and graphophone (which could record and play back sound).

43 See Totaro for a discussion of the relationship between Part 8 of *Twin Peaks: The Return* and 1950s science-fiction alien invasion movies.
44 Boulègue links this image—the orb containing Laura Palmer as "cosmic seed" but also BOB and the frog-moth creature that "parasites the girl"—to occult and religious mythological accounts of "the fertilization of an otherworldly embryo," the latter being connected with a messianic return of the gods in times of great evil and discord.
45 The shot where the Woodsmen enters the studio office and confronts the receptionist is an homage to Edward Hopper's painting, *Office at Night* (1940).
46 Raechel Dumas, "It is Happening Again: Traumatic Memory, Affective Renewal, and Deferred Resolution," *Twin Peaks: The Return*, *Quarterly Review of Film and Video* 36, no. 4 (2019): 327–43.
47 Cf. Agent Tammy Preston's concluding philosophical reflections "Final Thoughts" in her FBI report to Special Agent Gordon Cole (David Lynch): "Is the evil in us real? Is it an intrinsic part of us, a force outside us, or nothing more than a reflection of the void? How do we hold both fear and wonder in the mind at once? Does staring into this darkness offer up an answer, or resolution? What does it give us to hold on to? Does it reveal anything at all? Or can the simple, impossible act of persisting to look at what's in front of us finally pierce the blackness and reward us with a glimpse of something eternal beyond?" Frost, *Twin Peaks*, 143–4.
48 Assuming that the undecideable relationship between cinema and television in *Twin Peaks: The Return* can be resolved. See Boulègue, *The Return of Twin Peaks* for a discussion of this idea.

CONTRIBUTORS

John Caruana is Associate Professor of Philosophy at Toronto Metropolitan University, Canada. His research is in phenomenology, continental philosophy of religion, and film-philosophy. He has published on various philosophers, including Deleuze, Kierkegaard, Kristeva, and Levinas. His publications in film-philosophy include work on the film thinker André Bazin and several filmmakers, such as Bruno Dumont, Terrence Malick, and the Dardenne brothers. He is the coeditor with Mark Cauchi of *Immanent Frames: Postsecular Cinema Between Malick and von Trier* (2018).

Mark Cauchi is Associate Professor in the Department of Humanities, the Graduate Program of Social and Political Thought, and the Graduate Program of Communication and Culture at York University, Canada. He is the coeditor with John Caruana of *Immanent Frames: Postsecular Cinema Between Malick and Von Trier* (2018), the editor of special issues in *Symposium*, *Sophia*, and *European Legacy*, as well as the author of several articles in film-philosophy, continental philosophy, religious studies, and social and political theory.

Francisca Cho is Professor of Buddhist Studies at Georgetown University, United States. Her research focuses on East Asian Buddhism through the media of popular culture, particularly literary fiction, poetry, and film. Her most recent book is *Seeing Like the Buddha: Enlightenment Through Film* (2017).

Sarah Cooper is Professor of Film Studies at King's College London, UK. Her books include *Film and the Imagined Image* (2019), *The Soul of Film Theory* (2013), *Chris Marker* (2008), and *Selfless Cinema? Ethics and French Documentary* (2006). She has also edited special issues of the journals *Philosophies*, "Thinking Cinema—with Plants" (2023), *Paragraph*, "New Takes on Film and Imagination" (2020), and *Film-Philosophy*, "The Occluded Relation: Levinas and Cinema" (2007).

Walid El Khachab is Associate Professor and Coordinator of Arabic Studies at York University, Canada, and the co-director of ACANS, the Arab Canadian Studies Research Group. He edited the volume, *Arabs: Out of the Impasse?* (2004). Since then, he has published more than fifty chapters and academic articles on Arabic cultures and Islam in English, French, and Arabic, particularly on national identities and modernity, the politics of mysticism, and cinema and popular culture.

Nikolas Kompridis is the author of *The Aesthetic Turn in Political Thought* (2014), *Critique and Disclosure: Critical Theory Between Past and Future* (2006), *Philosophical Romanticism* (2006) and has taught at universities in Canada, the UK, and Australia. He is now in the "post-institutional" phase of his career, affiliated with the Center for Humanities and Social Change at the Humboldt University, Berlin, Germany, and the Centre for Ethics at the University of Toronto, Canada.

Kathryn Lofton is Lex Hixon Professor of Religious Studies, American Studies, and History and Divinity at Yale University, United States. She is the author of *Consuming Religion* (2017) and *Oprah: The Gospel of an Icon* (2011).

Sheila J. Nayar is Adjunct Professor of Film and Media Arts at the University of Utah. Her research interests include the interplay of narrative, phenomenology, orality and alphabetic literacy. She is the author of *The Sacred and the Cinema: Reconfiguring the "Genuinely" Religions Film* (2012) and *Cinematically Speaking: The Orality-Literacy Paradigm for Visual Narrative* (2010), as well as articles in *Film Quarterly*, *JAAR*, and *PMLA*. Currently, she is completing a monograph on Indian secularism and Hindi popular cinema, as well as a Fulbright-Nehru research project in Mumbai on how unlettered individuals engage with mobile technology.

Robert Sinnerbrink is Associate Professor of Philosophy at Macquarie University. He is the author of *New Philosophies of Film: An Introduction to Cinema as a Way of Thinking* (2021), *Terrence Malick: Filmmaker and Philosopher* (2019), *Cinematic Ethics: Exploring Ethical Experience through Film* (2016), *New Philosophies of Film: Thinking Images* (2011), and *Understanding Hegelianism* (2007). He has edited *Emotion, Ethics, and Cinematic Experience: New Phenomenological and Cognitivist Perspectives* (2021) and co-edited *Contemporary Screen Ethics* (2023). His articles have appeared in journals such as *Angelaki*, *Necsus: European Journal of Media Studies*, *Projections: The Journal of Movies and Mind*, and *Screen*.

Catherine Wheatley is Reader in Film and Visual Culture at King's College London, UK. She has published widely on questions pertaining to film, ethics and aesthetics, and religion. Catherine is the author of *Stanley Cavell and Film: Scepticism and Self-Reliance at the Cinema* (2018), the BFI Classics book on *Caché* (2013), and *Michael Haneke's Cinema: The Ethic of the Image* (2009), as well as the editor of a number of essay collections and special issues.

INDEX

Althusser, Louis   7, 47–9, 53–4
Amar Akbar Anthony
   the expression (also AAA)   163–4, 170, 172, 177
   the film (Dir. Manmohan Desai, 1977)   163, 166, 177
America   11, 19, 21, 31, 36, 43, 71, 89, 182–206, 242–5, 251, 257, 259 n.6, 262–3 n.33
animism   36, 40–2, 44, 58 n.53, 110
anthropomorphism   227, 230–5
Arendt, Hannah   120–1, 137
   natality   134, 137
Asad, Talal   10, 12, 54 n.1, 144

Bad Times at the El Royale (Dir. Drew Godard, 2018)   101–2
Bazin, André   43–4, 52, 69, 216–17, 223 n.44, 230
belief   6, 9, 10, 16, 20, 35, 36, 38, 51–2, 59 n.57, 62 n.112, 72, 74–5, 210, 212–13, 215, 218
Benjamin, Walter   35, 41–3, 70
Birth of a Flower, The (Dir. F. Percy Smith, 1911)   225–35, 241 n.46
Bollywood   163–81
Bordwell, David   7, 11, 54
Buddhism   13, 16–17, 19, 33, 86–106
   Buddha-nature   87, 95, 97
   images   97–100

capitalism   18, 20, 32, 41, 50
care   115, 117, 121, 134, 135
Christianity   8, 11, 16, 33, 40, 43–5, 47, 67, 75–8, 87, 147, 150, 152–5, 157–60
colonialism   88, 111, 118–19, 142 n.1, 183, 189, 194, 200, 247

Dalits   173–4
Dao, Daoism   86, 88–90
decolonization   111, 121, 135–6
Deleuze, Gilles   15–16, 64–85, 145
   action-image   70, 71
   classical cinema   70, 71, 81, 83 n.16
   time-image   66, 73, 76, 78, 81
Dhoom 3 (Dir. Vijay Krisha Acharya, 2013)   169
Direct Cinema (or observational cinema)   182, 185–90
disenchantment   13, 18–21, 31, 33, 34, 37, 39–42, 44, 51, 52, 66, 124, 137, 147, 149, 217, 218, 251, 252
divinization   227, 231, 234, 235
Divyāvadāna   97–9
documentary   19, 182–206
   and religion   182–3, 185
Durkheim, Emile   140–1, 176

Eliade. Mircea   117–18
emptiness (Buddhist concept of)   90–2, 99, 100, 105 n.15
enchantment   19–20, 31, 34, 37, 51, 147–8, 150, 151, 210, 214, 217–19
Epstein, Jean   40–1
Europa '51 (Dir. Roberto Rossellini, 1952)   78–81

faith   67, 72–4, 76–7, 80, 84 n.24, 84 n.26
Fanon, Frantz   111, 119–21, 130, 138
Fatima, Marika and Rachel (Dir. Helmy Rafla, 1949)   150, 152–5

INDEX

fetish, fetishism 7, 31, 50–1, 62 n.110
film studies 4–6, 10, 15, 29–30, 35, 38–9, 45, 46, 52–4, 57–8 n.44
Foucault, Michel 140

Gandhi, Mahatma 164, 174, 177
gender 112, 115, 121, 133, 134, 153, 169
Geroulanos, Stefanos 46–7, 53
Gunning, Tom 20, 35–8, 54, 210, 212–16

Habermas, Jürgen 9, 64
Hassan, Marcus and Cohen (Dir. Fouad El Gazaerli, 1954) 150, 156–60
Hinduism 33, 40, 89, 96, 242, 245–6, 251
Holy Ghost People (Dir. Peter Adair, 1967) 185, 188, 192–6

immanence 1, 29, 145, 146
India 89, 93, 97, 103 n.14, 104 n.20, 163–81
Islam 7, 11, 19, 111, 145–6, 148–51, 170–2

Judaism 40–3, 152–5, 157–60
Jurassic Park (Dir. Steven Spielberg, 1993) 209–10, 214, 215, 221 n.8, 224 n.58

Kafka, Franz 243, 246, 249–51, 258
Kal Ho Naa Ho (Dir. Nikhil Advani, 2003) 168–9
Kashmir Files, The (Dir. Vivek Agnihotri, 2022) 171
Kiarostami, Abbas 7
Kierkegaard, Soren 74, 75, 84 n.26
Koepnick, Lutz 216–17

Latour, Bruno 6, 10, 15, 21, 29–31, 34, 40, 47, 48, 52, 55 n.5, 228, 234, 236
Liberal, liberalism 7, 21, 41, 67, 150, 160, 247–9
Life of a Plant, The (Dir. F. Percy Smith, 1926) 231

Lotus Sutra 95–6
Lynch, David 21, 242–64

Maciak, Phillip 6, 9, 37–8, 57 n.42, 214
magic 6, 32, 34, 36, 41, 42, 44, 52, 99, 110, 210, 212–15, 217, 218
Marder, Michael 229, 234–7, 241 n.39
Marion, Fulgence 212, 219
materialism 89–91, 218
melodrama 150–2, 187
metaphysical. *See* transcendence
Metz, Christian 7, 35, 50–2
Middle East, The 7, 18, 144–62
Minh-Ha, Trinh T. 182, 200
Moolaadé
  the concept 110, 114, 130
  the film (Dir. Ousmane Sembène, 2004) 109–43
Mulvey, Laura 6–7, 11, 53
Münsterberg, Hugo 36, 39
mystery 6, 218, 219, 223 n.44, 242, 244, 250, 251
myth, mythical, mythology 6, 34, 35, 48, 69, 72, 242, 248, 257–8

nature 30, 32, 40, 44, 59 n.56, 90, 228–32
Nietzsche, Friedrich 65, 67–8, 71, 75, 82 n.7, 245, 248

plants 225–41
Plato 91–2, 211
PlayTime (Dir. Jacques Tati, 1967) 1–2, 4, 10, 22 n.1, 22 n.2
pluralism (diversity) 82 n.10, 144, 148, 150, 152, 153, 159, 160, 164–7, 169, 174, 175, 180 n.36
postsecularism 9–10, 21–2, 31, 66, 214, 242–3, 246–50, 250–1 n.15, 257–8
Primary (Dir. Robert Drew, 1960) 188, 189, 199

race 11–12, 26 n.52, 32–3, 51, 56 n.15, 187, 190–2, 201
ritual 92–102, 110, 114, 130, 165, 196

INDEX

romanticism 89, 219, 220
Rossellini, Roberto 75, 77–81

sacred 17, 20, 110, 117–18, 124–5, 130, 141, 144, 145, 184
  desacralization 130, 136, 140–1
Salesman (Dirs. David Maysles et al., 1969) 185, 188, 196–9, 202 n.14, 203 n.29
science 5, 7, 20, 34, 39, 47–52, 88–90, 211–13, 215, 218, 219, 224 n.58
science fiction 210, 214, 221 n.8, 224 n.58, 225, 226, 228, 230, 254, 255
secularism 4, 12, 29, 64–9, 82–3 n.10, 87–90, 100, 110, 126, 133, 144, 146, 148, 164, 183, 184, 217–19, 226–8, 230–6, 238, 242–3, 246–9, 257–8
  Indian 163–6, 174
  invisibility of 4–12, 29, 44–5, 47, 49, 54, 54 n.1, 65–6
  and Race 11–12, 26 n.52
  secularization 6, 18, 19, 31, 35, 36, 45–6, 51–2, 54, 56 n.17, 147, 149, 159–61, 183
Sembène, Ousmane 17–18, 109–45
separation of religious and secular 30–4, 67, 74, 81, 86–8, 91, 93, 111, 118
sexuality 92, 100, 131, 149, 156, 160, 195, 202 n.12
Sikhism 166–7, 172, 175, 178
Smith, F. Percy 20–1, 226–41
soul 39, 45, 228–31, 235–6, 238
Spielberg, Steven 20, 210, 214, 215, 222 n.20

spiritualism 33, 36–7, 39, 42, 242–4, 248, 257
spirituality 88–90, 184, 190, 192, 193, 195, 213, 218, 227, 234, 236
supernatural 35, 36, 40, 42–4, 90, 243–6, 252–4, 258
Śūraṅgama Sutra 96–7

Tati, Jacques 1–2
Taylor, Charles 6, 12, 13, 20, 33, 36, 64, 66, 218
  subtraction story 6, 87
technology 69, 70, 81, 151, 229–31, 233, 235, 243, 249, 257, 259 n.4, 262–3 n.33
Tiger Zinda Hai (Dir. Ali Abbas Zafar, 2017) 165, 168–70, 176
Time for Burning, A (Dir. Jersey and Connell, 1966) 185, 188, 190–2
transcendence 36, 56 n.17, 144–8, 150, 151, 220, 236, 242–4, 246, 248, 250, 251, 257–8
Twin Peaks: The Return (Dir. David Lynch, 2017) 242–64

Uncanny, the 9, 13, 21–2, 33, 36, 37, 56 n.17, 242–64

visibility of religion 1–3, 182

War (Dir. Siddarth Anand, 2019) 170, 172, 175
Weber, Max 13, 32–4, 39–42, 147, 218
wonder 20–1, 209–24, 228, 233, 238

www.ingramcontent.com/pod-product-compliance
Lightning Source LLC
Chambersburg PA
CBHW050323020526
44117CB00031B/1665